THE EIGHT PER CENT SOLUTION

ADVANCE PRAISE FOR THE BOOK

'Nikhil Gupta has written a highly insightful book, impressive for how its analysis connects the dots between different parts of the economy—households, financial sector, corporates (listed and unlisted), and the government—as well as for laying out in a transparent manner how they all interact with each other and the global economy. I particularly admire the emphasis on the role of household savings, the importance of the unlisted economy to get an accurate employment picture, and complex interactions between the domestic and the external economies. Highly recommended for all wanting to understand the Indian economy, in-depth while covering all of its breadth'

Viral Acharya
Former deputy governor, RBI

'This book will be a useful bridge between hard-core textbooks and purely journalistic writing. Nikhil explains the basic concepts lucidly, and more importantly, he stands out in a world full of two-handed economists by taking a position and giving his readers something definitive to disagree with'

Dr D.V. Subbarao
Former governor, RBI

'Nikhil Gupta not only takes apart the economy for us, gives us a peek into its moving parts, explains what makes it tick and demolishes quite a few hallowed myths, but he also charts a way forward for India clinically, without either chest-thumping or breast-beating'

Manas Chakravarty
Group Consulting Editor, *Moneycontrol*

'Nikhil Gupta does a tremendous job of explaining the nitty-gritty of how the Indian economy works and what needs to be done to achieve a very high rate of economic growth'
Vivek Kaul
Economic commentator and author

'Nikhil Gupta has written a useful book on the key issue of how to get back to a regime of 8 per cent growth, if that is possible at all. His approach is to analyse the strengths and weaknesses of the financial balance sheets of the three important sectors of the economy. Linking the financial dimensions and real dimensions runs into many definitional problems. However, the freshness of Nikhil Gupta's approach deserves recognition and further study'
Dr C. Rangarajan
Chairman, Madras School of Economics; former chairman, Economic Advisory Council to the Prime Minister; and former governor, RBI

'Usually books on macroeconomics are extremely boring. But now comes this extremely provocative book by Nikhil Gupta, a young economist whom I have known for over a decade. Without revealing too much of the suspense in the book, here are three excerpts from the book which will set you thinking about commonly held notions about the Indian economy.

> ... Even with such low headline debt-to-income ratio, the debt service ratio of Indian households is much higher than in other economies, which have 2–3x household debt...

> ... A careful analysis confirms that the fiscal consolidation in India has been too slow—down from 9.3 per cent of GDP in the 1990s decade to 8.5 per cent of GDP in the 2000s decade to 7.7 per cent of GDP in the 2010s decade...

> ... Government policies in India during the pre-COVID-19 years were largely geared towards encouraging consumption, which too contributed to lower household savings in the country...

'This is not the book for the conventional thinkers. This is the book for people who interpret the world far differently from the average'

Shankar Sharma
Veteran market investor, and founder, GQuant

'Nikhil Gupta's approach to complexities of the macroeconomic phenomenon is refreshingly different. Rather than be cowed down or get perplexed by these complexities, he has bravely gone about simplifying them to make them accessible to the lay reader. His "Theory of Everything" is an endearing example of this approach. This ability to simplify concepts and communicate them in a straightforward manner surely comes from being in the midst of equity traders who have to take split-second decisions without the luxury of interminable arguments. I highly recommend reading the book if only for its bold yet simply stated conclusions'

Rajiv Kumar
Chairman, Pahle India Foundation, Delhi;
and former vice chairman, NITI Aayog

'Nikhil Gupta's *The Eight Per Cent Solution* is a concise guide on the Indian economy. The book's main approach is to look at the economy from a balance sheet perspective. The book discusses various related topics on the Indian economy, including the significant but often overlooked household sector, the contributions of corporates, the government, and the external sector in driving economic growth. Practitioner-oriented explanations of basic economic identities are useful as an anchor for understanding the macro canvas. The book also seeks to dispel myths non-economists have and provides perspectives on competing policy strategies for driving the economy'

Navneet Munot
Managing Director and CEO, HDFC AMC

'A wonderful book delving into the different entities involved in the economies and how the interplay creates economic trends. It raises relevant challenges of how leverage and deleveraging trends are important to understand trends in the economy. In short, a nice read for someone who wants to understand the intricacies of the Indian economy'

Sankaren Naren
Chief Investment Officer, ICICI Prudential AMC Ltd

'Nikhil has managed to simplify a complex subject to such an extent that non-economists can understand not only this book but also how the economy works. He delivers the key message that for sustainable growth India should defer gratification in a very rational, easy-to-understand and powerful manner. A non-consensus view clearly, but there is no rule that says that minority opinions are incorrect. And that's why this is a compelling read'

Prashant Jain
Chief Investment Officer, 3P Investment Managers; and former Chief Investment Officer, HDFC AMC

'Written in an engaging style, this book by Nikhil Gupta demystifies difficult economic concepts, analyses a few recent macroeconomic policy interventions of the Modi government and identifies half a dozen lessons that should always be heeded. A refreshing take on economic policymaking'

A.K. Bhattacharya
Editorial Director, *Business Standard*; and author of *India's Finance Ministers: From Independence to Emergency (1947–1977)*

'Nikhil has explained economics in the common man's language. I have learned a few things about economics from this book. A good book to read for non-economists before one has an opinion on economic issues'

Raamdeo Agrawal
Co-founder and Chairman, Motilal Oswal Financial Services

THE EIGHT PER CENT SOLUTION

A Strategy for India's Growth

Nikhil Gupta

Foreword by
Dr Rathin Roy

BLOOMSBURY
NEW DELHI • LONDON • OXFORD • NEW YORK • SYDNEY

BLOOMSBURY INDIA
Bloomsbury Publishing India Pvt. Ltd
Second Floor, LSC Building No. 4, DDA Complex,
Pocket C – 6 & 7, Vasant Kunj,
New Delhi 110070

BLOOMSBURY, BLOOMSBURY INDIA and the Diana logo are
trademarks of Bloomsbury Publishing Plc

First published in India 2023
This edition published 2023

Copyright © Nikhil Gupta, 2023

Nikhil Gupta has asserted his right under the Indian Copyright Act
to be identified as the Author of this work

All rights reserved. No part of this publication may be reproduced or
transmitted in any form or by any means, electronic or mechanical,
including photocopying, recording or any information storage or
retrieval system, without the prior permission in
writing from the publishers

The book is solely the responsibility of the author and the
publisher has had no role in creation of the content and does not have
responsibility for anything defamatory or libellous or objectionable.

Bloomsbury Publishing Plc does not have any control over, or
responsibility for, any third-party websites referred to or in this book.
All internets addresses given in this book were correct at the time of
going to press. The author and publisher regret any inconvenience
caused if addresses have changed or sites have ceased to exist,
but can accept no responsibility for any such changes

ISBN:PB: 978-93-56403-59-8; eBook: 978-93-56403-55-0
2 4 6 8 10 9 7 5 3 1

Printed and bound in India by Thomson Press India Ltd

To find out more about our authors and books, visit
www.bloomsbury.com and sign up for our newsletters

'*I have thought it my duty to exhibit things as they are, not as they ought to be.*'

A. Alexander Hamilton
one of the founding fathers of the United States,
in letter dated 13 August 1782

CONTENTS

Foreword by Rathin Roy — xiii
List of Abbreviations — xvii

1. The Curtain Raiser — 1
2. The Heavy-Lifter but Highly Ignored Household Sector — 57
3. The Listed and the Lesser-known Unlisted Corporate Sectors — 103
4. The Government Sector: Believe It or Not, but It Has Its Limits — 151
5. The Connection between Domestic Participants and the External Sector — 192
6. Indian Economy: Past, Present and Future — 233
7. Role of Financial Markets in the Real Economy — 267
8. Lessons for the Future from the Past — 304

Appendices

Appendix 1: Household Financial Position in Nominal/Current Terms since 1950–51 — 341
Appendix 2: Household Financial Position since 1950–51 — 345
Appendix 3: Estimation of Debt Service Ratio for Indian Households — 350
Appendix 4: Deriving India's Corporate Profits from the Theory of Everything — 352
Appendix 5: Financial Position of India's Corporate Sector — 354
Appendix 6: Major Receipts Components of the Combined Government — 356

Appendix 7: Understanding the Economic Classification of Central Government Spending — 360

Appendix 8: Economic Classification of General Government Spending — 362

Appendix 9: Major Spending Areas/Components of the Combined Government — 364

Appendix 10: Understanding the Formal Accounting System of India's Government — 367

Appendix 11: Estimating Adjusted Fiscal Deficit from Reported Fiscal Deficit of the Central Government — 369

Appendix 12: Reconciliation of the Different Estimates of Union Government Liabilities and Estimation of the Adjusted Debt — 372

Appendix 13: Key Concepts in BoP and International Investment Position — 375

Appendix 14: India's Merchandise Trade Deficit by Broad Baskets — 379

Acknowledgements — 383
Notes — 385
Index — 397
About the Author — 401

FOREWORD

It has become commonplace for analysts to proclaim, proudly, that they are 'data driven'. This worries me. To use data in analysis and to draw inferences is one thing, to be driven by it quite another. The lack of an analytical framework within which to seek and utilize data can lead to moronic conclusions. A 'best fit' polynomial in three degrees does not automatically constitute a business cycle.

Mumbai is populated by economic analysts who are data driven. This is partly to please their bosses who want short-term responses to structural phenomena as their concern is purely with the business bottom line. I was, therefore, pleasantly surprised when I read this book. Its raison d'être is to set out a policy-relevant analytical framework within which to analyse the Indian economy.

Nikhil Gupta lays out a simple and tractable analytical framework, which is not novel in that it does not deviate from known textbook identities. In the quest to be data driven, these identities have been lost in the rush to use purely stochastic techniques to draw policy inferences. This book starts with the basic relationships between the participants in economic activity in a country—organized formal businesses, households (including not-for-profits), government and the rest of the world. Their interactions take place in two domains: they exchange goods and services, and they undertake financial transactions to facilitate these exchanges and the consequences of these exchanges (savings, consumption, foreign exchange transactions, etc.). As Gupta shows, these are compatible with settled and known macroeconomic and national accounts identities—but invoking these identities and dynamically tracing their evolution over time enables him to draw policy inferences that data-driven and stochastic approaches simply cannot do.

In this sense, this book belongs firmly in the Keynesian tradition though emphatically not its Hicksian IS-LM vulgarization which is mistakenly taught to generations of Indian students of economics as the Keynesian policy toolkit. Rather, Nikhil Gupta follows in the tradition of Kahn, Kaldor and Kalecki, tracing the interplay of stock flow relationships between macroeconomic aggregates and the response of the different sectors to this evolution. It is by this process that Kahn was able to so effectively define the multiplier (in contrast to the 'fiscal multipliers' so beloved to empirical vulgarian economists, which are analytically empty and therefore meaningless), and Kalecki distinguishes between macroeconomics of advanced and developing countries.

The book has six analytical learnings. Each of these is consistent with received macroeconomic theory but confused by 'data-driven' economists. Thus, the fact that a household buys equity in a firm may well mean savings for the household—but not for the economy, if the firm is making losses and the equity is consumed entirely by these losses.

The author also cautions against another tool favoured by the analytically illiterate, data-driven analyst: cross-country comparisons. On reflection one finds that there is nothing particularly unique about the Chinese growth model, but its replicability specifically to India is of limited value, as Nikhil Gupta explains eloquently and persuasively.

I will leave the reader to discover the other learnings, but note that each of them is consistent with textbook macroeconomics. Their contemporary novelty is only because the data-driven bias has caused this important pillar of policy tradecraft to rust everywhere, especially in India.

Nikhil Gupta titles his book *The Eight Per Cent Solution* because the punchline conclusion is that consistent 8 per cent growth is a necessary (if not sufficient) condition for India to transform the lives and well-being of the vast majority of its citizens. But what of the '15 per cent malaise'—that current macroeconomic performance is heavily reliant on the economic activity of the top 10–15 per cent of the population?

Nikhil Gupta argues that before aspiring to 8 per cent growth, India needs to urgently implement fundamental structural changes. He says that doing both is not an option. This will be difficult to put to any politician or businessman who wants to see India's growth story evolve here and now. However, the task of getting our house in order will bring an important dividend—the end of the 15 per cent malaise—which requires doing many of the things Nikhil Gupta advocates based on his analysis, such as strengthening the financial position of the household sector, paying attention to the health of the corporate sector beyond listed companies, paying attention to home market demand and not fantasizing about exports. All this will broad-base the 6 per cent growth that we will see as we implement these reforms and, by doing so, end the 15 per cent malaise. Even fiscal consolidation will contribute to this broad-basing. So much public money is currently used to compensate citizens for the failure of the economy to improve their prosperity and resilience, such that, as I have written elsewhere, the development state in India is now reduced to a compensatory state. A hard budget constraint on the compensatory state will force action to address the drivers of deprivation and lack of prosperity rather than its consequences.

I therefore consider this book an important addition to the stock of knowledge on Indian economic policy tradecraft. It has an analytical framework and offers a real alternative to sterile and erroneous 'data-driven' conclusions. It comes from Mumbai and is therefore genuinely grounded in the realities of exchange and finance. It is nested in important textbook propositions but uses these to address complexity in analytically relevant ways. It comes to concrete conclusions about the course that economic policy should adopt going forward.

For all these reasons, the book is refreshingly different, and will provide the economic policy ecosystem much that is new to reflect on in these uncertain times.

Dr Rathin Roy
Managing Director, ODI; former director, National Institute of Public Finance and Policy; and member, Economic Advisory Committee to the Prime Minister, Seventh Pay Commission

ABBREVIATIONS

ADB	Asian Development Bank
AEs	advanced economies
AFD	adjusted fiscal deficit
AGM	American growth model
ATBs	auction treasury bills
BE	budget estimate
BIS	Bank for International Settlements
BJP	Bharatiya Janata Party
BLR	base lending rate
BoP	balance of payments
BPCL	Bharat Petroleum Corporation Ltd
bps	basis points
BSR	Basic Statistical Returns of Scheduled Commercial Banks in India
CAD	current account deficit
CAG	Comptroller and Auditor General of India
CAs	chartered accountants
CAS	current account surplus
CBC	Central Bank of the Republic of China, Taiwan
CBs	corporate bonds
CFI	Consolidated Fund of India
CGA	Controller General of Accounts
CHF	Swiss franc
CIS	change in stocks
CoE	compensation of employees
COFOG	Classification of the Functions of Government

CPI	consumer price inflation
CPs	commercial papers
CPSE	Central public sector enterprises
CSO	Central Statistics Office
DBT	direct benefit transfers
DDT	dividend distribution tax
DILRMP	Digital India Land Records Modernisation Programme
DSR	debt service ratio
E&O	errors and omissions
EAGM	East Asian growth model
EBRs	extra budgetary resources
ECBs	external commercial borrowings
ED	external debt
EGM	economic growth model
EMEs	emerging market economies
EMI	equal monthly instalment
ETI	EMI to income
EXIM	Export-Import Bank
FCI	Food Corporation of India
FDI	foreign direct investment
FIIs	foreign institutional investments
FIs	financial Institutions
FPIs	foreign portfolio investments
FPO	follow-on public offer/further public offer
FRBM	Fiscal Responsibility and Budget Management
FSBs	fully serviced bonds
FXR	foreign exchange reserves
GATT	General Agreement on Tariffs and Trade

GBP	Great Britain pound
GCF	gross capital formation
GDP	gross domestic product
GDS	gross domestic savings
GFCE	government final consumption expenditure
GFCF	gross fixed capital formation
GFS	gross financial savings
GoI	Government of India
GST	goods and services tax
GVA	gross value addition
HFCs	housing finance companies
HPCL	Hindustan Petroleum Corporation Ltd
HPI	house price index
HPTI	house price to income
ICOR	incremental net capital output ratio
IDBI	Industrial Development Bank of India
IDR	Indonesian rupiah
IIP	International Investment Position
IL&FS	Infrastructure Leasing & Financial Services
ILO	International Labour Organization
IMF	International Monetary Fund
INR	Indian rupee
IOC	Indian Oil Corporation
IPO	initial public offering
IT	information technology
ITBs	intermediate treasury bills
IWG	Internal Working Group
JPY	Japanese yen
KRW	South Korean won

LMIC	lower-middle-income countries
LTI	loan to income
LTV	loan to value
LVB	Lakshmi Vilas Bank
MCA	ministry of corporate affairs
MCLR	marginal cost of lending rate
MCs	municipal corporations
MEIS	Merchandise Exports from India Scheme
MGNREGA	Mahatma Gandhi National Rural Employment Guarantee Act
MMT	Modern Monetary Theory
MoF	ministry of finance
MSMEs	micro, small and medium enterprises
MSS	market stabilization scheme
MXN	Mexican peso
NBFCs	non-banking financial companies
NDA	National Democratic Alliance
NFCs	non-financial companies
NFS	net financial savings
NGNF	non-government non-financial
NHAI	National Highways Authority of India
NHB	National Housing Bank
NIA	National Income Accounting
NSSF	National Small Savings Fund
NZD	New Zealand dollar
P&L	profit and loss
P&PFs	provident and pension funds
PAs	private allotments
PAT	profit after taxes

PBoC	People's Bank of China
PBs	payment banks
PbSBs	public sector banks
PBT	profit before taxes
PDI	personal disposable income
PFC	Power Finance Corporation
PFCE	private final consumption expenditure
PLIs	production-linked incentives
PMC	Punjab Mercantile Co-operative Bank
PMGKY	Pradhan Mantri Garib Kalyan Yojana
PM-KISAN	Pradhan Mantri Kisan Samman Nidhi
PPF	Public Provident Fund
PRC	People's Republic of China
PSUs	public sector units
PvSBs	private sector banks
QE	quantitative easing
QIPs	Qualified institutional placements
R&D	research and development
RAPMS	residential asset price monitoring survey
RBI	Reserve Bank of India
RE	revised estimate
RFD	reported fiscal deficit
RLLR	repo-linked lending rate
RoDTEP	Remission of Duties and Taxes on Export Products
RoW	rest of the world
RPPI	residential property price index
SCBs	scheduled commercial banks
SFBs	small finance banks

SGBs	sovereign gold bonds
SNB	Swiss National Bank
SPVs	special purpose vehicles
TFP	total factor productivity
UNCTAD	United Nations Conference on Trade and Development
UPA	United Progressive Alliance
UPI	unified payments interface
USD	US dollar
UTs	union territories
WIP	wages and salaries, interest payments and pensions
WNDR	weighted nominal deposit rate
WRDR	weighted real deposit rate
WTO	World Trade Organization
YoY	year on year
ZAR	South African rand

Chapter 1

THE CURTAIN RAISER

Non-economist: Huh . . . another book on economics. Why do we need that? Don't you know that we know that economists don't know that they don't understand anything? Nassim Nicholas Taleb puts it succinctly: 'As a general rule, whenever your intuition conflicts with that of an economist, bet on your intuition. Economists are reverse indicators: they are ~always wrong.'

Me: I dedicate this book to the Indian economy, in which I deeply feel there is a large vacuum. As far as betting on your intuition against an economist's, this is exactly what appears to have happened in the past four decades. And see where we are.

Non-economist: What do you mean? Don't you know that poverty has fallen at the fastest pace in the past few decades?

Me: Of course it has. But don't you know that income inequality within countries[1] has also risen substantially in the past few decades?

Non-economist: Whatever. But we would have definitely been worse off had we allowed economists to take charge.

Me: Well, I think by 'worse off', you mean slower growth. If so, you need to check your data because statistics suggest that per capita world economic growth[2] has weakened from 2.7 per cent between the 1960s and the 1970s decades to 1.3 per cent each in the 1980s and the 1990s, before picking up to 1.7 per cent in the 2000s decade. The slight improvement, to 2.0 per cent average growth, in the decade of the 2010s was largely supported by large fiscal stimuli and liquidity infusion by central banks, without which the global economy could have just collapsed like a house of cards. Do you really feel this is a sign of strength?

Non-economist: Anyway. What we need now is to move to a higher growth phase as soon as possible. What are your recommendations?

Me: 'If I had an hour to solve a problem, I'd spend 55 minutes thinking about the problem and 5 minutes thinking about solutions,' said Albert Einstein. Read the book and you will get your answers.

An economy consists of only four participants: the household, government, corporate and external sectors. It also consists of only three activities: consumption, savings/investments and external trade. But two facts make it complicated: the interconnectedness of these economic participants and the rising role of financial markets. In spite of the deep connectedness among the economic participants, economic analysts/policymakers pay little attention to the finances of the household sector and the unlisted corporate sector. There is also a serious lack of understanding regarding the connections between the real economy and the financial economy. This book intends to bridge these gaps.

The key conclusions and findings of this book are shared in this chapter, which also lists six key learnings which create the basis of the thought process behind this book and are extensively used in it.

On 20 September 2019, at around 11 a.m., the Government of India (GoI) took an unprecedented step. I was, coincidentally, in New Delhi that day on one of my regular trips, meeting a few experts on the Indian economy and adding to my knowledge while gauging the general mood among the intellectuals in the capital. Nirmala Sitharaman, the finance minister under the second innings of the Bharatiya Janata Party (BJP) government, announced that any new domestic manufacturing company incorporated on or after 1 October 2019, making fresh investments in manufacturing and commencing production on or before 31 March 2023, will have an option to pay income tax at the rate of only 15 per cent, down from the existing 30 per cent, subject to the condition that they will not avail of any exemption or incentive (the last date for commencement of manufacturing or production was extended by one year to 31 March 2024 in the Union Budget 2022–23). The effective tax rate for these companies, thus, would be 17.01 per cent, inclusive of surcharges and cess, down from the existing effective rate of 26–27 per cent. Further, the income tax rate on existing domestic companies was also reduced to 22 per cent (making for an effective tax rate of 25.17 per cent), provided they did not avail of any exemption/incentive. At the end of her statement,[3] the minister said: '. . . the total revenue foregone for the reduction in corporate tax rate and other relief estimated at ₹1,45,000 crore (or ₹1.45 tn).' This announcement attracted a lot of attention from domestic and global manufacturing companies, and it was hoped it would give a real boost to economic activity in India.

With the privilege of working in one of the largest brokerage firms in the country, I could see that the impact of this tax cut would be nothing less than a godsend for the industry. All my colleagues—not to mention equity analysts in other equity brokerage houses—lifted the earnings estimates of their coverage companies, boosting the stock market. After all, if tax rates fall, a company will be able to retain a larger share of its earnings, which can then be distributed to its shareholders (in the form of dividends) or ploughed back into the company as investments (called retained earnings). But economists are generally known as party-poopers, and I totally lived up to that reputation on that occasion. Let me give you a glimpse of how my (an economist's) mind was trying to understand the economic impact of this big announcement back then.

Let's consider an example. If the GoI announces tomorrow that every individual income taxpayer in the country would be eligible to receive 5 per cent of their annual tax payments in cash back into their bank accounts, the first question that would come to my mind would be, *'Where will the government get this money from?'* Of course, since the cash-back will come from the taxes paid by individuals, the GoI doesn't have to find new money; it will just have to return 5 per cent of the tax collection to the taxpayers. However, the Indian government has run a fiscal deficit historically, which means that its total expenditure has always been higher than its total receipts (if spending is lower than/equal to total receipts, it is called fiscal surplus/neutral). If the GoI returns 5 per cent of the income tax collected to the taxpayers, it will have only two options: (1) to keep total spending and other receipts unchanged, which would lead to a higher fiscal deficit; or (2) to keep its fiscal balance unchanged by hiking tax rates on other participants (such as excise duties on petrol/diesel, etc., or income tax rate on companies) and/or by rationalizing total spending.

Similarly, when the GoI announced the corporate income tax rate cut in September 2019, the first question that came to my mind was, *'Does the government accept that this will lead to a higher fiscal deficit?'* Although Sitharaman said the tax cut would cost the government ₹1.45 tn (or 0.7 per cent of GDP), there was no explicit mention of the expansion in fiscal deficit due to the corporate income tax cut.

The answer to this question is at the heart of gauging the *net economic* impact of the cut in corporate income tax rates—or of any other fiscal policy, for that matter. If the government keeps its fiscal deficit unchanged, it is very difficult to make a case for positive economic impact from the new policy. This is because while the GoI has cut the tax rate for companies, it will have to either increase other tax rates and/or cut other spending to keep the fiscal deficit intact. For instance, the government can choose to hike individual income tax rates or reduce some subsidy to offset the losses due to the corporate tax cut. If so, with lower disposable income (the amount of income left with the earner after paying taxes to the government, also called take-home income) or higher prices of non-subsidized commodities, households would cut back on their spending, almost entirely offsetting the impact of the lower corporate income tax rate. In short, while the GoI has given to companies with one hand, it has taken an equivalent amount from some other sectors (household, in this example) with the other. The net economic impact, thus, may be negligible.[4]

On the contrary, if the government accepts a higher fiscal deficit, which means it neither increases any other tax rate nor adjusts its expenditure downwards, cutting the tax rate on corporate income is effectively a transfer of resources from the government to the corporate sector in an economy.[5] However, there is a certain time lag and high uncertainty (sometimes calling for a leap of faith) involved in all such policies. While the GoI did immediately accept a higher fiscal deficit (due to lower receipts), higher corporate profits may or may not lead to higher investments and employment. In the same way that a 5 per cent cash-back to all individual taxpayers will not make all of them buy a new house, lower corporate income tax rate is not the only determinant for companies to accept or reject investment proposals. The broader economic environment, domestic demand, labour costs, the logistics infrastructure, other government policies and international competition are some of the other factors considered by companies when it comes to investing.

Therefore, even though the fiscal deficit widens, companies may choose to retain their higher profits (or profit after taxes, PAT) as savings rather than spend it. If companies decide to invest those savings at a later stage in the domestic economy, it would lead to higher production, higher employment, higher household income and, eventually, higher government taxes. Nevertheless, the immediate impact would be a higher deficit with no change in private spending.

If the GoI accepts a higher fiscal deficit resulting from a corporate income tax cut, the second question that would come to my mind is, *'How would the government finance a higher fiscal deficit?'* There are only two possible options—either by borrowing from the domestic market or by borrowing from the external (or foreign) markets. Both options have their own macroeconomic consequences, which, as I explain in this book, could be more complex than the headlines suggest.

While all this was playing on my mind, the equity markets were going berserk. This was not irrational but a totally sensible reaction from the equity market participants. One certain impact of a cut in corporate income tax rate was the transfer of resources to the corporate sector, which is what equity markets are concerned about. Even if the positive *net economic* impact was unclear, the positive impact on the bottom line of companies was certain, rightly pushing their stock prices higher.

Therefore, while an economic policy may have an immediate positive impact on the equity market, it may or may not have a beneficial impact on the economy. This is one reason why economists are generally more conservative in their analysis of situations and less optimistic than others, especially financial market participants. The latter are concerned about the *gross* impact of an economic policy (on companies in the case of equity/corporate debt market participants and on the government in the case of sovereign debt market participants), while the former (economists, like me) are concerned about the *net* impact[6] of these policies on the economy. Both concerns are sensible and rational.

Also, while such policies cheer equity market participants, fixed income (or debt) participants are less enthused.[7] Different asset classes, thus, reacted differently to the finance minister's announcement. In the week (quarter) following the finance minister's announcement, while the benchmark equity market index, the Nifty50, rose 7.5 per cent (14.5 per cent), the benchmark 10-year government bond fell as the yield rose by 14 (26) basis points (bps, one basis point being one-hundredth of a percentage point). The Indian rupee (INR) was broadly stable against the US dollar (USD).

Let's discuss one more example. These months before the 2019 general elections, the GoI launched the Pradhan Mantri Kisan Samman Nidhi (PM-KISAN) scheme in its Interim Budget presented on 1 February 2019. Under this scheme, vulnerable landholding farmer families with cultivable land of up to 2 hectares were promised unconditional direct income support of ₹6,000 per year. This would benefit around 120 mn small and marginal farmers. Recent Budget documents show there was an outlay of ₹124 bn in FY19[8] (as the scheme was announced retrospectively, with effect from 1 December 2018), ₹487 bn in FY20, ₹667 bn in FY21, ₹668 bn in FY22, a revised estimate (RE) of ₹600 bn in FY23 and a budget estimate (BE) of ₹600 bn in FY24.

Unlike in the previous example, this fiscal policy entailed an effective transfer of resources from the government to the farmers (or agricultural households) in the country. From this perspective, rural demand was expected to improve, leading to higher consumer spending and thus higher GDP growth. Further, with direct income support, the small- and marginal-farmer community also became a target for micro-finance companies.

But although the GoI announced an additional scheme costing ₹124 bn, total spending amounted to ₹23.1 tn in FY19, lower than the budgeted estimate (BE)/revised estimate (RE) of ₹24.4/24.6 tn. Still, the fiscal deficit in FY19 was higher—₹6.49 tn, against the BE/RE of ₹6.24/6.34 tn. This means that the higher deficit was on account of lower receipts and not higher spending (despite the new announcements).

It is thus possible that the *net economic* impact of this scheme was negligible because while the government decided to transfer additional resources to small and marginal farmers, lower total spending meant that some other expenditure was reduced (there were no new tax-related announcements). Effectively, these resources were transferred to the small and marginal farmers from either other individuals or companies.

Therefore, it is difficult to establish any significant positive impact of this announcement on the economy. The rural sector, however, certainly benefited.

These two examples reveal some important features of an economy. First, the gross impact of any fiscal/economic policy could be very different from the net impact. The targeted policies are likely to have a direct positive impact on a certain section of the society. However, the *net economic* impact could be at wide variance with the gross impact. Second, higher government spending may or may not represent a stimulus, depending on whether it leads to a rise in total spending, and thus a rise in the fiscal deficit. If total spending is unchanged or lower, it is unlikely to lead to higher economic activity on a net basis. The fiscal deficit may rise because of lower receipts rather than because of higher spending. Third, the various agents in an economy are interlinked. Any fiscal policy will affect economic activity by changing the behaviour of these agents. A change in economic behaviour in one participant tends to lead to a series of changes in the behaviour of other economic agents, which will eventually decide the *final economic* outcome. Fourth, while analysing the economic impact of any policy, one needs to look beyond the obvious and peel off several layers to understand the true economic impact. Most of the time, we stop at the *gross* impact and ignore the *net* impact. However, the latter, not the former, will determine the economic impact of a policy.

In this book, I focus on those sections of the economy which are less discussed in the mainstream, because of lack of data or lack of interest or knowledge. For instance, while everyone knows about the four sectors of the economy that I mentioned earlier, discussion on the household sector in India is mostly focused on the farmer (or agricultural) community because of its size. However, it is widely acknowledged that though this sector employs 45 per cent of India's workforce, it generates only 15 per cent of the national output. Further, the importance of non-farm rural and urban households has increased tremendously over the past few decades. Therefore, it is pertinent to understand the financial position of the entire household sector in India rather than focus on one community within the sector.

Similarly, most of the analysis on India's corporate sector focuses on the listed companies, and when it comes to the government sector, largely covers only the Union/Central government. A comprehensive analysis must include the unlisted corporate sector and the state governments because they account for the majority of India's corporate and government sectors, respectively. Any analysis missing these larger sections within these broad sectors could throw up highly misleading conclusions.

I am worried not only about the poor finances of the farmers but also about the deteriorating financial position of the entire household sector in the country. Although listed companies are having a gala time post-COVID-19, it is more a reflection of the rising concentration of power and economic activities within India's corporate sector rather than anything else. This is because the financial position of the much larger unlisted corporate sector has deteriorated to such an extent that, in the aggregate, the corporate sector in India has weakened in the post-COVID-19 period.

Further, higher spending by the Central government may happen on account of inadequate sharing of tax receipts by the Union government to states. Since the state budgets collectively are bigger than the Union budget, lower spending by the former could entirely offset higher spending by the latter. If so, the entire narrative of the fiscal stimulus based on only the Union government finances could be highly misleading. In order to gauge the true fiscal policy in India, one must combine Central and state finances. Unfortunately, there is no centralized or regulatory agency that shares or collects data from India's local, municipal or panchayat levels. The Reserve Bank of India (RBI), however, did a fantastic job of publishing[9] the first report on municipal finances in late 2022, compiling and analysing budgetary data for 201 municipal corporations (MCs) across all states.

Lastly, in this globalized world the interactions between the domestic economy and the external sector are extremely important. Although market participants will be aware of the headline data in terms of India's current account balance, exports, imports and foreign inflows, it is equally important for them to be aware of how the economic decisions of domestic participants affect the external sector. What are the true implications of foreign capital inflows on domestic economic growth? Under what circumstances do higher flows lead to positive growth, and what factors may mean adverse growth implications?

I firmly believe that 'reaching 8 per cent-plus growth' is the most important economic objective of the country. This book explains these less-discussed or rarely debated behind-the-curtains nuances in an economy. Without these nuances, any economic analysis will be incomplete and will likely culminate in misleading conclusions, and thus bad economic policies. Since the economic behaviours of the many participants are highly interlinked, we must arrive at the *net* impact of their behaviours from their *gross* impact to understand their true economic impact. This book aims to spread awareness about the weakening financial positions of the Indian household and unlisted corporate sectors among policymakers, investors and economic commentators. Without an improvement in the financial positions of these two sectors, the 8 per cent growth target looks distant.

Key Conclusion and Findings of the Book

We are living in a 20-20-format world. Not many cricket fans have the patience to sit and watch Test cricket these days. We want quick results. Therefore, I list the key conclusions and findings of this book upfront.

2020s the 'Healing Decade', or We Lose Precious Time

My analysis answers the key question *'How can India get back to 8 per cent-plus growth for a longer period of time?'* I argue that there are two possible scenarios that could shape the 2020s and the future decades. In the first scenario, which I hope does not materialize and is not my base case, the domestic economic participants and Indian policymakers ignore the lessons from the pandemic and continue to behave in a financially irresponsible manner. If so, consumption will remain the key growth driver and gross savings will continue to plummet over the next few years. Investments, thus, will continue to weaken, unless supported by foreign savings (also called current account deficit), creating external imbalances. Although real GDP growth may remain high (say 6–7 per cent) for a few years under this scenario, it will soon fizzle out, leading to much slower average growth over the late 2020s and the subsequent decades. This will not only leave us with limited time to mend our ways and to grow strongly on a sustainable basis but will also likely lead to slower growth in potential output in the subsequent decades, unless the structural issues are addressed.

Alternatively, I hope that several economic policies are adopted in line with a multi-decade strategy, which we discuss in this book. It is very likely that the benefits of these will not be reaped immediately, but only after a few years. If so, the 2020s decade should be accepted as the 'Healing Decade' for the Indian economy, wherein the authorities and domestic agents work towards addressing the structural domestic issues instead of focusing on achieving high GDP growth. Consequently, real GDP growth could ease to 4–6 per cent during the rest of the 2020s decade. This may seem outrageous and politically unacceptable. However, since this can lead to a sustainably higher growth of 6–8 per cent in the 2030s decade, and further, 8–10 per cent growth in the subsequent decade(s), it may encourage policymakers to consider this strategy.

Unlike in most other major economies of the world, India's demography is in its favour and the authorities must work towards yielding 'dividends' out of it rather than turning it into a 'burden'. According to the United Nations,[10] the working-age population (15–59 years) in India is expected to peak around the mid-2040s, after which it will start declining. This means that the nation has about two decades to ensure sound domestic fundamentals and achieve high growth. Spending the 2020s decade to set the stage and prepare ourselves for a brighter future will be more like Test cricket rather than a 20–20 match. This may sound like a big ask; however, I believe that this is an absolutely necessary condition to achieve sustainable high growth over a long period of time. We must have a long-term strategy and the patience to strengthen our roots, and then build at a faster pace.

My recommendation, thus, is for the authorities to use the 2020s decade to work extensively on improving the financial position of all the domestic economic agents, which will unlock the potential to grow at a higher pace on a sustainable basis. There are no short cuts to grow at 8 per cent on a sustainable basis, and that is why only a handful of nations in the world have achieved this feat. Higher growth in the near term, as explained in the first scenario, may prove to be unsustainable and is thus better avoided.

Now that I have told you about the destination, the more interesting part is the journey. This book uses sectoral financial balance sheets and the Theory of Everything identity to understand the Indian economy. In simple language, I analyse the financial positions of three domestic sectors—household, corporate and government—and discuss their linkages with the rest of the world (RoW = external/foreign sector). This approach helps me understand the Indian economy in a manner that is different from the usual value-addition methodology covering the agriculture, industry and services sectors. Given below are my four key findings.

1. *The Indian Household Sector's Financial Position Has Weakened Dramatically*

An analysis of household income, consumption, savings, investments and debt over the past seven decades indicates that the household sector's financial position has deteriorated dramatically during the past decade. Since it is the most pervasive and important sector in any economy, the absence of this realization in public debates is remarkable. It is well acknowledged that household consumption was the primary driver of economic growth during the pre-COVID-19 years. But for the first time in the past seven decades, household income growth has lagged behind household consumption growth. Consequently, household savings have fallen persistently since 2013, marking their first such fall in the past seven decades, and household leveraging has risen.

So what if India's household savings have fallen and debt has risen during the past decade? The former are still among the highest in the world while the latter is among the lowest. This is a very normal rebuttal used by many renowned economists in the country to shrug off these trends. Such comparisons and conclusions, however, are highly misleading. Even with such low headline debt-to-income ratio, the debt service ratio (DSR) of Indian households is much higher than in other economies, which have 2–3x household debt. The combination of high effective interest rates and low maturity leads to a higher service ratio for the Indian household sector, which makes the comparison of headline ratios meaningless. The analysis in this book suggests that the threshold for Indian household leverage is only 60–80 per cent of personal disposable income (PDI), much lower than in most other major economies of the world. At the current rate, Indian household debt will reach this threshold by the early 2030s decade.

Overall, the current financial position of India's household sector is equivalent to that of a company which is growing its spending quickly but garnering lower profits (= savings) and accumulating more leverage. My confidence in India's high economic growth based on household consumption is as low as my conviction to invest in such a company. This is, by far, one of the most important, and unbelievably most ignored, characteristics of the Indian economy, and one which has only worsened because of COVID-19. This raises a lot of serious questions on India's ability to grow fast on a sustainable basis in the future decades as it presents an important structural constraint for higher growth. Higher growth in the short term, if achieved, is very likely to happen at the cost of further deterioration in the financial position of the household sector, making the country's economic growth weaker in the subsequent decades.

2. *Listed Companies Strong, but Aggregate Corporate Sector Has Weakened*

COVID-19 has turned the tables for the two-member corporate sector in India. The listed universe accounts for 25–35 per cent of the entire corporate sector in terms of gross value addition (GVA), investments, leverage (debt), profits and (goods) exports. It means that the lesser-known, unlisted corporate sector is much larger than the listed universe. The listed companies were losing market share in the pre-COVID-19 world, but this trend appears to have reversed since mid-2020. Although the listed companies have benefited and have come out stronger from the pandemic, the unlisted corporate sector has suffered to such an extent that the financial position of the aggregate corporate sector has deteriorated in India.

More important, there seems to be growing evidence suggesting the weakening relationship between profits and investments in the corporate sector. During the first two decades of the twenty-first century, global corporate profits rose sharply (led by the US). However, corporate investments have either been stable or their increase has lagged pick-up in profits. This book argues that while investments drive profits, the relationship has weakened the other way round because of the changing nature of the global economy. One of the major factors responsible for the weakened virtuous cycle between investments and corporate profits is the large economic stimulus (fiscal and monetary), helping the corporate sector to thrive amid weak economic growth. The current economic environment is fragile, and the inevitable normalization in economic policies may quickly dissipate the good times for the corporate sector.

Notwithstanding decadal high profits and the large deleveraging of listed companies, the weak financial position of the aggregate corporate sector (lower profits and higher debt) in India in the post-COVID-19 period and the structural weakness in the general investment mood globally do not point to the possibility of an investment-led recovery in the country.

3. *Fiscal Consolidation Means Weak Growth in Government Spending in the 2020s Decade*

Along with household consumption, it was government spending that supported India's economic growth during the pre-pandemic period. Just like the corporate sector, there are two key players in the government sector—the Centre (or the Union) and the states. The financial position of the Central government is in much better shape than that of the state governments; however, what matters for the economy is their combined financial position. A careful analysis confirms that the fiscal consolidation in India has been too slow—down from 9.3 per cent of GDP in the 1990s decade to 8.5 per cent of GDP in the 2000s decade to 7.7 per cent of GDP in the 2010s decade. This implies that the government sector absorbed almost the entire household surplus in the 2010s decade, against less than 70 per cent in the mid-2000s decade.

Government policies in India during the pre-COVID-19 years were largely geared towards encouraging consumption, which too contributed to lower household savings in the country. The pandemic worsened the situation. To save the livelihoods of the citizens, the government had to increase its revenue expenditure (also called current or consumption-related spending) substantially at the cost of its capital expenditure (which primarily includes investments) in FY21. This, however, reversed quickly and the growth in the Central government's investments and their share in the total expenditure increased substantially in FY22 and FY23.

The Indian government's response to COVID-19 was initially highly criticized but then gradually drew praise. There is, however, no doubt that the COVID-19-related fiscal stimulus was much smaller in India than the response of most other nations in the world (including many other emerging markets). Since the spending of the government translates into receipt/income of the Indian private sector, the latter suffered more than their counterparts in other economies, which may have a long-lasting impact over the next few years. Notwithstanding the lower stimulus provided by India, the country, like other nations, is likely to remain in the fiscal consolidation mode over the 2020s decade as the aggregate adjusted fiscal deficit is expected to fall from 13.2 per cent of GDP in FY21 to 6–7 per cent by the end of the decade. Like household consumption, then, it is very likely that growth in government spending will be muted over the next many years compared to the pre-COVID-19 years.

4. *Can Exports Be the New Growth Driver? Unlikely, Given Other Discordant Economic Policies*

Lastly, the strong growth in India's merchandise exports during the past few quarters has brought with it a new ray of hope. After stagnating at $300 bn for almost a decade, India's merchandise exports rose to more than $420 bn in FY22 and further to $447 bn in FY23. As in the case of most successful Asian nations, it is believed that exports could be the next engine of growth in India, leading to 8 per cent-plus real GDP growth. This argument is so discordant with the other economic policies of the nation that it is an outright impossibility.

Looking at exports in isolation is inappropriate because the resources required to produce exportable goods and services are also used to produce domestic goods and services. Exports growth, thus, is not independent of the behaviour of domestic economic participants.

Further, exports can drive economic growth only if imports remain contained. GDP measures the value of goods and services produced within the geographical boundaries of a country. Exports represent the value of those goods and services that are produced domestically but absorbed by the external sector. Similarly, imports represent the value of those goods and services that are produced outside the domestic geographical boundaries but are used domestically. Imports, thus, are either consumed or invested (used further in the production process), because of which they are deducted from the sum of consumption, investments and exports to arrive at GDP. Several studies have found that a significant portion of imports is used as raw material in India, a part of which is then re-exported. It is, therefore, not surprising that exports and imports move in tandem in India. Not only did exports rise to an all-time high in FY23, but imports have also posted all-time high levels. Consequently, India's merchandise trade deficit also increased, rising to an average of $20–25 bn in the last few months of FY22 and the first half of FY23. What matters for economic growth, therefore, is not (gross) exports, but net exports (or current account balance).

Rising exports played a critical role in the successful transition of the four 'Asian Tigers' between the 1960s and 1990s into high-income countries, and in China's growth miracle since the 1980s. However, there are only two ways in which higher external demand can be met: by reducing domestic demand or by increasing imports (through higher debt or otherwise), or both. As we explain later in the book, the current policies do not suggest that the authorities want to achieve the former, and the latter is highly uncertain as net exports may or may not increase. A careful study of successful East Asian nations reveals two interesting facts: (1) countries like South Korea and Singapore witnessed high current account deficit (CAD) during the initial stages of their economic progress; and (2) even after three decades of double-digit growth in these economies, debt-to-GDP ratio in South Korea and Taiwan was less than 120 per cent of the GDP in the early 1990s.

Effectively, external trade (led by exports) can drive economic growth if and only if other economic policies (such as the treatment of the household sector, preference to the corporate sector [producers] and the fiscal deficit) are also in line with this model. This is not the case in India and is unlikely to happen anytime soon.

Too Many Objectives with Limited Resources: What Will We Give Away?

Overall, one of the biggest challenges with India seems to be that the authorities are trying to achieve too many objectives with limited resources. We want decent consumption growth, rising farm incomes, a buoyant corporate sector, higher investments, lower inflation, lower CAD, a largely privatized financial sector, lower presence of the government, contained fiscal deficit, etc. There is no economy in history that has been able to achieve all these objectives at the same time. Under the East Asian growth model the household sector was seriously suppressed to replace domestic demand with exports, and these countries had high CAD in the initial phases of their development. The financial sector was largely dominated by the government in these nations during their high-growth decades, and fiscal discipline was a major priority.

I am not rooting for re-nationalization of India's banking sector or for suppression of India's household sector (any more than has already been done). However, a careful study of the established economic growth models suggests two things: (1) the transition to high income was not achieved by any one single economic policy but by a combination of various policies, most of them working with each other and reinforcing the impact; and (2) several lessons learnt from such models are totally irrelevant or impractical for implementation by any nation, including India, in today's world.

In short, no nation can achieve everything and every nation needs to decide what to give away. In this book, I recommend that giving away a portion of economic growth for a few years in the current decade, while strengthening the financial position of domestic agents, will help India achieve higher growth over the subsequent decades on a sustainable basis. I see no other way for the Indian economy to grow at 8 per cent or higher on a sustainable basis. Here is a summary of the key recommendations suggested in this book to achieve sustainably high GDP growth:

1. India's gross domestic savings (GDS) must rise led by higher household savings, higher corporate profits and lower fiscal deficit.
2. There are only two ways to achieve higher household savings: either private consumption growth slows down (leading to slower GDP growth) or PDI starts growing faster than consumption. Further, the more the rise in household savings comes from financial savings, the better it is. Physical savings, at the same time, must not fall.
3. Although household leverage is low in India, its debt service ratio is very high. A combination of higher residual maturity and lower effective interest rate must be targeted to make household debt more sustainable. Lower savings, however, make it difficult to reduce interest rates.
4. Serious deliberations are required to incentivize the corporate sector to invest more. As and when that happens, the space created by higher GDS and lower CAD (or

surpluses) will allow investments to push GDP growth higher in the initial years without creating any economic imbalances.
5. The unlisted companies must witness a rise in their profits. Higher investments, not fiscal stimulus or lower household savings, should be the primary driver of higher corporate profits in India, hopefully rising back to at least 10 per cent of GDP.
6. The fall in fiscal deficit must at least be in line with the present decline in household savings. Lower fiscal deficit will clear the space for the private sector to borrow more domestically and increase its investments, as and when that happens.
7. The corporate sector, and not the household sector or the government, should be the primary driver of rising leverage in the country.
8. It may be futile to hope for export-led growth in India, which requires complementing policies to suppress the domestic consumers (that is, households) and incentivize the producers (that is, corporate sector). Without an increase in efficiency, higher exports can be attained only by replacing domestic demand or by higher imports, or both. Targeted policies, thus, must be adopted to reduce oil-related trade deficit so that larger deficit can be tolerated on the non-oil basket, which may be needed initially when investments rise faster.
9. The policymakers have introduced a number of policies to try to push labour productivity higher, which must be implemented with the same enthusiasm, as it may reap benefits only over a long period of time. An improvement in total factor productivity (TFP) growth and labour quality (better education) can help India attain 8 per cent growth with an investment rate of 32–33 per cent. However, this is no substitute for strengthening the financial balance sheet of economic agents.

10. The RBI must explore how to distance itself as much as possible from the currency markets, allowing the Indian rupee to be market-determined, and reduce the need to accumulate foreign exchange reserves (FXR). With the RBI solely focused on the government securities market, it will get better control over domestic fundamentals and reduce India's dependence on the US monetary policies.

All these policies must be pursued simultaneously, starting with a clear path to bring down fiscal deficit in a gradual but definite manner by the policymakers and avoiding policies that incentivize consumption over savings or retail debt over corporate debt. Excess focus on one policy, ignoring the other requirements, may not lead to high growth on a sustainable basis. Extremely delicate balance is needed to achieve this task, and it has been mastered by only a handful of economies in the world.

There Is One Other Way, Which One Can't Rely Upon

Real GDP growth can also be defined as a function of employment and labour productivity. Therefore, any changes or policies leading to better productivity will boost GDP growth. There are three sources of growth in labour productivity: labour quality (through better education), capital deepening (that is, higher investment per unit of labour) and total factor productivity (TFP). Much of the optimism about India's higher growth stems from a perceived improvement in its labour productivity.

According to the India KLEMS[11] database, capital deepening accounted for as much as 75 per cent of the average labour productivity growth during the period FY82 to FY18, followed by TFP growth (15–17 per cent) with better labour quality contributing less than 10 per cent.

The efforts of the Central government to promote capital deepening are notable. For more than a decade, the share of capital spending in total expenditure was in a stable, narrow range of 10 to 14 per cent, averaging around 12 per cent. During the past few years, however, it surged from 12 per cent in FY21 to 17.4 per cent in FY23RE and is budgeted to rise to an almost two-decade high of 22.2 per cent in FY24. The Centre's investments are, thus, budgeted to almost double from 1.7 per cent of GDP in the decade preceding the pandemic to 3.3 per cent of GDP in FY24.

This, however, is insufficient. To witness an improvement in labour productivity growth, India's total investment rate has to rise. Clearly, there was a concerted investment push by the Central government from FY22 onward; however, this reflects a shift of capex from the Central public sector enterprises (CPSEs), rather than additional capex. Aggregate public sector investments (including the Centre, state governments and CPSEs), thus, was at an eight-year low in FY23, as per my estimates. This, effectively, can be linked with the thesis of this book, which recommends that India must move away from consumption-led growth to investment-driven growth, which may need some sacrifice in the short term.

Further, many policies have been implemented to push TFP higher. TFP refers to all productivity gains that are not explained by either of the two production inputs. Though this area is not directly linked with the framework used in this book, it deserves a mention. A massive wave of digitalization has swept through the economy in the past few years. India's digital payment systems, such as the unified payments interface (UPI), have attracted a lot of attention across the globe. Not only has this helped reduce the cost of fund transfers and remittance payments but it has also greatly increased convenience. Besides, the government has been making efforts to remove various impediments in several areas, such as the single-window clearance initiative. The opening up of bank accounts under Jan Dhan Yojana, reforming the government's delivery system in welfare schemes through direct benefit transfers (DBT), linking PAN card with Aadhaar number and digitizing land records under the Digital India Land Records Modernisation Programme (DILRMP) are just few examples of this massive wave of digitalization in the country. There are numerous examples from a regular Indian's daily life, where this wave of digitalization is amply clear. All these incremental changes have led to immense convenience for citizens over the past many years. It is, thus, possible that TFP may increase in the future, giving a boost to labour productivity growth too. However, since these gains are highly uncertain and one does not know if they will be offset by other factors (such as weak employment growth or lower investments), it would not be advisable for the policymakers to bank on this.

What Constitutes an Economy?

Before proceeding to the key learnings, it is important to understand the constituents of an economy. An economy consists of only four participants—the corporate sector (private and public financial and non-financial companies), the government sector (the Central and state governments, including local and municipal-level authorities), the household sector and the external sector. Households consist of individuals (like you and me), the non-profit institutions serving households and unincorporated enterprises. The small shops at the corner of the street, the self-employed population providing numerous services, such as tailors and cobblers and street vendors also form part of the household sector. Similarly, the hundreds of thousands of professionals, such as doctors, chartered accountants (CAs), financial planners, etc., who are self-employed are also part of the household sector.

Economic growth is the outcome of the decisions of the three domestic participants (the corporate, government and household sectors) in terms of consumption, savings, investments and leverage. The foreign (or external) sector also influences and gets influenced by the economic decisions of these domestic participants. Stated in the simplest terms:

Gross domestic product (GDP) = Private final consumption expenditure (PFCE) + Government final consumption expenditure (GFCE) + Gross capital formation (GCF) + Exports – Imports

This means that an economy consists of only three activities: consumption, investment and foreign trade. Households are the primary consumers, accounting for more than 80 per cent of total final consumption expenditure in India. Unlike in most developed and developing economies, the household sector in India is also an important investor (primarily in residential real estate, but also in machinery and equipment [by unincorporated enterprises]), accounting for anywhere between 30 per cent and 40 per cent of total investments (called GCF in the equation above) in the economy. Effectively, therefore, the household sector accounts for approximately 70 per cent of GDP in India.

In contrast, companies (or the corporate sector) don't consume. The non-financial companies (NFCs) are the primary investors in India, accounting for roughly half of the economy's GCF, and the government sector accounts for the remaining 10–15 per cent of total investments. Broadly speaking, then, **households are the major consumers in the economy; NFCs are the major investors; and the governments do a bit of both.**

Of course, export and import of goods and services are transactions between the domestic economy and the external world. The balance of payments (BoP) figure presents a comprehensive account of all transactions of the domestic economy vis-à-vis the outside world, of which export and import of goods and services are only a part.

An obvious question at this stage would be, *'What about savings?'* While consumption and investments by various economic participants (called institutional sectors in national income accounting [NIA] parlance) gets captured in the GDP, how are savings accounted for? Savings are the residual of income after consumption spending. Savings hold a special and important place in economic analysis. As you will notice, the savings decisions of the various economic participants are discussed at multiple stages in this book. In fact, savings are one of the intrinsic elements of my analysis. They don't directly enter into GDP calculations; however, they are captured indirectly. In a closed economy, investments will always be equal to domestic savings. Since closed economies do not exist in today's globalized world, investments can be higher or lower than domestic savings, depending on whether an economy borrows from or lends to the outside world. This, as discussed later in this chapter, can be formulated into a powerful economic equation/identity.

Besides NFCs, there are financial companies too, including banks, non-banking financial companies (NBFCs), housing finance companies (HFCs), mutual funds, insurance companies, the RBI and pension funds. These companies act as intermediaries in an economy, and their primary purpose is to help mobilize funds from the savers (or surplus sector) and channel them to the borrowers (or deficit sector). The role of the financial sector has evolved during the past few decades. Traditional wisdom has it that banks use the deposits they receive from households or other sectors to create bank lending. However, as the Bank of England has stated,[12] the process of money creation is actually the reverse. Bank lending creates deposits rather than the other way round.

Notwithstanding this reverse modern theory of money creation, loans and deposits must not be confused with savings and investments in an economy. Bank lending creates deposits, not savings. And a portion of total borrowings is used to finance consumption rather than investments. Commercial banks are the true money creators in the modern economy, not the central banks. The process of money creation is totally different from the actual economic decisions that involve savings and investments made by the various participants in an economy. When a central bank eases monetary policy by cutting interest rates and/or by purchasing financial securities, also called quantitative easing (QE), it encourages spending by the private sector. However, whether this happens or not will be determined by the private sector.

In a nutshell, the household sector consumes, invests and saves, but since its savings are higher than its investments, the sector is a net saver (or net lender) in India. The corporate sector invests and saves, and under normal circumstances corporate savings are lower than corporate investments. The corporate sector, thus, is a net borrower (or a deficit sector); however, the corporate sector can also be a net lender (with savings higher than investments) during periods of weak confidence. And the government both consumes and invests, and since in most cases its consumption is more than its income, it is likely to be a net borrower (or in deficit mode) even without investment spending. In our normal discussions, we may use government savings and fiscal deficit interchangeably; however, these two terms are very different from the NIA perspective. Overall, households are the primary net lenders in the economy while governments are net borrowers. Of course, there are other nations where governments run fiscal surpluses and thus could be net savers (or lenders) in the same way that the corporate sector can also be a net lender. This is a very important point which will be repeated many time through this book.

Economic policies primarily work through redistribution of resources from one sector to the other—household to corporate, or government to household—or within a sector, say, from prosperous to poor households, or from less-leveraged companies to leveraged firms. All economic policies—be they fiscal, monetary or trade-related—work through changing the spending or saving (or investment) behaviours of the household, corporate and/or government sectors.

Six Learnings

Now I list six important economic rules which have shaped my analysis in this book.

Learning#1: Financial Savings Are Different from Physical Investments

One of the biggest surprises for me in my career has been the massive confusion among highly intelligent people regarding the distinction between financial/physical savings and financial/physical investments in an economy. While it took me some time to understand the confusion, its widespread nature made the reasons clear.

Let's first understand *financial* savings and investments. In daily life we use the terms 'savings' and 'investments' interchangeably. Almost all the time, we are referring only in financial terms. However, these two things are different in NIA terms. If I earn ₹100, of which I spend ₹70, the residual (₹30) is called my savings. In simple terms, the excess of income over consumption is the savings of an individual or entity. By default, a large part of our savings lies in bank accounts. In our daily lives, when we choose to shift a portion of our savings from bank deposits to, say, the financial markets or to insurance or pension funds, it qualifies as 'investment'. In short, when an individual shifts a portion of his savings into various investment instruments to earn higher interest, with some degree of risk, we call it investing. NIA standards, however, are different.

Under NIA standards, there is no concept of financial investments. All income in excess of consumption is referred to as savings, irrespective of whether it is parked with banks, the financial markets or some other instrument. It has nothing to do with the risk the 'investment' entails or the returns prospect; any money over and above consumption spending is called 'savings', not investments. Thus, 'savings' under NIA standards (as used by economists) is a much broader concept compared with the term 'savings' used in regular life.

However, there is an exception. If the individual chooses to buy an immovable asset, such as a home or land, or if a company (or a proprietor) decides to purchase machinery, these acts are investments. As a rule of thumb, in national accounting, investments represent the creation of fixed assets while savings are purely financial in nature. In NIA, fixed asset investments are also called physical savings. By definition, thus, the physical savings of an individual are the same as her investments.

Under NIA, unless money is spent to create a fixed asset—be it real estate, or machinery and equipment, or research and development, or intellectual property rights—it is either consumed or saved. Therefore, when a general statement is made, such as *'I have invested one hundred rupees in stocks today,'* or *'I have bought insurance'*, one has made savings, not investments, as per NIA, because no fixed asset has been created.

In other words, transactions involving fixed assets count as investments in the national accounts, and all financial transactions that do not create fixed assets are savings. I will explain it in greater detail when the financial position of Indian households is discussed in Chapter 2.

Similarly, while foreign direct investment (FDI) and foreign institutional/portfolio investments (FIIs/FPIs) are called investments in our daily discussions, they are not counted as investments in the national accounts because they do not necessarily create any fixed asset. This confusion is almost entirely because of the nomenclature of FDI and FIIs/FPIs.

FDIs and FPIs may or may not lead to higher investments in an economy, depending on a number of factors. They are inflows of foreign savings (capital/financial accounts under BoP) into the country; however, unless they are translated into goods and services (current account under BoP), they cannot be counted as investments in the national accounts. In simple words, abundance of foreign capital flows, even if it is in the most preferred form of FDI, does not guarantee an increase in total investments in the economy.

In recent times, as the global economy has become flush with liquidity, all emerging markets, including India, have seen large inflows of foreign capital. However, rather than this money getting spent on imported goods and services, thus leading to a lower current account balance and higher investments, it has simply added to the country's foreign exchange reserves and affected the financial markets. This is why it is important to segregate (financial) savings from (physical) investments.

Learning#2: Remember the Theory of Everything Identity in Economics

Economic analysis can be complicated or can lead to highly misleading conclusions if you are not aware of some rules that intend to make it easy. I believe that one of the easiest ways to understand the *economic* impact of any policy is through an identity, which I call the Theory of Everything in economics. This identity connects income, consumption, investments, savings and foreign trade in an economy and is very easy to derive and understand. What's more, it holds true for all economies under all circumstances. It is an ex-post equation, which means that when the national accounts are prepared at the end of any period (monthly, quarterly or yearly), this identity must hold, though there may be a very transitory disequilibrium. The Theory of Everything states that the total investments in an economy are always equal to the sum of domestic savings and foreign savings (measured as CAD):

Total investments = Domestic savings + Current account deficit (CAD) ...(1)

This is true for all open economies. In closed economies, total investments must equal domestic savings. All income in such a country will either get consumed or saved. Since there is no external or foreign sector in a closed economy, domestic or total investments are equal to domestic savings in the country. In a modern, open economy, however, total investments could be different (higher or lower) from domestic savings. The latter could be higher or lower than investments, depending on whether the economy lends to or borrows from the external world. If a country is a net borrower from the rest of the world, that is, it absorbs foreign savings, its total investments will be higher than domestic savings, and it thus will run a current account deficit. In contrast, if a country is a net lender to the RoW, total investments will be lower than domestic savings, and it will run a current account surplus.

Most economics students would be aware of this equation; however, since I hope this book gets read by non-economists

---

Box 1.1: Derivation of the Theory of Everything

A country's total domestic income (Y) is measured by the gross domestic product (GDP), which is the sum of private final consumption expenditure (Cp), government final consumption expenditure (Cg), private investments (Ip), government investments (Ig) and foreign trade (exports [X] and imports [M]) conducted by the household, corporate, government and foreign sectors. GDP, thus, is the sum of domestic consumption, domestic investments and net external trade. Total income, thus, can be expressed as:

$$Y (GDP) = Cp + Cg + Ip + Ig + (X - M) = C + I + (X - M)$$

Alternatively, income is simply the sum of consumption and savings:

$$Y = C + S$$

Equating both equations, we get: $C + I + (X - M) = C + S$

Or, $I = S - (X - M)$

Where, I = domestic investments, S = domestic savings and (X - M) = net exports of goods and services

Since current account balance is the sum of the trade balance of goods and services (X - M) and net income from abroad (R), the above equation can be rewritten as:

$$I + R = S - \{(X - M) + R\}$$

Total/national investments = domestic savings − current account balance

Or,

Total investments = domestic savings + CAD

too, the derivation is provided in Box 1.1. It is not difficult to make sense of the equation. Theoretically, it states that all investments in an economy must either be financed through domestic savings or through foreign savings. In other words, if investment demand in an economy is strong enough to outpace domestic savings, investors will buy goods and services from abroad, leading to CAD and foreign capital inflows. On the other hand, if domestic savings overtake investments, the excess savings will be exported to the RoW, leading to capital outflows, and thus current account surplus.

Generally, the Indian economy falls in the former category, wherein investments are higher than domestic savings. This difference between investments and savings is met through higher CAD, financed by foreign capital inflows. Other economies, such as the People's Republic of China (PRC) and Germany, on the contrary, fall in the latter category, with excess savings exported to the RoW and running current account surpluses.

Though the equation is well known and accepted, understanding the policy implications through this identity holds the key. As Dr Pronab Sen, the first chief statistician of India, told me once, 'I can actually finish an economics course in just three classes; however, understanding the behaviour and interlinkages between various sectors and activities is what is time-consuming and complicated.'

A question I am most often asked on this identity is, *'Why do we use CAD, and not foreign capital inflows?'* If I am talking about the financing of total investments in an economy, shouldn't I include foreign capital rather than the current account balance? Although I address this issue later in the book, the answer lies in Learning#1, discussed earlier. Investments in the national accounts mean transactions creating fixed assets. Since all foreign capital inflows do not do that, not all of it gets counted as investments.

Consider the case of the Indian economy: if the foreigners bring in capital inflows worth $2 bn in a year, it can have two possible implications. First, if the amount of foreign capital inflows is large enough to affect the domestic financial markets by reducing the cost of funds and pushing spending higher, it will lead to an increase in demand for foreign goods and services. Since higher investments or lower savings lead to higher CAD, such foreign capital inflows could boost GDP growth. Nevertheless, the growth impact would be equivalent to the extent of widening of the CAD rather than of foreign capital flows. This is because if CAD widens by, say, only $1 bn—only half of foreign capital flows—the remaining $1 bn would add to the country's foreign exchange reserves, which will eventually get invested in foreign securities and do not affect investments domestically. Therefore, it is CAD, and not foreign capital inflows, that forms a part of the identity.

Second, if the amount of foreign capital inflows is not large enough to push spending higher and is entirely sterilized by the RBI, CAD will largely remain unchanged because neither savings nor investments will be affected. In such a scenario, economic growth will also be unaffected. However, if foreign capital flows are included in Equation (1), it will lead to disequilibrium because neither investments nor savings change. Therefore, CAD and not foreign capital flows makes for the difference between savings and investments in a country.

Learning#3: The Corporate Sector Is Much Bigger Than the Universe of Listed Companies

As the Indian economy has an exceptionally large informal or unorganized sector, most national account statistics are regarded with some scepticism. Most of the analysis on India's corporate sector is based on either the BSE-500 companies or a larger listed corporate sector (with less than 3,000 actively traded companies) for which quarterly data is available. *'What is happening in the unlisted corporate sector and how strong or weak is it?'* is a question rarely debated.

I discuss this important characteristic in Chapter 3. The analysis clearly suggests that (1) the share of all the listed companies is less than 30 per cent of total corporate investments in the country; (2) the gross value addition (GVA) of listed companies is also about 26 per cent of the GVA of the entire corporate sector; and (3) the listed companies account for only about 34 per cent of outstanding corporate debt in the country. In fact, India' corporate profits (based on its listed companies) fell almost continuously from its peak of 6.2 per cent of GDP in FY08 to a two-decade low of less than 2 per cent of GDP in FY20, before picking up since the second half of FY21. While this is true, it does not take into account the large unlisted corporate sector.

The Theory of Everything equation helps me estimate the true aggregate corporate profits in India based on the macroeconomic aggregates. Equation (1) above can be reclassified and rewritten as:

Corporate profits = Total investments − Corporate depreciation + Dividends paid − Household savings − Government savings − CAD ...(2)

This equation not only helps us estimate the profits of India's entire corporate sector but also helps us identify the sources of these profits. Since the economy consists of only four sectors (household, corporate, government and external) and three activities (consumption, savings/investments and trade), corporate profits (PAT, which is a part of corporate savings) is dependent on the net investments in a country, its household savings, government savings and CAD. Corporate profits are primarily driven by investments in a nation and are inversely correlated with household and government savings. Further, the better the external trade balance (or the lower the CAD), the higher the corporate profits, and vice versa.

Using Equation (2), I find that India's aggregate corporate profits were not 2–3 per cent of GDP in FY18 and FY19 but 8–9 per cent of GDP, comparable to corporate profits in the US and the UK. It means that the unlisted corporate sector was not only highly profitable but highly resilient as well. There is enough evidence to support this hypothesis. These findings confirm that any analysis made without an understanding of the unlisted corporate sector will be partial and may lead to misleading conclusions.

Learning#4: Targeting Fiscal Deficit in Isolation Is Likely an Ineffective Strategy

High fiscal deficit is undesirable for any economy. Many nations—developed and developing—put an explicit cap on fiscal deficit, while others follow a soft target. India adopted the fiscal deficit target almost two decades ago; it was, ironically, achieved only once (in FY08) since.

The Fiscal Responsibility and Budget Management Act (FRBM Act), 2003, was passed and implemented in India to ensure long-term macroeconomic stability by removing fiscal impediments in the effective conduct of monetary policy and prudential debt management consistent with fiscal sustainability through limits on Central government borrowings, debt and deficits. The main purpose was to eliminate revenue deficit of the country (building revenue surplus thereafter) and bring down the fiscal deficit to a manageable 3 per cent of the GDP by March 2008. (Notably, the act was amended in the light of COVID-19, by shifting the target to achieve a fiscal deficit of 3 per cent of GDP by 31 March 2021 and by removing the commitment to achieve revenue surplus.)

The Theory of Everything, however, tells us that targeting fiscal deficit in isolation is a totally unfruitful exercise because the government is only one of the economic participants—and one that usually responds to the strengths or weaknesses of the private sector. Since private spending is the primary driver of growth in a nation, the fiscal deficit and government policies are usually a reaction to it. The stronger the private spending, the faster and better fiscal consolidation a government can practise; the weaker the private spending, the greater the fiscal expansion that would be required to support economic growth. Fiscal deficit, thus, is heavily dependent on private spending, which accounts for 80–85 per cent of GDP in India. The targeting of fiscal deficit is irrelevant, because if private spending is strong, the government may not have any other option but to consolidate to avoid the economy from overheating. On the contrary, if private spending is weak, the government must accommodate a higher fiscal deficit to support economic growth.

Let us understand it in some more detail. Equation (1) can be reclassified and rewritten as:

Government investments – Government savings = Private savings – Private investments + CAD
Or, *Core fiscal deficit*[13] *= Private sector surplus + CAD* . . .(3)

The equation implies that core fiscal deficit is equal to the sum of private surplus and CAD. If a country tries to achieve a particular target of fiscal deficit, it is effectively fixing the right-hand side as well. This sort of targeting has serious implications for economic growth.

Generally speaking, a lower core fiscal deficit led by lower private surplus and higher CAD is the most pro-growth scenario for an economy; however, a lower CAD will be more sustainable in today's environment. Lower private surplus implies higher private spending (consumption or investments), leading to higher GDP growth. In such a scenario, the government may take a back seat, relax and focus on fiscal consolidation. This could be achieved by either an unchanged CAD or a slight widening of it—lower than the fall in private surplus. This is exactly what happened in India during the FY04 to FY08 period. In fact, the government would do better to consolidate so that overheating is avoided.

If the government continues to expand its deficit—say, either because it decided to do so earlier and ignores the changing environment, or it just feels that it should be doing so, or simply because it is politically difficult to roll back extensions announced earlier—it is certain to end up overheating the economy. This would mean higher growth, higher inflation, higher CAD and a higher fiscal deficit. This is exactly what happened in the early 2010s decade in India. In the wake of the great financial crisis, private sector investments fell from their all-time peak of 32.4 per cent of GDP in FY08 to around 30.5 per cent of GDP in FY09 and FY10, and private sector savings rose slightly, from 36.3 per cent of GDP to 36.8 per cent of GDP. Consequently, the net surplus (savings less investments) of the private sector rose from around 4 per cent of GDP in FY08 to 6 per cent of GDP in FY10. During this period, the government supported economic activity as its deficit widened from around 5 per cent of GDP to 10 per cent of GDP. Nevertheless, these trends turned out to be temporary. Between FY11 and FY13, private investments rose back and touched all-time high levels, while private savings were maintained too. As a result, the private sector's surplus reduced quickly, from 6 per cent of GDP in FY10 to a two-decade low of 3.3 per cent of GDP during the three-year period. At the same time, the government was too slow to roll back its deficit, which was around 8 per cent of GDP during FY11 and FY13. As a result of higher aggregate investments and stable savings, CAD expanded and inflation rose sharply. Lower surplus reflects that the private sector was much more confident at that stage than was believed. This is a key reason why real GDP posted its all-time high and only double-digit growth in FY11, indicating that the economy was overheating.

These episodes (in the mid and late 2000s decade and early 2010s) suggest that fiscal deficit must be anti-cyclical instead of following any predetermined path. As private spending and economic growth were strong in the mid-2000s decade and early 2010s, fiscal consolidation was necessary to avoid overheating of the economy. In contrast, as private sector weakened immediately after great financial crisis in the late 2000s decade, the government should have supported the economy (as it did) and expanded its fiscal deficit. Any strict targeting of fiscal deficit during such difficult times restricts economic growth.

This indicates that a flexible approach is much more helpful than a binding fiscal deficit target. If the government is flexible and conscious of the economic growth, the fiscal policy will be anti-cyclical—expanding during downturns and tightening during boom periods. This has been practically true in almost all cases across the world.

However, there is no free lunch. There are limits to fiscal expansion in an economy. When the government expands its fiscal deficit, it is generally financed by domestic borrowings, which are funded through private savings. If the expansion in fiscal deficit is more than the increase in domestic private savings, the government either borrows from foreigners or, as has become a practice since 2008 in many nations, the central bank buys government securities (also called 'quantitative easing'). All these options have associated costs, which must be analysed carefully along with their expected benefits.

Learning#5: No External Policy Works without Affecting the Domestic Equilibrium

Lesson no. 5 also derives directly from the Theory of Everything. It tells us that current account balance is simply the difference between domestic savings and total investments. Current account records flows of goods, services, primary income and secondary income between the residents and the rest of the world. It shows the difference between the sum of exports and income receivable and the sum of imports and income payable. So any change in a country's current account balance will have to be led by a change in either total investments or domestic savings, or both, to match the identity. In other words, if external policies are effective in influencing foreign trade balance, it cannot be achieved without affecting the equilibrium between savings and investments.

CAD = Total investments − Domestic savings ...(4)

As discussed in detail in Chapter 5, this implies that a change in import tariffs affects a country's CAD by influencing the savings and investment behaviour of the domestic economic agents. While an imposition (or an increase) of tariff on an imported item changes the price of that commodity, its impact on a country's trade balance (or CAD) is determined by the decisions of the economic participants on their savings (or consumption) and investments. If tariffs are effective in narrowing CAD, it can be achieved only by reducing investments or by increasing savings, or both. There are no two ways about it.

This is true for any policy which is adopted to influence the foreign trade balance. Although it is not a directly intended consequence, a policy to encourage exports by providing targeted subsidies or to substitute imports by imposing/raising tariffs on commodities or by intervening in the foreign exchange market would invariably affect the savings and investment decisions of the economic participants in a country. The actual impact of an external policy, thus, could be very different from the intended consequences, depending on the impact of numerous other factors (domestic/external) on savings and investments in an economy.

For example, when the Indian government suggests that the production-linked incentives (PLIs) scheme introduced in 2020 will help narrow the CAD and boost investments, it is implying a sharp surge in domestic savings. Without a commensurate increase in savings, it is not possible to achieve this combination of lower CAD and higher investments. However, the PLIs enthusiasts fail to include this requirement in these arguments.

Learning#6: Cross-Country Comparisons Could Be Exciting but May Be of Limited Utility

It is commonplace to compare India with China. Led by Deng Xiaoping, China's economic liberalization began in 1979. The country stagnated in the late 1980s on account of the 1989 Tiananmen Square protests but revived soon after, in 1992, around the same time that India's liberalization process began. According to the World Bank, China's per capita GDP (in US dollar terms) was 82 per cent of India's during the 1980s decade—at $250, vis-à-vis $300 in India. In 1992, China overtook India, and the gap between the two countries has since widened exponentially over the past three decades. India's per capita GDP was only around 20 per cent of China's in recent years. Such a fantastic economic performance by China provides many lessons for any nation, including India.

But the economic, cultural, geographical and political differences between the two nations could make a highly successful policy in China totally impractical for adoption in India. This being so, the desire to witness high growth and follow China's growth model may tempt Indian policymakers to follow an unsustainable path, which may not only waste extremely precious and limited resources but may also end up harming the economy.

In Chapter 8, I discuss why China's economic growth model[14] is not unique. It is broadly a replica of the Japanese economic growth model, which was followed by almost all the successful East Asian economies too. Be it South Korea or Taiwan, from the 1960s to the 1980s, the broad outline of their economic growth models was similar and is known as the 'East Asian growth model', on which a large amount of literature is available. The lessons for India, thus, are neither new nor unknown. The question to be asked is, *Can India, even after knowing its pros and cons, follow this growth model in the 2020s and beyond?* Do the current economic realities provide an opportunity to India to replicate the successes witnessed by various nations during the past several decades? Does the present political structure in India support this growth model? If the answer to any of these questions is no, such comparisons have only limited utility. I explain why it is almost impossible for India at this stage to follow the East Asian growth model.

My scepticism does not come from my dislike of growth models or that their details are unknown, but from the simple fact that the world economy and its structure have evolved tremendously during the past few decades. The 2020s will not be comparable even to the 1990s, let alone the 1960s or 1970s. Simple comparisons of not only economic growth models but also of the debt-to-GDP ratios across nations may also be highly misleading. Any cross-country comparison, in general, must be made with proper knowledge and sufficient caution, since changes in the economic and political environment could render them unfruitful.

These six interlinked economic learnings are the fulcrum of this book. If you decide to proceed further, you have to accept these rules, or else you will not be in line with any of the analyses and conclusions contained in this book.

What Makes Economic Analysis Complicated?

It is often said that economics is for aliens. I mostly laugh away such statements because they are outright funny and I don't know of any other way to respond. However, deep down I feel sad (not angry). While we may not realize it, all of us are highly connected through the numerous economic policies affecting our decisions on a daily basis. Almost every decision taken by every person is based on its economic viability, and still we resist understanding of economics more accurately on a macro basis. I make my best attempt to explain these nuances in this book. However, it is also equally important to be aware of what makes economic analysis complicated. There are two facts: the interconnectedness among the different economic participants and the rising role of the financial markets.

Interlinkages between Different Economic Participants

Using two examples, I have showed how different the *gross* and *net* impact of an economic policy could be. This is a key reason why economists are generally less enthused by policies which may prove to be exceptionally beneficial for a particular (targeted) segment. What matters for economic growth is the *net* impact of an economic policy, which may turn out to be negligible or outright negative, even if it is positive for one section of society.

As explained in the second example, the government implemented a policy to shift resources within the household sector—from the non-agricultural people to the small and marginal farmers. Now, the objective of such a policy is clearly social in nature. The government wants to improve the livelihood of small and marginal farmers and also wants to work within its financial constraints. Therefore, while fiscal borrowings and the deficit were kept unchanged, the non-agricultural society (part of the household sector in an economy) transferred resources to the agricultural section (another part of the household sector).

Now, one could argue that the *net* impact of this policy could be negligible because household income broadly remains unchanged, along with government finances. However, this is not so. It is well accepted that the inclination of a poor person to spend is much higher than that of a high-income person. In economics parlance, the marginal propensity to consume (additional consumption from an additional unit of income) is much higher among the poor than among high- or middle-income people. Therefore, when income is transferred from the latter to the former section of the household sector, the actual impact would be higher consumption. This is because a loss of, say, 1 per cent of income for the high- or middle-income section is likely to reduce their savings rather than their consumption. On the contrary, higher income for the poor or low-income segment would most likely boost their consumption, with no-to-marginal rise in their savings. Therefore, the economic impact of such a policy would be to boost private/household consumption in the economy, equivalent to lowering household savings.

If the economy is suffering from low consumption demand and high savings, such a policy is appropriate. However, if the economy is already operating with strong consumption growth and if savings are lower than the desired level, such an economic policy would be more harmful. This is because lower savings would eventually result in either lower investments (via higher interest rates) or a higher CAD to sustain a similar level of investments as earlier (remember the Theory of Everything discussed in Learning#2). If so, the positive impact of higher consumption on economic growth could be easily negated by lower savings/investments. Also, if consumption growth was already strong and savings have already been falling for some reason in this economy, this is a definitely to-be-avoided policy.

These considerations involving both the interlinkages between the sectors and within a sector are exactly what make economic analysis complicated. This is also why most economic analysis (if comprehensive) includes a number of different scenarios rather than a focus on only one scenario. Different probabilities may be assigned to these scenarios. An analysis that ignores the many possibilities of a situation would be incomplete. I have explained the role of these interlinkages in India's economic growth over the past couple of decades in Chapter 6, which also lists the various economic scenarios likely to play out over the next couple of decades, with probabilities assigned to them.

Similarly, when one explains economic changes by focusing narrowly on credit growth, one is limiting the argument to only the assets side of the financial sector. Not surprisingly, then, many market participants will suggest monetary easing to increase the supply of funds without focusing much on the demand side. But what is happening in the non-financial sector of the economy is at least as important, if not more important. For more than a decade now, almost all developed economies in the world have practised massive, unprecedented and almost uninterrupted monetary easing and have created a liquidity glut. Still, they continue to suffer from deficient demand, and lending growth continues to remain tepid. The credit-to-deposit ratio of banks in major developed economies (including the US) in 2019 (pre-COVID-19) was lower than in 2007. Monetary policy, thus, cannot be expected to do all the heavy lifting. Live examples of this policy in more than twenty-five advanced economies in the world for more than a decade make this amply clear.

The complexity also arises from the fact that almost every economic policy decision has an opposite effect on the other side of the equation. Any economic policy encouraging consumption growth (without commensurate growth in income) implies lower savings or investments, and vice versa. Similarly, monetary easing by the cutting of policy interest rates may boost investments/consumption spending at the cost of savings. This book discusses the question, *'How can these contradictions be managed pragmatically?'*

Interaction between the Financial and Real Economies

Apart from these interconnections between the economic participants and among different sections within an institutional sector, the massive expansion of the financial markets has made economic analysis extremely complex. Since the important role that financial markets play in the economy is a relatively new phenomenon, it is an area of continuous learning and improvement. Therefore, I would not be surprised if I get a lot of pushback on this section. In fact, I will be eagerly awaiting your feedback on it.

Financial markets are not new to the world economy, but their rapid expansion and increasing discussion in mainstream economics is. 'Planet Finance is beginning to dwarf Planet

Earth. And Planet Finance seems to spin faster too,' stated Niall Ferguson[15] in his 2008 masterpiece, *The Ascent of Money*. An updated version of data used in his book suggests that the world economic output in CY21 was about $96 tn. Global equity market capitalization crossed $100 tn for the first time at the end of CY20, reaching an all-time high of 128 per cent of GDP, and stayed at 127 per cent of GDP in CY21 as well. The total outstanding value of debt (loans + domestic and international debt securities) amounted to $230 tn, or 264 per cent of GDP, in CY21, and the outstanding amount of derivatives is estimated to run into the quadrillions. Since CY06 (the last year used as reference in Ferguson's book), global economic output has increased by almost 85 per cent, equity markets have risen by 2.5x and debt markets have risen by 2.3x. In short, expansion of the financial markets has outpaced that of the real economy by a factor of anywhere between 2.7x and 2.9x.

Though financial markets are more than the stock/equity markets, I choose to start my discussion with the latter since I am connected with the equity brokerage industry. Stock markets are probably the most volatile and noisy of financial markets, and they are generally smaller than other financial markets The primary channel through which the stock market supports economic activity is by providing an additional venue to companies to raise funds/capital. There are several ways in which a company can raise funds through the stock markets—an unlisted company (or a private company) can choose to go public by offering shares in a new stock issuance called initial public offering (IPO); an existing listed company could offer new issuance to investors through a follow-on public offer or further public offer (FPO); a company can raise funds through a rights issue (offered at a discounted price) to existing investors or shareholders; and a company can choose to issue shares to a large private equity fund or a set of pre-identified qualified institutional investors in private placements.

In India, there were 2.46 mn registered[16] companies with the ministry of corporate affairs (MCA) as of 31 January 2023, of which 62 per cent (that is, 1.52 mn) companies stand active. Of these active registered companies, only about 5 per cent (that is, 71,485) are public limited, of which only 6,754 (0.4 per cent) were listed in the country. There are no official statistics available on the total assets or turnover of the whole of India's corporate sector. However, based on the authorized (or paid-up) capital, public limited companies make up for 64 per cent of the total authorized capital of all registered companies in the country. The listed companies may account for almost half of total authorized capital.

The secondary channel through which the stock market supports economic activity is the 'wealth effect'. The higher (lower) the stock markets, the greater (or less) the wealth of shareholders. This wealth effect has gained massive attention in recent years with the rising role of stock markets. There has been growing evidence, especially in the US economy, that the wealth effect plays a very important role in economic growth. Thus, the stronger the equity market, the better the economic growth.

The importance of equity markets to economic activity, however, could be very different for different nations. There are at least four factors that determine the potency of the impact of equity market movements on economic growth. First, what determines the role of the different financial markets in economic growth is the widespread participation of retail individuals. All countries are different, and so are the behaviours of their people. Since stocks are risky assets, the stock market participation ratio in a country would depend on the risk appetite of its people. The more risk appetite the people have, the more they save their money in the stock markets and the bigger and more crucial equity markets become for an economy. Therefore, if households save primarily in debt instruments (such as bank deposits, insurance and pension funds) rather than in the equity markets in a country, the latter have a relatively smaller role in economic activity in the country. In fact, since stocks are risky assets, it is also fair to assume that the stock market is primarily dominated by the high- and upper-middle-income sections of the society.

Second, as explained in the two examples discussed earlier, equity market performance would be closely related to the impact of an economic policy on the corporate sector rather than on the entire economy. In the first example, when the government announced a cut in the corporate tax rate, it was almost a no-brainer that the stock markets would cheer the announcement, irrespective of what the economic impact would be. Over a period of time, if the interlinkages among the different economic participants do not lead to higher economic growth, and thus a sustained rise in corporate profits, the exuberance may come down. However, the immediate impact of such an economic policy, which undoubtedly benefits listed companies, will be a rise in the stock markets. Another example could be stock markets getting a boost when listed companies decide to cut employee costs by, say, 10 per cent in a particular year. The immediate impact of lower costs would be to add directly to the bottom line of these companies, leading to higher profits for them. But lower salaries and wages for employees and lower advertising or raw material procurement (in volume terms) would hurt household income (the unincorporated enterprises) and/or the unlisted corporate sector, which will eventually come back to haunt the producers, or the listed corporate sector.

Third, the recent policy of quantitative easing adopted by almost the entire world economy has led to a massive glut of global liquidity, which has invariably found its way into the financial markets. The movements in debt and equity markets used to be in contrast to each other in the pre-2008 era. A buoyant economic environment would see much better returns in the equity markets and subdued returns in the debt markets, and vice versa. However, this gush of liquidity from the central banks has led to almost all financial markets moving in a similar direction. Sooner or later, these banks will be forced to normalize their monetary policies. Unless the economic fundamentals are strong enough to support these buoyant financial markets without the support of central banks, the co-movements in the various financial markets imply that their collapse could also be aligned. Any unwanted policy decision could then create more havoc in the financial markets, and thus in the global economy, which would make 2008 a relatively benign scenario. This is exactly what partly unfolded in 2022.

Finally, it is important to understand the scope of listed companies in a country's corporate sector, especially in a country such as India. With the unorganized sector as ubiquitous as it is in India, it is very likely that the share of unlisted or unregistered companies in the country's total investments or employment or gross value added would be much higher than that of listed companies. It would therefore be highly misleading to consider trends in the listed corporate sector as representative of the entire corporate sector.

Apart from equity markets, there is the debt or fixed income market, which is usually bigger in size than equity markets almost everywhere in the world. The wealth effect from the equity or debt market is based on the participation of retail investors. If the citizens of a country are more conservative in their approach and have a low risk appetite, as in India, the debt market may have a higher wealth impact than the equity market. If so, it may be futile to compare the findings for another market, say, the US, which has much higher risk appetite and thus broader retail participation in the equity market, with India's.

These nuances are discussed in greater detail in Chapter 7. With the rising role of financial markets in the world economy, no economic discussion is complete without an understanding of their role.

Together, the interconnectedness and the rising role of financial markets have seriously complicated the economic discussion over the past couple of decades. A sincere attempt is made to un-complicate them in this book.

Objective and Flow of the Book

As you may have realized by now, many preconceived notions will be seriously challenged and debated throughout this book.

It is well acknowledged that India's growth has weakened consistently during the past few years, even before the COVID-19 pandemic hit the world economy. India's real GDP growth weakened sharply from an average growth of 6.7 per cent in CY17 and CY18 to just 4.6 per cent in CY19 (before COVID-19), the lowest growth in eighteen years and even lower than the 5 per cent growth in CY09 (during the great financial crisis). The 2010s decade thus ended on a more gloomy note, with under 5 per cent growth—in stark contrast to a very solid 9.5 per cent average growth in CY10 and CY11, at the beginning of the decade. What changed so dramatically during this decade? A serious debate was underway on whether the slowdown represented a cyclical or structural slowdown. The discussion, however, changed dramatically after COVID-19, and the debate now is whether the economic recovery seen in CY21 and CY22 is more durable or transitory. These questions are connected. An answer to this debate will not only decide the future path of India's economic growth but will also help us understand what the required policy responses should be.

An equity investor analyses several financial accounts—profit and loss (P&L) statements, balance sheets, cash flow statements, etc. It is widely agreed that if Company A has a very strong balance sheet, it would be preferred over Company B with a weak balance sheet, even if the P&L of the former is weaker than the latter's. If the investor is taking a long-term view, she is more likely to be drawn towards Company A than Company B.

This book is almost entirely based on the analyses of India's sectoral financial balance sheet. As far as my knowledge goes, this is the first attempt to analyse the Indian economy through such a lens. Through this book, I intend to explain and examine India's economic growth through the financial accounts of the four economic participants—the household, corporate, government and external sectors. How has the financial position of these sectors moved during the past few decades, especially since liberalization? What does it imply for India's economic growth? Instead of looking at the agricultural, industrial and services sectors in the economy, which is how most of the economic analyses on India has been conducted so far, I look at how the country's individuals have spent and saved their income, how the country's companies have earned and invested their revenue, and how the government has spent its taxes. On top of that, I have covered how the domestic participants have interacted with the foreign sector and how inflows of foreign capital affect the Indian economy. Of course, it is pertinent to understand the evolving role of the burgeoning financial sector on the real economy. How influential are the equity and bond markets in India's economy, and how strong is the connection between the financial and real economies?

Once we understand the financial position of each participant, it is relatively easier to understand and differentiate between the areas of comfort and the areas of concern. The required economic policies, thus, should help strengthen the comfort areas and address the concerns with extremely targeted measures.

The analysis contained in this book also helps us understand the role of debt/leverage in an economy. Since the 1980s, leverage has become an almost inevitable and consistently growing part of the economic system. As mentioned earlier, there is a serious dearth of official statistics on India's total outstanding debt, although there has been some development on this front. Although the Central government publishes details of its borrowings on a monthly basis and its outstanding debt on a quarterly basis, there is no regular database on either corporations or state governments. Through various proxies, it is widely believed that India's leverage ratio is very low, especially compared with other economies. Do these comparisons make sense? Is India's debt really low? If yes, what is the scope to increase India's leverage, and how can we achieve that? If no, what is the threshold level, and how far or near is India to that? More important, it is necessary to realize that debt can be sustainable or unsustainable, based on its utilization. Therefore, the efficiency of investments is an important metric for an economy and its growth.

In the following four chapters, I discuss in detail the financial accounts of India's four economic participants. I choose to begin with the omnipresent household sector of the economy in Chapter 2. Just as with all other major economies, the household sector represents the backbone of the Indian economy as well. I feel that there is a serious vacuum in terms of analysis of India's household sector. By no means is the analysis contained in this book exhaustive, but I try my best to begin this process of giving the household sector as much importance in our economic analysis as we give to the corporate or government sector.

Using data from the past seven decades, I highlight the trends in income, consumption, savings, investments and debt of the Indian household sector and make cross-country comparisons where necessary. I argue that the finances of the Indian household sector have weakened considerably during the past decade. This deterioration has happened for the first time post-Independence. Worryingly, it rarely gets a place in public debates. Luckily, it has not yet reached an alarming level, and there is time to change course.

India's corporate sector is discussed in Chapter 3. I explain the interactions between the corporate and household and other participants. How do the various decisions taken by the households, on an aggregate basis, affect corporate profits, and vice versa? I discuss the various factors that affect corporate profits and how only some of these conditions are conducive for boosting economic growth.

Most of the analyses on India's corporate sector is limited to listed companies, for which quarterly/annual data is easily and regularly available. Chapter 3 highlights the importance of the unlisted corporate sector in India. As in the case of households, long-term historical data is produced on various important parameters related to India's corporate sector. Further, I discuss the relationship between corporate investments and their profits, using global database.

In Chapter 4, India's public finances and fiscal policies are discussed in detail. This is one of the most widely tracked and analysed sectors of the economy, but several recent developments, some of which are first-time entries, warrant special attention. In an effort to add further value to this densely researched topic, numerous direct and indirect effects of several economic policies undertaken by the governments on Indian household/corporate behaviour are discussed. While the Indian household balance sheet has weakened in recent years, public finances have worsened significantly.

Also, there is serious disagreement over the true extent of India's fiscal deficit, and thus debt. A comprehensive analysis is made to help understand what the most appropriate contribution of the government to India's economic growth has been. In fact, while the finances of the Central government remain in focus, state budgets are much bigger and their spending is closer to the people of India. Therefore, state finances are analysed in as much detail as the Centre's. What is more, the role of central public sector enterprises, which borrow on their own books rather than the Union government borrowing to finance their capital outlays (called off-balance sheet spending), has changed rapidly in the past few years. Though most CPSEs are included in the corporate sector, some special companies cannot be classified under this sector, and they should not be excluded from the government sector.

In this truly globalized environment, the impact of relatively freely flowing capital on the financial and real economy of the recipient nation can be complicated. Being one of the most favoured investment destinations globally, India has received large amounts of foreign capital in the past few years. However, its implication for the real economy may or may not be as significant. Most important, all external policies work primarily by changing the equilibrium among domestic participants. Chapter 5 is dedicated to understanding these connections between external policies and domestic players.

The lessons from the previous chapters are summarized in Chapter 6 and possible implications for the Indian economy are discussed. Apart from decoding the growth trends of the past decade, various possible scenarios that could play out over the next two decades are also listed. The structural analysis of the past many decades is combined with the changes brought in by COVID-19 in 2020 and 2021. Four key areas of improvement, which require urgent attention to strengthen the underlying economic fundamentals and help the economy achieve 8 per cent real growth on a sustainable basis, are discussed. As mentioned above, I call the 2020s decade the 'Healing Decade', wherein the authorities must attempt to address the country's structural issues. Without this healing, it would be extremely difficult for India to witness strong growth in the subsequent decades. Although healing implies low growth in the 2020s decade, the economy will reap the benefits of these adjustments over the 2030s and 2040s decades, with India's demography remaining favourable until the mid-2040s. None of these steps are low-hanging fruits, and policymakers may be well aware of most of these measures. Nevertheless, I firmly argue that without their implementation it would be nothing more than a dream to expect India to grow faster and witness a repeat of the economic performance of the 2004–2008 period.

There is, however, a possibility that rather than addressing these issues the economic participants may behave more aggressively and irresponsibly to go back to the pre-COVID-19 trends. If so, while economic growth may show some strength in the near future with a highly likely scenario of lower growth in potential output over the years, the economy will also become increasingly unsustainable and prone to serious accidents. That is why the 2020s decade is so important for India.

Chapter 7 examines in detail the second complication—the interactions between the financial and real economies. How do financial markets affect GDP growth? What are the different channels through which different financial assets affect the behaviour of economic participants? How strong are these channels in India? How does the global monetary policy affect financial markets, and what could be its implications? How can India isolate itself from such severe interconnectedness? These questions are addressed in this chapter.

Using some interesting data to gauge the risk appetite of Indian households vis-à-vis the world's other major economies, I explain why the wealth effect may not be very strong in India. Nevertheless, there is no denying that India is part of the highly connected global economy and that turbulence in the US (or major advanced economies) will seriously affect India too. It is, therefore, even more important to adopt policies to mitigate the adverse impacts of the global monetary policies, which, of course, involves some serious thinking and difficult decisions.

Lastly, after understanding India's domestic economy through the lens of economic participants and their interlinkages, various economic growth models (EGM) followed by successful Asian economies (including China and Japan) and Anglo-Saxon nations are discussed in the final chapter. What are the various learnings from these EGMs for the Indian economy and what model, if any, is being adopted in India? Or is India developing and following a new model? If so, is India's unique EGM sustainable? It is worth contemplating whether

India's stage of development and the changing globalization landscape allow us to follow established paths. In Chapter 8, I compare India's growth model, which is termed as 'unique' by various commentators, with two established growth models in the world economy. Key lessons from established theories suggest possible options for Indian policymakers to choose from, if we want to achieve high growth for decades.

Key Lessons from the Chapter

- Every policy decision has a *gross* impact, likely on the targeted segment, and a *net* impact, called the economic impact. To understand the economic impact of any policy, one must understand its influence on all participants in an economy. It is possible that the positive effects of a policy on one segment could be entirely negated by its adverse impact on another participant, creating negligible or negative economic impact.
- I hope the Indian authorities utilize the 2020s decade as a 'Healing Decade' to strengthen the financial position of the domestic economic agents. Although this implies that average growth may plummet to around 5 per cent (or lower) during this decade, it will certainly set the stage for much higher growth on a sustainable basis over the subsequent decades. However, if we remain focused on achieving high growth in the near term, it is very likely that India's potential growth would continue to decline, leading to slower growth in the 2030s and 2040s decades. In short, unless the domestic structural issues are addressed comprehensively, it is highly unlikely that India will post high growth (say, 8 per cent-plus) over a long horizon.
- An economy consists of three domestic agents or participants—the corporate sector (private and public financial and non-financial companies), the government sector (the Central and state governments, including

- local and municipal-level authorities) and the household sector. Households comprise individuals (people), the non-profit institutions serving households and unincorporated enterprises. The fourth participant is the external sector.
- An economy consists of only three activities—consumption, investment and foreign trade. Households are the major consumers in the economy; NFCs are the major investors; and the government does a bit (relatively) of both. Households are key investors in the case of India as well.
- The analysis contained in this book is based on six lessons:
  - **Financial savings versus physical investments:** There is nothing like financial investments in the national accounts. Everything that is not spent out of income is called savings. And investments are only those spendings that create new fixed assets.
  - **Remember the Theory of Everything identity in economics:** Derived from the GDP equation, this identity holds the potential to explain the likely economic impact of almost every policy in a country. It is stated as:

    Total investments = Domestic savings + Current account deficit (CAD)
  - **The corporate sector is much bigger than the universe of listed companies:** Most of the analysis on India's corporate sector is focused on the listed companies, probably because of lack of interest in other companies and data limitations. The unlisted corporate sector, however, is much larger than the listed universe, not only in terms of investments and GVA but also in terms of profits. Using the Theory of Everything, I explain and estimate India's aggregate corporate profits at 8–9 per cent of GDP against the 2–3 per cent in FY18 and FY19 for the listed companies.

- **Targeting fiscal deficit in isolation is likely an ineffective strategy:** Since fiscal policies are a reaction to the behaviour of the private sector, targeting fiscal deficit in isolation without considering the economic environment in infeasible. When the private sector is buoyant, higher economic growth will allow the government to consolidate. But during a slow economic growth period on account of weakness in the private sector, the government must ideally stimulate the economy by expanding its fiscal deficit.
- **No external policy works without affecting domestic equilibrium:** Most trade policies, like other economic policies, impact the external sector (say, CAD) by influencing the behaviour of the domestic participants. Import tariffs, export subsidies or currency manipulations, all are effective only if they affect the savings–investments equilibrium in the domestic economy. It is easy to explain this using the Theory of Everything identity.
- **Cross-country comparisons could be exciting but may be of limited utility:** Any cross-country comparison must incorporate the economic, political and demographic differences between the countries. Today's Indian economy is more comparable with that of the nineteenth-century US or late twentieth-century South Korea or Taiwan, rather than the twenty-first century US or Korea. Similarly, all comparisons between China and India must be made with caution.

- There are two complications that make economic analysis more complex than otherwise: interconnection among economic participants and the rising role of financial markets.

Chapter 2

THE HEAVY-LIFTER BUT HIGHLY IGNORED HOUSEHOLD SECTOR

Non-economist: Good choice. I agree with you. We must start our discussion with the consumers. After all, they are KING.

Me: This chapter is not only about consumers. We intend to discuss the household sector in detail.

Non-economist: Alien language. Huh, what's the difference? Aren't households consumers?

Me: Of course they are. But they are much more than consumers. They are the key savers in the country, who bear almost the entire burden of all bailouts, directly or indirectly. And therefore, their consumption spending should be in line with their income. What is more, in India they are a major investor and their leverage has risen sharply during the past decade.

Non-economist: What are you saying? You are complicating a simple thing. That's what economists do. That's why nobody listens to you . . .

Me: Well, I am not complicating things. But you are right—nobody listens to us.

Non-economist: Whatever! And what difference does it make if consumption spending is higher than income? We need consumption growth. And consumer debt is so low in India that it must rise. Look at household debt in other economies.

Me: When consumption grows faster than income, it simply implies a drawdown of household savings. Lower savings in a young nation such as India is very peculiar and could have serious implications. Also, a comparison of the headline household debt in different nations is almost meaningless. What matters is the debt-service ratio, which is very high for Indian households compared to those of most other nations. Overall, household finances have weakened drastically over the past few years and it does not bode well for Indian economy. Let me explain . . .

Using data from the past seven decades, the trends in income, consumption, savings, investments and debt of the Indian household sector are discussed in this chapter, and cross-county comparisons are made where necessary and possible. It is argued that the finances of the Indian household sector have weakened considerably during the past decade. This deterioration has happened for the first time post-Independence in the economy, and worryingly, it rarely gets a place in public debates. But the situation is not dire yet, and thus the sooner policies are implemented to change course, the better it will be.

My friend Saurabh is a young and passionate professional who has been working in India's buoyant services sector for the past few years. His gross annual income is ₹10 lakh, implying a monthly income of about ₹83,000. In Union Budget 2021–22 presented on 1 February 2021, the GoI introduced an optional new personal income tax structure while retaining the old tax structure. The catch is that if a taxpayer chooses to switch from the old to the new tax structure, he/she will have to let go of almost all exemptions attached to the old structure. If Saurabh chooses to opt for the new individual income tax regime and let go of all available exemptions, his tax payout will be higher; therefore, he chooses to stay with the old tax regime and avail of the exemptions.

Since Saurabh is a well-educated guy, he is a good financial planner and knows how to minimize his tax liability. He chooses to park a portion of his annual income, say, totalling ₹1,75,000, in various life and medical health insurance schemes, in the Public Provident fund (PPF) and other available options under Section 80C and 80D to avail of the available exemptions and reduce his taxable income to ₹8,25,000. Under the old tax slab, this implies a total tax liability of ₹80,600 for the year. Accordingly, from Saurabh's total income of ₹10 lakh, his disposable (or take-home) income for the year is ₹9,19,400. This is called disposable income because this is what is left at his disposal after paying taxes to the government. In short, disposable income is equal to the difference between total income earned and taxes paid to the authorities.

Out of his disposable income of ₹9,19,400, he decides to park ₹1,75,000 in various tax-saving instruments. These count as his (financial) savings. Although in daily life we call these transactions 'investments' to reduce our tax liability, they count as 'savings' in the National Income Accounting. So, the total money now left with Saurabh is ₹7,44,400.

Of this, Saurabh spends roughly ₹1,80,000 on groceries, ₹1,50,000 as housing rent, ₹60,000 on clothing and footwear, almost ₹1,20,000 on transport, and ₹1,50,000 on other items, such as entertainment, recreation and other activities. In total, Saurabh spends about ₹6,60,000 on consumption.

So, in a nutshell, Saurabh's annual income is ₹10 lakh, out of which he has paid total taxes of ₹80,600 and made a consumption expenditure of ₹6,60,000 during the year. After all these expenses, he saves ₹2,59,400, of which ₹1,75,000 was saved in various tax-saving instruments and the remaining ₹84,400 maybe in banks, the equity market, debt market and as cash in hand. Assuming he earns interest at 5 per cent on his financial savings, he receives an interest income of ₹12,970 during the year, taking his year-end gross financial savings (GFS) to ₹2,72,370. Since there are no loans (or financial liabilities), his net financial savings (NFS = GFS − financial liabilities) are also the same.

All these transactions are shown in Exhibit 2.1 under Year 0, illustrating the accounting of personal transactions under NIA. Saurabh's effective tax rate is 8.1 per cent of his gross income and his personal savings are 29.6 per cent of his disposable income. Also, since his savings exceed his investments, Saurabh is a net lender with a net financial surplus equal to his NFS.

Now, let's bring in some complications. One fine day, Saurabh decides to take a home loan, say, totalling ₹10 lakh, to buy a new house. How does that get accounted for in the national income accounts and what are its implications for Saurabh's financial position?

Saurabh takes a loan of ₹10 lakh in Year 1, but his income, assume for simplicity, remains unchanged at ₹10 lakh. There are two possible utilizations of this new loan. Under the first option, Saurabh buys a new house, which will be counted as household investment (or physical savings) rather than consumption. Under the national accounts, any creation of fixed assets is classified as investment, and since buying a new house implies a new residential construction, it comes under investments in the country rather than under consumption. In India, as I explain later in the chapter, household savings have two components—financial savings and physical savings (or investments). Thus, with the new loan, Saurabh's physical savings and, therefore, total savings, rise by ₹10 lakh.

This transaction, however, creates a chain of events, all of which are captured in Exhibit 2.1. When Saurabh takes a loan to buy a house and invests a portion of his own money in the house, his financial position changes significantly in Year 1 vis-à-vis Year 0. Given below are the various changes:

1. **Interest payments (line item 6)** – Assuming the home loan is for five years and at a 10 per cent rate of interest, Saurabh will have to pay ₹92,696 (or 9.3 per cent of his gross income) towards interest payments in Year 1. The interest payments, as under any equal monthly instalment (EMI) loan repayment plan, will fall in the subsequent years and the entire loan will be repaid by the end of Year 5.

Exhibit 2.1: An illustration of how personal transactions are accounted for in the National Income Accounts

	Year 0	Year 1	Year 2	Year 3	Year 4	Year 5
Total income (1)	1,000,000	1,000,000	1,050,000	1,102,500	1,157,625	1,215,506
Tax saving instruments (2)	175,000	175,000	175,000	175,000	175,000	175,000
Taxes paid# (3)	80,600	61,319	75,253	90,078	105,857	125,492
Disposable income (4) = (1) − (3)	919,400	938,681	974,747	1,012,422	1,051,768	1,090,014
Personal Consumption (5)	660,000	610,000	640,500	672,525	706,151	741,459
Net interest paid (6)	−12,970	89,010	71,742	52,687	31,665	8,609
Interest receipts^ (6.1)	12,970	3,686	3,964	4,247	4,533	4,680
Interest paid on loans* (6.2)	0	92,696	75,706	56,934	36,198	13,289
Total savings (7) = (8) + (9)	272,370	239,671	262,505	287,210	313,951	339,946
Net financial savings (8)	272,370	−760,329	262,505	287,210	313,951	339,946
Gross financial savings (8.1) = (4)−(5)−(6)	272,370	77,403	83,245	89,180	95,183	98,271
Less: Financial liabilities~ (8.2)	0	837,732	−179,260	−198,030	−218,768	−241,675
Physical savings (9)	0	1,000,000	0	0	0	0
Net lending (+) / borrowings (−) (10) = (8)	272,370	−760,329	262,505	287,210	313,951	339,946
Investments (11) = (9)	0	1,000,000	0	0	0	0
Outstanding debt@ (12)	0	837,732	658,472	460,442	241,674	0
Savings rate (13) = ((7) / (4))% − 100	29.6	25.5	26.9	28.4	29.8	31.2
Debt ratio (14) = ((12) / (4))% − 100	0.0	89.2	67.6	45.5	23.0	0.0

#Using the individual income tax rates under the old regime
* Assuming rate of interest @10% for 5 years
@ After timely payment of principal loan obligations
^ Assuming 5% interest rate on GFS
~ Net liabilities = New loans minus repayments

Source: Author's estimates

2. **Tax liability (line item 3)** – Since interest paid on home loans (up to ₹2,00,000 per annum) qualifies for tax benefits in the country, Saurabh's tax liability will go down from ₹80,600 in Year 0 to ₹61,319 in Year 1. The effective tax rate thus falls from 8.1 per cent in Year 0 to 6.1 per cent in Year 1. As interest payments decline from Year 2, tax liability, and thus the effective tax rate, will inch up.
3. **Disposable income (line item 4)** – With unchanged gross income and lower taxes, Saurabh's disposable income would rise to ₹9.39 lakh in Year 1. Assuming higher gross income from Year 2, tax liability increases with the fall in interest payments, leading to higher disposable income vis-à-vis Year 1.
4. **Personal consumption (line item 5)** – Unlike in Year 0, Saurabh spent 9.3 per cent of his gross income to make interest payments in Year 1, which means that in spite of higher disposable income, total money available to consume and save was only about ₹6.71 lakh, against ₹7.44 lakh earlier (excluding money parked in tax saving instruments). With Saurabh having his own home, he does not need to spend on housing rent now. Accordingly, his consumption goes down by ₹1,50,000. However, with a new house he needs to buy furniture and some other household stuff totalling ₹1,00,000, which he was not required to spend on earlier. Overall, his consumption falls from ₹6,60,000 in Year 0 to ₹6,10,000 in Year 1.
5. **Financial savings (line item 8)** – Although Saurabh's income was unchanged and his consumption went down, his financial savings took a serious hit because he had to make interest payments on his loan. Therefore, his gross financial savings (GFS, line item 8.1) turned from positive ₹2,72,370 (including interest receipts) to just ₹77,403 (adjusted for net interest paid). His net financial savings will be much lower, as we need to adjust GFS with the net financial liabilities (line item 8.2). With new loans totalling

₹10 lakh and principal repayment totalling ₹1,62,268 in the same year, Saurabh's net financial liabilities stand at ₹8,37,732. This means that his net financial savings will be a negative ₹7,60,329.

6. **Physical savings (line item 9)** – Since Saurabh has bought a new house, his investments go up, which are, by definition, equal to his physical savings. Therefore, while Saurabh's net financial savings are a large negative, his physical savings are significantly positive.

7. **Total savings (line item 7)** – As total personal savings are a sum of net financial savings and physical savings, Saurabh's total savings will be ₹2,39,671. As a percentage of disposable income, his total savings will be 25.5 per cent in Year 1, lower than 29.6 per cent in Year 0.

8. **Net lending (+)/borrowings (–) (line item 10)** – Since Saurabh didn't have any investments in Year 0 and had positive savings, he was a net lender. However, as his total savings are lower than his investments in Year 1, he will become a net borrower (equal to his net financial savings because physical savings are the same as investments). From Year 2, as financial savings rise and there are no further loans, he turns into a net lender again.

Therefore, when a person takes a loan, a series of changes happens in his financial statement. We all know this implicitly, through our own experience or from hearing about it from friends and families. Exhibit 2.1 explains how the changes take place in the NIA. From Year 2 to Year 5, Saurabh doesn't take any new loans and pays off his loan in time. The changes in his financial statement are shown in Exhibit 2.1.

Alternatively, instead of buying a new house, Saurabh may choose to go on a foreign trip or buy a new car with his loan. If so, there are no investments because no new fixed asset has been created. However, personal consumption gets a major boost. A different series of changes would occur in Saurabh's financial statement. With no tax benefits on personal or car loans, his disposable income would remain unchanged in Year 1, while higher consumption and an increase in financial liabilities would lead to a sharp erosion in his savings.

The purpose of beginning the chapter with this example is twofold:
1. to explain certain terminologies (disposable income, financial savings, physical savings, difference between consumption and investments, etc.), and
2. to show how various transactions are recorded in a financial statement, which eventually helps in preparation of the national income accounts.

There are a few important lessons from this example that need to be remembered before I proceed further:
1. Money parked in all sorts of financial instruments is classified as 'financial savings', not investments. In fact, there is no concept of financial investments under the NIA (Lesson#1 in Chapter 1).
2. Interest payments are neither consumption nor savings but eat up a portion of your disposable income (that is, borrowings in Year 1 eats up your future income).
3. Loans provide additional resources for spending, either on consumption of goods or on investment items; however, they do not change one's income. In effect, loans help the borrower spend from his future income, and they are repaid over their tenure.
4. The borrower's consumption or savings or both tend to grow slowly or decline in the first few years of the loan. In our example, Saurabh's personal consumption and savings in Year 3 were lower than in Year 0. This is primarily because a part of the disposable income was used to make interest payments, which were high in the initial years.

5. Savings are nothing but unspent income. If Saurabh's consumption grows faster than his disposable income, his savings rate will fall.
6. And lastly, leverage and savings are inversely correlated. Higher leverage will lead to repayment obligations, which will reduce disposable income for the borrower. Since consumption cannot be reduced dramatically in a short period of time, savings will take a larger hit.

With these terminologies and lessons in mind, I think we are now ready to discuss the financial position of India's household sector. In this chapter, the objective is to provide as much detail on the financial position of Indian households as possible, with crisp analysis. Most of the data used in this chapter is from official sources; however, at some places I have used my own derived estimates (with detailed explanations and assumptions) and have made conclusions based on them. Overall, this chapter seeks to analyse five major activities of households—earning, consumption, saving, investment and borrowing (Appendix 1 and Appendix 2 provide the nominal and real data for these activities for the past seven decades). All these activities are directly linked with each other. This chapter includes more-than-usual data points, primarily because the existing analysis on India's household sector is very thin. Long historical series (for the past seven decades in most cases) and cross-country comparisons are also used at several junctures to substantiate my arguments and conclusions.

Household Income: Components and Trends

The household sector consists of all the domestic economic entities except the corporate sector (financial and non-financial) and the government sector (Centre and the states, including local and municipal-level authorities). In other words, the household sector includes not only individuals but also the non-corporate (or the unincorporated) private sector.

Think of it this way: the small shops at the corner of the street (famously called 'kirana stores'), the self-employed population providing numerous activities such as tailors and cobblers, the hawkers serving delicious street foods such as chaats in north India, vada pav in Mumbai, dosa/idlis in south India and puchkas in east India, etc., also form a part of the household sector. Similarly, hundreds of thousands of professionals, such as doctors, chartered accountants (CAs), lawyers, financial planners, etc., are also part of the household sector.

In developing economies such as India, which have a large informal and/or unorganized sector, it is very difficult to directly arrive at statistics for the household sector because of its pervasiveness. Not surprisingly, then, it is mostly estimated as residual in India. Every economy in the world has a few peculiar characteristics which make it stand out from the rest of the world. Although almost all economic principles broadly work the same way everywhere in the world, it is these idiosyncrasies that alter the exact impact of economic policies in a particular nation.

Household income is directly dependent on the employment profile of the nation. According to the 2023 periodic labour force survey, the total number of workers in India was about 542 mn (or 39.6 per cent of the population) in the year ending June 2022.[1] Of these, about 300 mn (or 55.8 per cent) are self-employed (entrepreneurs, or those who run own-account enterprises) and the remaining 44 per cent almost equally distributed between casual and regular employees. Self-employed persons earn mixed income or operating surpluses; casual employees earn daily wages or irregular salaries; and regular wages/salaries are earned by only 21 per cent of all workers in India. Such an employment profile makes estimation of PDI for India a challenging task, and that's why most of the statistics on the household sector are residual.

If you compare these figures with what obtains in the world's other major nations, the share of regular workers in India is in the second lowest decile. Of the total 196 countries for which such data is available with the International Labour Organization (ILO),[2] India was positioned at #168 in 2019 (and #164 in 2021) in terms of the share of regular employees in the country. The percentage of regular employees in India's workforce is less than half of the world's average of around 53 per cent, lower than the 36.4 per cent of the lower-middle income countries (under which India gets classified, as per the World Bank) and the 29.6 per cent of South Asia.

According to the 2023 periodic labour force survey, about 45 per cent of all workers in India were engaged in the agricultural sector in 2021–22, most of whom are classified as 'informal workers'. Of the non-agricultural workers, 67–68 per cent are classified as 'informal workers' in India, implying that around 82 per cent of all workers in India are in the informal sector. In fact, the share of informal workers in India has remained steady at around 82 per cent for more than a decade. ILO data[3] confirms that the share of informal workers in India is the sixth highest among eighty-nine countries for which such data is available for the year 2019.

Due to the challenges presented by these characteristics of India's working population, PDI is estimated as residual in India's national income accounts, which is, more correctly, the income level of the non-corporate, non-government sector of the economy. The Central Statistics Office (CSO), however, does the challenging task of estimating household income in India on an annual basis, but with a lag of almost ten months. Data for the year ending March 2021 was published on the last working day of January 2022 (in 2023, this data was published on the last working day of February).

A comparison of PDI and GDP growth suggests that the two variables (in nominal as well as real[4] terms) moved in line with each other for more than five decades post-Independence.

Between FY51 and FY00, real GDP growth and real PDI growth averaged 4.5 per cent each (and 11.5 per cent each in nominal terms). But the two indicators have shown divergent growth paths during the past two decades. In contrast to the second half of the twentieth century, in the 2000s decade, household income (or PDI) growth outpaced GDP growth, while in the 2010s decade, the former lagged behind the latter. As against average real GDP growth of 6.9 per cent each in the first and second decades of the twenty-first century, real PDI grew faster, at 7.5 per cent, in the 2000s decade, and much slower, at 6.0 per cent, in the 2010s decade.

The CSO provides the break-up of PDI into various components, which are made publicly available with a further lag of four to six months. PDI primarily has four components—compensation of employees earned by regular and casual workers; operating surplus/mixed income earned by the large self-employed pool of workers engaged in the massive unincorporated sectors like partnership/proprietorship firms; property income; and current transfers. This practice is uniform across nations, and a cross-country comparison throws some interesting facts. For the purpose of simplicity, we combine the last two components—property income and current transfers—as 'others'.

According to the most recent data made available by the CSO in the documents titled 'First Estimates of India's National Account Statistics' on 28 February 2023,[5] household income in India amounted to ₹185 tn (or $2.5 tn) in FY22. The details (available up to FY21) confirm that compensation of employees (CoE)—comprising wages and salaries before taxes and social contributions are deducted and social contributions paid by the employers—accounted for less than 40 per cent of total household income in India. Another 35 per cent of personal income is accounted for by mixed income (which accrues to self-employed households) and operating surplus (which accrues to partnerships/proprietorships, etc.). The remaining household income (around 26 per cent) is attributed to 'other' income earned from property, current transfers, etc. The share of CoE is only slightly higher than the share of mixed income/operating surplus in India.

In most major economies the share of CoE accounts for 60–70 per cent of income, while the share of mixed income/operating surplus is not above 20 per cent. In short, a very low share of CoE and a very high share of mixed income/operating surplus in household income is a unique characteristic of the Indian economy, and it has the potential to alter the impact of various economic policies in India vis-à-vis other economies.

These details reveal the vulnerability of India's working population. A very high share of vulnerable employment (defined as non-regular workers) in the total workforce, a very high share of entrepreneurial income and among the lowest share of regular employees in total household income are the characteristics which are likely to have hurt the Indian economy extraordinarily hard during exceptional circumstances, such as during the COVID-19 pandemic. I will discuss the impact of COVID-19 on household finances in detail later in this chapter.

Household Consumption: Components and Trends

In most economies, private (or personal/household) final consumption expenditure (PFCE) accounts for the largest portion of GDP. Of the total nominal GDP amounting to ₹235 tn ($3.2 tn), PFCE accounted for 61 per cent (₹143 tn or $ 1.9 tn) in FY22. The share is at a similar level for many other major economies of the world such as the US, Indonesia, Malaysia, Greece, Italy, the UK, Germany, Japan, France and Spain. China is at other end of the spectrum, with PFCE accounting for less than 35 per cent of the national economic output.

The share of PFCE in India fell from more than 90–95 per cent in the post-Independence decade (that is, 1950s) to 65 per cent of GDP at the end of the twentieth century. The share fell further in the first decade of the twenty-first century before reversing the trend and rising in the 2010s decade. The share of PFCE stood at 64.6 per cent of GDP in FY01, falling to its all-time low of 56 per cent in FY11 before rising to 61 per cent in FY20 and staying there till FY22. The last time PFCE saw a rise in its share of GDP was in the late 1970s, when it increased from 76 per cent of GDP in FY77 to 79 per cent of GDP in FY81. In other words, real PFCE growth has outpaced real GDP growth consistently for the past few years. Real PFCE growth averaged 3.7 per cent in the 1950s, 3.2 per cent in the 1960s, 2.8 per cent in the 1970s, 4.7 per cent in the 1980s, 4.8 per cent in the 1990s and 6.4 per cent in the 2000s decade. Real GDP growth had always averaged more than real PFCE growth—close to 4 per cent each in the 1950s and 1960s, 2.9 per cent in 1970s, slightly below 6 per cent in the 1980s and 1990s, and 6.9 per cent in the 2000s decade. For the first time in the past seven decades, real PFCE growth (at 7.2 per cent) averaged higher than average growth in real GDP (at 6.9 per cent) in the 2010s decade. In nominal terms, PFCE growth (at 13.2 per cent) averaged higher than average growth in real GDP (at 12.4 per cent) in the 2010s decade.

This suggests that the 2010s was the first decade in the post-Independence period, or since the 1950s, when investments growth lagged GDP growth. In other words, consumption was the primary driver of higher GDP growth in the 2010s decade, which was not the case in the previous decades. This is probably one reason why we hear so many accusations of overestimation of GDP growth in the country.

Using CSO data, one can classify PFCE between discretionary and non-discretionary items. By and large, discretionary items are non-essential goods and services, while non-discretionary items are essential spending. Going by the age-old adage of *roti, kapda aur makaan*, we include food (and beverages, if separate data not available), clothing and footwear, and housing to estimate the share of non-discretionary/essential items in total PFCE. The remaining items, such as transport, education, health, recreation, goods and services, household goods and services, etc., classify as non-essential or discretionary spending.

In India, the spending on discretionary items has grown much faster than non-discretionary spending during the past half a century, due to which its share has risen from 25 per cent in the mid-1980s to 40 per cent in early 2000s decade, and further to 52.1 per cent in FY20. During the most recent decade (data ending 2019–20), while nominal spending on essential items grew at an average of 12 per cent, discretionary spending grew at an average of 14 per cent, which led to an increase in the share of the latter from 48.6 per cent of PFCE in FY10 to 52.1 per cent in FY20. Of course, while discretionary spending contracted due to the pandemic, non-discretionary spending increased in FY21.

A comparison of the share of discretionary versus non-discretionary spending across select nations suggests that the share of discretionary spending in PFCE ranges from 42 per cent in China to almost 70 per cent in the US, with India sitting near the lower end, at close to 52 per cent.

Why does it matter? Well, the higher the share of discretionary items in total PFCE, the more the fall in total PFCE during difficult times. Similarly, the higher the share of non-discretionary items, the lower the decline in PFCE during recession periods such as the COVID-19 pandemic. The fact that the US economy is on one extreme, with more than two-thirds of total private consumption in discretionary items, and China is on the other extreme, with only about 40 per cent consumption of discretionary components, the adverse impact on total PFCE during a recession would also be very different in the two economies. Since the share of discretionary and non-discretionary items is almost equal in India, any adverse impact in India will be lower than in the US but higher than in China.

Household Savings: Components and Trends

Let's take a pause and sum up the facts we have learnt above. For the first time in the past seven decades, household income has grown slower than GDP and personal consumption. Between FY11 and FY20, real PDI growth averaged 6.0 per cent, real GDP growth averaged 6.9 per cent and real PFCE growth averaged 7.2 per cent. A direct consequence of lower growth in income vis-à-vis consumption is lower savings (remember the lessons from Saurabh's financial statement?). After all, savings is the difference between income and consumption. However, estimation of household savings in India is done indirectly—by the summation of financial savings (estimated by 'flow of funds' approaches) and physical savings (estimated by 'commodity flow' and 'residual' approach).

The Report of the High Level Committee on the Estimation of Savings and Investment, 2009 (Para VI. 7, p. 94), under the chairmanship of Dr C. Rangarajan,[6] explains it thus:

> Savings of an economic unit can be estimated either from the income account as earned surplus, being the difference between current income and current consumption and taxes (as followed in the US for households) or from the balance sheet as earned net worth, being the difference between changes in financial assets and liabilities (as followed in India for households' financial savings). In the US and the UK, both the estimates are available, which help in cross-validating the income-expenditure survey based direct estimates of savings. But in India, only flow of funds based estimation is available for household financial savings and commodity flow based estimation is available for household physical savings. In the absence of income-expenditure survey, there is no direct estimation of household savings . . .

The Household Sector

Many eminent economists have recommended adoption of direct estimation of household savings in the country based on integrated household income–expenditure surveys. Once such an attempt was made by the National Sample Survey Office (NSSO) in the 1950s; however, the data obtained were unreliable and thus the existing practice of indirect estimation survived. The 2009 report refers to the NSSO attempt in 1983–84 to conduct a pilot inquiry with an objective of arriving at a feasible and technically sound methodology for the household income surveys. The results, however, were as disappointing. The NSSO Report (September 1995)[7] states:

> It should be clear from the overview of results presented above that the Pilot Survey on Income, Consumption and Savings did not settle all issues connected with the methodology to be followed for household income surveys in India. It is, therefore, essential to conduct further pilot surveys for resolving these issues with a view to arriving at a satisfactory methodology.

No more such surveys have been conducted since.

Although household savings are estimated indirectly in India, a comparison of household savings using the two different methods—direct (by deducting PFCE from PDI) and indirect—during the past three decades suggests that while there are differences between the two estimates, they tend to move in a similar direction. Notably, while the indirect approach resulted in a higher estimate of household savings for the entire first decade of the twenty-first century, it has returned lower figures than the direct estimate since FY12. The change in the definition[8] of household sector in the new revised base of the national accounts to 2011–12 may have also played an important role in this. Nevertheless, rather than fixating on the exact numbers in the national accounts, it is more useful to focus on the trends or the direction in which savings are moving. And the results are very clear. There is no doubt that household savings have fallen significantly during the past many years, irrespective of the methodology used.

The household sector in India, as in many other nations, has been the major saver in the nation. A glance at the long-term historical data suggests that household savings have broadly been increasing post-Independence. For almost six consecutive decades running between the 1950s and the 2000s decade, the household savings rate (defined as the ratio of household savings to PDI) rose gradually from less than 10 per cent in the 1950s to 20 per cent in the mid-1990s, and further to more than 25 per cent in the early 2000s decade, touching its all-time peak of 32.2 per cent in FY10. In the 2010s decade, however, household savings fell to 23 per cent in FY16 before recovering gradually to 23.8 per cent in FY20 and further to 26.8 per cent of PDI in FY21, supported by the pandemic. It fell again to 24.9 per cent in FY22.

Household savings in India have two components—financial savings and physical savings. Household gross financial savings include seven components: currency, deposits (banks and non-banks), insurance funds, pension and provident funds, shares and debentures, claims on government, and others. An estimate is made for household borrowings (or liabilities) as well, which is then deducted from GFS to arrive at household NFS.

Household physical savings primarily consist of investments in 'construction and building' by individuals and unincorporated enterprises, and investments on 'machinery and equipment' and 'research and development (R&D)', primarily by unincorporated enterprises. By definition, household physical savings are equivalent to household investments.

A big misconception in the minds of market participants, including many subject experts, is that gold is part of household savings. But strictly speaking, gold is a negligible part of household physical savings. Most of the gold demand—say, roughly 85–90 per cent of total demand—in the country is met through imports. By definition, imported goods and services can never be part of domestic savings, which is simply equal to the excess of income over final consumption. This fact is borne by the new 2011–12 national account series. In the new series for household savings, household savings have a third component called 'valuables', which includes savings in gold that is extracted domestically. Since only about 10–15 per cent of gold demand is met through domestic production, 'valuables' under savings do not account for more than 0.3–0.4 per cent of GDP, or 1–1.5 per cent of total household savings.

Household Financial Savings

Although the final responsibility of furnishing details on India's gross domestic savings lies with the CSO, the RBI provides an estimate of household financial savings. The CSO now publishes India's GDS estimates in February of the following year (that is, with a lag of eleven months); the RBI used to produce household financial savings estimates with a five-month lag, by August of the year, in its annual report. More recently, the RBI started publishing household financial savings data on a quarterly basis with a lag of a few months (available up to Q4FY22 as of end-March 2023). According to the CSO, household net financial savings dropped to 9.7 per cent of PDI in FY22, similar to the levels seen in the pre-pandemic period and down from 13.8 per cent of PDI in FY21. Physical savings (including valuables), however, increased to 15.3 per cent of PDI in FY22, similar to the levels seen in FY18 and FY19 but higher than 13.1 per cent of PDI in FY21.

Household GFS is adjusted with the financial liabilities to arrive at the net financial savings. Whether one should look at GFS or NFS depends on the objective. If one is concerned with the evolution of the financial sector, GFS is more relevant. However, if someone, like me in this book, is more interested in understanding the relationship between domestic savings and economic growth, then NFS is more pertinent. This is because total household savings include an estimate of physical savings as well, which are acquired through the borrowing or by the incurring of liabilities by households. To avoid double counting, it is necessary to adjust GFS with financial liabilities (you may want to go back to the beginning of this chapter to read about Saurabh once again).

For the first six decades post-Independence (that is, from the 1950s to the 2000s), household GFS was moving in only one direction, that is, north-east. From an average GFS of 4 per cent of PDI in the 1960s, it crossed 10 per cent of PDI for the first time in the late 1980s. It crossed 15 per cent in the early 2000s and touched an all-time high of 23 per cent of PDI in FY07. Since then, it has fallen almost continuously: to 13 per cent of PDI in the mid-2010s before stabilizing at 14–15 per cent of PDI in the pre-COVID-19 years. It surged to a fourteen-year high of 18.5 per cent of PDI in FY21, before falling again to 14 per cent in FY22. As mentioned earlier, there are seven components of GFS.

Deposits (banks and non-banks) have been the predominant choice of household savers in the country since the 1970s. On an average, during the past half a century, out of every ₹100 saved by a household in financial instruments, almost ₹46 has been deposited, primarily in a bank. The share of deposits in household GFS stayed in a very narrow range of 30–35 per cent in the last three decades of the twentieth century. It increased sharply to 43 per cent in the 2000s decade and averaged even higher, at 47 per cent, in the 2010s decade, as bank deposits got an exceptional boost in FY17 owing to demonetization. It increased to 41 per cent in FY21, before falling to 32 per cent in FY22.

Households also hold 10–15 per cent of their GFS as **currency** to be used for immediate consumption or for other purposes. The share of currency has also remained stable around this range since the 1980s. It was around 12.5 per cent between FY19 and FY21, before falling to 10.4 per cent in FY22.

Among two long-term instruments—**insurance funds and pension and provident funds (P&PFs)**—the share of insurance funds has risen consistently from the low double-digits in the second half of the twentieth century to 15–20 per cent in the past two decades. In contrast, the share of P&PFs fell from almost one-third of GFS in the 1960s to an all-time low of around 9 per cent in FY09 before rising back to around 20 per cent in recent years, especially post-demonetization in FY17.

Indian households invest a relatively small share of their financial savings in risky assets such as shares, debentures, mutual funds and commercial bonds—together called **shares and debentures**. During the best equity market periods in the first decade of the twenty-first century, households parked only 1–2 per cent of their GFS in shares and debentures, and they reduced their exposure in these markets. The best decade for the financial markets from the perspective of retail participation was the 1990s, especially the first half, when the average share of shares and debentures was as high as 19 per cent of GFS. This category witnessed higher inflows post-demonetization and has averaged 7 per cent since, with 8.2 per cent share in FY22.

Households have also reduced their direct exposure to the government through the public provident fund (PPF), small savings, etc., during the past one and a half decades. For three decades, from the 1980s to the 2000s, as much as 13 per cent of household financial savings were parked under the category called **claims on government**; this reduced to 1–2 per cent in the late 2000s and early 2010s decades. However, it rose once again after demonetization, towards 10 per cent of GFS.

To sum up, the share of deposits in GFS was extremely low in the 1950s and 1960s, and it picked up only in the 1970s, probably led by the nationalization of Indian banks. In the 1950s, long-term instruments (such as PPFs) were very popular and currency was predominant in the 1960s. Since the 1970s, deposits have been the predominant choice for parking of financial savings of Indian households, followed by long-term instruments such as insurance funds and P&PFs.

Household NFS, which is arrived at after adjusting GFS with financial liabilities, moved in line with GFS during the second half of the twentieth century. However, NFS failed to match the rapid rise in GFS in the first decade of the twenty-first century. While GFS rose from 13.5 per cent of PDI in FY01 to 18 per cent in FY11 (down from its peak of 23 per cent in FY07), NFS rose modestly from 12 per cent at the beginning of the century to an all-time peak of 13.3 per cent of PDI in FY11. This is because household borrowings started rising rapidly from the beginning of the twenty-first century. Financial liabilities of households rose from 1.7 per cent of PDI in FY01 to an all-time high of 8.5 per cent in FY07 before falling to 4.7 per cent in FY11. During the 2010s decade, household liabilities averaged 4.3 per cent of PDI every year, implying that household NFS has remained below or close to 10 per cent of PDI for most of the decade. In fact, NFS was just around 10 per cent of PDI in the pre-pandemic period, close to the lowest level in the past two and a half decades, before witnessing a pick-up to 13.8 per cent of PDI in FY21, which fell again to 9.7 per cent in FY22.

Overall, household GFS rose sharply from around 13 per cent at the end of the 1990s to an all-time peak of about 23 per cent of PDI in the first decade of twenty-first century. However, during the past decade, household GFS averaged 14 per cent of PDI, lower than the 17.5 per cent of the previous decade. On the contrary, financial liabilities of households averaged 4.3 per cent of PDI in each of the past two decades. As a result of lower GFS and stable liabilities, NFS averaged 9.9 per cent of PDI during the 2010s decade, much lower than the 13.3 per cent in the 2000s decade.

Household Physical Savings or Investments

Apart from financial savings, household savings include physical savings. By definition, household physical savings are equal to household investments. In fact, household physical savings are estimated from the investment statistics. Since a large part of the household sector consists of unincorporated bodies, 'machinery and equipment' also forms part of household investments, and thus of physical savings. Still, the majority of household investments are in construction (primarily residential), while other components hold a smaller role.

Household physical savings are estimated by a mix of 'commodity flow' and 'residual' approaches. The Report of the High Level Committee on Estimation of Savings and Investment, 2009 (Para IX.16, p. 201) explains it thus:

> The estimates of gross capital formation for the public sector & private corporate sector are also prepared by expenditure approach on the basis of analysis of budget documents and annual reports of enterprises. These estimates of public sector plus private corporate sector including co-operatives by type of assets (construction and M&E) are subtracted from the corresponding overall estimates compiled through the commodity flow method to arrive at the estimates for household sector as a residual.

In short, first, aggregate estimates of gross fixed capital formation (GFCF) and change in stocks (CIS)—and thus, gross capital formation (GCF)—are prepared using various high-frequency indicators on a quarterly basis for quarterly GDP data. On an annual basis, then, aggregate estimates of GFCF and CIS are classified by type of assets—construction, machinery and equipment, cultivated biological resources and intellectual property rights—and separate estimates are prepared for the public sector (including Central and state governments and departmental and non-departmental commercial undertakings) and the private corporate sector from the financial accounts prepared by these sectors. The estimates for household investments in construction, machinery and equipment and others are then arrived at as residuals, which are then added up to prepare estimates of household GFCF and CIS. By definition, household investments (or GCF = GFCF + CIS) are equal to physical savings (see Exhibit 2.2).

Exhibit 2.2: Household physical savings are estimated as 'residuals'

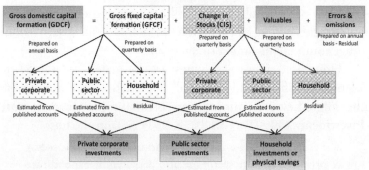

Source: CSO, author's design, Motilal Oswal Financial Services Ltd

The share of physical savings is much higher than that of financial savings in total household savings. If you recall our example at the beginning of this chapter, when Saurabh decided to take a loan to buy a house, his physical savings went up sharply since housing is, by far, the biggest expenditure any individual can ever incur. Overall, while Indian household NFS has been around 10 per cent of PDI in the 2010s decade and averaged 13.3 per cent during the 2000s decade, physical savings have never been below 12 per cent of PDI in the past two decades. In fact, physical savings picked up precisely when household liabilities started to rise.

Household physical savings witnessed a massive rise in the 2000s decade but fell sharply in the 2010s decade. Between FY51 and FY99, physical savings crossed 12 per cent of PDI only once (12.3 per cent in FY91) and never touched 13 per cent of PDI. In contrast, it has never been below 12 per cent of PDI in the 2000s and 2010s decades. From the high single digits till the mid-1990s, household physical savings comfortably moved into the teens in the beginning of the twenty-first century and stayed at around 15 per cent of PDI till FY08. The five years immediately after the great financial crisis saw the highest physical savings on record and peaked at 20 per cent of PDI in FY12. Since FY14, however, it eased off and stabilized at around 15 per cent of PDI up to FY22.

The boom in the residential real estate sector was perhaps the primary contributor to high growth immediately after the great financial crisis hit the world economy in 2008–09. Between FY09 and FY15, household physical savings averaged 18 per cent of PDI, almost double the level in the 1990s decade.

Therefore, while total household savings have fallen almost continuously during the 2010s decade, the fall in the first half was attributed to financial savings while the fall in the second half was led by physical savings. More recently, both financial and physical savings have stabilized at relatively lower levels.

India's Residential Real Estate: Role of Households in Investments

With investment-to-GDP rate at above 30 per cent for more than fifteen years now, India's investment rate is second only to China's among the world's major countries. What, however, is unique to India is the very large share of the household sector in the country's total investments. In most of the world's major economies, the corporate sector is by far the largest investor. However, household investments account for more than a third of total investments in India, against less than 15 per cent in other emerging markets such as China, South Africa and Indonesia. Interestingly, the share of households in total investments in a few advanced economies such as Australia, Italy and Germany is close to 30 per cent—relatively on the higher side, but still lower than in India. The only other country with very high share of households (around 35 per cent) in total investments is Canada.

The real estate sector is generally a reflection of economic activity—the better the income (or GDP) growth, the better the property market. For most part of the past seven decades, the two have shared a good positive correlation. Between FY09 and FY13, when the entire world economy was going through one of the worst financial-cum-economic crises since the 1930s, the Indian economy hardly budged, at least in part courtesy its real estate sector. The only five-year period since the 1950s when India's real GDP growth averaged around 9 per cent (on a 2004–05 base) was from FY04 to FY08; however, the only year with real double-digit GDP growth in India was FY11 (almost immediately after the great financial crisis).

The strong growth in physical savings, however, didn't sustain for long. Between FY13 and FY17, average growth in household investments was only 3.5 per cent, marking the lowest five-year average growth in any period since the early 1960s. Real GDP growth, however, continued to grow impressively, at an average of 7 per cent during the corresponding five-year period. As explained above, this was primarily because household (and government, as we will see in Chapter 4) consumption grew strongly during this period. The only two other episodes of disconnect between real estate and GDP growth were during the early 1980s and early 1990s, when physical savings remained weak notwithstanding higher income growth.

If the real estate sector is so large and important for an economy, the question that arises is, *'What are the key drivers of the residential real estate sector in India?'* One cannot argue that this is an industry where Say's Law—supply creates its own demand—prevails. Due to the very high initial costs and fixed investments for a developer, without demand the industry is unlikely to take off, let alone thrive. If so, demand for residential real estate projects is the primary indicator which decides the future of this industry. If there is sufficient demand for any type of dwelling, supply will happen.

The four key parameters that affect the residential property market in India are **the potential buyer's income, house prices, borrowing interest rates and rental income**. If an individual has sufficient confidence that he can maintain his income, the person can likely buy a house within his income constraints. In an uncertain environment, however, buyers are most likely to go into wait-and-watch mode and delay purchase.

Moreover, higher house prices tend to reduce demand. This is particularly true in the case of end-user demand, wherein the transaction is by first-time buyers for their own use. However, since houses are also seen as an investment, higher house prices could also boost housing demand. Therefore, if house prices are not rising or are falling, investment-related transactions could slow down while end-user demand may increase. It is equally important to understand the drivers of housing prices. If the fall in prices is driven by an economic meltdown, housing demand is unlikely to witness any boost.

Further, since these transactions generally involve loans, borrowing costs could also be an important factor. According to the National Housing Bank (NHB),[9] the outstanding individual housing loans of scheduled commercial banks (SCBs) and housing finance companies have increased from 0.7 per cent of GDP in FY87 to 10.6 per cent of GDP in FY22. India's mortgage loan market, however, is very small compared to the US's (at around 50 per cent of GDP), the UK's 65 per cent and China's 30 per cent of GDP.

Finally, higher rent not only encourages tenants to buy new houses but also encourages existing home owners to buy additional houses, which could then be let out in the market. In the metropolitan areas in India, where property rights are well defined and upheld in the courts of law, higher rents could boost the market for residential real estate in India.

Among the other factors that drive housing demand, the most important is individual wealth. A rise in the number of high-net-worth individuals or any significant positive shock to an individual's income can also lead to higher housing demand.

The long-term historical as well as recent trends in real PDI growth have already been discussed. Notably, house prices in India have also weakened considerably. A look at the annual percentage change in RBI's house price index (HPI) during the past decade suggests that the appreciation in house prices has weakened from 25 per cent at the start of the 2010s decade to 2–3 per cent in the recent quarters (Exhibit 2.3). Why, then, someone may ask, is there no revival in demand for residential real estate? Well, this is because although the growth in house prices has weakened remarkably over the past decade, housing affordability has worsened during the period. Apart from collecting data on house prices in ten cities and preparing the HPI, the RBI also conducts a quarterly residential asset price monitoring survey (RAPMS[10]) on housing loans disbursed by select banks and HFCs across thirteen cities—Mumbai, Chennai, Delhi, Bengaluru, Hyderabad, Kolkata, Pune, Jaipur, Chandigarh, Ahmedabad, Lucknow, Bhopal and Bhubaneswar. Generally, thirty-two select banks/HFCs participate in the survey, although this number may vary due to non-reporting/participation by banks/HFCs or non-inclusion of data due to quality-control issues. This survey collects data on various

Exhibit 2.3: House prices growth has weakened considerably in the past decade

Source: RBI

measures to prepare time series on select ratios, such as (1) loan to value (LTV) ratio, a measure of credit risk on housing loans; (2) EMI to income (ETI) ratio, representing loan eligibility; (3) house price to income (HPTI) ratio, reflecting affordability; and (4) loan to income (LTI) ratio, another affordability measure. Also, the house price index used in this survey is not RBI's HPI but a different all-India residential property price index (RPPI) based on house transactions backed by property loans.[11]

Unlike in the case of the HPI, the RBI has published the results from RAPMS only two times. Although the RBI has been conducting RAPMS since July 2010, the first publication was released only in May 2015 (with data from the quarter ending June 2010 to December 2014) and the second publication was released in July 2019 (with updated data up to March 2019).

Based on the RAPMS data, there are two affordability measures—the house price to income ratio and the loan to annual income ratio. HPTI indicates the average number of monthly incomes required to own a house, and LTI indicates the amount borrowed for housing in terms of the annual income of the borrower.

Although house price growth in India has weakened sharply from around 25 per cent YoY in 2011–12 to just 2–3 per cent currently, house affordability has worsened during the past few years. HPTI increased from below 60 in the period prior to 2015 to 62 in 2018–19, while the LTI ratio rose from 3.0 in FY16 to 3.4 in FY19, the latest reading available from RBI's RAPMS (Exhibit 2.4). Therefore, while HPI growth has moderated sharply, HPI appears to continue to grow faster with respect to growth in borrowers' income during the past many years. Not surprisingly then, the loan amount borrowed for housing has also gone up in terms of annual income.

A look at the city-wise data in the HPI and affordability suggests that while house prices had weakened in all eight major cities, house price affordability had worsened everywhere up to

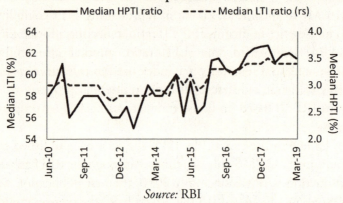

Exhibit 2.4: Housing affordability has worsened during the period

Source: RBI

March 2019. Although we don't have HPTI data post March 2019, it is likely that it has fallen in the past few quarters, helping to improve affordability. But it may be unwise to second-guess, since it would have been difficult to imagine that housing affordability had worsened between FY16 and FY19 without this evidence.

Lastly, lower interest rates also bode well for household investments. Not surprisingly, then, EMI-based housing affordability indices show massive improvement. However, the low interest rate environment is behind us now. Going forward, this is going to be an increment headwind for the residential property market in India.

It is not that the authorities are unaware of this fact. To address the malaise in India's residential real estate sector, a number of measures have been announced and implemented to address the structural issues. Importantly, household investments appear to have bottomed out in 2017 or so. There were improvements in cement production, steel consumption, construction activities, stamp duty and registration charges collected by the states in 2018 and 2019. However, neither was the recovery very strong nor did it last for very long to start reversing the economic slowdown. The pandemic led to an economic standstill in mid-2020, although various factors such as stamp duty benefits, lower interest rates, lower house prices and surging stock markets together helped revive household investments in CY21/CY22. All these incentives/benefits, however, have peaked. It would, thus, be interesting to watch if the revival in the residential real estate market continues or if it falters in the near future.

Household Debt: Estimation and Trends

Till recently there were no official estimates of historical household debt in India. If one googled 'household debt in India' till recently, two very different and highly misleading estimates would appear on the screen—3–4 per cent of GDP or 11–12 per cent of GDP. The first estimate of household debt of 4 per cent of GDP represents the annual flow of financial liabilities and the second data was from the Bank for International Settlements (BIS). However, the BIS, like all other agencies and participants, used data on 'personal loans' by Indian banks as household debt, which is only one part of debt. In its March 2018 Monthly Bulletin, the RBI published for the first time quarterly estimates of Households' Financial Assets and Liabilities for the period Q1FY16 to Q2FY18. The press release said: 'This is the first release of quarterly data on household financial assets and liabilities, as a precursor to our endeavour to move towards quarterly compilation of FoF accounts.' While the attempt was highly appreciated, the next version came out after more than two years, in June 2020, which had updated data up to March 2020. The official data, thus, was available for five years, from FY16 to FY20. The most recent data now available is for Q4FY22 (quarter-ending March 2022), published in the Monthly Bulletin of September 2022. Household debt, as per RBI data, stood at 35.3 per cent of GDP in FY22, down from 39.3 per cent in FY21 but higher than 33.5 per cent in FY19.

What about the historical data? How has household debt evolved in India during the past many decades? For this, I have used two techniques. The first methodology uses RBI data on 'Flow of Funds' to prepare an estimate of household outstanding debt during the past seven decades, while the second methodology helps us prepare an estimate for the past fifteen years (since FY05) on a quarterly basis. Both methodologies yield similar estimates.

The first technique (Method#1) is to add up the annual flow of liabilities, which is available since FY52, to estimate household debt (see Appendix 1). Since liabilities don't have any valuation changes and the annual flow of liabilities is net incurrence of liabilities, the cumulative data will provide us with the stock of household liabilities. The only assumption to make is on the starting point—outstanding household debt in FY51. Since the Indian economy was very small in FY51 (₹10,400 crore or just 0.05 per cent of FY20 GDP), it doesn't matter whether we assume Indian household debt at 1 per cent or 100 per cent of PDI at that time. When we add up the flows for the past seventy years, the difference is trivial. Therefore, assuming household debt at 10 per cent of GDP in FY51 and adding up the annual flows of household liabilities every year, we learn that India's household debt was 45.2 per cent of PDI in FY22, up from 42.2 per cent in FY19 and 20 per cent in FY03.

The second methodology (Method#2) is a bottoms-up approach, wherein the lenders' exposure to Indian households is analysed. If any individual or non-corporate non-government entity wants to borrow in the country, there are only three possible formal/institutional lenders—banks, NBFCs and HFCs. Banks are the primary source of borrowings for households in India. Using data from RBI's 'Basic Statistical Returns of Scheduled Commercial Banks in India (BSR)', we find that the total exposure of the banks to the Indian household sector amounted to ₹67.3 tn or 55 per cent of bank loans. Household debt, thus, was *at least* 36 per cent of PDI in FY22.

Data from the NHB reveals HFCs' outstanding loans at about ₹13.4 tn each (or 5.7 per cent of GDP) in FY22, of which household (or individual) loans amounted to ₹8.1 tn (or 4.3 per cent of PDI). Similarly, RBI data suggests that the share of the household sector in the NBFCs' loan book has risen consistently, from 18 per cent in FY16 to 30 per cent in FY22. It implies that ₹8.8 tn (or 4.8 per cent of PDI) was lent by NBFCs to the household sector in FY22. Assumptions are made to arrive at such data prior to FY16 for which no such break-up is available.

The aggregate of the exposures of SCBs, NBFCs and HFCs to the household sector (Method#2) thus suggests that household debt in India was ₹84.2 tn in FY22 or 45.4 per cent of PDI (and 35.9 per cent of GDP). This methodology suggests that household leverage has risen from 31.8 per cent of PDI each in FY09 and FY10.

Although Method#1 provides long-term reliable data on household debt, there are three clear benefits of Method#2. One, it provides quarterly estimates of household leverage with a lag of just two to three months. Two, it provides additional details regarding the lenders—banks, HFCs and NBFCs. Banks account for 80 per cent of total household debt. It has, however, reduced from 87 per cent a decade ago. Three, it helps in further classification of household debt under a few major activities—mortgage/home, vehicles/automobile and agricultural loans. Housing loans account for almost 30 per cent of household debt, followed by agricultural loans (approximately 21 per cent) and vehicle loans (around 9 per cent). These three categories thus account for almost 60 per cent of all household leverage. The share of agricultural loans has fallen consistently in the past few years and that of automobile loans has increased.

Although household debt has almost tripled from around 16 per cent of PDI at the turn of the century to 45 per cent of PDI currently, it is still very low compared to household debt in other major economies. However, is it the right way to compare headline household debt? Is there any way to estimate the threshold for household debt in India, beyond which it will become a concern?

Is Household Debt in India at a Threatening Level?

This is not an easy question to answer, considering the limited data availability in India. An answer to this question requires a detailed analysis of the profile of borrowers by income, occupation, wealth and other characteristics. Nevertheless, there are two ways in which we can arrive at some imperfect answers to this very difficult question.

The first method is to find out if the recent spurt in household debt is led by 'credit widening' or 'credit deepening'. The former implies that expansion in debt is led by an increase in the borrower base (higher number of borrowers), while the latter represents a higher concentration of household debt (same borrowers getting more loans). A priori, expansion in debt led by credit widening is more desirable[12] than expansion led by credit deepening. There are no details available for the number of loan accounts under household debt with NBFCs and HFCs; however, such information is available for banks. Since SCBs account for about 80 per cent of the household debt in the country, this exercise is worth it.

An analysis of the drivers of banks' household debt suggests that expansion in household debt during the past nine years has almost entirely been on account of credit widening (Exhibit 2.5). This is in sharp contrast to what led the previous periods of expansion. Based on the available data for more than two decades, from FY99 to FY22, it is clear that between FY09 and FY13 (the period of highly unbalanced growth for the Indian economy), almost 80 per cent of all the growth in

Exhibit 2.5: 'Credit widening' vs. 'Credit deepening' in household debt in India

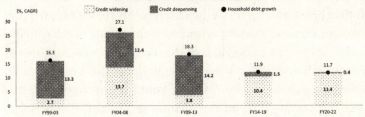

'Credit widening' implies higher debt growth driven by more loan accounts and 'Credit deepening' means higher loan per account
Source: RBI, author's estimates

banks' household debt was on account of credit deepening. A sharp increase in 'loan per account' implies concentration of household debt in the country, which reflects a build-up of risk. The situation was not different at the turn of the century (between FY99 and FY03), when around 82 per cent of the expansion in household debt was on account of increasing concentration.

During the past nine years (FY14–FY22), things have moved to the other extreme. While banks' household exposure has risen by an average growth of 11.8 per cent per annum during the period, loan-per-borrower (or 'credit deepening') increased only marginally, from ₹1,97,848 in FY14 to ₹2,17,130 in FY22. This implies that only around 10 per cent of the growth in household debt was contributed by credit deepening. Credit widening was thus almost entirely responsible for the expansion in household debt between FY14 and FY22. The number of loan accounts more than doubled, from 135.4 mn in FY14 to 309.9 mn in FY22.

The limitation of this analysis, however, is that RBI publishes data on the number of accounts, not on the number of borrowers. It is possible that the same borrowers may be taking new loans by opening new accounts. However, there is no way to address this issue with the publicly available data we have.

The second procedure to gauge if household debt is reaching a tipping point is to estimate the debt service ratio for India's household sector. A look at the DSR trends over the past two decades and its comparison with the trends in other major countries give us a good idea of the picture to draw conclusions from. BIS released a working paper[13] on the limitations in estimating this ratio for different countries; nevertheless, it is worth spending time on this analysis because of its superiority over the previous method.

The BIS defines DSR as the ratio of interest payments plus amortizations to income. However, since data on amortization is generally not available, the BIS follows an approach used by the US Federal Reserve Board to construct DSR for the household sector. It explains the approach thus:

> At the individual level, it is straightforward to determine the DSR. Households and firms know the amount of interest they pay on all their outstanding debts, how much debt they have to amortise per period and how much income they earn. But even so, difficulties can arise. Many contracts can be rolled over so that the effective period for repaying a particular loan can be much longer than the contractual maturity of the specific contract. Equally, some contracts allow for early repayments so that households or firms can amortise ahead of schedule. Given this, deriving aggregate DSRs from individual-level data does not necessarily lead to good estimates. And such data are rarely comprehensive, if available at all. For this reason, we derive aggregate DSRs from aggregate data directly.

The formula used by the BIS to estimate the DSR for sector j (households in our case) at time t is:

$$DSR_{j,t} = \frac{i_{j,t}}{(1-(1+i_{j,t})^{-S_{j,t}})} * \frac{D_{j,t}}{Y_{j,t}}$$

where, $D_{j,t}$ denotes the total stock of debt, $Y_{j,t}$ the aggregate income available for debt service payments, $i_{j,t}$ the average interest rate on the existing stock of debt and $s_{j,t}$ the average remaining maturity across the stock of debt.

The People's Bank of China used the BIS methodology to arrive at the DSR for China's household sector and compared it with the DSR of other nations as estimated by the BIS.[14] For the Indian economy, the task is even more complicated. Not only do we not have any available data on amortizations but there is also no official data providing aggregate interest payments or the average maturity profile of Indian household debt.

Using disaggregated official data from the RBI and the NHB, however, the DSR for Indian households can be estimated with some assumptions (see Appendix 3 for details). My calculations suggest that Indian households use about 11.5 per cent of their disposable income to service their debt. A comparison of this ratio against those of other major economies suggests that while household debt to income ratio is the lowest in India (at 45 per cent in FY22), and less than 25 per cent of the ratio in Nordic countries (such as Norway, Denmark and Sweden), the DSR for Indian households is exceptionally high (Exhibit 2.6).

How is that possible? Why is Indian household DSR so high despite India having the lowest debt ratio? As the BIS formula suggests, the lower the interest rate (i) and the higher the maturity (s) are, the lower the DSR will be for any given level of household debt to income ratio (D). Although household debt to income ratio in India is the lowest compared to other nations, its DSR is much higher than that of many other nations, including China, due to the combination of very high effective interest rates and the average maturity of about five years. In other countries, the effective interest rates are much lower and maturity much higher. For instance, in China, the effective interest rate was around 5 per cent and the average maturity about eighteen years in CY19.

Further, while the DSR has fallen for most nations (or stabilized at lower levels) during the past many years as interest rates fell dramatically in the 2010s decade, the DSR for Indian

Exhibit 2.6: Despite lower debt to PDI ratio, DSR is very high for Indian households . . .

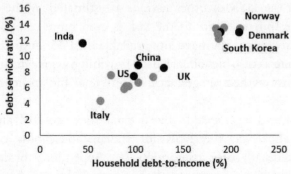

March 2022 data for all except South Korea (CY21) and China (CY20)

Exhibit 2.7: . . .which has risen gradually during the past decade

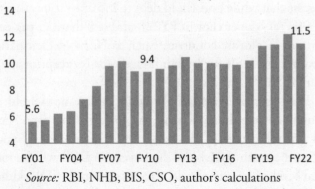

Source: RBI, NHB, BIS, CSO, author's calculations

households rose from 5.6 per cent at the turn of the century to 9.4 per cent in FY10 to about 11.5 per cent in FY22 (Exhibit 2.7).

The BIS research working paper noted:

> . . . the DSRs' peak levels are surprisingly similar across countries and time despite different levels of financial development. As a broad rule of thumb, the graph panels suggest that a DSR above 20–25% reliably signals the risk of a banking crisis. [However, there are exceptions] . . . for some countries, such as Korea, the DSR typically exceeds this level without any crisis occurring. Equally, some countries, like

Germany or Greece (not shown), have much lower values. This is likely to be driven by country-specific factors, such as the age distribution, the rate of home ownership, industrial structure and income inequality.

Although DSR is not a perfect measure for prediction of economic crises, higher DSRs significantly increase the severity of recessions and also provide an early warning indicator of crises. The BIS working paper concluded that 'if the DSR is 5 percentage points higher, the recession is about 25% more severe, as real output would on average drop by 5% rather than 4%' and that 'a rapid rise in the DSR above 6% (relative to a 15-year average) is a very strong indication that a crisis may be imminent'.

Comparing Indian household DSR with these thresholds indicates that the household leverage in India is not alarmingly high. While the DSR is at 11.5 per cent for India, the fifteen-year average crossed 10 per cent in recent years. Further, a look at the historical DSR for several nations confirms that the threshold is not uniform across nations. For instance, household DSR has been much higher, at around 15 per cent, for decades in many advanced nations such as Denmark, Norway, Australia and the Netherlands. On the contrary, household DSR was 11.5 per cent at its peak in CY07 in the US (similar to what it is in India now), when the subprime crisis was triggered.

Doing some reverse calculations and assuming 10.4 per cent and 15 per cent annual growth in PDI and household debt respectively in the future (same as in the pre-COVID-19 period), with the current maturity (that is, 5.2 years) and unchanged interest rates (that is, 10 per cent), DSR for Indian households will touch 15 per cent/20 per cent at a debt to income ratio of only 59 per cent/78 per cent. Such DSR was reached in the Nordic countries only at debt to income ratios of more than 200 per cent. Assuming that average maturity increases gradually to 5.5 years (or six years) and the effective interest rate falls to 9.5 per cent (or 9 per cent), the threshold of 15 per cent/20 per cent DSR would shift to debt to income ratio of 62 per cent/83 per cent (or 67 per cent/90 per cent). It is, therefore, safe to conclude that the threshold for Indian household debt is only 60–80 per cent of PDI, much lower than in Western nations.

The fact that household debt to income ratio is very low in India compared to other economies does not necessarily imply that there is nothing to worry about on that front. While we can take some comfort in the fact that the recent spurt in household debt is primarily linked to widening of the borrower base rather than higher concentration of debt, in the absence of any details about the profile of borrowers, this conclusion is not sacrosanct. Instead, the fact that the service ratio of lower household debt in India is very high compared to many other nations is a matter of concern, though not alarming yet. In many European nations, while the household debt ratio is almost 100 per cent, it consumes only about 6–7 per cent of the household disposable income. Even in the US and China, while the debt ratio is 90–100 per cent, the DSR is 7.5 per cent to 8.5 per cent, much lower than the 11.5 per cent in India.

While more analysis with detailed data is required to be done by the regulators (since it is impossible to conduct this exercise without detailed data in public domain), the key lessons are:

1. since the cost of servicing debt is much higher and the average maturity is very low in India, the headline household debt to income ratio is not comparable with that of other nations;
2. with unchanged maturity and effective interest rate, if DSR of 15 per cent is considered as the tolerable limit for India, the threshold of India's household debt is estimated at less than 60 per cent; this threshold increases to 78 per cent if DSR of 20 per cent is considered as the tolerable limit;

3. the best way to make higher household debt more sustainable in India for a longer period of time is to prolong the average maturity and/or reduce the cost of debt.

Our analysis concretely confirms that household leverage in India is not as low as most public forums, market commentators and many leading multi-international organizations believe and argue it to be. However, it is not at alarming levels even at this stage, which provides a window to policymakers to attempt the required manoeuvres to make it more sustainable.

Impact of COVID-19 on Household Finances in India

During any economic recession, as demand for goods and services comes down, companies retract their production, leading to higher unemployment and lower income for the employed. This leads to further reduction in demand for goods and services, creating a vicious cycle. Unless a stabilizer such as fiscal and/or monetary support comes in, the situation may go from bad to worse very quickly. The COVID-19 situation, however, was like no other economic recession, and the policy decisions were swift. Still, as a consequence of the national lockdown, the economic impact was very real and huge.

The immediate impact of COVID-19 on household finances was colossal. In light of the quickly spreading virus, a national lockdown was announced in the last week of March 2020. As the lockdown took everyone by surprise, incomes dropped (especially for the self-employed and casual/daily workers) immediately in Q4FY20. Since it created some panic among the general public, citizens reacted by hoarding essential items, leading to higher consumption and a dip in their savings. As the lockdowns extended into the next couple of quarters, discretionary spending was severely impacted. Accordingly, consumption started falling along with income, but people's savings increased.

As mentioned earlier, household savings in India consist of two components—financial savings and physical savings. Due to COVID-19, though financial savings (particularly bank deposits) surged, physical savings (or investments in real estate) almost dissipated in the first two quarters of the pandemic.

There is no quarterly official data on either household physical savings (investments) or household income. RBI has published quarterly estimates on household financial savings and household outstanding debt, which is available up to the quarter ending March 2022 (Q4FY22). An estimate of household investments on a quarterly basis, and thus household total savings, can be prepared from the 'stamp duty and registration charges' collected by state governments. Then, using the direct methodology (unlike the official methodology), PDI can be calculated by adding personal consumption (available from quarterly GDP) and household total savings (RBI's/my own estimates).

Against an average growth of 10.5 per cent YoY from FY18 to FY20, nominal PDI grew only 2.0 per cent YoY in Q4FY20 before declining by about 8 per cent YoY in H1FY21. This means that instead of a 10.5 per cent growth in FY21 (assuming the average of the previous three years), PDI grew by just 2.4 per cent in FY21, implying an income loss of about ₹13.1 tn (or 6.6 per cent of actual GDP in FY21).

In contrast, after declining by a strong 8 per cent YoY in Q4FY20, household savings grew marginally in H1FY21. Within savings, net financial savings surged while physical savings (primarily residential real estate activity) fell by almost a third in H1FY21.

Household debt, interestingly, continued to grow decently every quarter in FY21. After growing at an average of 15.3 per cent YoY every quarter between FY16 and FY19, household debt growth weakened to 10.8 per cent in FY20 and grew slowly at 8.3 per cent in H1FY21.

As the economy started unlocking, the economic situation started improving. Things normalized further in H2FY21, just before a ferocious second COVID-19 wave hit the nation in March 2021. Unlike in the first wave, there were no national lockdowns during the second COVID-19 wave. Therefore, although the highest daily number of confirmed COVID-19 cases was four times the number recorded during the first wave, the economic impact was only 15–20 per cent of the impact resulting from the first.

The financial position of households normalized further in FY22, and reflected the pre-COVID-19 trends. Household savings fell to about 25 per cent of PDI, similar to that in FY18 and FY19. Real consumption growth was strong at 11.2 per cent, higher than real GDP growth of 9.1 per cent, which was stronger than real PDI growth of just 5.6 per cent YoY in FY22. According to the second advance estimates of the Government of India,[15] these trends continued in FY23 as well.

Indian Household Finances Have Worsened Massively

The household sector is by far the largest, most pervasive and most important economic participant in any economy. In spite of this, most public debates on economics assume that the only responsibility of the household sector is to consume. As discussed above, household income, savings, investments and debt are also facets of the economy that are as important as household consumption. An excessive focus on consumption, disregarding other important parameters, could have highly damaging consequences.

'Buy till you die', as they say—and it appears that Indian households have practised this during the past few years. Consequently, the finances of the Indian household sector have deteriorated substantially during the past decade. A graphic representation of the entire analysis in this chapter is provided in Exhibit 2.8. It shows the average growth in household finances—real income, real consumption, financial savings,

Exhibit 2.8: Household finances have deteriorated significantly in the last few years

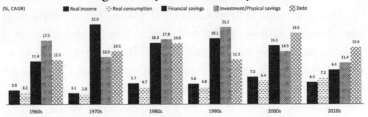

Please see Appendix 1 and 2 for data
Gross financial savings, investments and debt are in nominal terms
Source: CSO, RBI, author's estimates

investments (that is, physical savings) and debt—over the past six decades. The key findings are summarized below:

1. For the first time post-Independence, household consumption growth has outpaced household income growth. While income growth in the 2010s decade was lower than in the previous decade, private consumption growth was the highest ever.

2. As a result of higher growth in consumption than in income, household savings suffered in the 2010s decade. Gross financial savings grew at the slowest pace in the past five decades, while average growth in net financial savings was in the single digit for the first time since the 1960s decade.

3. Also, this was only the second time in the past five decades when net financial savings grew slower than physical savings. The average growth in the latter in the 2010s decade was also the weakest in the past six decades.

4. Although debt growth was also lower than in the previous decade, it grew at the fastest pace compared to other activities of the household sector in the 2010s decade.

5. Household debt in the country has risen from around 32 per cent of PDI in FY11 to 45.2 per cent in FY22, while household savings have fallen from their peak of 30.5 per cent to 25 per cent during the corresponding period.

Consequently, the ratio of household debt to household savings has risen from 1.1x a decade ago to 1.8x in FY22. It means that while a year's worth of household savings was sufficient to pay off the entire household debt a year ago, it now takes almost 1.8 years' worth of savings to achieve the same feat—a deterioration of 70 per cent in a single decade.

These facts make the consumption-driven growth model highly unsustainable. Higher consumption growth is not worrying per se; however, since it outpaces income growth, it is supported by withdrawal of savings and incurrence of higher leverage, and this presents the perfect cocktail to push the soul of this economy into serious trouble—financial stress.

Lower savings may be bad news for households and for the future economic growth trajectory. But it helps companies/producers to post good sales, and thus profits. In the same way that households are dependent on the corporate sector for employment, companies are also reliant on the household sector for demand for the goods and services they produce. Irrational behaviour on the part of one economic participant could benefit another participant. How? Let's see in the next chapter.

Key Lessons from the Chapter

- The household sector includes individuals and unincorporated enterprises such as sole proprietors and partnerships. Thus, it is pervasive in an economy.
- Private final consumption expenditure is only one activity of the household sector, and it should always be analysed along with its other activities such as earning, saving, investment and borrowing, which are as important.
- During the 2010s decade, household consumption in India grew faster than household income, marking the first such decade since the 1950s. Consequently, household savings have fallen persistently for the past six to seven years,

marking their first such fall in the past seven decades. These worrying trends have continued in the post-COVID-19 years as well.
- In sharp contrast to the widely held belief (till about a couple of years ago) that household debt in India is 10–12 per cent of GDP, the official estimates (from RBI and our calculations) suggest that it is more than three times that (35 per cent of GDP and 45 per cent of PDI).
- The combination of lower savings, rising leverage and weakening income growth vis-à-vis strong consumption growth present the perfect cocktail to push the soul of the economy into serious trouble—financial stress in this case.
- Unlike in most other economies, households in India are exceptionally large investors too. Weak household investments in residential real estate have made the economy suffer during the past many years. Lower interest rates may help boost real estate demand; however, unless housing affordability improves (with lower house prices and/or stronger income growth), the residential real estate sector may remain subdued.
- Lastly, although India's household leverage is the lowest compared to most other nations', the higher cost of servicing debt (due to lower maturity and higher interest rates) render such cross-country comparisons of the headline ratios worthless. Neither is household leverage in India as low as most public forums suggest, nor is there massive room left to expand it in the future.

Chapter 3

THE LISTED AND THE LESSER-KNOWN UNLISTED CORPORATE SECTORS

Non-economist: A nation cannot become a superpower without a vibrant corporate sector, which must be incentivized and supported at all costs and at all times. It is both the major employer and investor in the economy. It builds nations.

Me: No one is doing any social service. Companies are doing what they do in return for profits. The objective of companies is to maximize profits/sales and generate wealth for its shareholders/promoters. It is not the moral duty of the government to support companies unless their objectives align with the national objectives, which tend to be more social in nature.

Non-economist: Profits lead to higher investments. Without profits, how will companies grow, and why will they invest? Corporate profits in India had fallen to a multi-year low of 2–3 per cent of GDP in the pre-pandemic years. Where was the incentive for companies to invest? This is why the corporate sector has deleveraged in the past few years.

Me: India's aggregate corporate profits averaged 9 per cent in the 2010s decade, not 2–3 per cent. Also, investments drive profits, not the other way round. And expectation of profits drives investment decisions. This expectation, in turn, is dependent on economic buoyancy. If profits rise without economic buoyancy, which has happened in the past decade or so, it is highly unlikely to lead to higher investments.

Non-economist: Higher profits without economic buoyancy? Where does 9 per cent come from? And what do you mean by 'investments drive profits, not the other way round'? Care to elaborate?

Me: Of course. Let me explain . . .

Whenever one speaks of the corporate sector in India, more often than not the reference is to the listed/BSE500 companies. This is why India's corporate profits are believed to be as low as 2–3 per cent of GDP, when it is approximately 9 per cent of GDP in reality, comparable to corporate profits in the US and the UK. The huge difference between the listed companies and the aggregate corporate sector in India is not only in terms of profits, but also in terms of leverage, investments, gross value addition and (merchandise) exports. This being so, an analysis/discussion based only on listed/BSE500 companies may lead to misleading conclusions, especially from the macroeconomic perspective. In this chapter, the financial position of India's aggregate corporate sector is discussed with a special focus on the unlisted sector. COVID-19 has made the differences between the listed and unlisted corporate sectors starker. An analysis of the key determinants of corporate profits helps explain the relationship between profits and investments. A comparison of India's current corporate deleveraging vis-à-vis historical global episodes also throws up interesting facts. Overall, this analysis does not point to any imminent strong revival in corporate investments in India.

Do you remember my friend Saurabh? When he spends on domestic goods and services in the country, it becomes revenue for the producers. The producers can be part of the household or corporate sector. However, Saurabh also derives his income from these producers or manufacturers of goods and services. Therefore, there is a very strong circular connection between the household and corporate sectors. In effect, the latter—on an aggregate basis—is largely an employer of the consumers of its own goods and services. Confused? Let's discuss it.

As I have mention earlier, this book is about the connections between the different economic participants in the nation.

In this chapter, we extend our main theme by bringing the corporate sector into focus. How does the household sector influence the finances of the corporate sector? How leveraged is India's corporate sector? What is the role of the corporate sector in India's GDP growth? These are the key questions addressed in this chapter.

By definition, a company doesn't consume. Therefore, corporate disposable income is broadly equal to the sector's savings.[1] If corporate savings are lower than corporate investments, the sector will be a 'net borrower'—borrowing from other domestic savers, especially households, or from abroad (by importing capital and thus, widening current account deficit, CAD) or from both. On the contrary, if corporate savings are higher than corporate investments, the difference will be either lent to the domestic net borrower (that is, the government) or exported abroad (capital outflows or current account surplus).

The corporate sector consists of two types of companies—non-financial companies and financial companies. The primary economic activity of the former is investment, while the latter acts as an intermediary between the net savers (households, generally) and net borrowers (government and/or corporate sector). Recently there has been a lot of discussion on India's financial sector and several books[2] have been written on the subject. In fact, during the past few years we have had many central bankers who have been more vocal than their predecessors about the health of India's financial sector. Also, the financial sector, especially considering the expanding role of central banks, is so wide that it is difficult to contain any discussion on it in a few pages.

Therefore, in this chapter I focus on NFCs and their role in India's economic growth through the investments they make. Households—via real estate—account for a significant share of investments in India. Not surprisingly then, the share of the corporate sector in total investments in India is among the lowest—only about half—among other economies. Since corporate investments are the most efficient investments, their lower share in total investments affects the efficiency of India's investments.

One of the most important metrics for gauging the performance of the corporate sector in any economy is its profits. Unfortunately, there is no official data on India's corporate profits. Therefore, I use my own estimates (and describe my methodology) for India's corporate profits. Similarly, while the RBI has started publishing household outstanding debt on a quarterly basis, there are no official estimates of quarterly corporate debt. In July 2019, the RBI released its report 'Financial Stocks and Flows of the Indian Economy 2011–12 to 2017–18', with its first official estimates of corporate (financial + non-financial) debt in India.[3] The data was updated with 2020–21 data in its March 2023 publication. Although there is no domestic official quarterly data on India's corporate debt, BIS provides quarterly estimates for FY08 onward. Therefore, RBI's annual data and BIS's quarterly data are used wherever India's corporate debt is discussed in this chapter. Both estimates are very close, and the latter is updated up to Q3FY23 (quarter ending December 2022). It is well known that India's corporate sector has deleveraged sharply during the past decade; however, a comparison with historical global corporate deleveraging episodes throws up some interesting insights.

Before I delve deeper into the NFCs in India, let me briefly discuss India's financial sector. India has traditionally been a banking-dominated society; banks attract more than half of the total financial assets of households and account for more than half of the total institutional lending to the non-government sector in the economy. The importance of banks, however, has reduced dramatically in the past few years with the emergence of non-banking financial companies and housing finance companies and the rise of the corporate bonds market. Growth in the NBFC/HFC sector has fizzled out over the past three or four years (following the default by Infrastructure Leasing & Financial Services [IL&FS] in September 2018), but it continues to be an integral part of India's financial stability because of its interlinkages with the traditional banking sector and the corporate bonds market. It is not a surprise then that the two recent RBI governors (Dr Raghuram Rajan and Dr Urjit Patel) and a former RBI deputy governor (Dr Viral Acharya) have been outspoken about the financial sector reforms in the country.[4]

I restrict my discussion on India's financial sector to two major developments in this area which have broad economic implications—the rising importance of the non-banking financial sector and the shift from public sector banks (PbSBs) to private sector banks (PvSBs).

India's Financial Sector

A stable and strong financial sector acts as an intermediary to channel funds from the savers (households) to the borrowers (NFCs and the government), and it is almost impossible for any nation to grow at a high pace on a sustainable basis without a robust financial sector.

As we have seen, more than half the GFS of households are parked in the banking sector. Further, banks have an even more important role to play in the credit market. Based on my estimates of non-government non-financial (NGNF) debt in the country, banks accounted for as much as 70 per cent of the total debt in the country at the turn of the twenty-first century. The non-bank lenders and market instruments—comprising NBFCs, HFCs, commercial papers (CPs), corporate bonds (CBs) and external commercial borrowings (ECBs)—accounted for less than a third of total lending to the NGNF sector. Their contributions to NGNF debt growth were also similar, at the 70:30 ratio, in the first decade of the twenty-first century.

However, things started to change in the 2010s decade. The share of banks in NGNF debt eased to 65 per cent in FY14, reducing consistently to less than 60 per cent in FY17 and to a multi-decade low of 55.6 per cent in FY19 before rising slightly for the first time in thirteen years to 56 per cent in FY20 and staying there in FY22. In contrast, the share of the so-called shadow banks (NBFCs and HFCs) increased continuously, from about 15 per cent in FY10 to its peak of 21.8 per cent in FY19. Further, the share of borrowings through bonds issued by NFCs also doubled, from just 6 per cent in the late 2000s decade to around 12 per cent in the second half of the 2010s decade. Short-term borrowings raised through CPs remained trivial in NGNF debt; however, their share too crossed 1 per cent of outstanding debt for the first time in FY16 and has stayed there since. To put this in perspective, the share of banks in NGNF debt in the US has been only around 30 per cent since the 1980s.

The contribution of the traditional (that is, banks) and new lenders (NBFCs + HFCs) to NGNF debt growth has also moved commensurately. The contribution of banks to NGNF debt growth fell from more than 65 per cent in the 2000s decade to less than 50 per cent for the first time in FY16 and to a two-decade low of 34 per cent in FY18. Thus, while banks accounted for 56 per cent of NGNF debt, their contribution to NGNF debt growth fell to almost one-third in FY18, when NBFCs and HFCs were highly aggressive.

In other words, when banks were cleaning their balance sheets by resorting to slow credit growth, building adequate capital and recognizing bad assets, NBFCs and HFCs replaced banks as the major contributors to NGNF debt in the country. While the new lenders accounted for just 21 per cent of NGNF debt in FY18, they contributed 40 per cent to NGNF debt growth during the year. It is, however, unfortunate that the asset quality of the new lenders turned out to be bad, leading to the IL&FS collapse in September 2018. For the next few years,

India's financial sector remained in trouble. The IL&FS default was followed by scares in YES Bank, Punjab Mercantile Co-operative (PMC) Bank and Lakshmi Vilas Bank (LVB), and many other lenders have been in the news for all the wrong reasons. Therefore, while the banking sector was making (or being forced to make) the required adjustments, the financial sector remained weak as a result of the fresh weaknesses witnessed among the non-bank lenders.

In Chapter 2, when we discussed household debt and the major lenders to households, we had said that banks account for about 80 per cent of total household debt in the country. However, the share of banks in corporate debt has fallen consistently, from as high as 60 per cent in the 2000s decade to 50 per cent by the mid-2010s and to as low as 40 per cent in recent years. Notwithstanding the regulatory changes, this shift in role among lenders from banks to non-banks is remarkable in such a short period of time. After the IL&FS default in September 2018, a liquidity crunch was triggered in the housing finance sector. The RBI took over the regulation of HFCs from the National Housing Bank (NHB) by amending the National Banking Act in 2019.

Second, there has been a massive change within the banking sector as well during the past few years. Not only has the banking sector lost to the non-bank lenders, but within the banking sector, public sector banks have lost substantially to private sector banks. The share of PvSBs in total deposits was extremely stable, at 17–18 per cent, between FY04 and FY14; this increased to 20 per cent in FY15 and rose further, to 31 per cent in FY22. In the case of loans, the share of PvSBs rose from 17–18 per cent in the 2000s decade to 25 per cent in FY17 and further to 37 per cent in FY22.

Worse, due to massive recapitalization of PbSBs to the tune of ₹2 tn in the pre-COVID-19 period, government holding has increased further in several PbSBs. Comparing the performance of PbSBs and PvSBs, Dr Urjit Patel showed that not only were PbSBs worse than PvSBs in their asset quality, but the former's high non-operating expenses to earnings ratio, higher incidence of frauds owing to poor operational risk management and low capital adequacy also differentiated them from the latter.[5]

Both these large changes in India's financial sector—the shift from banks to non-banks and the shift from PbSBs to PvSBs within the banking system—imply that (1) although non-bank lenders had an extremely good run for a few years, they have become highly vulnerable since the IL&FS default in FY19, bringing back focus on the traditional banking sector, (2) private banks are better governed than government-owned banks, and (3) it is imperative to reduce the dominance of PbSBs.

Amid all this, the RBI released a report[6] of its Internal Working Group (IWG) to Review Extant Ownership Guidelines and Corporate Structure for Indian Private Sector Banks in November 2020. The report generated intense reactions when it said, 'Large corporate/industrial houses may be allowed as promoters of banks only after necessary amendments to the Banking Regulations Act, 1949.'

The Indian banking sector has evolved continuously since 1993. To increase competition and diversity, the RBI allowed on-tap licensing, and fourteen licences for universal banks have been issued in the private sector since 1993, of which ten banks are currently in operation. Further, two new categories of bank licences were introduced—small finance banks (SFBs) and payment banks (PBs). As of end-2022, twelve SFBs and six PBs have been licensed. Additionally, foreign investment up to 74 per cent in PvSBs is allowed.

Why then should large corporate/industrial houses be allowed into banking? This was the question asked by Dr Viral Acharya and Dr Raghuram Rajan in a research note on RBI's IWG report.[7] The authors argued that industrial houses should not be allowed into banking, primarily for two reasons: (1) the well-known issues of connected lending and misallocation of credit would invariably be disastrous, and (2) it would further exacerbate the concentration of economic (and political) power in certain business houses.

Both these situations have been experienced by the Indian economy, and therefore the RBI proposal raised concerns. Relating to the first reason, Amol Agrawal, assistant professor of economics at Ahmedabad University says:[8]

> The then Prime Minister Indira Gandhi listed 'the removal of control by a few' as one of the major reasons for nationalisation. She further added that by 'severing the link between the major banks and the bigger industrial groups which have so far controlled them', the government will be able to professionalise the banking sector.

Agrawal also notes that six of the fourteen banks that were issued licences since 1993 have faced trouble. Of these, four were run by professionals, one was controlled by a corporate and the sixth by a financial institution.

As Professor C.P. Chandrashekhar from the Centre for Economic Studies and Planning, Jawaharlal Nehru University, New Delhi, wrote in 2011:[9]

> In the years preceding nationalisation, when leading banks were part of business groups, an excessively large and disproportionate share of advances by these banks went to firms in which directors had [a direct or indirect interest] . . . Influence rather than project screening was clearly determining lending and leading to overexposure to a few clients.

The second reason cited by Acharya and Rajan is even more pertinent. Incidentally, about a week before the RBI report was published for public viewing on 20 November 2020, the *Financial Times* ran a story titled '"Modi's Rockefeller": Gautam Adani and the Concentration of Power in India'.[10] The pithy title clearly suggests what the content of the article is. In fact, as we will see later in this chapter, data shows that while the corporate sector has deleveraged massively, NIFTY50 companies have taken on more debt during the past five years. India's corporate debt has risen from ₹85 tn in FY16 to ₹117 tn in FY20, and approximately 25 per cent of this increase (amounting to ₹8.2 tn) is accounted for by thirty-nine NIFTY50 NFCs. The share of non-financial NIFTY50 companies in total corporate leverage increased from 12.6 per cent by FY16 to 16 per cent in FY20.

Interestingly, while the RBI report said, 'All the experts except one were of the opinion that large corporate/industrial houses should not be allowed to promote a bank', the change was still recommended.

If this recommendation is adopted, the true impact will be visible only after many years (probably after more than a decade). At this stage, India's financial sector has witnessed a substantial improvement in its balance sheet, especially after COVID-19, which certainly takes away the supply-side issues in India's credit growth. What remains, however, are the self-restrictions on the part of lenders because of low confidence in the economic recovery and weak credit demand. Although confidence among retail borrowers and demand from them is still strong, the corporate loan book and corporate demand, which play an important role in India's economic activity, have weakened considerably over the past decade.

What Are India's Aggregate Corporate Profits and What Are Its Determinants?

The primary economic role of NFCs is to borrow and invest. But why do people become entrepreneurs or start an enterprise? There could be many reasons. To begin with, an enterprise would be a source of income for the owners (or founders), just as jobs are for workers who get wages or salaries. Instead of working for someone else, an entrepreneur works and earns for himself or herself. Like labour and capital, entrepreneurs are also one of the factors of production in the economic system, and their payments are called profits. As his flow of income stabilizes, an entrepreneur may choose to expand, turning a proprietary or partnership firm into a large company with many employees. Many entrepreneurs, however, choose to remain small, and that is why own-account workers and/or micro, small and medium enterprises (MSMEs) are a major segment in most economies, including in India. Since most of these employers-cum-employees don't register themselves under the Corporate Act, they become part of the household sector of the economy.

Many, on the other hand, choose to take the risks and rewards associated with becoming large. With the company becoming a separate entity from the owner, its objectives obviously change. From being a source of income to the owner initially, companies and large businesses tend to have very different objectives. Some choose to be more socially responsible by contributing to the nation's development; some companies are purely a result of the passion of their entrepreneurs who want their brainchild to grow and become a legend; while the purpose of some businesses is to grow their clout and power in the political/economic circles to seek economic rent. However, one common thing that helps companies to exist, survive and thrive is the profits. At no stage can the owner or the company survive with continuous losses (unless, of course, it is a shell company, a cover-up for some other activities). Therefore, profits are not only the rightful reward to entrepreneurs for their hard work but are also necessary for their very survival.

Depending on the market structure, corporate profitability is an indicator for measuring the efficiency with which resources are used in a country. In a highly competitive environment, higher corporate profits can only be achieved through constant innovation and better productivity, while monopolistic or highly controlled markets tend to boost profits with higher levels of inefficiency. Higher profits are likely to sustain in the former environment, while it will fade off sooner or later with serious unintended consequences in the latter.

It is disappointing that there are no official data on India's corporate profits. If the question is '*What are India's corporate profits and how have they evolved over the years?*', the most likely answer would be '2–3 per cent of GDP in the pre-COVID-19 period, down from its peak of around 6 per cent of GDP in FY08'. While this statistic is definitely true, it is incomplete and highly misleading.

The profits of India's listed corporate sector increased from 2 per cent of GDP in the early 2000s decade to its peak of 6.2 per cent of GDP in FY08. It gradually but consistently fell in the 2010s decade to a two-decade low of 1.6 per cent of GDP in FY20 before improving to a decade high of 4.5 per cent of GDP in FY22.

Was India's corporate profits just 2–3 per cent of GDP? Is it possible that India's corporate sector makes only 20 per cent (or 25 per cent) of the profits its counterparts in the US, Germany or the UK make relative to their GDPs? Is high inefficiency or the heavy-handedness of the state pulling down profits? Such questions are commonplace but mostly remain unanswered. However, these questions are baseless because, as I have said earlier, India's corporate profits are not 2–3 per cent of GDP, but were around 9 per cent of GDP for the past decade before falling in recent years. If so, it is similar to corporate profits in advanced economies.

We know that India's listed universe is very small. As of 31 January 2023,[11] the total number of registered companies in India was 2.46 mn, of which 1.52 mn (62 per cent) were active companies. Of these, only 71,485 companies are public limited, of which only 6,754 companies are listed. Therefore, only about 0.3 per cent of the total number of companies in India are listed, and 99.7 per cent are unlisted. With such a large unlisted corporate sector, it should not come as a surprise if overall corporate profits are significantly different from that of the listed sector in the country. The gap has widened further, especially after quasi-corporations were included in the national accounts as part of 'private corporations' under the new 2011–12 base; they were included in the household (or unorganized) sector under the previous (2004–05) base.

To estimate India's corporate profits, we need to understand its determinants. Profits are simply an excess of receipts (or turnover or sales) over expenditure for a company. Higher receipts or lower expenditure could thus boost corporate profits. However, the ways in which higher profits are achieved will determine whether the profits will sustain or are likely to fade over the medium term.

Let's take a simple example. If companies decide to lower total expenditure by reducing employee costs, it can be achieved in two ways—by lowering the employee count or by cutting the compensation given to employees. The former will lead to higher unemployment and the latter to lower labour income. In either scenario, the purchasing power of the people (or the household sector) will diminish, reducing their ability to purchase the goods and services produced by the companies. Thus, the lowering of costs by companies to boost profits in the immediate future will lower demand for their products over a period of time, which will reduce their revenue, keeping profits at either the same or lower levels than if they had not cut employee costs.

Similarly, if companies decide to hike the prices of their final goods and services to increase their turnover, and thus profits, it is unlikely to be effective since higher prices will reduce demand for their products. Even if the companies hiking prices enjoy a monopoly in their field or if the demand for their products is price-inelastic, higher inflation will reduce the purchasing power of the general public, reducing the overall demand for goods and services.

Therefore, while it is easy to argue that profits could be increased by cutting costs or by increasing prices, it is not as straightforward as it seems. The best way to boost profits is to increase productivity or efficiency, for which firms need to invest. Investments are thus, the primary determinant of profits. Let's see how.

Remember the Theory of Everything we discussed in Chapter 1, which links income, consumption, savings and investments? Total investments in an economy are equal to the sum of gross domestic savings and current account deficit.

Total investments = Domestic savings + Current account deficit (CAD) ...(1)

Let's rearrange this equation to understand the determinants of corporate profits. Total investments and savings are equal to the sum of investments and savings done by each sector. So, we can expand the right side (rs) of Equation (1) as

Total investments = Household savings + Corporate savings + Government savings + CAD ...(2)

Since I am interested in finding out the determinants of corporate profits, let's bring corporate savings to the left side (ls) and take investments to the right. Rewriting Equation (2), we get:

Corporate savings = Total investments – Household savings – Government savings – CAD ...(3)

Since corporate savings are equal to the sum of retained earnings (or net savings) and depreciation, I can rewrite the Equation (3) as:

Corporate retained earnings (net savings) + Corporate depreciation = Total investments – Household savings – Government savings – CAD

Or, *Corporate profits – dividends paid = Total investments – Corporate depreciation – Household savings – Government savings – CAD*

Or, *Corporate profits = Total investments − corporate depreciation + dividends paid − Household savings − Government savings − CAD* ...(4)

In short, since retained earnings are undistributed corporate profits, the Theory of Everything tells us that corporate profits are the sum of total investments and dividends paid, after deduction of corporate depreciation, household savings, government savings and CAD.

In the context of the Indian economy, there are four components in total investments—gross fixed capital formation (GFCF), change in inventories, valuables, and errors and omissions (E&O). The sectoral break-up into household, corporate and government is available for the first two components—GFCF and change in inventories. Therefore, we can rewrite Equation (4) as:

Corporate profits = (Corporate investments + Household investments + Government investments + Valuables + Errors & omissions) − corporate depreciation + dividends paid − (Household net financial savings + Physical savings) − Government savings − CAD

Or, *Corporate profits = (Corporate investments − corporate depreciation) + Valuables + E&O + dividends paid + (Household investments − Household net financial savings − Physical savings) + (Government investments − Government savings) − CAD* ...(5)

Since household physical savings are equal to household investments and the difference between the government's investments and savings is equal to the core fiscal deficit, we can rewrite Equation (5) as:

Corporate profits = Net corporate investments + Valuables + E&O + dividends paid − Household net financial savings + Core fiscal deficit − CAD ...(6)

Therefore, corporate profits are positively linked with corporate net investments, dividends paid and the core fiscal deficit, but they are inversely correlated with household net financial savings and CAD (or foreign savings). This is a powerful equation and therefore needs more explanation. Let's look at each component in detail (for a succinct explanation, non-economists may refer to a 1997 research paper by the Jerome Levy Forecasting Center, LLC).[12]

How do 'corporate investments' lead to higher profits? This is the simplest of all the questions to answer. Investments, in economic terms, are the sum of gross fixed capital formation, change in inventories and net acquisition of valuables. As mentioned earlier, in the national accounts or in macroeconomics, investments include only physical investments, not financial transactions. When a company buys a building or installs machinery and equipment, it either expands its balance sheet by adding fixed investments on the assets side and debt on the liabilities side or replaces one asset (cash) with another (fixed investment). With no expenses generated, the net worth of the company after the creation of new fixed assets remains unchanged. However, since the sellers of these fixed assets are also part of the business or corporate sector, their revenue goes up, leading to higher profits and pushing their net worth higher. The higher the corporate investments, the higher the corporate profits.

Why does 'depreciation' lead to lower profits? Although creation of fixed assets does not lead to any expense at the time of transaction, the total value of the investment is expensed in full over the life of the fixed asset. In exact contrast to fixed asset creation, there is no revenue related with depreciation provisions and therefore this expense is simply a drag on total profits. Depreciation is also called 'capital consumption allowances' in many economies, which is more appropriate.

How do 'dividends paid' lead to higher profits? Unlike in many countries, dividends paid by a company to its shareholders were taxed in India, and the tax was to be paid by the domestic company sharing its profits. In the Budget 2020, the finance minister abolished this tax and it was subsumed under personal income taxes. This means that the incidence of dividend income taxation was shifted to shareholders from companies. An analysis of more than 4,000 listed companies reveals that total dividends paid from FY18 to FY22 amounted to 1.3–1.4 per cent of GDP and has been in the range of 1.1 per cent to 1.6 per cent of GDP over the past two decades. However, unlisted companies may also pay dividends, for which no data is available.

To prepare an estimate of the total dividends paid by the corporate sector, I use the dividend distribution tax (DDT) paid by India's corporate sector[13] to the Government of India. The DDT rate has been constant at 15 per cent during the past fifteen years, before which it changed frequently. The gross dividends are calculated using the total collections under DDT and the tax rate. I deduct taxes on dividends paid from the gross dividends to arrive at the distributed dividends paid by the corporate sector to shareholders in the country. This exercise reveals that unlisted companies pay very little dividends to its shareholders.

When part of the profits is distributed as dividend among shareholders, who are a part of the household sector in the economy, it adds to personal disposable income. Depending on the marginal propensity of these recipients to consume, a part of these dividends gets consumed in purchase of goods and services from the corporate sector. Therefore, the higher the dividend payments, the higher the household income, the higher the personal consumption and the higher the revenue of companies, leading to higher corporate profits.

How do 'household net financial savings' lead to lower corporate profits? Just as higher household income leads to higher consumer spending, and thus higher corporate profits, higher household savings have the reverse impact. Household savings, in general, are nothing but the difference between income and consumption. For any level of income, the lower the consumption, the higher will be the savings. Higher household savings thus imply lower demand for goods and services, and thus lower corporate revenue and profits.

How does 'core fiscal deficit' lead to higher profits? All other things being constant, a higher core fiscal deficit (higher government investments and lower savings) leads to better corporate profits. Fiscal deficit can be expanded in two ways—by lower receipts (primarily taxes) and by higher expenditure. If the government reduces production taxes or corporate income taxes, it will directly lead to higher corporate profits. And if the government reduces indirect taxes or personal income taxes, it will add to the purchasing power of households, leading to higher consumer spending, which, as discussed above, is also profit accretive. If the government increases its expenditure, that too will lead to higher corporate profits, either directly (by government purchase of more goods and services) or indirectly (from the government announcing new income schemes or increase in subsidies). Therefore, whenever the government chooses to expand its fiscal deficit, it is almost equivalent to expanding corporate profits in an economy. Lower savings by one participant means higher income for another.

How does 'CAD' or 'foreign savings' lead to lower profits? The only exception to 'lower savings by one participant meaning higher income for another participant' is if the first entity spends it on foreign goods and services. Not only does this not increase demand for goods and services produced by the domestic companies, but by buying foreign goods domestic buyers also spend their income outside the country. Therefore, whenever a nation runs a deficit on the current account, there is a net transfer of domestic wealth to the rest of the world. Any such transfer of wealth overseas implies a loss to the domestic business sector. Since CAD leads to higher foreign income at the expense of the domestic participants, it is also referred to as 'foreign savings'. On the contrary, if India exports more than it imports, there is a net transfer of foreign wealth into the domestic economy, increasing domestic corporate profits. The higher the CAD (or foreign savings), therefore, the lower the corporate profits (we discuss balance of payments in detail in Chapter 5).

So a reclassification of the Theory of Everything reveals that investments are the primary and largest source of corporate profits, which also benefits from higher core fiscal deficit. On the contrary, corporate depreciation, household net financial savings (which is equal to household surplus) and CAD are a drag on corporate profits. There are three other important lessons from this identity:

1. While any one firm (no matter how large) can decide its investment spending, it is unlikely to influence total corporate investments in the country. Consequently, no one firm can influence corporate profits in any nation. This is important to remember because many a time when we hear or read about a large investment decision by a firm, we tend to argue that this would boost total investments in the country. As the equation suggests, this is not true.
2. Since corporate profits and personal savings are inversely correlated, it confirms that consumer spending is also a key driver. Household savings are an excess of income over consumption. The lower the consumer spending, the higher the savings for any given level of income. From the economy's perspective, however, investments need domestic savings.
3. By expanding its fiscal deficit, irrespective of how it does it, the government supports corporate profits, which stabilizes the corporate sector during a downturn. Since consumers are most likely to reduce their spending and increase their savings sharply during any slowdown, the government is the only source of support for the corporate sector. If

the fiscal deficit is not raised, a slowdown will turn into a recession, and then into a depression.

The identity confirms that higher investments lead to higher profits. However, is the relationship virtuous in nature, with the probability that higher profits can also lead to higher investments? It may or may not happen. Equation (6) above suggests that while higher investments are a key driver of corporate profits, they are not its only determinant. There could be an episode when lower investments and higher profits can coincide, supported by a higher fiscal deficit, lower household savings and/or lower CAD. Depending on the starting position, however, higher profits may or may not lead to higher investments. For instance, if the economy had a high fiscal deficit and low household savings to begin with, further expansion in fiscal deficit and reduction in household savings will boost corporate profits; however, this will tend to worsen the economic environment at the same time. This may lead to scepticism among the corporate sector, and even higher profits may not lead to higher investments. On the contrary, if the nation runs a fiscal surplus and has very high household savings to begin with, higher spending may lead to higher corporate profits, which may bring about confidence among the corporate sector in the sustainability of economic growth, converting into higher investments. Therefore, higher profits may or may not lead to higher investments. However, as shown in Equation (6), higher investments definitely lead to higher profits. Investments, in other words, are driven by profit expectations, which, in turn, are dependent on the economic environment.

Now, using Equation (4) or Equation (6), let us compile data to estimate India's aggregate corporate profits. As mentioned earlier, corporate profits are different from what is suggested by India's listed (or BSE500) companies. My estimates of India's corporate profits for the past three decades are provided in Appendix 4. The five key highlights are:

1. India's corporate profits increased from its lows of 2 per cent of GDP in the 1980s to above 4 per cent of GDP by the late 1990s and early 2000s. The high-growth phase in the 2000s decade led to further gains in corporate profits, which touched an all-time high of 12.3 per cent of GDP in FY08, which was then interrupted by the great financial crisis. After falling to 8.4 per cent of GDP in FY12 and FY13, corporate profits picked up and stayed at around 9.5 per cent of GDP till FY18. It, however, averaged 8.5 per cent of GDP in the two years (FY19 and FY20) prior to COVID-19.
2. When we break up India's corporate profits by listed and unlisted companies, we find some interesting facts: (1) the combined profits of all listed companies have fallen by about 75 per cent, from their peak of 6.2 per cent of GDP in FY08 to just 1.6 per cent of GDP in FY20. This was the lowest profits for listed companies in almost two decades; (2) Although the profits of listed companies fell sharply during the past decade, the profits of unlisted companies (including quasi-corporates) rose from 6 per cent of GDP in FY08 to 6.5 per cent in the pre-COVID-19 years. It fell in the interim period to around 4 per cent of GDP between FY09 and FY13 before recovering; (3) The inclusion of quasi-corporates in private non-financial corporations partly explains the fall in the share of listed companies in India's corporate profits, and (4) within listed companies, while the profits of BSE500 companies (a commonly used benchmark for listed companies) fell almost consistently—from their peak of 5.1 per cent of GDP in FY08 to 2 per cent of GDP in FY20—non-BSE500 companies posted aggregate losses during the six successive years prior to COVID-19. The profits of non-BSE500 listed companies have moved from their peak of 1 per cent of GDP in FY08 to losses of 0.4 per cent of GDP in FY19 and FY20.

3. Although corporate profits as a percentage of GDP touched the double digits for three consecutive years in the 2000s decade and have been in the high single digits since, they averaged 9.0 per cent of GDP in the 2010s decade vis-à-vis 8.1 per cent of GDP in the 2000s decade. A comparison of the two decades confirms that while higher net corporate investments and lower household financial savings added to corporate profits, they were partly negated by a lower fiscal deficit and a wider CAD. In fact, the contribution from lower household savings was same as from higher investments in the 2010s decade. This is how strongly the household and corporate sectors correlate with each other.

To understand it better, let's divide the past two decades into four episodes. It is apparent that the more-than-tripling of the corporate profits to GDP ratio, from 3.3 per cent in FY00–FY04 to 10.8 per cent in FY05–FY08, was largely because of higher investments. However, the ratio averaged 9.2 per cent of GDP during the pre-pandemic period (FY15–FY20), implying a fall of 1.7 percentage points (pp) of GDP from the FY05–FY08 period. Notably, net corporate investments fell by 3pp of GDP during the period, more than half of which was offset by a sharp drawdown (of 1.9 pp of GDP) in household financial savings.

4. Despite sharp fall in investments and rise in household savings, India's aggregate corporate profit declined only slightly in FY21, though BSE500 companies posted six-year-high profits. Total corporate profits stood at 8 per cent of GDP in FY21, down from 8.5 per cent of GDP in the previous two years; however, it increased to 3.2 per cent of GDP for listed (and BSE500) companies. This implies that the profits of unlisted companies fell to a seven-year low of 4.7 per cent of GDP in FY21. Aggregate corporate profits increased to 8.4 per cent of GDP in FY22; however, unlisted sector continued to suffer as listed companies

posted a decadal high profits of 4.5 per cent of GDP during the year.

5. Unlike in most developed nations, the dividend payout ratio in India averaged only about 15 per cent of profits and between 1.1 per cent and 1.6 per cent of GDP during the past three decades. There were only minor differences in the 1990s vis-à-vis the 2000s and 2010s decades. It was the highest, at 21.4 per cent, in the 2000s decade and 18.7 per cent in the 1990s and down to 15.4 per cent in the 2010s decades (despite 23.7 per cent in FY21). This means that unlike in the US, where a large part of higher corporate savings is transferred to households since their dividend payout ratio is 60 per cent, it is not the case. Given the very low dividend payout ratio, the bulk of corporate savings stay with the companies as retained earnings (or net savings).

Before proceeding, let's summarize what has been discussed above. Contrary to the widely held belief that corporate profits amount to 2–3 per cent of GDP, India's aggregate corporate profits averaged 9 per cent of GDP in the 2010s decade and were at their peak of 12.3 per cent of GDP in FY08. This means that while profits from listed companies have fallen almost consistently from their peak of 6.2 per cent of GDP in FY08 to less than 2 per cent of GDP in FY20, the unlisted sector has not only been able to maintain its profits but also saw its profits peaking at 6.7 per cent of GDP in the FY16–FY20 period. The situation has reversed since the pandemic, as listed companies posted profits at an eleven-year high of 4.5 per cent of GDP in FY22, while the unlisted sector's profits were at an eleven-year low of 3.9 per cent of GDP. Within the listed sector, though, profits from BSE500 companies fell from their peak of 5.1 per cent of GDP in FY08 to 2 per cent of GDP in FY20, and non-BSE500 listed companies posted losses in the six consecutive years since FY15, from their peak profits of 1 per cent of GDP in FY08. Further explanation is provided below to support these facts.

Share of Listed Companies in Corporate Tax Collection

Although there are no official statistics on corporate profits in India, the regular data on corporate taxes collected by the GoI helps us get a fair idea of the trends in the share of listed and unlisted companies in India's aggregate corporate profits. After collecting the data on direct taxes paid by listed companies and comparing it against the corporate income taxes received by the GoI, one can deduce the share of unlisted companies as the residual. Since the share of listed companies has fallen in India's aggregate corporate profits (as discussed above), we can expect a significant fall in its share in corporate taxes too.

Exhibit 3.1 plots the share of listed companies in total corporate income taxes collected by the GoI during the past two decades. Since the government accounts are prepared on cash-basis (that is, income and expenses are recorded only when cash is received or paid), the data for listed companies has also been taken from cash flow statements rather than from their profit and loss statements (which is prepared on accrual basis, that is, income and expenses are recorded when they are incurred instead of when money changes hands).

From as high as 53 per cent in FY08, the share of listed companies in corporate income tax collections fell below 47 per cent in the pre-pandemic years. During the corresponding period, the share of listed companies in India's aggregate corporate profits (measured by profits before taxes, PBT) declined from 60 per cent to 57 per cent. The Union Budget documents provide aggregate PBT of India's corporate sector based on the filing of income taxes. This analysis is conducted using PBT data for only profit-making companies (available in the Budget documents from FY06 to FY21, which is then compared with the listed companies' data), which would be eligible to pay taxes.

Exhibit 3.1: Share of listed companies in corporate income taxes has come off, in line with the fall in their share in profits

*Only profit-making listed companies as per January 2023
Listed corporate taxes data from cash flow statements
Source: Budget documents, MOFSL, author's calculations

This analysis provides more credence to the fact that not only did the unlisted corporate sector pay higher direct taxes than the listed companies almost every year during the past fifteen years but also that the rise in its share in direct taxes is in line with the increase in its share in corporate profits.

Are New-Age Cash-Burning Companies Included in This Model?

A question posed during a presentation I made to my clients was about the coverage of this macroeconomic identity. Paralleling the evolution of the nature of the economy, from agriculture to manufacturing to services in general, the nature of the corporate sector too has evolved dramatically during the past two decades. A large number of start-ups have entered the arena with the sole objective of creating massive disruptions with their deep pockets. From taxi aggregators (such as Uber and Ola) in the initial years to retail e-markets (such as Amazon and Flipkart) to food aggregators (such as Zomato and Swiggy), all these companies have had broadly similar evolution models: grab as much of the customer base as possible with massive discounts and promotions, which eventually leads to consolidation in the industry after a few years. Therefore, these start-ups witness huge losses in the initial years (perhaps ten or fifteen years) and are likely to post their first profits only after many years of burning cash.

Over the years, these companies have provided large-scale employment to the unskilled population (primarily working as delivery agents/transporters), but their aggregate losses run into billions of dollars. Are these companies included in the Theory of Everything equation? Are their huge losses year after year captured in this model? When I first received this question, I was confused and went back to the basics to understand it. However, after some time I was convinced that such start-ups and their losses are indeed captured in this model.

If you remember, the Theory of Everything identity suggests that corporate profits are not only dependent on investments but also on household savings, government savings and CAD. Therefore, it includes the behaviour of all economic participants in any nation. Now, let's assume there is a start-up company which is not like Amazon or Zomato but an old-age manufacturing company, which struggles to become profitable in the initial years as it is building up its customer base and creating a brand for itself. The new-age e-company model of burning cash is not new. It is not that all traditional companies turn profitable in their first year; however, they pay their employees/promoters from the first month of operations and may also choose to offer discounts to customers (meaning less profits, or higher losses, depending on the competition). Therefore, like new-age companies, traditional manufacturing companies may also have suffered losses in the initial years of their operations. However, even if companies fail to make profits from the first year, they have to make salary payments to their employees and also pay their dues to their suppliers. Thus, not only do they contribute towards household income but they also bring higher revenue to the aggregate corporate sector.

The aggregate profits of the corporate sector, nevertheless, may be lower, higher or unchanged, depending on the discounts received/given by the start-up companies.

Thus, by paying salaries and wages to their employees, new companies do add to the aggregate demand, which further leads to higher demand for goods and services in the economy, leading to higher revenue for other companies meeting consumers' demand. The government may also benefit through higher personal income taxes (if salaries and wages are higher than the tax exemption limits). All these effects are captured in the Theory of Everything identity, along with the losses made by the start-up companies. The entire cycle plays itself out, irrespective of whether the start-up is an old-economy participant or a new-age company. Even though these companies take losses on their books, they support household income, and thus consumption, add to the revenue (and thus profits) of the rest of the corporate sector and may also contribute to the exchequer. The coverage of this equation is thus highly comprehensive.

How Big Is India's Listed Corporate Sector?

So India's corporate profits are very different and much higher than the profits of its listed companies. In fact, the share of the latter had fallen dramatically, before recovering post-pandemic. Is this an exception? I just showed that it's not. The share of listed companies in corporate income taxes had also fallen commensurately. But what about the share of listed companies in India's corporate investments? Or in exports, for that matter? What is the share of listed companies in India's corporate debt? Can we estimate the GVA of listed companies and find out their share in the corporate GVA, and thus the national GVA in the country? Yes, we can.

This exercise will help us get an idea of how representative the listed corporate sector or the BSE500 or NIFTY50 companies are to understand the finances of India's corporate sector. This exercise is done using six indicators—outstanding debt, gross value addition, investments (gross fixed capital formation), exports, profits and direct (or corporate income) taxes. While the first three indicators are estimated for NFCs only, we have included the financial sector for analysis on the latter three indicators. This analysis is done for the year 2011–12, which is the base used for NIA, and for 2019–20, the last year before COVID-19. The difference between the data for the corporate sector and for the listed company sector is the data for the unlisted corporate sector. The summary of our findings is provided in Exhibit 3.2:

Given below are the key findings:

1. **Corporate debt** is the only indicator that did not show a decline in the share of listed companies during the past decade. The outstanding debt of listed NFCs almost doubled from ₹21 tn in FY12 to ₹40 tn in FY20, implying that their share in outstanding corporate debt was unchanged at 34.3 per cent of GDP in the two years. More important, the share of NIFTY50 companies increased from 11 per cent to 16 per cent (from ₹7 tn to ₹19 tn) during the same period, confirming the concentration of corporate debt in the 2010s decade. It also implies that NIFTY50 companies accounted for almost half of outstanding debt by all listed companies in FY20, up from a third a decade ago in FY12.

2. **Corporate GVA** – Although the share of listed companies in corporate debt was unchanged, it has fallen against almost all other indicators, including GVA, defined as the sum of all factor payments (that is, labour, capital and entrepreneur); the share of listed companies fell from 34 per cent in FY12 to 26 per cent of corporate GVA in FY20. Notably, the share of BSE500/NIFTY50 companies fell slowly during the period, which means that the share of non-BSE500-listed companies declined faster. It also

implies that unlisted companies witnessed higher GVA growth during the period, due to which their share increased from 66 per cent in FY12 to 74 per cent of corporate GVA in FY20.

3. **Corporate investments** – With the improvement in the financial position of large listed companies, their potential to drive investment revival in the country has been widely debated. Here also, the share of listed companies fell sharply in the 2010s decade. From as high as 52 per cent of corporate investments in FY12 (notably, FY12 was an exception as it was 36.4 per cent in FY13), the share of listed companies fell to 28 per cent in FY20. The share of BSE500 companies also declined, from 37 per cent in FY12 (27 per cent in FY13) to 28 per cent in FY20. However, the share of NIFTY50 companies fell only slightly, from 18.2 per cent to 17.1 per cent of corporate investments during the period. In other words, listed companies account for around 13 per cent of total investments in the country.

4. **Corporate exports** – Not only has the share of listed companies fallen in India's GVA and investments but the contribution of listed companies to India's exports also declined in the 2010s decade. In absolute terms, total exports (of goods only) by listed companies increased from ₹6.5 tn in FY12 to ₹7.2 tn in FY20; however, with higher growth in India's total exports, their share fell from 45 per cent in FY12 to just 33 per cent in FY20. BSE500/NIFTY50 companies followed the same pattern during the past decade. Non-BSE500 companies have also lost their share in India's total exports. It means that the non-corporate sector (primarily MSMEs, which are a part of the household sector) has witnessed an improvement in its share in India's total exports in the past decade.

5. **Corporate profits** – As mentioned earlier, the share of listed companies in corporate profits before taxes fell

Exhibit 3.2: Share of listed, BSE500 and NIFTY50 companies in corporate NIA in FY20 (and FY12)

	Unit	Debt[1]	GVA[1,2]	Investments[1,4]	Exports[5]	Profits (PBT)[3]	Direct taxes[3]
All listed companies	% of aggregate corporate sector	34.3 (34.2)	26.3 (34.2)	28.3 (51.7)	32.6 (44.6)	52.0 (58.3)	44.2 (48.7)
BSE500		26.9 (22.7)	23.6 (27.9)	28.2 (37.3)	27.2 (38.5)	47.1 (50.8)	40.0 (43.0)
NIFTY50		16.1 (11.2)	14.4 (16.9)	17.1 (18.2)	14.2 (25.6)	28.3 (30.5)	23.2 (26.0)
Non-BSE500 listed		7.4 (11.5)	2.7 (6.3)	0.0 (14.3)	5.4 (6.0)	4.9 (7.3)	4.1 (5.8)
Unlisted companies		65.7 (65.8)	73.7 (65.8)	71.7 (48.3)	67.4 (55.4)[6]	48.0 (41.7)	55.8 (51.3)
Aggregate Corporate sector	INR tn	117.2 (61.2)	73.1 (31.4)	28.2 (14.7)[7]	22.2 (14.7)	17.8 (9.9)	5.6 (3.2)
	% of GDP	58.3 (70.1)	39.8 (38.8)	14.1 (16.8)	11.0 (16.8)	8.9 (11.3)	2.8 (3.7)

Data for FY20 (FY12 in parentheses)

[1] Only for non-financial companies (NFCs)
[2] Estimated as the sum of factor payments = employee costs, interest paid, depreciation, profit before taxes
[3] For only profit-making companies (financial and non-financial)
[4] Estimated using balance sheet (net block/fixed assets, capital work-in-progress, inventories) and profit and loss statement (depreciation) data
[5] Exports of goods (or merchandise) only
[6] Share of the rest of the economy (including household sector)
[7] Based on listed/BSE500/NIFTY50 companies in January 2023

Source: CSO, RBI, Budget documents, MOFSL, author's calculations

sharply in the past decade—from 58.3 per cent in FY12 to 52 per cent in FY20 (pertaining to only profit-making companies). Further, the share of BSE500/NIFTY50 companies was down from 51 per cent/30 per cent in FY12 to 47 per cent/28 per cent in FY20 (broadly stable at 52 per cent/30 per cent during the FY16–FY19 period). Notwithstanding lower aggregate corporate PBT, the share of the unlisted sector surely went up before the COVID-19 pandemic.

6. **Corporate taxes** – One of the clearest ways to confirm whether the non-listed corporate sector is as large as other macro-data suggests is to look at the share of listed companies in the gross corporate taxes collected by the Central government. Here also the trend is similar. Listed companies account for less than half of total corporate taxes paid in the country, and their share fell from 49 per cent in FY12 to 44 per cent in FY20. The share of BSE500/NIFTY50 companies in corporate income taxes also fell during the past decade.

Lastly, total employment by all listed companies was only 7–8 mn each in FY18 and FY20 (which is likely to have risen to 8.5–9.5 mn in FY21–FY22), accounting for a mere 3–4 per cent of total non-farm employment in the country. Since this data is highly sketchy and cannot be used to make comparisons (IT companies may include onsite/offshore workers, different companies may have included or excluded casual workers, etc.), it is not included in the above analysis. Total employment by NIFTY50 companies was about 2.5mn in the past few years, accounting for around 1 per cent of total non-farm employment in the country. While it is well known that large organized companies are built on productivity efficiency, the meagreness of their share in India's non-farm employment is remarkable.

Overall, this analysis proves that listed companies (more than 3,000 common samples) account for 25 per cent to

35 per cent of the entire corporate sector in India on most macroeconomic indicators (except taxes paid). What is more, not only has their share in total corporate profits fallen dramatically in the past decade, the same is true of other important indicators too (except debt).

The share of NIFTY50 companies is even lower—14–17 per cent—on most indicators except profits and taxes, where the share is closer to 25 per cent. However, their share in corporate debt has increased during the past decade.

Next time, therefore, if one talks about corporate statistics in the country, the reader should be mindful of the large gaps between the BSE500 (the most likely benchmark for corporate data) companies and the true corporate universe in India. The trends under different indicators among the two samples—listed companies and the entire corporate sector—could be similar to or divergent from each other. In fact, I will return to this important characteristic of India's corporate sector towards the end of this chapter again, when I present my analysis on the impact of the COVID-19 pandemic.

What Is Corporate Debt in India and How Strong Is the Deleveraging?

The financial balance sheets for the corporate sector were produced for the first time in India by RBI in mid-2019 (and then updated in mid-2022 and early 2023); however, historical data series covering the flow of funds from the 1950s and onward are available. Since liabilities are fixed in nature (and it is free of any valuation effect), India's corporate debt[14] can be estimated for the past seven decades, starting FY52. According to RBI estimates, corporate debt in India peaked at 70 per cent of GDP each in FY11 and FY12. It fell to 62 per cent of GDP by FY16, after which it fell to around 58 per cent of GDP in FY19 and FY20, before rising to 61 per cent in FY21, the last period for which RBI data is available (see Appendix 5). Assuming the same yearly growth as suggested by the updated

BIS estimates, India's corporate debt fell to 55.6 per cent of GDP in FY22.

Within the corporate sector, BSE500 companies account for about a quarter of total outstanding corporate debt in the country. Interestingly, while the aggregate corporate sector deleveraged substantially during the past decade (up to FY19), the debt to GDP ratio of the large listed companies was extremely stable during the period. The debt to GDP ratio of BSE500 companies almost doubled from just 8.5 per cent of GDP in FY06 (similar to what it was at the turn of the century) to 16 per cent of GDP in FY12 and has hovered around that level during the past decade. At its peak, the leverage of BSE500 companies touched 16.8 per cent of GDP in FY14, which eased to 14.1 per cent in FY18. Due to the pandemic and corresponding decline in nominal GDP, BSE500 rose to 15.7 per cent of GDP in FY20, before easing to 15.4 per cent of GDP in FY21. This suggests that the deleveraging has happened entirely in the non-BSE500 corporate sector and the unlisted sector. The debt to GDP ratio of non-BSE500 listed companies has almost halved from 8.1 per cent of GDP in FY12 to 4.3 per cent of GDP in FY20, and further to 4.1 per cent of GDP in FY21. For the unlisted corporate sector, this ratio declined from 46.1 per cent to 38.3 per cent of GDP during the same period, before recovering to 41.5 per cent in FY21.

NIFTY50 companies (of which thirty-nine are NFCs) do not show similar trends. Their debt to GDP ratio fell from 8.7 per cent of GDP in FY15 to 7.8 per cent each in FY16 and FY17 before it started rising again to its new peak of 9.4 per cent in FY20 (and remained high at 9.1 per cent in FY21, before easing to 7.8 per cent in FY22). Not surprisingly, then, the share of NIFTY50 companies increased from 10 per cent of corporate debt in FY11 to 16.1 per cent of corporate debt in FY20, before falling to 14.9 per cent in FY21 and further down to 14.2 per cent in FY22.

The outstanding debt of NIFTY50 companies quadrupled from ₹5.3 tn in FY11 to ₹18.9 tn in FY20. This implies that while these companies accounted for only 15–16 per cent of outstanding corporate debt, they accounted for as much as 25 per cent of the increase in corporate debt in the country between FY16 and FY20.

A fall in India's corporate debt ratio by almost a fifth (from 70 per cent to 58 per cent of GDP) in just eight years is remarkable. However, there are two important questions to consider: (1) How strong is India's corporate deleveraging vis-à-vis historical global episodes? and (2) What are its economic implications?

A 2015 IMF working paper[15] examined the impact of private sector (households + non-financial corporate) deleveraging on output changes in the post-deleveraging period. It found larger deleveraging to be associated with positive growth in the subsequent period, and greater intensity in deleveraging, that is, higher per annum reduction in leverage, was associated with faster subsequent growth. However, it also found that the more stretched the time spent in deleveraging, the lower the subsequent growth.

I rework the updated database (from BIS) to verify the two conclusions of the working paper. Although the IMF paper focused on private sector leverage, I focus only on corporate debt here. Using data for forty-four countries available for the period since 1960, seventy episodes of corporate deleveraging are found—fifty in twenty-eight advanced economies and twenty in sixteen developing nations. Exhibit 3.3 provides a summary of these episodes and comparison of real GDP growth during the deleveraging period vis-à-vis average growth rates in the pre- and post-deleveraging three-year periods.

Broadly, growth rates picked up after corporate deleveraging in both advanced and developing economies, with the averages reflecting similar cycles across the two. For advanced economies, the average fall in corporate debt during deleveraging cycles

Exhibit 3.3: Summary of corporate deleveraging episodes in the world during the past six decades

Country	Period	Real GDP growth (% per annum)			Cumulative fall in NFCs debt-to-GDP	Average duration (years)
		Pre-deleveraging	Peak-to-trough	Post-deleveraging		
Advanced economies	50 episodes	2.9	3.5	3.7	14.0	4.6
Developing economies	20 episodes	3.4	2.1	3.8	12.4	4.0
Corporate deleveraging episodes lasting 7 or more years						
Argentina	1998–2014	5.8	2.3	1.2	23.4	16.0
Belgium	1979–86	1.9	1.6	3.5	5.3	7.0
Colombia	1998–2005	2.0	2.4	5.6	12.5	7.0
Czech	1997–2004	3.4	2.6	6.3	36.7	7.0
Germany	2003–14	0.3	1.4	2.1	13.3	11.0
India	FY12–FY19	7.2	7.0	2.0	12.7	7.0
Israel	2007–15	5.1	3.4	4.3	23.8	8.0
Italy	1972–83	3.6	3.2	3.0	30.4	11.0
Japan	1972–79	4.5	4.1	3.4	14.7	7.0
Japan	1993–2004	1.2	1.2	1.6	48.4	11.0
Japan	2009–17	0.7	1.6	–1.4	11.7	8.0
Mexico	1994–2001	3.5	2.8	1.8	23.0	7.0
Norway	1988–96	1.8	3.3	3.3	16.3	8.0
Portugal	1983–90	1.2	4.2	1.1	63.5	7.0
Singapore	1997–2006	7.7	5.1	3.7	22.9	9.0
South Korea	1994–2001	7.9	5.2	5.1	33.0	7.0
Taiwan	1996–2003	6.7	4.5	6.0	7.2	7.0
Thailand	1997–2007	3.7	3.9	2.8	68.7	10.0
UK	1967–79	2.2	2.9	–0.3	5.0	12.0
UK	2008–15	1.6	2.4	2.0	20.7	7.0
Average	20 episodes	3.6	3.3	2.9	24.7	8.7

Pre-deleveraging and post-deleveraging growth rates are 3-year averages
Source: BIS, RBI, author's calculations

was 14pp of GDP and the average duration was 4.6 years. Real GDP growth improved from 2.9 per cent in the pre-deleveraging years to 3.7 per cent after the deleveraging.

Similarly, the average fall during the corporate debt deleveraging cycles in developing nations was 12.4pp of GDP and the average duration was four years. Real GDP growth improved from 3.4 per cent in the pre-deleveraging years to 3.8 per cent after the deleveraging. In other words, the rate of average corporate deleveraging in both advanced and developing economies was almost similar, at 3pp of GDP per annum, and average growth in the post-deleveraging period was better than in the pre-deleveraging period.

Thus, the first conclusion of the IMF working paper can be easily verified and confirmed. Larger deleveraging was found to be associated with positive growth in the subsequent period, and greater intensity in deleveraging, that is, higher per-annum reduction in leverage was associated with faster subsequent growth.

Let's test the second conclusion now. Of the seventy episodes from forty-four countries, only twenty episodes lasted seven or more years. The details of these episodes are also provided in Exhibit 3.3. Of these twenty episodes, real GDP growth in the post-deleveraging period (three-year average after the trough of corporate debt to GDP ratio) was higher than in the pre-deleveraging period (three-year average before the peak of corporate debt to GDP ratio) in only seven episodes. This means that if the deleveraging cycle is prolonged (seven years or more), growth in the subsequent period is lower than in the pre-deleveraging period in almost two out of three cases and was higher only in one-third of the cases.

This suggests that the second finding in the IMF working paper, that the more stretched the time spent in deleveraging, the lower the subsequent growth, also holds. The IMF cited this as the *trade-off against the time spent deleveraging*. The longer the deleveraging cycle continues, the lower will be the gains after the adjustments.

As noted above, RBI data reveals that India's corporate debt peaked in FY12 at 70 per cent of GDP and troughed at 57.4 per cent of GDP in FY19 before recovering in FY20 and FY21. This means India's corporate deleveraging episode lasted seven years, which was much longer than the average deleveraging period (of 4 years) among developing economies. The cumulative fall of 12.7pp of GDP in India's corporate debt during the period was similar to the average decline (of 12.4pp of GDP) among developing economies. Thus, India's corporate deleveraging was prolonged and it was not very intense.

This analysis, thus, confirms that policies should be geared towards facilitating up-front deleveraging or balance sheet adjustments. Although these policies will likely lead to weak growth in the short term, the sizeable gains over the medium term could offset the costs of that.

Also, it is broadly argued that corporate deleveraging is over now. As listed companies have come out stronger from the pandemic, it is believed they will start expanding capacities soon and add more leverage since their cash flows have improved and their balance sheets have shed their extra flab. I am not sure if the pandemic triggered an end to India's corporate deleveraging or just led to a pause in it. However, since listed companies account for only 25–35 per cent of corporate investments and debt in the country, it is pretty clear to me that corporate investments are unlikely to grow substantially in the immediate future since the unlisted corporate sector has weakened due to the COVID-19 pandemic.

Impact of COVID-19 on Corporate Sector's Financial Position

To gauge the financial impact of any event or policy on India's corporate sector, the sector must be divided into two segments: listed companies and unlisted companies. COVID-19 has had very different impacts on these two segments of the corporate sector. As expected, corporate profitability collapsed in the quarters, that is, Q4FY20 and Q1FY21, immediately following the pandemic. Nevertheless, recovery in the corporate sector was quicker than in the household sector. India's aggregate corporate profits were back to pre-COVID-19 levels by Q2FY21, and listed companies' profits rose to multi-year highs.

After being stable at 2.0–2.5 per cent of GDP, the profits of listed companies entirely disappeared (i.e. 0.0 per cent of GDP) in Q4FY20 before recovering to the second lowest level of 0.5 per cent of GDP in Q1FY21. However, it has witnessed an impressive turnaround since then. The profitability of listed companies increased to 3.8 per cent of GDP in Q2FY21, the highest in seven years, and has stayed at or more than 4 per cent of GDP right up to Q3FY23. Nevertheless, as discussed above, India's aggregate corporate profits (including that of unlisted companies) fell slightly from about 8.5 per cent in pre-COVID-19 period to 8 per cent of GDP in FY21 and 8.4 per cent in FY22.

Using our Theory of Everything, the profitability of the unlisted sector was arrived at as residual. While listed companies' profitability increased from a two-decade low of 1.6 per cent of GDP in FY20 to a decade high of 4.5 per cent of GDP in FY22, they gained at the cost of the unlisted/unregistered corporate sector. My calculations suggest that profits of the latter fell to an eight-year low of 4.7 per cent of GDP in FY21 and down further to 3.9 per cent in FY22 (see Appendix 5).

As shown in Appendix 4, a higher fiscal deficit and the first current account surplus in seventeen years added to India's corporate profits in FY21. However, they were more than offset by higher household savings and a fall in net investments in the country.

Not only was there stark divergence between profits of the listed and unlisted corporate sectors, but the trends in their leverage were also different. FY21 and FY22 annual reports show the leverage of BSE500 companies declined 3 per cent in FY21, before increasing by just 2 per cent in FY22. Comparing these with the RBI/BIS estimate of aggregate corporate debt, we find that the outstanding debt of the remaining corporate sector (including non-BSE500 listed companies and the unlisted corporate sector) grew 5.4 per cent in FY21 and again 10.1 per cent in FY22, since aggregate corporate debt increased 3.1 per cent and 8.1 per cent in the two years.

It means that while the profits of listed companies improved and they deleveraged, the opposite was true for the larger unlisted/unregistered corporate sector, which registered weaker profits and higher debt. Thus, while cash flows improved for listed/BSE500 companies and their financial position improved dramatically due to COVID-19, the financial position of the aggregate corporate sector in India was not as benign.

Since listed companies account for less than a third of corporate investments in the country and the remaining is accounted for by the unlisted/unregistered companies, the deterioration in the financial position of the aggregate corporate sector in India is worrisome. If better cash flows, higher profitability and lower debt make the argument for listed companies to invest in the near future, the worsening of these parameters for the unlisted/unregistered companies indicates lower investments by them.

Moreover, just because listed companies have better cash flows, it does not mean they will invest more or expand their capacities. Several relevant indicators, such as low capacity utilization, a continuously falling fixed asset turnover ratio, a weak new order book to sales ratio and inventory to sales ratio, confirm that the listed companies are unlikely to increase their investments in the immediate future.

What Is the Role of the Corporate Sector in Economic Growth?

Do higher profits lead to higher investments? While higher investments increase profitability, historical data suggests that the relationship has failed to hold the other way.

During the past few decades, corporate profits have only risen almost globally. US corporate profits during the 2010s decade averaged 9.7 per cent of GDP and was not below 8.9 per cent of GDP in any year during the decade. Before the great financial crisis in 2008, and since 1960, US corporate profitability has never touched the level of 9 per cent of GDP. It crossed 8 per cent of GDP for the first time in CY04, and the peak before the great financial crisis was 8.9 per cent of GDP in CY06.

Similarly, corporate profitability in South Korea, one of the four 'Asian tigers', rose sharply from an average of 4–5 per cent of GDP during the 1970s, 1980s and 1990s (the roaring period for the economy) to an average of 10.6 per cent of GDP in the 2010s decade. The same was true for the UK, where corporate profitability averaged 10 per cent during the 2010s decade vis-à-vis 8.5 per cent in 1980s and 1990s; in Japan it averaged 7.5 per cent of GDP during the past two decades vis-à-vis 2.5–3.5 per cent of GDP during the preceding two decades.

India was no different. After Independence, corporate profitability in India stayed low at about 2 per cent of GDP for the next four decades, between the 1950s and 1980s. The situation changed with the opening up of the economy. Corporate profits almost doubled to 4.4 per cent of GDP in

Exhibit 3.4: Corporate profits have increased sharply almost everywhere in the 21st century . . .

Germany and China data since 1991 and 1992, respectively
For India, CY2000 = FY01
Source: Various national sources, author's estimates

the 1990s decade, doubled again to an average of 8.1 per cent of GDP in the 2000s decades and rose further to 9 per cent of GDP in the 2010s decade. This rising trend in corporate profitability across nations is captured in Exhibit 3.4.

China is the only exception among the world's major economies (for which such data can be prepared) where corporate profits in the 2010s decade were much lower than that in the 1990s and 2000s decade. China's data is available since 1992.

Notwithstanding falling China's corporate profits in the 2010s decade, rising trend in other large economies drove global corporate profits to average 8.7 per cent in the 2010s decade, higher than 8.2 per cent in the 2000s decade, which was sharply up from 6 per cent in the 1990s and 5.1 per cent in the 1980s decade (Exhibit 3.5).

At the same time, however, global investments, which, as discussed above, are the primary driver of corporate profits, increased to an average of 26.8 per cent of GDP in the 2010s

Exhibit 3.5: . . . leading to a consistent rise in global corporate profits in the past few decades

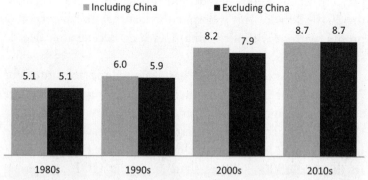

Including the US, Eurozone (since 1999), the UK, Japan, India, China (since 1992) and South Korea. Prior to 1999, Germany (since 1991), France and Italy/Spain (since 1995) are used, instead of Eurozone
Source: Various national sources, author's estimates

Exhibit 3.6: Global investments, however, have failed to match the rise in profits

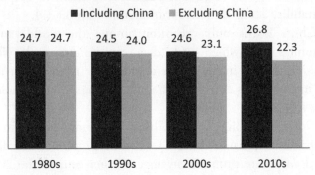

Germany and China data since 1991 and 1992, respectively
Source: Various national sources, author's estimates

decade, after remaining at a broadly unchanged average of about 24.6 per cent of GDP in the previous three decades (Exhibit 3.6). China, however, has made an immense contribution to this rise in the 2010s decade (and stability in the previous decades). Excluding China, global investments fell almost continuously during the past three decades—from 24.7 per cent of GDP in the 1980s to 24 per cent in the 1990s to 23.1 per cent in the 2000s decade and further to 22.3 per cent in the 2010s decade. This is despite the fact that global corporate profits (with or without China) increased decade after decade since the 1980s.

It is then not surprising that China alone accounted for 29 per cent of global investments in 2021, up from 20 per cent a decade ago and just 5 per cent at the turn of the century (Exhibit 3.7). This is in contrast to the fact that China's share in global GDP has increased slowly to 18.5 per cent in 2021. In the mid-1980s, China's share in global GDP and global investments were similar at just 2 per cent each. For the sake of comparison, the share of the US in global investments has fallen faster relative to its share in global GDP. From close to 30 per cent each at the turn of the century, the US's share in

Exhibit 3.7: China alone accounted for 29% of global investments in 2021

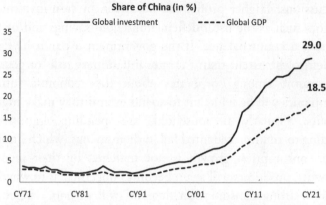

Source: Various national sources, World Bank, IMF, MOFSL

global investments declined to 19 per cent in 2021, while it was 24 per cent in terms of global GDP. In other words, China's growth model is heavily dependent on investments, while the US economy followed a consumption-led (non-investments) growth model (discussed in detail in Chapter 8).

Therefore, the argument that low corporate profits had constrained the ability of companies to invest is clearly not true. Corporate profits were at an all-time high in most nations across the globe during the 2010s decade, while global investments continued to weaken (or did not increase to match the rise in profits). Thus there is no doubt that while higher investments lead to higher profitability, higher profits have not led to higher corporate investments.

But why don't higher profits lead to higher investments? After all, if companies do not invest, does it not raise doubts as to their ability to generate future profitability?

As explained earlier, companies invest not when they have earned profits but when they are confident that there will be further profits from the new investments. If they are confident about the economic environment, they will feel assured about their profitability, and investments will follow. Thus, it is *expectation* of profits and not higher profits in the recent past that leads to higher investments. This is often ignored in daily discussions. Higher profits can be driven by non-investment factors such as the fiscal deficit, household savings and/or the current account balance. If the government expands its fiscal deficit to the extent that it creates inflationary risks or general discomfort among corporates about the economic future, companies will be reluctant to spend even if they make higher profits. Similarly, if households are spending aggressively, leading to an unprecedented fall in their savings (which implies that consumption growth is not matched by their income growth), producers will again become concerned as to whether such a strong consumption demand will sustain. Therefore, they will be cautious about expanding their capacities beyond a point.

This is exactly what appears to have happened in India. Not only has India's fiscal deficit remained wide during the past decade (as will be discussed in Chapter 4), but household finances have also deteriorated substantially during the past decade (discussed in Chapter 2). What will then inspire confidence among Indian companies to invest?

In fact, while NFCs are reluctant to invest, the financial companies are busy lending to the retail sector, creating higher credit growth and thus consumption demand. It is amazing how almost all lenders in the country have patronized the retail sector during the past few years while industrial loans have faced tremendous tightness. During the past five years, while the corporate sector has deleveraged, the household sector has loaded up on debt. Between FY15 and FY20, households accounted for half of the total rise in private non-financial debt in the country. In other words, while corporate debt has grown at just 7.7 per cent per annum during the period, household debt has risen at 15.6 per cent per annum in the second half of the 2010s decade. In absolute terms, household debt has doubled from ₹34 tn in FY15 to ₹70 tn in FY20. Higher leverage helps the household sector to consume now, leading to potential risk to savings in the future if income growth continues to lag.

Consequently, while companies are making more profits or witnessing higher savings, they are not utilized towards higher physical investments but parked in the financial markets. I will be discussing the role of the financial markets in India's economic growth in detail in Chapter 7, but it will not be unfair to state that managing their stock prices has been of paramount importance to listed companies. In his 1962 classic, *Capitalism and Freedom*,[16] Milton Friedman wrote, 'There is one and only one social responsibility of business—to use its resources and engage in activities designed to increase its profits so long as it stays within the rules of the game, which is to say, engages in open and free competition without deception or fraud.' The primary objective of any listed company (and of most unlisted companies too) is to maximize returns for its shareholders. This objective may or may not be linked with better economic growth and the company's contribution towards economic growth. This is where the big disconnect lies.

Lack of synchronization between the objectives of the government and those of companies is a key reason for the conundrum. When the government announces or implements fiscal stimuli in the hope of boosting economic activity, while corporate profits get an immediate boost, a pick-up in the economic activity may or may not happen. When the government increases spending or provides tax incentives to companies, it is hoped that the corporate sector will utilize the resultant higher profits or savings to boost economic activity by increasing hiring/employment, raising employees' income and/ or increasing production. The combination of higher corporate profits and weak investments confirms that the former has not led to the latter.

This gap between the national objectives (that is, of the government) and those of the corporate sector is wide and has widened further in recent years, as higher support to companies has effectively been utilized to increase returns for a handful of shareholders rather than to share them with the broader economy. This is because the objective of creating wealth for shareholders can be achieved by companies without making any contribution to the wider economy. A few decades ago, this was not the case. Only companies with the ability to deliver extraordinary earnings due to their competitive edge or some unique technology were able to command a great premium. That is not the case now. In fact, investors are very sceptical of companies with high debt, and this leads to extra discomfort for capital-intensive companies. Such companies usually have higher expense charges on account of depreciation (or consumption of fixed capital), which reduces their profitability (remember the Theory of Everything).

Therefore, one way to ensure channelling of the fiscal support provided to companies towards better economic growth is to align corporate objectives with the national objectives. Is there any way the authorities can force companies to utilize their profits for economic development? Yes, there are ways, but they are controversial and will be in direct conflict with the free-market theories. For instance, highly profitable companies are increasingly choosing to distribute their earnings among shareholders as dividends or to announce buybacks of their own shares at a premium. Can the authorities create a better incentive structure to route at least a part of those earnings into economic development? Can the government make it more unattractive for companies and their shareholders to distribute profits as dividends rather than reinvesting them? Is there any way it could be made more attractive for capital-intensive companies to earn higher profits with higher investments?

There are no easy answers to these questions. But with appropriate deliberations and incentive structures, better results can definitely be achieved. The government plays an important role in economic growth, not only by spending but primarily by creating an environment where higher contribution to economic growth by each economic participant is incentivized and encouraged. What has India's fiscal policy during the past few years been? Have these policies helped push growth higher or have they only contributed to the structural concerns we have discussed so far? I discuss this in the next chapter.

Key Lessons from the Chapter

- As far as India's financial sector is concerned, apart from the usual asset quality issue, two major changes have taken place. Banks are being replaced by non-bank lenders and public sector banks are losing to private sector banks. These changes have contributed significantly to the shift from lending to industrial/infrastructure businesses to lending to the consumer/retail sector, which comes with its own set of problems.
- Listed companies in India are not a comprehensive representative of India's corporate sector. While the profits of BSE500 companies have fallen continuously from a peak of 5.1 per cent in FY08 to around 2 per cent of GDP in FY20, India's aggregate corporate profits stayed at close to 9 per cent of GDP in the 2010s decade, lower than its peak of 12.3 per cent of GDP in FY08. This means that the unlisted corporate sector in India enjoys very high profits in the country.
- Profits are positively correlated with investments and core fiscal deficit, and they are adversely affected by household financial savings and CAD. Therefore, while higher investments lead to higher profits, increase in profits (led by non-investment factors) may or may not lead to higher investments.
- Listed companies not only had less than 50 per cent share in India's aggregate corporate profits in the pre-pandemic period, but their share in corporate GVA, corporate

investments, corporate debt and goods exports in the country was also between 25 and 35 per cent in recent years. They, however, accounted for about 45 per cent of corporate direct taxes paid in the country.
- The share of listed companies has not only fallen in terms of profits, but its share of total investments, GVA, income taxes paid and savings of the corporate sector also shows a similar trend. Their share in the country's corporate debt, however, has been stable.
- India's corporate debt fell from a peak of 70 per cent of GDP in FY12 to less than 58 per cent in FY19. This implies a cumulative deleveraging of about 20 per cent since FY11, which amounts to prolonged deleveraging. An analysis of such global episodes indicates that in 70 per cent of cases where deleveraging continued for more than seven years, growth was slower than in the post-deleveraging period.
- Lastly, the combination of rising corporate profits and weak investments during the past few decades suggests that low profits are not a constraint when it comes to increasing investments. Serious deliberation is required to create a new incentive structure to encourage companies to spend their higher profits and contribute to economic development. Without these efforts, the gap between the primary objectives of the government and those of corporate sector will widen further, leading to ineffectiveness of any fiscal support provided to boost economic growth.

Chapter 4

THE GOVERNMENT SECTOR: BELIEVE IT OR NOT, IT HAS ITS LIMITS

Non-economist: Ooh, the government . . . the torch bearers in an economy. They bear the burden of running the economy. But the Indian government runs very high deficits and high debt.

Me: No, households bear the burden of running an economy. The government is more like a referee. And do you know what India's true fiscal deficit and debt are?

Non-economist: How does it matter? The Indian government has always favoured the poor as elections near. Lousy politics . . . How can we ever become a rich country?

Me: Let me explain how it matters. In fact, eventually, it is all about the numbers. Government policies have far-reaching implications for the entire economy—

Non-economist: But they only think about politics. India's corporate sector is not buoyant because of them. The government has no business to be in business.

Me: The government has no business to be in business? Then why do they have to take full responsibility to save the economy during a crisis? What sort of lop-sided responsibility is this? Unless we understand how fiscal policies affect the behaviour of other participants in the economy, we can never appreciate the government's role . . .

Non-economist: OK, OK.

Me: . . . and it is equally important to know what our country's true fiscal deficit and debt are. We must understand clearly how much of the domestic resources are absorbed by the government. Being the largest borrower, its debt sustainability is of paramount importance. Let me explain . . .

Public finances attract the most research in economic analyses in India; however, the focus is largely on the Union government. In this chapter I examine the consolidated finances of the general government (Centre + states) during the past five decades and discuss the direct and indirect effects of several fiscal policies on the economic behaviour of the private sector. As discussed, there is serious debate over the true extent of India's fiscal deficit, and thus debt, which is expected to be settled in this chapter. Here I explain why the skewed expectations of market participants and other experts from the government are bound to fail. Contrary to the new narrative of modern monetary theory, there are genuine limits to fiscal support in India, as the government already absorbs almost the entire pool of household surplus.

Public finances are one of the most researched segments in the Indian economy. No other macroeconomic event gets as much attention as the Union Budget, currently announced on the first day of February each year. Since actual policies can be announced on any day of the year, the exclusivity of the Union Budget has fallen over the years. Data shows that the bigger action happens through the state governments, which rarely gets as much attention.

Including the transfers and devolution of taxes by the GoI (or the Union government) to the state governments, the states together account for about 60 per cent of all government receipts (excluding borrowings or debt receipts) collected in the country. Consequently, the total expenditure of all the state governments is also around 60 per cent of all government spending. Total spending by the general government, that is, the Centre and state governments, amounted to ₹53.9 tn (or 26.8 per cent of GDP) in FY20, of which only 40 per cent, amounting to ₹21.5 tn (or 10.7 per cent of GDP) was spent by the GoI[1] and the remaining 60 per cent by the states. In spite of this, state Budgets do not get as much attention as received by the Union Budget. Subsequent analyses of India's fiscal policy are also largely based on the data released by the GoI on a monthly basis. Such analyses can be highly misleading, and it reflects lazy (or ignorant) analysis on the part of us economists. Unlike the Union Budget, the documents for which are easily and conveniently available at one place in proper order, it is a mammoth task to maintain and follow the annual Budgets of the country's twenty-eight states and eight Union Territories (UTs). The only exhaustive annual study on state finances is released by the RBI, but it is available with a lag of almost eighteen months—actual accounts for FY21 was available in the publication released in January 2023 with revised estimates for FY22 (FY22RE) and Budget estimates for FY23 (FY23BE).

The task is further complicated because monthly data for the states/UTs is not available on a fixed schedule or in a uniform manner. However, the monthly reporting on states' finances has improved dramatically in the past few years. Just like the controller general of accounts (CGA) publishes monthly data on the Centre's finances, the comptroller and auditor general (CAG) of India produces monthly data on most Indian states except Goa, that is, for more than 93 per cent of all states (data for the UT of Delhi is also not available on a monthly basis).

To understand the quality of government spending, state government finances are more relevant because the GoI transfers grants to the states (amounting to ₹5.3 tn in FY20, which increased to ₹6.4 tn in FY21), which are spent by state governments through allocations to various departments/ministries.

A comprehensive analysis of the general government (or government, hereafter) has become even more important after the introduction of the goods and services tax (GST) in India with effect from 1 July 2017. States were assured of 14 per cent compounded growth over the base year 2015–16 for loss of revenue arising on account of GST implementation for a period of five years ending June 2022. Therefore, the GoI levied a 'compensation cess' on certain GST items, which is eventually credited to the Compensation Fund for apportioning to states once every two months. However, in the wake of the COVID-19 pandemic, there was a large shortfall in the Compensation Fund, which increased the gap between the guaranteed and actual receipts of states. To meet the shortfall in GST compensation to be paid to the states, the GoI borrowed ₹1.1 tn from the market under the special window in FY21 and passed it on to the states as loans. The Centre borrowed another ₹1.59 tn under the special window in FY22 and passed it on to states as back-to-back loans in tranches.

As GST collections posted strong growth in FY22, which continued into FY23, the GoI released the entire amount of GST compensation payable to states (₹869 bn) up to 31 May 2022 on 31 May 2022.[2] On 25 November 2022,[3] the government released an additional amount of ₹170 bn towards the balance GST compensation for the period April to June 2022.

Since there were some months when the GoI did not clear its entire dues to the states, a standalone analysis of the GoI finances would overestimate fiscal spending in the country because a part of that spending should ideally have been transferred to the states on account of the GST shortfall. When the GoI spent the money that should have been allocated to the states, it curtailed the ability of the states to grow their spending. Therefore, only an inclusive analysis will help us understand the true picture.

In this chapter, therefore, the combined finances of the government[4]—the Centre and state governments together—are analysed to understand the true fiscal policy in India. Four broad topics are covered in this chapter. The role of government spending in India has increased in recent years and its contribution to real GDP growth has also risen. We first analyse total receipts and total expenditure of the government during the past three decades—FY91 to FY20 (FY21 and FY22 are avoided because of the pandemic). This section looks at how the government has increased or decreased its spending in some of the most important areas such as social development (education, health and sanitation), defence, mandatory or non-discretionary spending (interest, salaries and pension), popular schemes (such as subsidies) and investments. This will also help us understand the improvements made in government spending since the 1990s and the existing gaps.

Second, a detailed analysis is provided on the widening gap between the reported fiscal deficit (RFD) and the actual or adjusted fiscal deficit (AFD) of the government. What matters from the economy perspective is the AFD and not the RFD. Followers of macroeconomic trends will be aware of this growing debate on India's public finances. The fiscal deficit of the GoI had reduced from 6.5 per cent of GDP in FY10 to 3.4 per cent of GDP in FY19; however, there had been a growing and large quantum of spending—and thus, borrowings—by the CPSEs, called below-the-line or off-Budget transactions, which do not affect the fiscal deficit but get reflected in the outstanding liabilities of the Central government. There are two very important implications of AFD: (1) the higher the aggregate borrowing requirements of the government, the more it will absorb from the available pool of funds (savings), especially since external borrowings are very limited; and (2) the financial markets also react to the actual fiscal burden rather than to the reported numbers. The comparison of AFD vis-à-vis the surplus of the household sector is revealing.

Third, a closer look at the various fiscal policies adopted by the Central and state governments during the past few years helps us understand their macroeconomic implications. How have these policies affected the behaviour of households and the corporate sector? I find it extremely disturbing that government support for economic activity during the past few years appears to be highly biased towards current or consumption-related spending, discouraging the savings potential of the citizens. Linking this with the analysis contained in Chapter 2, it may be argued that these fiscal policies could have contributed to the deteriorating financial position of India's household sector, which has now become one of the most serious challenges to be overcome for sustained higher growth. Understanding the context in which these policies have been adopted will help us appreciate some of the challenges faced by the governments.

Lastly, a discussion on the impact of COVID-19 on government finances reveals that notwithstanding the limited fiscal support implemented in India, government finances deteriorated substantially, partly because the starting position was not favourable. In any case, the inability of the government to stimulate the economy will have a long-lasting impact on India's growth.

Where Do Governments Earn from and What Do They Spend On?

No economy can function in peace unless the government maintains law and order and sets clear rules of operation for any participant undertaking any economic or non-economic activity in the country. Besides, as the only authority in a geographically defined nation to tax activities, the government has unmatched power to incentivize or dis-incentivize production and consumption of certain goods and services. A part of the taxes is required for the government to spend on essential public services; however, through taxation, the government can favour one segment of the society over others. Apart from taxation, the government has the power to decide to spend on and/or subsidize some industries/sectors over others. Therefore, while direct consumption and investments by the government accounts for less than 20 per cent of India's GDP, there are several indirect ways in which the government can affect the behaviour of other economic participants.

During the past five decades, the share of government (direct) spending—including consumption and investments—ranged between 12 per cent and 17 per cent of GDP, and its direct contribution to real GDP growth averaged 14 per cent (or 0.9pp) during the period. As the private sector turned cautious on investments in the late 2010s decade, the government has done some heavy lifting. The government's direct spending (consumption and investments) contributed only about 8 per cent (or 0.6pp) to real GDP growth between FY11 and FY14, which doubled to an average of 16 per cent (or 1.2pp) during the next five years (FY15–FY19) before the pandemic reduced its contribution in FY20 (see Exhibit 4.1). Government spending increased in FY21, while real GDP contracted, and it contributed as much as 24 per cent (or 2.1pp) to GDP growth in FY22.

Exhibit 4.1: Contribution of government spending to real GDP growth

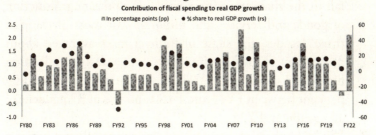

Spending = Consumption + Investment
Source: MOSPI, Budget documents, various national sources

An obvious question is, '*Where do the governments spend?*' Before answering this question, we must understand its receipts or income sources, which are discussed next (also see Appendix 6). In general, there are only four sources of income for the government—taxes, non-tax revenue receipts (such as dividends from CPSEs, interest receipts, etc.), non-debt capital receipts (such as divestment of the government's stake in companies and recovery of loans and advances) and debt capital receipts (also called fiscal deficit). Further, taxes are divided into two categories—direct and indirect taxes. The key highlights are:

1. The share of direct taxes (that is, personal income taxes and corporate income taxes) in India has risen sharply and

consistently from 7 per cent of all government receipts in the late 1980s to 17 per cent in FY05 and to a peak of 26 per cent of all receipts in FY19 (same as in FY08) before falling back to 22 per cent in FY22. Within direct taxes, growth in corporate income taxes has been much faster than in personal (non-corporate) income taxes. The share of corporate income taxes rose from 3 per cent of all receipts in FY91 to 9 per cent in FY05 and further to 13 per cent in FY19 (peak of 15 per cent in FY08) before falling back to 10 per cent in FY22. In contrast, the share of personal income taxes increased from 5 per cent of all receipts to 8 per cent and to peak of 12 per cent in FY19, and remained unchanged at 12 per cent in FY22.

2. The higher share of direct taxes, however, doesn't imply a fall in the share of indirect taxes (on domestic production of goods and services and imports). For most of the past three decades, the share of indirect taxes averaged about 39 per cent of total receipts and was at a post-liberalization high of 43 per cent in FY07. Its share remained around 39 per cent between FY13 and FY20 and was at 37 per cent of all receipts in FY22.

3. While the share of direct taxes has risen and that of indirect taxes has been broadly stable, the share of non-tax non-debt receipts (revenue and capital) has fallen continuously, especially during the past two decades. After remaining stable at around 17 per cent of all receipts till the early 2000s decade, the share of non-tax non-debt receipts fell closer to 11–12 per cent in the early 2010s decade and has stayed there since. Notwithstanding all the attempts of the Central government to boost disinvestment receipts or to take away RBI's excess capital, the share of these receipts has stayed around 12 per cent during the 2010s decade and dropped to 9 per cent in FY22.

4. The government's debt capital receipts (or the reported fiscal deficit, RFD) have also fallen during the past three

decades. From above 30 per cent of all receipts, the share of debt receipts fell to an all-time low of 15 per cent in FY08, before the great financial crisis pushed it back to 30 per cent in FY09–FY10. In the 2010s decade, the share of RFD declined to 25 per cent, before rising to an all-time high of 42 per cent in FY21 and 31 per cent in FY22. The RFD was slightly below 6 per cent of GDP each in FY18 and FY19—only the second time in the past four decades (except in FY07–FY08), before the pandemic pushed it to a record high. However, as we will see later in this chapter, the lower RFD in the pre-pandemic years was due to the sharp increase in off-Budget spending, which ideally should be part of the fiscal deficit.

We now move on to examining the total spending by the government, which amounted to ₹53.9 tn in FY20, or 26.8 per cent of GDP. However, GDP data shows that the total spending (consumption + investments) of the government amounted to only around 15 per cent of GDP. This is because, increasingly, a larger portion of government spending is accounted for by transfers and loans, which are not counted under the government's final consumption expenditure or its investments (called gross capital formation). Therefore, if fiscal stimulus is in the form of transfer payments, say, one-off income payments or subsidies on selected commodities, it will not show up as fiscal spending in GDP. Rather, it would add to the recipient's income and would be part of private spending (or savings). This method of classifying the total spending of the government is called 'Classification of the Functions of Government (COFOG)' or referred to as 'socio-economic functions' (details are provided in Appendix 7). Under this classification, the total spending of the government is divided sector-wise into three parts—current expenditure, capital expenditure, and financial investments and loans. It can be further reclassified into four segments—final consumption (GFCE), investments (GCF), transfers (current and capital) and financial investments and loans. This data is available from FY81, and the data for FY 22 is provisional (see Appendix 8).

There are two more useful ways of classifying government spending—by nature and by purpose of spending. By nature, the total expenditure of the government can be divided into mandatory/committed expenditure, capital spending and other (non-committed) revenue spending. The higher the share of mandatory spending, the lower the flexibility the government possesses to manage its finances. Under purpose-wise classification, we look at government spending on different sectors, departments and/or ministries to understand the areas of priority. The key highlights of various categories of total government spending are:

5. During the 1980s and 1990s, consumption (such as employee compensation) accounted for the bulk of fiscal spending. The share of investments fell from 8 per cent of total spending in the 1980s to about 7 per cent in the 1990s decade. Transfers (current + capital) also rose during the period from about 32 per cent to 38 per cent of total spending in the 1990s, while the share of financial investments and loans declined. The composition of government spending changed further in the 2000s decade and the 2010s decade. The share of final consumption reversed and fell towards one-third of total spending in the 2010s decade; while it started increasing for investments towards the low double digits. Transfers, however, continued to increase further to almost half of all spending. Thus, while total government spending was more than 26 per cent of GDP in the 2010s decade, almost half of it consisted of current and capital transfers. The government's final outlays (consumption and investments) were less than

half of total fiscal spending, which is what gets captured in GDP as GFCE and government investments.

6. By its nature, almost half of government spending is mandatory or non-discretionary in nature, and this includes wages and salaries, interest payments and pensions (WIP). Of course, the share of WIP rises with the implementation of every pay commission; however, the ratio has been very stable, in the range of 45 per cent to 55 per cent, during the past two decades, averaging 48 per cent of all spending. The higher the share of mandatory spending, the lower the flexibility to manoeuvre during difficult times. The share of capital expenditure was more than 20 per cent of total spending in the early 1990s, which fell to a trough of 13 per cent at the turn of the century but recovered quickly to 18 per cent in FY08. During the 2010s decade, however, it stayed stable at 14–15 per cent, before rising to 16 per cent in FY22. The remaining 40 per cent of all spending is, thus, accounted for by other non-mandatory revenue spending, including items such as subsidies and expenses on other welfare schemes. The share of mandatory spending is higher for the Central government than for the states. During the past few years, the share of committed expenditure has accounted for 40–45 per cent of total spending by state governments; however, the share of such spending is as high as 53–57 per cent for the Union government (adjusted for grants/transfers to the states).

7. A classification of the total expenditure by purpose reveals that spending on interest payments and the education and health sectors are the highest, together accounting for more than a third of the total spending of the general government (see Appendix 9). Notably, the share of education and health has remained stable, at 16–17 per cent, during the past three decades. However, the share of interest payments started rising in the late 1980s, peaking at 22 per cent of total spending in FY02. It has fallen since

and has been 17–18 per cent during the 2010s decade. Rural development, national security and pension are the next big components. The share of spending on national security has fallen gradually, from 13 per cent in the 1990s to less than 10 per cent in recent years. However, rural development has accounted for between 10 per cent and 15 per cent of total spending during the past three decades, with its share rising from 11 per cent in the 2000s decade to close to 14 per cent in recent years.

Pension has witnessed the highest rise during the past three decades, increasing from just 4 per cent of total spending in the early 1990s to 9–10 per cent in recent years. Of the total pension payments, two-thirds is paid by the state governments, with Central government employees accounting for the remaining one-third.

Overall, the nature of government spending in India is not exactly ideal. The share of education and health has been stagnant, at just 16–17 per cent, while it has declined for national security. This means that the additional resources saved through lower interest payments were absorbed by other areas such as rural development and pensions, which has seriously curtailed the ability of the government to spend on more productive areas such as infrastructure. The share of capital spending has thus remained broadly stable, at a low level of 15 per cent during the 2010s decade.

What Are India's True Fiscal Deficit and Outstanding Government Debt?

The difference between the total receipts and total spending of the government is known as the 'fiscal balance'. If receipts are higher than total expenditure, the government is said to be running a 'fiscal surplus', and if receipts are lower than total expenditure, there is a 'fiscal deficit'. The reported fiscal deficit of the government in India has averaged 8.3 per cent of GDP during the past four decades (FY81–FY22). It narrowed to an average of 6.8 per cent of GDP during the 2010s decade (FY11–FY20). Neither the Union government nor the states (on combined basis) have had a single year of fiscal surplus during the past half a century. Several individual states, however, have posted fiscal surpluses in some years.

During the past few years, there has been growing debate among economists regarding the true extent of the gross fiscal deficit of the GoI. This issue has come to the fore because of various off-Budget[5] or below-the-line transactions which the Union government has resorted to in recent years. Interestingly, the existence of such entries is as old as the concept of fiscal deficit itself in India. However, the magnitude of these transactions increased significantly in the past few years, implying that the gap between AFD and RFD has widened.

It is important to know the AFD (or true fiscal deficit) because, regardless of whether the government counts it in its fiscal deficit or not, higher government borrowings through the markets or otherwise imply that these resources would be unavailable to the private sector (primarily corporate). As in many other nations, AFD in India is primarily financed through household savings, as foreign (external) borrowings by the government are limited—less than 5 per cent of India's sovereign bonds are held by foreigners, in contrast to 40–50 per cent in the case of many rich nations. Therefore, the higher the fiscal deficit, the more the government absorbs household savings in the country, leaving little for the corporate sector to borrow domestically. For a developing country like India, such dependencies act as a natural constraint on government borrowings. It also helps us explain why the Modern Monetary Theory (MMT) is not applicable in India.

In an ideal situation, the gross fiscal deficit of the GoI must be equal to the difference between the outstanding debt (or liabilities) of the government at the end of the current and previous year. This is, however, not true for India. One of the major causes of the discrepancies between the fiscal deficit and the change in the GoI's outstanding debt is that while the former is almost entirely concerned with the Consolidated Fund of India (CFI), the latter also includes transactions in the public account, valuation changes and a few other transactions (explained in detail next), which are entirely out of the formal accounting system (see Appendix 10 to understand the formal accounting system of India's Union government).

Specifically, there are five adjustments which need to be taken care of while incorporating the various off-Budget transactions to estimate the AFD from the RFD (please note that this section deals with the GoI or the Central government only).

1. The Union government has recapitalized public sector banks and other government-controlled banking entities during the past few years. This has not affected the fiscal deficit but has been included in the government's liabilities. Such equity infusions in PbSBs have been done by deducting the debt received by the government from PbSBs from the equity investments made. The GoI issued recapitalization bonds worth ₹758/200 bn in FY20/FY21. They should be included in the fiscal deficit.

2. For more than two decades, the GoI has had arrears on account of its fuel and fertilizer subsidies. During the 2000s decade, the government issued bonds to oil and fertilizer companies to make up for these arrears. Like recapitalization bonds, these transactions were part of the public account, which pushes government debt higher but leaves the fiscal deficit unchanged. The annual reports of Bharat Petroleum Corporation Ltd (BPCL), Hindustan Petroleum Corporation Ltd (HPCL) and Indian Oil Corporation (IOC) confirm that their total receivables from the GoI amounted to ₹253/250 bn in FY20 and FY21. This is equivalent to the arrears on fuel subsidies.

In the case of fertilizer subsidies, while the official amount is not disclosed publicly, the carry-over liability appears to have fallen from ₹325 bn in FY19 to almost nil[6] in FY20. Further, while the arrears increased in early FY21,[7] the GoI increased its allocation to the fertilizer subsidy in FY21 to take care of these dues. Therefore, there were no arrears on account of fertilizers in FY20 and FY21. Further, the GoI took some great measures[8] to check the growing fertilizer subsidies. These arrears are entirely out of the formal accounting system and must be adjusted for to arrive at the AFD.

3. More recently, the GoI also deferred its cash payments to the Food Corporation of India (FCI) for carrying out its massive food subsidy programme. Instead, the FCI has been provided loans through the National Small Savings Fund (NSSF). These transactions[9] are a part of the public account, not part of CFI, and therefore, while they do not enter the fiscal deficit, they are included in the outstanding debt of the GoI. Besides, various other agencies, such as National Highways Authority of India (NHAI) and Power Finance Corporation (PFC), have also received loans from NSSF, which was never the case before FY15. Various NBFCs and the NHAI have their own streams of revenue from which they can repay NSSF and other lenders. The FCI, on the other hand, does not have any revenue stream of its own and is completely dependent on the GoI for all its operational expenses.

Financial support was extended to various CPSEs through loans from the NSSF totalling ₹1.41 tn in FY20. The net support, however, amounted to ₹949 bn, as an amount of ₹464 was adjusted towards redemption. The FCI was the major beneficiary of these loans and received as much as ₹1.1 tn on gross basis and ₹636 bn on net basis in FY20. These transactions are not included in the fiscal deficit. In FY21, however, the GoI decided to pay off all

outstanding FCI arrears and included them on its books, which pushed the RFD higher. Since these payments included arrears of the last few years, the RFD turned out to be higher than the AFD in FY21.
4. During the past few years, the GoI has issued fully serviced bonds (FSBs) for specific purposes. These bonds are entirely out of the formal accounting system of the GoI, being neither part of the CFI nor the public account. These are issued through some special purpose vehicles (SPVs) to pay for the government's expenditure. However, the interest and principal payments on these bonds are serviced by the GoI. The GoI issued FSBs, also called extra budgetary resources (EBRs), totalling ₹220/267 bn in FY20/FY21. These bonds are neither included in the fiscal deficit nor in the outstanding liabilities, and thus the RFD must be adjusted for these FSBs.
5. There are some securities issued to international multilateral organizations, such as the IMF and Asian Development Bank (ADB), and to some other financial institutions, such as Export-Import (EXIM) Bank and Industrial Development Bank of India (IDBI), which are excluded from the fiscal deficit. Securities totalling to ₹12/90 bn were issued to various agencies in FY20/FY21.

Therefore, the RFD of the GoI must be adjusted to take into account these five transactions every year to arrive at the AFD for the year. Appendix 11 lists the differences between the RFD and AFD of the GoI for the past four decades.

The conclusion is that while the RFD of the GoI was ₹9.3/18.2 tn (or 4.6/9.2 per cent of GDP) in FY20/FY21, after adjusting for these five off-Budget transactions totalling ₹2.2/–1.6 tn, the AFD will be ₹11.5/16.6 tn (or 5.7/8.4 per cent of GDP). These off-Budget entries, thus, amounted to as much as 1 per cent of GDP in FY20, pushing the AFD higher than the RFD. However, FCI repayments implied that the AFD was lower than the RFD in FY21.

Repeating the same exercise for all years of the past four decades suggests that the reliance of the GoI on these transactions has increased sharply during the past fifteen years. While off-Budget transactions averaged 0.4 per cent of GDP prior to FY06, they averaged 1 per cent of GDP during the next fifteen years (FY06–FY20) and as much as 1.5 per cent of GDP during the three years prior to COVID-19 (FY18–FY20). As the GoI paid off these arrears, the AFD was lower than the RFD in FY21. With no NSSF borrowings for the FCI, no recap bonds and no FSBs, AFD was on level with RFD in FY22. This improved transparency on the part of the GoI is highly appreciated.

This analysis confirms that (1) off-Budget transactions have gained prominence during the past fifteen years since the Fiscal Responsibility and Budget Management Act came into existence in 2003 to narrow India's fiscal deficit; (2) the AFD of the GoI was never 3 per cent of GDP or below—the target set under the FRBM Act. It was at 3.3 per cent of GDP in FY08, against the RFD of 2.5 per cent, and (3) After easing to 4.3 per cent of GDP in FY17 (the third lowest since 1980), the AFD of the GoI has risen by about 0.5pp of GDP every year to 5.7 per cent of GDP in FY20, marking the highest deficit in the past eight years.

Now we move from the Central government to the combined fiscal deficit estimation of the government. It requires four special adjustments on account of (1) grants from the Centre to the states, (2) interest payments by the states to the Centre, (3) loans and advances provided by the Centre to the states, and (4) repayment of loans by the states to the Centre. The RBI provides the combined fiscal deficit with all these adjustments. Keeping in mind these adjustments, a comparison of the RFD vis-à-vis the AFD of the government during the past four decades is shown in Exhibit 4.2. Coming back to what we stated at the beginning of this section, the RFD of the government averaged 8.3 per cent of GDP during

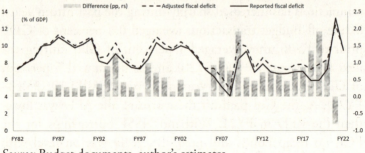

Exhibit 4.2: Comparison of the reported and adjusted fiscal deficit of the government in India since the 1980s

Source: Budget documents, author's estimates

the past four decades, easing to 6.8 per cent in the 2010s decade. The combined AFD, however, averaged 8.8 per cent of GDP during the past four decades, averaging 7.7 per cent of GDP during the 2010s decade. Although it is lower than the average of 9.5 per cent of GDP in the 1980s, 9.3 per cent of GDP in the 1990s decades and the average of 8.5 per cent in the 2000s decade, the combined AFD of 7.7 per cent of GDP is not low by any standard. Therefore, since reliance on off-Budget transactions has increased greatly during the past few years, the pace of fiscal consolidation is much slower than the general narrative.

Interestingly, while the FRBM Act recommends that Union and state governments narrow their gross fiscal deficit to 3 per cent of GDP each, recommending an implied combined fiscal deficit of 6 per cent of GDP, the AFD has been above the targeted deficit every year since FY04, except in FY08, when it was 4.8 per cent of GDP.

This exercise of arriving at the adjusted fiscal deficit brings us to the next obvious question: What are the true liabilities of the government? This exercise is even more interesting because there are three sources[10] that provide data on the outstanding liabilities of the GoI—the Union Budget documents, the Ministry of Finance (MoF, through Status Papers on Government debt) and the Reserve Bank of India. All three sources, however, provide different data on the outstanding liabilities of the GoI. According to the Budget documents, the GoI's liabilities in FY20/FY21 amounted to ₹102.2/120.8 tn (or 50.8/60.9 per cent of GDP); as per the RBI, it was ₹106.2/124.9 tn (52.8/63 per cent of GDP); and according to the MoF only ₹97.5/117 tn (48.5/59 per cent of GDP). What explains these differences and which source is accurate?

The outstanding liabilities of the GoI are divided into two parts—public debt and 'other liabilities'. The former, which is part of the CFI, includes internal and external debt, and the latter includes all liabilities which are part of the government's public account. There are three reasons for the differences in the data reported by the three agencies:

1. **External debt (ED)** in the Budget documents is according to book (or historical) value, while the RBI and the MoF include external debt 'at current value'. At book value, external debt stood at ₹3.0/3.9 tn in FY20/FY21, while according to current value it amounted to ₹5.9/6.6 tn. Ideally, one should include external debt at current value to estimate the outstanding liabilities of the GoI. This would increase the debt estimated in the Budget documents by ₹2.9/2.7 tn.

2. Since FY17, the GoI has incurred liabilities on account of **FSBs** or **EBRs**, which are not included in the debt estimates presented by the GoI in the Budget documents. In fact, the footnote in the Budget Statement 1(i) (which provides data on the liabilities of the GoI) in the Union Budget 2020–21 mentioned this clearly: 'In addition to above, Govt. liabilities on account of Extra Budgetary Resources (Govt. fully serviced Bonds), at the end of FY 2018–19 were ₹89,864.10 crore, which was about 0.47 per cent of GDP.' The RBI and the MoF include these EBRs in their calculations, which increased the outstanding debt by another ₹1.1/1.4 tn for FY20/FY21.

When we adjust the Budget estimates with these two items totalling about ₹4 tn each, the outstanding debt of the GoI (as per the Budget documents) becomes ₹106.2/124.9 tn, similar to what the RBI states. So, RBI makes only these two adjustments when presenting its estimates of outstanding liabilities of the GoI.

However, the MoF makes two more adjustments, as below:

3. The RBI and Budget estimates include all **liabilities under the NSSF**. There are five components in the NSSF— (i) investment in Central government special securities against outstanding balance as on 31 March 1999; (ii) investment in Central government special securities against collections net of withdrawals from the funds received thereafter in the Fund; (iii) reinvestment in Central government special securities out of the sums received on redemption of securities; (iv) investments in special state government securities against net collections from 1 April 1999 (NSSF – States); and (v) investments in public agencies from the NSSF (NSSF – PSUs). The liabilities under the first three components are considered borrowings by the GoI from the NSSF for financing its fiscal deficit and is shown under the head 'Public Debt' of the GoI, as 'Securities against small savings'. The last two items, however, are included under 'Other liabilities' of the GoI in the Union Budget as 'National Small Savings Fund'. The MoF adjusts the outstanding liabilities of the GoI with the last two items to estimate the liabilities actually owed on account of the operations of the GoI. These liabilities (NSSF – States and NSSF – PSUs) stood at ₹4.4/4.2 tn and ₹3.7/1.3 tn, respectively, in FY20/FY21, amounting to a total of ₹8.1/5.4 tn.

4. Finally, the MoF adjusts the GoI's debt with the **cash balances**, which have increased substantially in the last few years. The GoI held cash balances amounting to ₹0.6/2.4

tn in FY20/FY21, which should also ideally be reduced to arrive at the GoI's outstanding liabilities.

Thus, the RBI estimates of the GoI's outstanding liabilities are adjusted with a portion of the NSSF and cash balances. According to the MoF, thus, the GoI's total liabilities stood at ₹97.5/117 tn (₹106.2/124.8 tn − ₹8.1/5.4 tn − ₹0.6/2.4 tn) in FY20 and FY21.

So which one is an accurate estimation? Ironically, none of the three official sources presents the true outstanding debt of the GoI. While the RBI and the Budget documents overestimate the outstanding debt of the GoI, the MoF underestimates it. This is because the true debt of the GoI must include the NSSF loans to the FCI because they are undertaken to serve the purpose of the government and should be included in the fiscal deficit, along with the annuity obligations on account of various projects it rewards. The outstanding borrowings of the FCI through NSSF amounted to ₹2.5 tn in FY20, which was entirely cleared in FY21.

Lastly, the GoI also incurs liability in the form of annuity[11] on several projects it rewards. As at end March 2021, there were forty road projects for which outstanding annuity obligations amounted to ₹376 bn (₹418 bn in FY20). The liabilities accrued on these annuity projects should also be included in the GoI's outstanding debt.

Overall, thus, the adjusted outstanding liabilities of the GoI amounted to ₹100.5/117.5 tn or 50/59.2 per cent of GDP in FY20/FY21 (₹97.5/117 tn from the MoF + ₹2.5/0 tn on account of FCI debt + ₹0.4 tn each on account of annuity liabilities). Appendix 12 provides the adjusted estimates of the GoI's outstanding debt/liabilities during the past three decades, with all the details discussed above.

Since the GoI paid off all FCI arrears (on account of NSSF borrowings) in FY21, FCI debt disappeared this year, whereas it had amounted to ₹2.5 tn in FY20. Therefore, the difference between the GoI debt estimated by the MoF and the adjusted debt was minimal, and only on account of the annuity obligation towards various road projects in FY21. The Union Budget and the RBI still overestimate the debt.

What about the combined outstanding liabilities of the government? Just like some adjustments on account of intra-governmental transactions were required to arrive at the combined fiscal deficit of the general government, we have to make a few adjustments here also. While the RBI is the sole agency that provides detailed data on state deficits and liabilities, the MoF—using RBI's data on states' finances—also provides data on the combined liabilities of the government in India. There are only two adjustments that must be netted to arrive at the combined liabilities of the government:

1. Loans and advances from the Centre to the state governments, and
2. Investments by states in the 14-day intermediate and auction treasury bills (ITBs/ATBs).

According to the RBI, the outstanding liabilities of the general government amounted to 75.2/89.4 per cent of GDP in FY20/FY21RE, while it was 74.9/87.4 per cent after my adjustments. Therefore, although the RFD is very different from the AFD because the former misses a few items, the official estimates of the outstanding liabilities of the general government incorporate most of the required adjustments. The challenge when it comes to the latter is to understand which of the three official estimates of Union government liabilities represents the true level.

A look at the long-term trends in the outstanding liabilities of the government suggests that before COVID-19 it was stable at around 70 per cent of GDP in the 2010s decade, which cannot be considered low by any standard for a developing economy such as India (Exhibit 4.3). Further, although there was no large fiscal stimulus in India in FY21, the surge in government debt to a new peak of 87 per cent of GDP is substantial.

Exhibit 4.3: Combined liabilities of the general government in India since the 1980s (% of GDP)

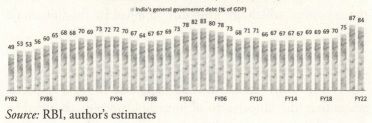

Source: RBI, author's estimates

How is it relevant? So what if India's adjusted fiscal deficit averaged 7.7 per cent of GDP in the 2010s decade instead of the reported deficit of 6.8 per cent of GDP? Why has so much trouble been taken to estimate and explain AFD and the combined liabilities of the government in India? The answer is that irrespective of whether the government counts its deficit and debt appropriately or not, the actual borrowing requirements are based on the all-inclusive (or adjusted) deficit. In simple words, whether the food subsidy is billed to the GoI or the FCI, while it makes a difference to the reported fiscal maths, both will be borrowing from the same pool of available funds in the domestic financial markets.

As stated repeatedly in this book, what makes economic analysis complicated are the strong interactions between the various participants. When the government runs a fiscal deficit, that is, its spending is more than its receipts, it has to borrow. It does not matter whether the government borrows from a bank in the form of loans or from the market by issuing securities, because every penny borrowed by it comes from the net savings of the private sector (primarily households) in the country. Of course, the government could borrow from the external sector (discussed in the next chapter); however, the share of foreigners in India's sovereign debt is less than 5 per cent.

Since households are the major (and often only) net savers in India, it implies that directly or indirectly the fiscal deficit is financed through household (net) savings. Thus, if fiscal deficit is high, as has been the case in India, the government tends to mop up a large part of the domestic funds available in the economy, which are primarily supplied by the household sector.

Data for the 2010s decade suggests that the AFD in India absorbed the entire household surplus (or net financial savings). This was broadly similar to what happened in the 1990s and worse than the 90 per cent of household surplus absorbed by the fiscal deficit in the 2000s decade. From an average of 9.3 per cent of GDP in the 2000s decade, household net financial savings fell to 7.8 per cent in the 2010s decade, while the combined fiscal deficit fell slowly, from 8.5 per cent of GDP to 7.7 per cent of GDP during the corresponding period.

A look at the annual trends reveals that the share of AFD to household surplus fell to 53 per cent in FY08, the lowest (or best) during the last four decades. Household surplus in FY08 amounted to 9 per cent of GDP while the combined AFD stood at a four-decade low of 4.8 per cent during the year. In contrast, while household savings stood at 7.7 per cent of GDP in FY20 and increased to 11.5 per cent in FY21, the combined AFD rose to 8.3 per cent/12.4 per cent of GDP. Between FY12 and FY19, household surplus averaged 7.5 per cent of GDP while the adjusted fiscal deficit averaged 7.7 per cent of GDP, implying an average absorption of over 100 per cent of household surplus by the government during the eight-year period.

As the government(s) ate up all surplus/funds supplied by the household sector, the corporate sector was left to rely on its own savings/resources or external borrowings. This has another serious implication. If the corporate sector feels more confident about spending or increasing its investments but the fiscal deficit doesn't reduce, the corporate sector will have to borrow from abroad, increasing India's current account deficit. Although India's GDP growth will improve dramatically, a combination of higher fiscal deficit and CAD (together called the 'twin deficit') will push inflation higher. This is exactly what gripped the Indian economy from FY10 to FY14.

Therefore, while we generally hope for higher investments, and thus higher GDP growth, the authorities must stand ready to create space for higher private spending (household + corporate) on a sustainable basis; because unless the fiscal deficit narrows to allow the corporate sector to utilize the household surplus, higher GDP growth will lead to serious economic imbalance in the form of external deficit and turn out to be temporary.

What Is India's Fiscal Policy and What Are Its Implications?

The first two sections in this chapter were dedicated to understanding India's government finances—Central and state—on a combined basis. In this section, the focus is primarily on the recently announced policies of the Union government and various states to understand their implications for India's macroeconomy. It is then linked with the data presented in the previous sections and with the core thesis of this book.

The present ruling party in India, the Bharatiya Janata Party, has been called by various names[12] in the past eight years—'*Suit boot ki sarkar*', '*Garibo ka masiha*', 'Anti-poor government', '*Robin Hood sarkar*', and much more. While it is one thing to build an image in favour of or against something, it is an altogether different story when one tries to match the image with the allocations made in the Budget. In this section, a sincere attempt is made to understand if the actions of the GoI have matched its words during the past few years.

'*Suit boot ki sarkar*' Or '*garibo ka masiha*'?

As mentioned above, Union Budgets are among the most widely covered annual events in India by the domestic and global media. The government's communication on the first day of February every year reflects its priorities as far as the image-building process is concerned. An analysis of the Union Budget speeches since 1999–2000, which includes four complete election cycles with five full Budgets and one Interim Budget each—those of NDA-I (1999–2004), UPA-I (2004–09), UPA-II (2009–14) and BJP-I (2014–19) and, in the current election cycle, BJP-II (2019–present)—has been made to understand if the government projects itself as a 'pro-poor government' or as a '*suit boot ki sarkar*'.

As a very simple exercise, we note the number of times the government has used the words 'farmer(s)/poor' in the Budget speech versus 'companies/banks'.

On average, the words 'farmer(s)/poor' were used 0.24 times per 100 words of Budget speeches during the BJP-I regime, more than the average of 0.1 times during UPA-II, of 0.14 times during UPA-I and of only 0.08 times during NDA-I. On the contrary, use of the words 'companies/banks' reduced from 0.49 times per 100 words during NDA-I to 0.31–0.34 times during UPA-I, UPA-II and BJP-I regimes.

Compared to the previous governments, the sharply higher frequency of use of the words 'farmer(s)/poor' and the lower use of 'companies/banks' make it clear that the BJP government used the platform for the presentation of the Union budget to project itself as a 'pro-poor government' rather than as a '*suit boot ki sarkar*'.

More interestingly, while observers would appreciate the government for its tight leash on the (reported) fiscal deficit during the past few years, 'fiscal deficit' was mentioned only 0.04 times per 100 words of Budget speeches during BJP-1, same as that by the UPA-I. Notably though, it was not mentioned at all in FY20 Budget, which was unusual.

A comparison of the occurrence of the words 'farmer(s)/poor' v/s 'companies/banks' in the past twenty-seven Budget speeches (including four Interim Budgets) confirms that the Interim Budget of 2018–19 presented on 1 February 2019 (just three months before the 2019 general elections) was exceptional. The finance minister of the time, Piyush Goyal, made an 8,000-word-long speech, which mentioned 'farmer(s)/poor' 0.48 times per 100 words, 4 times the average mention of 0.12 times per 100 words during the previous twenty-three speeches. In contrast, mention of 'companies/banks' was 0.26 times per 100 words, which was the third lowest since FY00 and lower than the average of 0.36 times between FY00 and FY23.

The long-term trend in mentioning these two segments in the Union Budget speeches indicates that while the focus on 'companies/banks' has fallen almost consistently, the mention of 'farmer(s)/poor' has been stable, with sporadic jumps.

Another interesting fact to note is that while 'farmer(s)/poor' got extraordinary mention in the FY18, FY19 and FY20(I) Budget speeches, the use of these words was scarce during the first four years of BJP-II. What's more, the focus on 'fiscal deficit' was the lowest, to 0.03 times per 100 words, of speeches during the past four Budgets.

Whether this image-building around being a 'pro-poor government' was matched by the government's actions (or allocation of resources) is more important from the economic implications perspective.

During the BJP-I regime, the combined spending of the general government grew at an average of only 10.9 per cent, the lowest growth seen during any election cycle since the 1990s. The sector-wise (or purpose) classification reflects that growth in rural spending (including expenditure on agricultural and allied activities, rural development and irrigation) has been the highest compared to the growth in spending on other sectors between FY14 and FY19.

Going by the same classification used in Appendix 9, average growth in government spending in different sectors is calculated for the last five election cycles of the post-liberalization period (Exhibit 4.4). Average growth in expenditure on rural development was 17 per cent during the BJP-I period (FY15–

Exhibit 4.4: Where has the government spent in recent years?

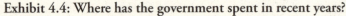
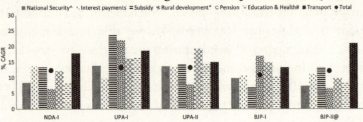

^ Defence and police
* Including agricultural and allied activities, rural development and irrigation
# Including water sanitation and supply
@ Up to FY22

Source: Budget documents, RBI, author's estimates

FY19), higher than the average growth of 10.9 per cent in total spending during the period. It was followed by a 14.8 per cent growth in the pension and a 13.4 per cent average growth in the transport sectors.

There have been three defining features which explain this phenomenon of prioritization of the rural sector during the past few years—farm loan waiver, direct income support and strengthening of social security benefits for the poor/unemployed sections of the society.

Farm Loan Waivers

For a few years before the pandemic, the Indian banking sector was under serious stress because of some high-profile corporate defaults. These instances became so popular worldwide that Netflix made a three-episode documentary on such loan defaults, featuring Vijay Mallya, the flamboyant Indian businessman and former member of Parliament, and Nirav Modi, another Indian businessman, also known as India's diamond king. While these high-profile industrial loan defaults were being discussed and intensely criticized, it appeared to have provided the grounds for some economic agents to seek loan waiver for the farmers across the country.

Commendably, the Central government stayed clear of announcing any sort of national-level farm loan waiver. However, the states couldn't handle the pressure. Between 2014–15 and 2020–21, as many as eleven state governments announced farm loan waivers totalling ₹2.55 tn. According to RBI's 'Study of State Budgets 2020–21',[13] the size of these state farm loan waivers since 2014–15 was significantly higher than those of the previous two nationwide debt waiver programmes—₹100 bn in 1990 (₹637 billion at 2020–21 prices using GDP deflator) and ₹525 billion in FY08 (₹1.08 tn at 2020–21 prices using GDP deflator) announced by the Central governments of the time. The economic impact of the current loan waivers on the states' finances, however, was limited because the waivers were staggered over three to five years and the actual costs incurred on account of these waivers was only about two-thirds, on average, of the announced amounts.

Direct Income Support to Farmers

More than 40 per cent of all workers in India are engaged in agricultural and allied activities in the country. Even so, the economy is still dependent on the rain gods every year since irrigation infrastructure in the country is very weak. Only about half of the net sown area in the country is under irrigation. The performance of BJP-I has been exceptionally weak in this area. Since 1901, there has never been a streak of five straight years of lower-than-normal rainfall from the south-west monsoon (SWM) during the June–September period except between 2014 and 2018. There was a pretty bad phase in the second half of the 1960s, but India has never had five consecutive years of shortfall in the past 120 years. The first two years of BJP-I saw a double-digit shortfall in the SWM, followed by a 3 per cent shortfall in 2016, a 5 per cent shortfall in 2017 and a 10 per cent shortfall in 2018. While the rain gods were not as angry in FY17, the demonetization of November 2016 came as an unprecedented shock to the economy. The terms of trade—estimated as the ratio of input prices and output prices—turned highly unfavourable for the farm sector, and not surprisingly, the agricultural society then became the Achilles heel for the incumbent government close to the 2019 general elections.

Because of the adverse impact of all this on the credit culture in the country amid an already weak financial sector and the moral hazard issue, farm loan waivers came under increasing scrutiny. Thus, as an alternative, as the RBI study of state budgets puts it, 'Income support schemes for farmers were for the first time announced by some state governments in 2018–19.' Karnataka, Odisha and Telangana were the first three states to announce and implement direct cash transfer to farmers in 2018–19. However, the scheme never took off in Karnataka, which saw a change of government in mid-2018.

Three months before the general elections, the Union government launched the Pradhan Mantri Kisan Samman Nidhi (PM-KISAN) in the Interim Budget announced on 1 February 2019 to provide assured income support of ₹6,000 per annum to all institutional landholders in the country. The Central government spent ₹12 bn in 2018–19, which increased to ₹487 bn and ₹610 bn in 2019–20 and 2020–21, respectively. In addition to Odisha and Telangana, five more states—Andhra Pradesh, Haryana, Jharkhand, West Bengal and Chhattisgarh—implemented unconditional income support schemes for farmers. Some states, such as Andhra Pradesh and Odisha, have combined their support with PM-KISAN's, while others have implemented their schemes over and above PM-KISAN.

Strengthening of Social Security Benefits

Alongside PM-KISAN, the GoI announced the launch of a mega-pension scheme, the Pradhan Mantri Shram-Yogi Maandhan, for the unorganized sector. Workers with monthly income of ₹15,000 or less and belonging to the age group of eighteen to forty are eligible under this scheme. Each subscriber will receive a minimum assured pension of ₹3,000 per month after attaining the age of sixty, for a monthly contribution of ₹55 at age eighteen, going up to ₹200 at age forty.

Why would states remain behind? As many as eleven states increased monthly pensions during the same year. In their 2019–20 state Budget speeches, Andhra Pradesh and Telangana announced the doubling of monthly pension amounts to ₹2,250 and ₹3,000 per month, respectively. Himachal Pradesh, Jharkhand and Rajasthan have also increased pension amounts. Andhra Pradesh reduced the pension age from sixty-five to sixty, and Telangana from sixty-five to fifty-seven.

Although these schemes and policies are attractive from the social and political perspectives, the economic implications of these measures could be multifold. There are three major ways in which these policies could hurt the country's economic progress.

1. **Adverse impact on productivity growth:** From the labour market perspective, real GDP growth is simply a function of employment and productivity. While most of the economic growth in developed economies is derived from the former (that is, employment), the latter is still the primary driver of real GDP growth in developing/emerging economies such as India, and thus there is weak-to-no correlation between employment and GDP growth in most developing/emerging economies. For example, in India as much as 93 per cent of GDP growth during the decade between FY05 and FY16 was contributed by productivity gains, with only around 7 per cent contribution by labour employment. Given this, and given the country's large informal or unorganized economy, any steps that are even incrementally adverse for productivity and/or lead to incentives, which thwart a shift in employment to the formal or organized sector, should be avoided at all costs.

These populist schemes do exactly the opposite of what is required.

The NABARD All India Rural Financial Inclusion Survey 2016–17 estimated the average monthly income of agricultural households in India at ₹8,931 in 2015–16; it ranged from ₹6,668 per month in Uttar Pradesh to ₹23,133 in Punjab. The disbursement of ₹6,000 per annum under the Centre's PM-KISAN scheme thus implies that the average direct income support would be 5.6 per cent of the annual income for farmers. However, it was close to or higher than 10 per cent in six states—Andhra Pradesh, Jharkhand, Odisha, Telangana and West Bengal—that have complemented PM-KISAN with their own income support schemes, and as much as 5 per cent for Haryana farmers, who are the second richest in India among all states. In fact, for Andhra Pradesh and Chhattisgarh, the income support could be around 15 per cent of agricultural household income. For instance, the average monthly income of agricultural households in Andhra Pradesh was ₹6,920 in 2015–16 (the second lowest among states), which amounts to ₹8,375 per month in 2019–20, after adjusting for four years of inflation. Since the Andhra Pradesh government has combined its income support scheme (called YSR Rythu Bharosa) with PM-KISAN, total income support to the state's farmers amounts to ₹13,500 per annum, or 13.4 per cent of the annual household income.

It would thus not be unfair to assume that these income support schemes could—probably only incrementally, though—affect productivity growth adversely. More worryingly, once these taps are open, it is extremely difficult to close them.

2. **Reduce fiscal flexibility:** At this stage, it is important to note that all these income schemes have been in addition to the various already existing subsidy programmes. If the

Union and state governments are using these unconditional income support schemes to replace subsidies over a period of time, these schemes may be worth considering. But the current policies are more a reflection of political compulsions, rather than economic wisdom.

As discussed above, during the past few years, more than half of the Centre's total spending (as much as 53–57 per cent) has been committed or non-discretionary (WIP) in nature. Another set of spending, such as subsidies and defence spending, can be classified as semi-discretionary (accounting for 20–25 per cent), due to their political/essential nature, which too are difficult to reduce or eliminate significantly at will. This implies that less than a quarter of the Centre's total spending is discretionary in nature, which puts serious constraints on its fiscal independence.

Similar exercises for the seven states which have announced direct income support to farmers confirm that the share of non-discretionary or committed expenditure has increased during the past few years. While the share of such expenditure in the total spending of all states, cumulatively, is around 42 per cent, the share of non-discretionary spending has increased from 27.3 per cent of total spending in FY16 for Rajasthan to as much as 51 per cent in FY21, and is as high as 58 per cent for West Bengal. The worry is that the state governments continue to remain extremely myopic, as confirmed by the recent decision of Rajasthan to return to the old pension scheme, along with four other states.

3. **Consumption versus savings:** Since most of these kinds of free income support accrues mainly to the poor households in the country, it will lead to higher consumption and lower savings in the country. Although some of this support is possibly used to purchase agricultural equipment such as

tractors or irrigation machinery, it is unlikely to form a large part of total spending among this category.

In poor-to-ordinary households with young members, a larger share of their income goes into consumption and their propensity to save is small. At the other extreme are the rich households and companies among whom propensity to save is very high. With the government's income support benefiting mainly poor or low-income households, it is highly likely that consumption will increase in the economy.

Similarly, with better and higher pension and free (or subsidized) health insurance schemes, these social security schemes tend to reduce the need for households to save. Although one could rightly argue that the targeted households were in any case not major savers in the economy, fiscal policies aimed at improving social security benefits, in general, reduce the need or requirement for households to save as much as they did earlier. By discouraging savings, these schemes automatically incentivize consumption.

These schemes are supposed to increase the income of poor households, which could boost overall income in the economy and thus help restart the growth engine. This is probably what the policymakers had in mind when they announced these schemes. However, what needs to be noted is that these income schemes are transfers from one section of the society to another. There are only two possible ways to implement these schemes. The first option is for the government to incur higher spending on this account by expanding its fiscal deficit, which will then be financed by borrowings. But the higher fiscal deficit of the government will lead to lower gross domestic savings, while higher resources with the poor will boost consumption.

Alternatively, the government may decide to keep its fiscal deficit unchanged, which means either the government has reshuffled its spending plan and its income schemes are a redistribution or the government has levied some taxes or duties to finance the higher spending on account of the income schemes. In the latter scenario, higher taxes can be collected only from middle-income households, rich households and companies. As higher tax outgo is unlikely to change the consumption habits of these sections, this implies that their savings will go down.

As discussed earlier, less than a quarter of government spending is discretionary, of which half is on the capital (non-defence) account. Therefore, if the government keeps total spending unchanged even after announcing new popular schemes, it is likely that the government has compromised on the quality of fiscal spending—moving away from investments and towards consumption.

In any case, these income supports are most likely to end up reducing the savings and/or investments potential in the country and giving a boost instead to consumption spending. If we link this back with what we had discussed about the Indian household sector in Chapter 2, we can see the profound implications of these fiscal policies. This is exactly what is happening in the economy and needs to change as soon as possible.

Not only has government spending towards the farmer/poor segment of the society risen faster, but low-income earners have also received tax benefits. The exemption limit for individual income tax payers has been increased from ₹2 lakh in FY15 to ₹2.5 lakh and the entry (or the minimum) tax rate has been reduced from 10 per cent earlier to 5 per cent. In fact, a resident individual whose net/taxable income does not exceed ₹5 lakh can avail of tax rebate capped at ₹12,500 under Section 87A. It means that all individuals with annual taxable income of up to ₹5 lakh effectively do not have to pay any tax.

The government introduced a new tax regime in 2020, and to incentivize individual taxpayers to shift away from the old regime, the scope of the full rebate on income tax under the new regime was expanded to ₹7 lakh in the 2023–24 Budget.

In contrast, the government has tried to make up for these tax losses to the exchequer in two ways: (1) by levying surcharges on the amount of income tax at various rates if the total income of the assessee exceeds ₹50 lakh, and (2) by imposing or hiking customs duty rates on various import items. The rate of surcharge ranges from 10 per cent for individuals with total income of ₹50 lakh to ₹1 crore, to as high as 37 per cent for individuals earning more than ₹5 crore (the peak rate was reduced to 25 per cent under the new regime in February 2023). Thus, the effective tax rate for individuals earning more than ₹5 crore has gone up from around 33 per cent to 42.7 per cent (39 per cent under the new tax regime).

The most important question to ask is, *Is the Indian economy at that stage of development where this strong redistribution policy can sustain and succeed?*

Lee Kuan Yew, former prime minister of Singapore and one of Asia's most respected leaders, talks about the necessary balance between equality and competitiveness in his book.[14] Here is an excerpt from it:

> At the end of the day, the basic problem of fairness in society will need to be solved. But first, we have to create the wealth. To do that, we must be competitive and have a good dose of the 'yang'. If we have too much of the 'yin' and over-redistribute the incomes of the successful, then we will blunt their drive to excel and succeed. . .

The Indian authorities must seriously consider if enough wealth has been created in the society to carry on with this redistribution path. Consumption is rising and savings have been falling in the economy for almost a decade now, and the redistribution policies tend to exacerbate these trends.

There is a widespread phenomenon among wealthy Indian families to send their children abroad for higher studies. The brain drain theory is not a myth in the country. If there is already a tendency to move out of the country, an incremental marginal tax of 42.7 per cent on individuals with income above ₹5 crore (39 per cent under the new tax regime) can lead to further exodus of the wealthiest from the country. These trends over a long period can prove disastrous and must be kept in check.

Impact of COVID-19 on Government Finances

As in most other nations, Indian policymakers too tried their best to contain the economic costs of this pandemic. The GoI announced multiple fiscal stimulus packages, which were supported by massive monetary easing by the RBI. GoI announced a series of support packages (financial and non-financial) since the end of March 2020. Beginning with relief measures relating to statutory and regulatory compliance matters on 24 March 2020 and the Pradhan Mantri Garib Kalyan Yojana (PMGKY) on 26 March 2020, the GoI got into action mode pretty quickly. Later, during the course of five days between 13 May 2020 and 17 May 2020, the GoI unveiled the five tranches under the scheme 'Aatmanirbhar Bharat Abhiyaan' to support the Indian economy in the fight against COVID-19. The package announced new measures totalling ₹11 tn. Including PMGKY, and with RBI's support, the policymakers announced a total support package worth ₹21 tn (over 10 per cent of GDP) for the Indian economy.

While this was comparable to the packages announced in many other countries, the details caused a lot of discomfort (as they did in many other major economies too). Most of the support was either in the form of additional liquidity injection by the RBI or credit/financial guarantee to MSMEs or credit enhancement to various parties. There were no major incentives in India for companies/MSMEs to retain employees or income support for people who lost their jobs. The effectiveness of the support was thus considered highly dissatisfactory, with the true fiscal stimulus being just 3–4 per cent of GDP, as per various estimates.

Like in other nations, the (reported) fiscal deficit of the general government expanded sharply in India as well—from 5.9 per cent of GDP each in FY18 and FY19 to a record high of 13.2 per cent of GDP in FY21. At the same time, the combined debt also surged from 70 per cent in the pre-COVID-19 years to 89.3 per cent of GDP in FY21.

While the fiscal deficit increased substantially, this was largely because of lower receipts rather than the result of higher spending. A comparison of budget estimates of FY21, which were prepared before the pandemic in February 2020, with the actual outcome for the year confirms that the total receipts of the government stood at ₹36.5 tn (25 per cent lower than BEs), while total spending amounted to ₹62.7 tn in FY21 (same as the BEs). One may rightly argue that spending would have been lower without the pandemic in FY21; however, the significance of lower receipts in pushing deficit higher cannot be denied.

While the Central government increased its spending dramatically in FY21—from the budgeted ₹30.4 tn to ₹35.1 tn—what is also important to note is that states' spending stood at ₹34.1 tn in FY21 vis-à-vis the target of ₹39.7 tn. In other words, while states' spending was around 30 per cent higher than the Centre's gross spending between FY16 and FY20, the former was lower than the latter in FY21. This is why it is important to analyse the combined finances of the Central and state governments.

Some other stark differences have emerged in the finances of the Central and state governments in the post-COVID-19 years, which demands attention. The quality of the Central government's spending has improved remarkably in FY22 and FY23, while it has weakened for states.

As discussed in Chapter 1, higher investments (or capital deepening) have been the key contributor to higher GDP growth in India over the past few decades. The concerted efforts of the Central government to push capex in the country during the post-COVID-19 period are commendable. Its infrastructure spending on defence, railways and roads and highways is budgeted to increase by 2.5x in three years, that is, between FY21 and FY24BE. If so, the share of capital spending in total expenditure increased from about 12 per cent in the previous decade to 15.6 per cent in FY22, 17.4 per cent in FY23RE and is budgeted to rise to an almost two-decade high of 22.2 per cent in FY24.

Such improvement in the quality of the Central government's expenditure is remarkable and has the potential to boost GDP growth in the country. Nevertheless, one must analyse it in conjunction with states and other relevant participants.

Unlike the Centre, the share of states' capex in their total spending is estimated to have averaged 15 per cent, lower than 17 per cent in the pre-COVID-19 years. Further, a large part of the increase in the Centre's capex is a reallocation from central public sector enterprises (CPSEs). Prior to the pandemic, a lot of capex was done through the CPSEs. Excluding the department of food and public distribution (which included expenditure by the Food Corporation of India), CPSEs' capex peaked at 3.3 per cent of GDP in FY09. It fell to 2.3 per cent of GDP in FY11 and remained there for the entire 2010s decade. In FY22, CPSEs' capex fell to 1.6 per cent of GDP and further to 1.3 per cent of GDP in FY23RE.

Thus, while the Centre's capex has increased, the aggregate public sector's capex stood at an eight-year low of 5.7 per cent of GDP in FY23, compared to 6.0–6.5 per cent in the pre-COVID-19 years. Since CPSEs are included in the corporate sector in this book, there is a clear connection between the fall in corporate investments and the rise in the Centre's capex. On net basis, since there was no rise in India's total investment rate, the boost to India's productivity growth due to the Centre's efforts is not definite.

Overall, COVID-19 not only hurt the government's ability to grow its spending faster in the post-COVID-19 period but also weakened the financial positions of the household and unlisted corporate sectors. Listed companies, on the contrary, came out much stronger from COVID-19. At the same time, the improvement in India's external position in FY21 was unparalleled. What do these improvements mean for India's growth? How are the economic decisions of the domestic participants connected with those in the external sector? This is what I discuss in the next chapter.

Key Lessons from the Chapter

- Although the GoI finances get the most attention, state Budgets are larger. Almost 60 per cent of all government receipts are apportioned to states, which also account for a similar share in the total expenditure of the government.
- Between FY91 and FY20, the share of direct taxes in the total receipts of the government (Centre + states) has increased, while the share of debt receipts has fallen.
- Interest and education and health are the two largest spending areas of the government and the share of the latter has remained stable at 16–17 per cent during the past three decades. The share of expenditure on national security has fallen from 12 per cent to 10 per cent during the period, while it has increased sharply on account of pensions, from 4 per cent in the early 1990s to 9 per cent.
- An analysis of adjusted fiscal deficit confirms that (1) off-Budget transactions have gained prominence during the past fifteen years since the Fiscal Responsibility and Budget Management Act came into existence in 2003 to narrow India's fiscal deficit; (2) the adjusted fiscal deficit of the Central government was never 3 per cent of GDP or below—the target set under the FRBM Act; and (3) after easing to 4.3 per cent of GDP in FY17 (the third lowest since 1980), the AFD of the Union government has risen

by 0.5pp of GDP every year to 5.7 per cent of GDP in FY20, marking the highest deficit since FY12.
- Although the RFD is very different from the AFD, the official estimates of the combined outstanding liabilities of the government incorporate most of the required adjustments. A look at the long-term trends in the outstanding liabilities of the government suggests that while the liabilities are lower than the peak of 83 per cent of GDP reached in the early 2000s, they have broadly gone nowhere during the past three and a half decades and have stayed at close to 70 per cent of GDP during the period. It, however, increased to an all-time high in FY21 on account of the pandemic.
- The BJP government presented itself as a 'pro-poor government' rather than as a '*suit boot ki sarkar*' during its first tenure between FY15 and FY19. This was also matched in action—with higher allocation towards rural spending, which has been in the form of farm loan waivers, direct income support and strengthening of social security benefits for the poor/unemployed sections of the society during the past few years.
- These schemes or policies are very attractive from the social and political perspectives; however, these schemes tend to affect productivity growth adversely, reduce fiscal flexibility and also incentivize consumption over savings.
- Notwithstanding the Central government's concerted efforts to boost capex, it is unlikely to create additional growth, as the aggregate public sector's capex was the lowest in eight years in FY23. Higher Centre's capex was a mirror image of lower corporate capex, as CPSEs' capex has declined sharply in the recent years.
- Overall, it is very likely that the average growth in the government's spending over the next few years will be slower than in the pre-COVID-19 years; this will help meet the fiscal deficit target at the cost of GDP growth.

Chapter 5

THE CONNECTION BETWEEN DOMESTIC PARTICIPANTS AND THE EXTERNAL SECTOR

Non-economist: India is such a conservative country. If there is a lack of investments, why can't we bring in foreign capital and increase investments? We need capital.

Me: Yes, we are a capital scarce country, but bringing in money would not necessarily lead to higher investments. Availability of finances is very different from investments.

Non-economist: Alien language again. If you get FDI, does that not lead to higher investments? India now has the fifth largest stock of foreign exchange reserves in the world. What are we doing with it? Why can't we use those reserves for domestic investments?

Me: No, large FDI inflows do not necessarily lead to higher investments. It depends on what happens to the existing investments in the country. Also, we must be careful about being complacent regarding high forex reserves. It is not so straightforward, to convert forex reserves into investments. The global economy has become fragile and exchange rate markets appear to be a new war zone.

Non-economist: Such conservatism will not take us anywhere.

Me: And what if too much aggression takes us down? Currency risks are very real and history suggests that such mistakes could be fatal for any nation. More important, external account transactions are way more complicated than suggested in daily discussions. The authorities must undertake serious deliberations and make their choices carefully.

In this truly globalized environment, the impact of relatively free-flowing capital on the financial and real economy in the recipient nation can be complicated. Being one of the most favoured investment destinations, India has also received a large amount of foreign capital in the past few years. However, its implications for the real economy may or may not be as significant. Most important, all external policies work primarily by changing the equilibrium among domestic participants. This chapter is dedicated to understanding the connections between external policies and the behaviour of the domestic agents.

The concept of a closed economy is unreal these days. All major economies in the world are open to foreign transactions. In the same way that fiscal accounts record all transactions of the government with the rest of the economy, balance of payments records all transactions done by a nation with the rest of the world (RoW). BoP consists of two major accounts: the current account and the financial (or capital) account. In a strict sense, capital account transactions record non-financial assets and liabilities and capital transfers which are different from those on the financial account, which records financial assets and liabilities. However, since capital account transactions are very small, these two accounts are used interchangeably throughout this book.

The sixth edition of the *Balance of Payments and International Investment Position Manual* (BPM6) published by the IMF says: 'The balance of payments is a statistical statement that summarizes transactions between residents and non-residents during a period. It consists of the goods and services account, the primary income account, the secondary income account, the capital account, and the financial account.' Appendix 13 provides a short description of all the major components of BoP.

The current account balance and the financial account balance, by definition, match each other inversely. It means that if a nation is a net importer of goods and services, it will be a net importer of foreign capital as well. If a nation runs a deficit on the current account, it has to run a surplus (or net inflows) on the financial account. This is why it is called the *balance* of payments account. The financial account is the obverse of the current account. This is true for all countries at any point in time. It is not possible for any nation to run a current account surplus with net financial account inflows, or vice versa. This is a simple but important point, which needs further explanation.

Consider a two-nation world—China and the US. Let's assume that China exports goods and services worth $500 bn to the US and imports goods and services amounting to only $300 bn from the US. This makes China a net exporter of goods and services amounting to $200 bn and the US a net importer of goods and services worth $200 bn. Let's assume for simplicity's sake that the income accounts—primary and secondary—are balanced (we will, however, see later that this assumption is incorrect). It would mean that China runs a current account surplus (CAS) of $200 bn and the US runs a current account deficit (CAD) of $200 bn.

The question then is, *'What would Chinese exporters do with the excess US dollars earned and, simultaneously, how will the US finance its CAD?'* Since Chinese exporters cannot use US dollars in the domestic economy, they have only one possible option. With excess US dollars at their disposal, Chinese exporters could become lenders to US importers, who will now become borrowers. In order to finance the CAD, US importers will issue financial securities (in the form of bonds, equity, debentures, etc.) to Chinese exporters. The latter, with their US dollar earnings, would be happy to invest in those financial assets to earn returns. However, these inter-border transactions would now be part of the financial account, not the current account. Chinese exporters will export their US dollar earnings and US importers will import capital to fund their CAD. Thus

China runs a surplus on the current account and is also a net lender to the US (or to the RoW, in this case), implying net capital outflows from China to the US. On the contrary, the US runs a deficit on the current account and it is also a net borrower on the financial account, implying net capital inflows. In short, a nation that runs a CAS is a net lender to the RoW, and a nation with a CAD is a net borrower (or has inflows) on the financial account.

When financial assets are exchanged between two countries, the lenders earn an interest income while the borrowers incur interest costs. These earnings and payments will reflect in the primary income accounts and the current accounts, respectively, of China and the US. Therefore, our earlier assumption of balanced income accounts was incorrect. These transactions will widen China's CAS and the US's CAD, which will either be offset via goods and services transactions within their current accounts or adjusted by obverse transactions under their financial accounts or by a combination of both these adjustments.

In any case, the BoP account will eventually *balance out* for both nations. The current account balance will be exactly matched by the financial account balance with the opposite sign, both cancelling each other and thus balancing out the BoP accounts of each nation with the RoW.

In the real world, however, there is another option available to exporters in many economies. Although US importers will have to issue financial securities to Chinese exporters, this could be done indirectly. As mentioned above, Chinese exporters could directly invest in US securities, and the BoP accounts of the two nations would balance out. However, with imperfect capital mobility in China, implying restrictions on capital account outflows, Chinese exporters can also convert their US dollar earnings into the local currency, called Chinese yuan or renminbi (CNY/RMB), at their central bank (or the monetary authority), the People's Bank of China (PBoC). This will lead to an increase in foreign exchange reserves held at PBoC, against which the central bank will have to release local currency.

The question, however, is, *'How will China's BoP then balance?'* When PBoC buys US dollars and increases its FXR, PBoC will invest its FXR in foreign currency assets (US dollar assets, in this case). The outflows from FXR will be recorded under 'reserve assets' within China's financial account. Thus, the outflows on China's financial account will once again match the surplus on China's current balance account. In other words, while China will add to its FXR, it will be recorded as outflows under BoP because China (via PBoC instead of via private players) has lent the money to foreigners. Also, PBoC is unlikely to invest directly in the US importers' securities. Instead, it will buy US treasuries, which will indirectly finance US's CAD.

This example is relevant for India too. Unlike the US Federal Reserve or the European Central Bank (ECB), the RBI intervenes in the currency markets via FXR. Notably, it is not true that only central banks of the emerging and developing economies intervene in the currency markets via FXR policies. There are many central banks in the developed countries—such as Central Bank of the Republic of China, Taiwan (CBC) and Swiss National Bank (SNB)—that intervene in their currency markets through their FXR policies. In simple words, FXR is an important tool for central banks for managing (or influencing) their own country's currency.

This is what the BPM6 says about reserve assets:

> Reserve assets are those external assets that are readily available to and controlled by monetary authorities for meeting balance of payments financing needs, for intervention in exchange markets to affect the currency exchange rate, and for other related purposes (such as maintaining confidence in the currency and the economy, and serving as a basis for foreign borrowing).

Unlike the central banks of China, Taiwan and Switzerland, the RBI does not manage the level of the Indian rupee against the US dollar, or any other currency. Instead, RBI intervenes in the currency market to manage sharp movements and volatility in the Indian rupee.

Further, while the current account is entirely open everywhere in the world, many countries—especially those that intervene in the currency markets—have restrictions on their financial or capital accounts. These restrictions are generally skewed against capital outflows, though capital inflows are relatively unrestricted (with few limits) in most economies. In contrast, countries that do not intervene in the currency market have perfect mobility in their financial account, and their current account deficit is determined by the financial account inflows. Countries such as the US, the UK, Spain and Greece fall in this category. If foreign capital inflows in these countries increase, their current account deficits will also rise accordingly, and vice versa. Nevertheless, as the Theory of Everything suggests, current account balances are a by-product of domestic savings and total investments. Therefore, in perfectly open nations, foreign capital inflows affect domestic savings (via consumption) and/or investments, which eventually get translated into current account balances.

For countries where the central banks intervene in the currency markets via FXR policies, although there are no restrictions on the current account, it can be effectively manipulated by their respective central banks, which will decide how much of the foreign capital inflows will be allowed to stay in the domestic markets. This manipulation is also effectively achieved by influencing domestic savings and investments.

For instance, if India witnesses net inflows of $100 bn a year, by choosing to add $50 bn to its FXR, the RBI effectively constrains India's CAD to $50 bn. Any decision to accumulate/reduce FXR is effectively a decision to restrict/widen CAD. Not only do these decisions affect domestic savings and investment balances but they also have implications for the INR and other domestic financial markets. The RBI's actions will not only decide the domestic liquidity, and thus its impact on various financial assets, but will also affect domestic savings, investments and, finally, India's CAD. The FXR policy thus becomes the most important indicator for understanding India's external sector.

It also suggests that foreign capital flows or financial account balances are more important than current account balances; more so because the exogenous factors (related to global liquidity and sentiments) are more influential when it comes to the financial account than the current account. Surprisingly, most of the research or economic arguments is focused on India's CAD (explaining the exports and imports) than on foreign capital flows (including FXR, FDI inflows, debt and equity flows).

Abundant foreign capital inflows can ensure a large supply of financing; however, whether it leads to higher domestic investments, and thus, GDP growth, is determined by the nature of the flows, the central bank's decision to allow those flows to stay in the domestic market, and their impact on financial assets. As discussed above, for countries where central banks are absent from the currency markets, the current account balance is determined by foreign capital inflows, which affect domestic savings and investments.

Because of these reasons, this chapter begins with a discussion on the role of FXR in India (or any other country where the central bank intervenes in the currency market).

Foreign Exchange Reserves and Domestic Money Supply

Unlike China, India is a net importer of goods and services and runs a CAD. In fact, although India is the fifth[1] largest FXR holder in the world—following China, Japan, Switzerland and Russia—it is the only nation among the top five FXR holders to have a CAD. All other large FXR holders run a surplus on their current accounts and are net lenders to the rest of the world. India, in stark contrast, is the only large FXR holder which is a net borrower from the rest of the world.

How did this happen? Foreign capital inflows in India have outpaced its CAD. For sixteen consecutive years up to FY20, India had run a persistent deficit on its current account. However, its financial capital inflows have outpaced its CAD, helping India to add to its FXR in thirteen of the past sixteen years. Between FY05 and FY20, India's aggregate CAD amounted to $545 bn. However, actual foreign capital inflows totalled $930 bn during the period, implying a net addition of $385 bn in India's FXR. India's total FXR has thus risen from $113 bn in March 2004 to $478 bn in March 2020.

A country can add to its FXR by either running a surplus on the current account or if its foreign capital inflows are more than its CAD. FXR, thus, is a balancing figure between foreign capital flows and the current account balance. If a country runs a CAD but witnesses higher foreign capital inflows, it means that its FXR has increased, which will be reflected as outflows in the financial account under BoP, since FXR is eventually parked in foreign assets/securities. Similarly, if the country runs a CAS and also attracts foreign capital inflows, the accretion to FXR would again enter into the financial account as outflows to balance the BoP account. Lastly, if foreign capital inflows are lower than the CAD or if foreign capital outflows are higher than the CAS, the country will lose its FXR, which will reflect as an addition (withdrawal from foreign assets) in the financial account under BoP.

Going back to the previous example of China and the US, there was a point when the PBoC collected US dollar and released CNY into the domestic market. This was the stage when the PBoC influenced the currency market. When China's BoP surplus is very high, and thus Chinese exporters are flush with USDs, the PBoC faces two choices: (1) convert those

USD earnings into CNY and add to its FXR, or (2) decide not to intervene. The latter option, however, is unavailable under an imperfect capital mobility regime. If PBoC does not allow exporters to freely invest their USD earnings in foreign assets, it is PBoC's responsibility to convert the earnings into domestic currency. Otherwise, Chinese exporters would have no incentive to export goods and services and earn FXR; or they will import an equivalent amount of goods and services using their FX earnings, which would have serious repercussions on China's economic growth. Therefore, PBoC has no option but to convert the foreign exchange earnings into CNY.

Under the first option, a nation's FXR policy has a direct bearing on its domestic money supply—narrow (M0) and broad (different nations have different measures of broad money supply: China and the US have M2; it is M3 in the eurozone and M4 in India and the UK). When India faces a deluge of foreign capital inflows that outpace its CAD, the RBI adds to its FXR and supplies an equivalent amount of domestic currency (INR) in the system. Higher demand of INR assets (leading to the deluge of FX inflows) leads to an appreciation bias in INR, which is at least partly negated by the RBI's actions to suck out dollar liquidity and supply rupees. However, the RBI may also choose to neutralize the expansionary effect of FXR on India's money supply by a process called 'sterilization'. Should the RBI not want to add further rupee supply in the domestic market but purchase USDs, the impact could be sterilized by selling an equivalent amount of domestic (government) securities. This will keep money supply unchanged, but will help reduce the USD supply in the domestic markets. It will, however, put pressure on the domestic bond market.

Exhibit 5.1 details the role of FXR (or acquisition of net foreign assets) in India's narrow (or high-powered) money supply, called M0. For any central bank, there are two options for creating money in the domestic market—by acquiring foreign assets and by acquiring domestic assets (generally government securities). When a central bank acquires these assets, it releases an equivalent amount of domestic currency, which creates money supply (M0). In India, it's the prerogative of the RBI to decide the rate at which it wants M0 to grow in any particular year. Of these two sources, foreign capital inflows are out of RBI's control. If there are excessive inflows in one year, the RBI will decide on the amount of foreign capital it wants to purchase and/or sterilize, depending on its likely impact on M0 and the rupee. To offset the appreciating pressure on the rupee (led by high foreign capital inflows), the RBI may choose to accumulate FXR, which will create M0, unless it is sterilized by reducing the RBI's holdings of government securities. Therefore, if there is a large supply of foreign capital inflows in the country adding to FXR, it becomes the primary tool for creating M0. If FXR accretion is less than the desired growth in M0, the RBI buys domestic assets to meet its M0 growth target. Foreign capital inflows, therefore, decide the ability of the RBI to purchase/sell domestic assets. This was apparent during FY21 when, notwithstanding almost unanimous demand from all sections of the economy, a strong surge in FX inflows curtailed the ability of the RBI to buy large amounts of government securities.

When India ran a CAS between FY02 and FY04, it also attracted foreign capital inflows. Consequently, India's FXR tripled from $40 bn in December 2000 to about $120 bn in April 2004, implying an average addition of $2 bn per month during that period. Since the acquisition of foreign assets was too large and too fast, the RBI sterilized those operations to avoid its expansionary impact on M0, and thus, on inflation. Consequently, while RBI's net foreign assets increased from ₹1.7 tn in December 2000 to ₹5 tn in April 2004, its holdings of government securities declined from ₹1.5 tn to ₹132 bn during the period. Further, RBI's other assets (loans and advances, and investments in non-government securities) also reduced, from ₹800 bn to ₹200 bn during the period. With

Exhibit 5.1: Domestic money supply, foreign exchange reserves (FXR) and INR–USD rate

	Change in reserve money (M0, INR tn)				Change in broad money (M3, INR tn)				Change in FXR stock (US$ bn)	INR–US$ rate* (% YoY)
	M0	Rupee securities	FX assets	FXR/M0 (%)	M3	Rupee securities	FX assets	FX assets/ M3 (%)		
FY00	0.2	0	0.3	131.3	1.4	0.5	0.3	19.4	5.5	3
FY01	0.2	0.1	0.3	137.7	1.9	0.7	0.4	23.4	4.2	5.4
FY02	0.2	−0.1	0.6	333.9	1.9	0.8	0.6	33.1	11.8	4.4
FY03	0.3	−0.3	1	314.1	2.2	0.9	0.8	37.6	22	1.5
FY04	0.5	−0.8	1.3	232	2.9	0.7	1.3	46.2	36.9	−5.0
FY05	0.8	−0.5	1.3	157.8	2.4	0.1	1.2	51.1	28.6	−2.2
FY06	0.8	0.2	0.6	72.7	4.7	0.1	0.8	16.2	10.1	−1.5
FY07	1.3	−0.1	1.9	148.9	5.9	0.7	1.9	31.7	47.6	2.2
FY08	1.7	−1.7	3.7	221	7.1	0.7	3.8	54	110.5	−11.0
FY09	0.8	2	0.4	56.2	7.8	3.8	0.6	7.3	−57.7	14.2
FY10	1.6	1.4	−0.5	−30.4	8.1	3.9	−0.7	−8.8	27.1	3.2
FY11	1.9	1.5	1	50.7	9	3.1	1.1	12.4	25.8	−4.0
FY12	1.4	2.2	1.4	102.6	8.8	3.9	1.5	17.1	−10.4	5.2
FY13	0.8	0.5	0.9	109.1	10	3.4	0.9	9.2	−2.4	13.5
FY14	2.2	1.1	2.4	112.2	11.3	3.4	2.9	25.5	12.2	11.2

	Change in reserve money (M0, INR tn)				Change in broad money (M3, INR tn)					Change in FXR stock (US$ bn)	INR–US$ rate* (% YoY)
	M0	Rupee securities	FX assets	FXR/M0 (%)	M3	Rupee securities	FX assets	FX assets/M3 (%)			
FY15	2	−3.3	3.2	165.9	10.3	−0.4	3.3	31.6		37.4	1.1
FY16	2.5	0.6	2.6	101.6	10.7	2.3	2.8	26.5		18.5	7.1
FY17	−2.8	2	0.1	−4.9	11.7	6.2	0.2	2.1		9.8	2.4
FY18	5.2	−1.4	3.6	70.1	11.7	1.4	3.6	31.1		54.6	−3.9
FY19	3.5	3.3	0.9	25	14.7	3.9	1.5	10.1		−11.7	8.5
FY20	2.6	1.9	7.4	286.2	13.7	5.7	7.3	53.4		64.9	1.4
FY21	5.7	1.1	6.1	106.8	20.4	8.9	7.8	38		99.2	4.7
FY22	4.7	3.5	2.4	51.8	16.5	6.3	2.8	16.7		30.3	0.4
FY23	2.6	0.0	1.4	56.8	18.5	6.9	−0.1	−0.5		−28.9	7.9

* A rise (fall) implies depreciation (appreciation) in INR against USD

Source: RBI, author's estimates

RBI almost out of government securities in 2004, the GoI introduced dated securities and treasury bills under the new market stabilization scheme (MSS) which were then used to carry out the sterilization operations and drain out the excess liquidity through RBI.

Although India returned to a deficit on the current account from FY05 onward, its accretion of FXR continued unabated till FY08. As can be seen in Exhibit 5.1, incremental FX assets accounted for more than 100 per cent of the increase in M0 every year between FY00 and FY08 (except in FY06, when it contributed 73 per cent to the change in M0) and more than 200 per cent from FY02 to FY04 and FY08.

Although the central bank holds control over the money printing machine, the true power of money creation lies in the hands of the commercial banks under the modern monetary system. This is clear from the fact that M0 (or the narrow money supply, entirely and solely controlled by a central bank) is only about 20 per cent of M3 (the broad money supply) in India. This is the case almost everywhere in the world. The saying that 'commercial banks can create money out of thin air' is true, because the modern monetary system allows commercial banks to create money through their power of lending, which can be done in a jiffy. What is more, there is no limit to this money creation by commercial banks. A classic research paper[2] by the Bank of England in 2014 shows, in sharp contrast to conventional wisdom, that loans create deposits, and not the other way round.

In India FXR not only accounted for more than 100 per cent of M0 but its average contribution to M3 was as high as 39 per cent between FY02 and FY08, and ranged from 16 per cent to 54 per cent during the period. Had RBI not sterilized those foreign capital inflows, India's money supply growth would have been much higher, creating inflationary pressures in the economy as too much money would have chased too few goods and services. With little FX interventions, it would have also strengthened INR and adversely impacted its external trade balance.

Changes in FXR have a bigger bearing on currency movements than on the current account balance. Economists are often accused of linking currency movements with the current account balance. That is not true. Had that been the case, the rupee would have depreciated every year since FY05. Movements in the domestic currency are related to foreign capital flows more than to CAD. Therefore, if capital inflows outpace CAD, RBI's intervention in the FX market and its (FXR) policies will determine its impact on the INR.

All this does not mean that FXR is the only variable that determines currency movements. Had that been the case, INR would have appreciated in fifteen of the last twenty years. In reality, the INR strengthened only six times between FY00 and FY23—FY04 to FY06, FY08, FY11 (when CAD was as high as 2.7 per cent of GDP) and FY18 (when CAD was 1.8 per cent of GDP). A number of factors impact currency movements. During the past two decades, India has witnessed a reduction in its FXR only five times—in FY09, FY12, FY13, FY19 and FY23. The rupee had weakened exceptionally (with an average of 10 per cent) during these years.

It is worth repeating that foreign currency inflows have a direct impact on the ability of a central bank to intervene in the domestic government securities (G-sec) market. If the accretion of FXR is large enough to push M0 growth higher than desired, the RBI's hands will be tied when it comes to buying G-secs. More likely in fact, the RBI will have to sell G-sec to manage the money supply. On the other hand, if foreign capital inflows are much lower than required to increase M0 at the desired pace, the RBI will have to conduct open market operations to buy government securities. The inevitable impact of these transactions on the bond market is only secondary.

The FXR policy is thus a primary tool for many central banks in the world to manage or influence the currency markets.

Rising FXR Brings Back an Old Debate

Prior to the exceptional FY21, the only year in its entire post-liberalization history when India added $100 bn in a year to its FXR was FY08, when it increased by $111 bn—from $199 billion at end-FY07 to $310 billion. The domestic growth miracle, amid the global boom, made India one of the fastest growing economies in the world. Although India ran a CAD of 1.3 per cent of GDP that year, the rupee strengthened 11 per cent against the US dollar in FY08, the only year in which it registered double-digit appreciation in the past two decades. Considering the strong rise in India's FXR, Justin Yifu Lin, then the top economist and a senior vice-president at the World Bank, suggested that India should use its large pool of FXR to fund infrastructure projects.[3]

Absolute changes, however, can be misleading. An increase of ₹10 over a base of ₹100 and of ₹1,000 can lead to very different conclusions. Similarly, while India added the highest amount to its FXR in FY08 and FY21, the pace of accretion to its FXR was the highest during the FY02–FY04 period when, as mentioned above, FXR almost tripled, from $40 bn to $120 bn. It was around this time that the idea of using FXR for domestic investments was first initiated by the Planning Commission. Since India's real GDP growth averaged only about 4 per cent from FY01 to FY04, P. Chidambaram, the finance minister between May 2004 and November 2008, floated the idea of setting up a special purpose vehicle (SPV) to utilize India's rising FXR to fund infrastructure projects in the Union Budget of 2005–06 (presented in February 2005). Although it was not implemented, the proposal was much debated during the years of high accretion to FXR. With India adding about $100 bn in FY21 and with an FXR stock of more than $600 bn by March 2022, the debate has got a new life again.

However, it is difficult to use FXR to fund domestic investments. Not only is the beneficial impact, in terms of real GDP growth, unlikely to be very large, but the related macro-adjustments may also not be acceptable to the policymakers.

Let's assume that the government funds infrastructure projects worth, say, ₹1 tn, and increases its fiscal deficit by an equivalent amount. However, to ensure that this additional deficit and borrowings do not lead to higher interest rates and crowd out private investments, the entire amount would have to be financed by the RBI. Instead of printing currency to finance a higher fiscal deficit and create inflationary pressures, the RBI could choose to keep its balance sheet unchanged by reducing FXR (say, by $12 bn in this case, assuming an exchange rate of USD1 = INR83) to fund the fiscal deficit. This would keep RBI's balance sheet unchanged, mitigate inflationary fears and also keep interest rates under check with an increase of ₹1 tn worth of new infrastructure investments. There is no agreement on the outcome of such a scheme.

Dr Shankar Acharya[4] argues that infrastructure investment largely focuses on the non-tradable sector and is not import-intensive. Thus the additional expenditure would not lead to a significant decline in FXR, and RBI's balance sheet would expand, leading to inflationary fears.

Dr Arvind Panagariya on the other hand says, 'the import intensity of infrastructure is virtually irrelevant to the final outcome'.[5] If infrastructure projects are import-intensive (a power project, for instance), he explained, the RBI can buy GoI bonds against $12 bn, and that $12 bn could be used to import the required goods and services for infrastructure projects. This would lead to higher CAD and a lower financial account, by $12 bn each. However, RBI's balance sheet would be unchanged, keeping inflation under check, and domestic interest rates would also be unchanged. The final outcome would be an increase in the infrastructure investments, in fiscal deficit, in government debt and in CAD, and lower FXR by $12 bn.

According to Dr Panagariya, even if the infrastructure projects carried out under this scheme are in the non-tradable sectors, the RBI can keep its balance sheet unchanged by selling $12 bn to the domestic agents and suck out ₹1 tn in exchange, which can then be used to buy GoI bonds to finance the infrastructure projects. The domestic agents then will be left with a reduced demand for domestic output and the holding of $12 bn. Since the market participants cannot utilize USD domestically, the reduced output of goods and services (worth ₹1 tn, which was sucked out by the RBI) will be met by higher imports (using $12 bn). Thus, CAD, fiscal deficit and government debt would rise with lower FXR.

The bottom line, therefore, is that irrespective of what happens, the infrastructure spending (or extra fiscal deficit) would eventually be financed by a higher CAD. The critical question, as put forth by Dr Panagariya in his book,[6] is 'whether the RBI is willing to follow an exchange rate policy that would allow injecting extra FXR into the economy each year'.

Further, as the RBI decides to inject the additional $12 bn into the markets, it could potentially lead to a stronger rupee (due to higher demand for INR). In this case, the private agents will be less willing to hold USD supplied by the RBI at the same exchange rate. A stronger rupee will make imports cheaper and exports dearer, creating conditions for a wider CAD.

These results can easily be arrived at using the Theory of Everything equation, where total investments in an economy are equal to the sum of domestic savings and CAD. Looking at the financing of domestic investments, the question may arise, *'Shouldn't the equation include foreign capital inflows (or the financial account balance) instead of CAD?'* The answer is no, because investments in the national account system imply physical goods and services (Lesson#1 in Chapter 1).

FXR is effectively the residual of excess foreign capital inflows over CAD, which is eventually invested in foreign assets and enters as outflows in the financial account under BoP. FXR, therefore, does not add anything to domestic investments. If the equation uses the financial account balance instead of CAD, it will include the changes in FXR, which is incorrect. Therefore, what matters for domestic investment is CAD, not foreign capital inflows.

Going back to the equation, it can be rearranged as:

Core fiscal deficit = Private surplus + CAD

The equation suggests that if the core fiscal deficit rises (as the government decides to spend an additional ₹1 tn on infrastructure projects—tradable or non-tradable), private surplus will go up or CAD will widen, the two outcomes that we arrived at in the above example. If the authorities (fiscal and monetary) wish to keep the private sector balance unchanged, CAD will widen. However, if the RBI chooses to keep CAD unchanged, it will result in higher private sector balance (by reducing private sector spending, since it is now left with USD, which cannot be used domestically).

Also, the addition of $100 bn in FY21, over and above the $108 bn of the previous three years, is not really too fast an accumulation of FXR. The jump in FXR stock from $413 bn in March 2019 to $607 bn in March 2022 implies an average growth of 14 per cent during the three-year period, which is less than half the average growth of 36 per cent seen during the four-year period between FY01 and FY05. Further, unlike during FY02–FY04, India's accumulation of FXR in recent years is on the back of higher capital inflows instead of on account of current account surpluses (except in FY21). There is a large difference between these two sources of FXR accretion. The former consists purely of borrowings, with an obligation to be repaid or withdrawn, depending on the nature of capital inflows. The latter, however, are the nation's assets. The former, therefore, are a weaker source of FXR accumulation than the latter.

Coming back to the debate on the use of FXR to fund domestic investments to push GDP growth higher, Deepak Lal, Suman Berry and Devendra Kumar Pant created a sensation in 2003 when they claimed that the RBI's policy of accumulating FXR cost the country 2.7pp to 3.7pp of GDP growth per annum during the 1990s decade.[7] Had the capital flows been entirely absorbed by the economy, the authors argued, India's average real GDP growth would have been 8.5 per cent per annum in the 1990s decade, against the actual average GDP growth of 5.8 per cent. Further, the authors claimed that real GDP growth would have averaged 9.5 per cent had the bond-financed fiscal deficit been eliminated.

However, Vijay Joshi and Sanjeev Sanyal refuted those claims as they pointed out huge errors in the conclusions reached by Lal, Berry and Pant.[8] In particular, Joshi and Sanyal estimated that the additional real GDP growth would only be about 0.4 per cent a year higher had all capital flows been entirely absorbed by the economy, and FXR would not have accumulated at all. They said:

> If the entire increase in reserves had been absorbed into investment each year, the ratio of investment to GDP averaged over the decade would thus have been 1.2 percent higher than it actually was. The incremental net capital output ratio (ICOR) in the 1990s was 2.8. This implies, assuming a constant ICOR, that the increase in India's growth rate of GDP would have equalled 1.2/2.8, or 0.4 percent a year (approximately) over the decade, a far cry from the Lal, Bery, and Pant estimate of 2.7 percent.[9]

The question then is, how did Lal et al. arrive at such high estimates?

Joshi and Sanyal highlighted the underlying fallacy in their assertion too. Lal et al. assumed that if capital inflows had been fully absorbed without any sterilization, S–I gap would have increased by the sum of the net capital inflows and private remittances each year. They missed the fact that a part of capital and remittance inflows (equaling CAD) was already absorbed and thus, S–I gap would increase only to the extent of foreign exchange accumulation.

Things have not changed much since. Although India has added FXR worth approximately 3.7 per cent of GDP in FY21 and average accretion was 1.7 per cent of GDP between FY18 and FY22, the increase in India's annual real GDP growth would have been 0.4 percentage points (with an ICOR of around 4.3x during the period, excluding FY21 when real GDP contracted) had all capital inflows been absorbed into the financial markets.

Even this small increase, however, represents the upper bound, as absorption of all FXR by the domestic economy would have altered India's exchange rate adversely—also highlighted by Joshi and Sanyal. Similarly, had India not added to its FXR during the past five years and entered COVID-19 with an FXR stock of $360 bn instead of $477 bn, the behaviour of foreign investors might have not been so favourable towards India.

In sum, using FXR for domestic investments will at best lead to a small increase in the country's GDP growth at the cost of higher CAD, higher fiscal deficit and higher government debt, and most likely a stronger rupee.

FDI as a Source of Higher Investments

Another live debate is about the composition of foreign capital inflows. Foreign portfolio investments (FPIs) are an example of short-term volatile capital inflows (also called 'hot money'), and foreign direct investments (FDI) are an example of stable, long-term money. The IMF defines FPIs as the flows that *provide a direct way to access financial markets, and thus can provide liquidity and flexibility*. FDIs, on the other hand, are defined as funds that *may supply additional contributions such as know-how, technology, management, and marketing.* The former, therefore, are volatile in nature, while the latter are a more stable form of foreign capital flows. Furthermore, enterprises in a direct investment relationship are more likely to trade with and finance each other, while portfolio investors typically have less of a role in decision-making at the enterprise. It is, therefore, argued that FDIs are the preferred form of foreign capital flows in any country. However, the beneficial impact of FDIs on economic activity is not guaranteed.

A look at the share of FDI in total outstanding foreign capital flows in major Asian economies suggests that their share in total foreign capital liabilities has increased in all nations in the 2010s decade compared to the 2000s decade, and they accounted for between 40 per cent and 50 per cent of all foreign capital liabilities in 2020. From as low as 20 per cent in the early 2000s decade, the share of FDI in India's foreign capital liabilities averaged 33 per cent in the 2010s decade and touched 40/39 per cent in CY20/CY21. In China it has been between 50 per cent and 60 per cent of all foreign capital liabilities.

Large FDI inflows are generally seen as a very good sign and as a source of domestic investments. But do they always boost GDP growth?

In a paper written in 1995, Dr Pronab Sen explained the specific set of conditions that must be obtained for FDI to make a positive impact on domestic output.[10] By linking the potential impact of FDI on interest rates, imports, domestic savings (or consumption) and investments, Dr Sen showed that FDI leads to deterioration in the trade balance (and thus, BoP), which is then required to be offset by various government initiatives to witness any positive output effect. This was his conclusion:

> The real benefit of FDI lies in augmenting the level of investments in the economy and thereby contributing to output expansion and growth. However, given the negative BoP effects, the government has to take collateral steps to

ensure that the economy does not run into a serious foreign exchange problem . . .

Among the possible counter-policies Dr Sen suggests that could be adopted by the government are: (1) higher foreign borrowings, (2) contractionary monetary policy, (3) lower public investments by the same quantum as the domestic component of FDI, (4) weaker currency, and (5) allowing foreign investors to remit more foreign exchange in the form of equity than is required for their direct imports. All these options are policies to neutralize deterioration in the BoP due to FDI inflows. However, some of these options (2 and 3) will achieve this by hurting GDP growth, thus effectively negating the positive impact of FDI on domestic output.

Dr Sen's paper was published before the East Asian crisis, when FDIs were considered a major source of domestic investments in the East Asian miracle from the 1960s to 1980s. His analysis suggested that the interlinkages between various participants—impact of external capital flows on the behaviour of domestic economic agents—matter more than the headlines.

While currency depreciation will be discussed later in this chapter, it is also important to note that a large part of FDI inflows in the recent years in most countries has been in the non-manufacturing sector (especially information technology [IT] and retail), which have a weaker positive impact on domestic growth.

The quality of FDI has deteriorated in the recent decades, and therefore its positive impact on growth has weakened too. The primary reason for this deterioration is the falling share of FDIs in the manufacturing sector and its rising share in the services sector (especially in retail and IT/telecom). Further, FDIs in the past many years have not led to significantly higher new investments in the recipient countries. Instead, a large part of these FDIs have been in the equity or mergers and acquisitions areas, which simply replace existing investments. In other words, recent FDI inflows are related more to brownfield projects than to greenfield projects.

China, in the 1990s and the early 2000s decade, is a striking example of how FDI can boost domestic investments, and thus growth. This was because (1) China's gross FDI inflows in the early 1990s were as high as 6 per cent of GDP—by far the highest among all Asian economies; and (2) more than 65 per cent of all FDI inflows between the early 1990s and 2006 were in the industrial (including manufacturing) sector. In contrast, FDI inflows for the East Asian tigers, such as South Korea and Taiwan, were rarely above 2.5 per cent of GDP during their high-growth phases between the 1960s and mid-1990s. Similar to China, however, more than 70 per cent of all FDI inflows in South Korea for the three decades between 1962 and the early 1990s and around 80 per cent of all FDI inflows in Taiwan for the four decades between 1952 and 1992 were in the industrial/manufacturing sector.

In India, notwithstanding FDI inflows of about $50 bn per annum in the past seven years (2015–2021) against average FDI inflows of $25 bn in the six years before that (2009–2014), they were a modest 1.6 per cent of GDP in the 2010s decade. More important, the share of the industrial sector in India's FDI in the second half of the 2010s decade was only around 30 per cent, similar to what it was in the second half of the 2000s decade. Interestingly, the share of FDI in the industrial sector fell towards 35–40 per cent in almost all countries in the 2010s decade. Newly industrialized countries (such as Malaysia, the Philippines and Thailand), however, still have a much larger share of FDI inflows (50–65 per cent) in the industrial sector.

During the past seven years (2015–21), almost a third of all FDI inflows in India (38 per cent in the past three years) has been in the retail, IT and telecom sectors. These FDI inflows are less effective than the manufacturing/industrial FDIs. Most of the current FDI inflows are a replacement of existing investments and do not entail the setting up of new capacities or factories. For instance, when Reliance Jio raised foreign capital and brought in almost $20 bn in CY20, it simply changed the form of its liability from debt to equity, which did not lead to any new investments in the country.

India's Current Account: Drivers and Implications

Overall, FXR—the residual in BoP—is the most important variable for understanding the external position of a country. However, like the financial account (which includes foreign capital flows), the current account also plays an important role in a country's output growth. The current account has four parts: goods/merchandise, services, primary income and secondary income. India runs a deficit on goods/merchandise, a surplus on services, a deficit on primary income and a surplus on secondary income. Overall, India has run a CAD for sixteen consecutive years up to FY20 before COVID-19 turned it into a surplus in FY21. However, it was back to CAD in FY22.

There are two important things to note: (1) Till about two decades ago, almost the entire deficit on India's current account was on account of fuel and petroleum products. There was a consistent surplus on non-oil items before FY04. (2) Until recently, India's foreign trade deficit on the goods/merchandise account was primarily on investment-related goods, and the country used to run a decent surplus on the consumption basket. This equation, however, has deteriorated in the past few years as India started witnessing a deficit on the consumption basket also.

Since the 1950s, India has been a consistent foreign-trade-deficit nation on merchandise. This means that its exports of goods have been lower than its imports of goods. During the past seventy-one years, India has run a surplus on its merchandise trade only twice—in FY73 and FY77. India has run a merchandise trade deficit uninterrupted for the past forty-four years, including in FY21.

India's dependence on oil imports is well known. The country imports as much as 80–85 per cent of its oil. In the 1970s and 1990s, net oil imports accounted for the entire merchandise trade deficit which rose to an all-time peak of 5.5 per cent of GDP in FY12–FY14 and averaged 3.9 per cent of GDP in the 2010s decade.

Let us examine India's non-oil trade balance. As against a surplus of more than 1 per cent of GDP at the beginning of the twenty-first century, it moved into deficit mode in the mid-2000s decade and has been in deficit for the past eighteen consecutive years. From an average surplus of 0.6 per cent of GDP in the 1990s decade, India's non-oil trade posted a deficit of 1.2 per cent of GDP in the 2000s decade and was as high as 3.2 per cent of GDP in the 2010s decade. In the second half of the 2010s decade, India's non-oil trade deficit averaged 2.9 per cent of GDP—higher than the oil trade deficit—for the first time in the past five decades.

Consumption versus Investment Trade

To get a better understanding of what has driven India's merchandise trade deficit in the post-liberalization period, I have divided its exports and imports basket into four parts—consumption, investments, oil and valuables. On the non-oil basket, India has run a consistent trade deficit on valuables (wherein, like oil, India imports the raw material [gold] and exports the refined products [jewellery]) and investments in the past two decades, while there had been a non-trivial surplus on the consumption basket until recently (Appendix 14 provides the details, along with definitions of consumption and investments trade basket).

The deficit on valuables has been under 1 per cent of GDP since FY98 (barring four years [FY10–FY13], when it was worse), before which there was a surplus on the valuables basket. In 2015, the authorities attempted to lure gold holders in the country to monetize their assets by investing in the sovereign gold bonds (SGBs) scheme. However, less than ₹100 bn was raised during the first four years (up to FY20) of the scheme. Due to COVID-19, the RBI was able to raise ₹160 bn through twelve tranches of SGBs in FY21. Further, the government has raised another ₹130 bn in ten tranches of SGBs in FY22. This means a total amount of ₹387 bn[11] (90 tonnes of gold) has been raised through SGBs in more than six years, which is a negligible amount considering the overall gold imports. It would be great if more incentives—financial or otherwise—are introduced to permanently reduce gold imports and recycle the huge stock of gold in the country (probably faster through gold-loan NBFCs).

On the investment basket, however, trade deficit has been more than 2 per cent of GDP or more every year between FY00 and FY20. However, the highlight of India's persistent merchandise trade deficit has been the consumption basket. India's surplus on the consumption basket averaged more than 3 per cent of GDP in the 1990s, which halved to 1.6 per cent of GDP in the 2000s decade. The deterioration continued in the first half of the 2010s decade, and eventually turned into a small deficit in the three years prior to COVID-19 (FY18–FY20), before posting a negligible surplus in FY21 (0.1 per cent of GDP). The consumption basket again posted a deficit (0.2 per cent of GDP) in FY22. In contrast, India's trade deficit on the investments basket was pretty stable—at 2.6 per cent of GDP in the 1990s decade, 2.1 per cent in the 2000s decade and 2.6 per cent in the 2010s decade (it fell to a three-decade low of 0.7 per cent of GDP in FY21, but widened to 1.5 per cent of GDP in FY22).

Details of the consumption and investment subcategories are also revealing. The reversal in consumption-related foreign trade from a surplus to a deficit was broad-based. Electronic goods category is not the only reason for the deterioration in India's consumption trade deficit, as it is sometimes believed to be. Although the surplus on India's consumption trade declined from an average of 1.2 per cent of GDP during FY11–FY15 to nil during FY16–FY20, implying a deterioration of 1.2 per cent of GDP, the deficit on electronic goods widened from 1.4 per cent of GDP to 1.7 per cent during the corresponding period. It means that electronic goods accounted for less than one-third of the deterioration in consumption-related trade during FY16–FY20.

The reduction in the trade surplus on textiles in the 2010s decade vis-à-vis the 2000s decade was as large a contributor to the worsening consumption trade deficit as electronic goods, and the fall in the trade surplus on agricultural and allied activities in the second half of the 2010s decade (FY16–FY20) vis-à-vis the first half (FY11–FY15) was as high as the combined deterioration in electronic goods and textiles.

Similarly, the general belief that the trade deficit on engineering goods is the primary driver of higher investments-related trade deficit is not true. Although the average investment trade deficit was 2.6 per cent of GDP in both the 1990s and 2010s decades, there was large change in the contribution of the subcategories. While the deficit on engineering goods narrowed from 1.6 per cent of GDP in the 1990s to 0.9 per cent of GDP in the 2010s decade, it was more than neutralized by the widening trade deficit in ores and minerals—from just 0.2 per cent of GDP to 1 per cent of GDP. The trade deficit on chemicals and related products also narrowed, and it was largely unchanged in the 'others' subcategory.

All these trends in the goods and services trade are in perfect sync with the thesis discussed in this book. There are four key lessons that emerge:

1. Overall, India's persistent trade deficit on the merchandise account since FY05 has been on account of the worsening non-oil trade balance. The deterioration in the merchandise foreign deficit beginning FY04 occurred with the start of the high-growth period. This is not a coincidence. As we

will see in Chapter 8, the worsening trade deficit (or CAD) in India in the 2000s and 2010s decades, along with faster economic growth, was thus neither a concern nor unique.
2. The shift in India's economic growth driver from investments in the 2000s decade to consumption in the 2010s decade is also reflected in the external account. The deterioration in India's consumption trade basket—from large surpluses in the 1990s to a small deficit in the late 2010s decade—was in line with the consumption-led growth in India.
3. The perpetual and sticky dependence of India on oil imports has worsened lately. Domestic production of crude oil in India peaked in FY12 and has fallen continuously every year since. Total crude oil production in India in FY20 was the same as in FY02. Similarly, domestic production of natural gas in India in FY20 was the least since FY05 (since when data is available) and 42 per cent down from its peak in FY11. At the same time, production of refinery products increased more than 6 per cent during the 2010s decade, supported by a similar growth in oil imports. To grow faster, India may have to accept a higher trade deficit on non-oil items. One clear way to make this sustainable is to reduce dependence on oil items and create space for a higher non-oil deficit. Although India is gaining momentum on renewable sources of energy, its continuous reliance on oil imports acts as a constraint to higher growth.
4. India has run a trade deficit on all four baskets—including on valuables—during the past few years. GoI had implemented physical restrictions on gold imports in 2013 to contain the deficit on valuables.

Overall, the deterioration in India's CAD during the past two decades has been more structural and deeper in nature than before. This means that the policymakers must find a way to reduce the oil and valuables' trade deficit, and it confirms that a consumption-driven growth model is not sustainable in India.

Policies Addressing the Trade Deficit: How Do They Work?

There are many tools available to a nation to address a persistent trade deficit. However, any policy implemented to influence foreign trade will also have an impact on domestic savings and investments. Remember, the Theory of Everything identity says:

CAD = Total investments – Domestic savings

CAD changes only if there are corresponding changes in either investments or domestic savings or both, because this identity has to match. If investments rise and savings are unchanged, CAD widens. If savings rise and investments are unchanged, CAD narrows. However, any change in CAD will happen only through changes in investments and domestic savings.

Two of the most commonly used policies to improve external trade balances are import tariffs and currency devaluation. There are some other trade interventions, such as physical restrictions on imports of particular commodities and direct subsidies to exporters. All these policies broadly work in the same way. If they are effective and the trade deficit narrows, it will happen only through corresponding changes in investments and/or domestic savings. When a country imposes import tariffs or decides to devalue its currency, it may not have any intention or objective to change investments or domestic savings. However, if CAD narrows, either domestic savings go up or investments decline or a combination of both happens.

Import Tariffs as a Tool to Address Trade Deficit/CAD

One of the policies that address persistent merchandise trade deficit in India, which has been used extensively by the GoI during the past few years, is to impose import tariffs, also called customs duties. For most of the period since India's liberalization in the early 1990s, trade liberalization has been the theme followed by the country. India has opened its borders gradually since the 1990s, because of which the average import tariff collection rate fell from its peak of 60 per cent in the late 1980s to around 6 per cent in FY14. The fall of as much as 90 per cent in the import tariff collection rate is the biggest confirmation of trade liberalization in India. During the past few years, however, the average import tariff rate has almost doubled, to 11.5 per cent in FY20, which marked the highest rate in sixteen years. It surged even higher, to 13.9 per cent in FY21, before easing to 12.1 per cent in FY23.

How does import tariff help reduce trade deficit? Well, this is pretty straightforward. Higher import tariffs mean the prices of imported items will go up. As imports become expensive, demand for those products should ideally reduce, helping to reduce overall imports, and thus, the trade deficit. This is what we generally hear from almost all market participants, including economists. Is it really so simple? Is this the correct and only possible explanation of how tariffs work?

Although the average import tariff collection rate has doubled from an all-time low of 6 per cent in FY14 to about 12 per cent in FY20 (pre-COVID-19), have imports also fallen to help narrow the trade deficit? Not really. Total merchandise imports grew at an average of 5 per cent between FY16 and FY20 against a decline of 6 per cent in the previous four years, between FY12 and FY16. Surprising, right?

The following points help us to understand the likely impact of higher tariffs on CAD and other variables:

1. The Theory of Everything identity, that is, CAD = Domestic investments – Domestic savings
2. All three variables—CAD, domestic savings and investments—used in this identity are based on current prices (nominal terms); and
3. Price elasticity of the imported commodities on which tariff rates are hiked.

The Theory of Everything implies that there is no *ceteris paribus*—other things do not remain constant. While higher tariffs may have a negative impact on demand for the targeted imported items, the actual outcome depends on how other things, such as demand for other imports (on which tariffs are unchanged) and/or consumption of domestic items, change. Higher import tariffs influence the external balance only by adjusting the domestic variables.

Although the higher prices of certain commodities will reduce the quantity of demand for that product, the import bill for that commodity—with the higher price but lower demand—may remain unchanged. Therefore, while tariffs will affect the real variables, the nominal variables may remain unchanged. And the merchandise trade deficit, CAD, domestic savings and investments (used in the identity) are all nominal variables.

Econ 101 tells us that higher prices reduce demand, and vice versa, for normal goods. However, there are certain types of items for which demand goes up as prices rise. In economics terms, these commodities are called 'Giffin goods'. If the authorities hike tariffs on such goods, it is not necessary that demand for them or imports of them will go down. In fact, a rise in their imports could lead to higher imports, exactly the opposite of the desired objective.

So, how do import tariffs work? When tariffs are imposed or hiked on some commodities, the prices of those imported items rise. The main purpose of tariffs is to discourage imports of certain items, which is to either support domestic production of those items (such steel manufactured in India) or to purely restrict imports of some non-essential items (such as gold). As the prices of these imported items go up, it is hoped that demand for them will reduce, and thus, the imports bill too. While this *may* happen, it may not necessarily happen.

Professor Michael Pettis explains in *The Great Rebalancing: Trade, Conflict, and the Perilous Road Ahead for the World*

Economy[12] that higher tariffs are expected to discourage imports, not because they raise the price of imported commodities but because they adversely affect households' real income in a country. Lower real income would ideally reduce personal consumption and thus push household and domestic savings higher. Assuming all other things as constant, this is how the trade deficit narrows when import tariffs are imposed.

Higher tariffs—just like inflation—act as a hidden tax on household income, reducing its value in real terms. As the purchasing power of consumers falls with lower real income, their real consumption—measured in the quantity of goods demanded—would also come down. However, the nominal household consumption—measured as the value of the quantity demanded—could be higher, lower or unchanged post the higher tariffs. While higher tariffs adversely affect the quantity of imported commodities demanded, the imports bill—measured in nominal terms—may increase, decrease or remain unchanged. What matters for the policy to be effective is for total spending on imports of those commodities to decline: the imports bill has to fall to narrow the trade deficit, and thus, CAD. This may or may not happen.

Assume that the government hikes import duty on a normal item and discourages households from consuming it. Although this reduces the quantity of demand for this good, the imports bill—in nominal terms—may remain unchanged. In that case, while real consumption growth will be lower than before, nominal consumption in the country may remain unchanged. With no change in the total imports bill, the trade deficit, and thus, CAD, will also remain unchanged. Further, since domestic consumption, production and investments remain constant, total savings will also be unchanged. Real growth, however, will be adversely affected.

Let's assume that after some time the authorities decide to hike the tariff rates on this item further, to an extent where the lower quantity demanded leads to a fall in the imports bill in nominal terms. In that case, with the lower imports bill, the trade deficit will narrow. With no change in consumer spending on other imports and domestic items, total consumption in the country would be lower. If domestic production and investments remain unchanged, it would imply that domestic savings—the difference between income/production and consumption—will rise in the country. The policy, thus, is effective; however, it hurts nominal as well as real economic growth.

This situation could quickly turn extremely complicated. Let's assume the government has hiked custom duties on mobile phones, as a result of which the demand for imported mobile phones goes down to such an extent that total spending on imports falls. If so, the importing domestic companies, along with the exporting foreigners, would lose their business. If domestic companies lose business, depending on the magnitude of the impact on them, lower corporate revenue may result, which could lead to a series of events resulting in lower domestic investments, shedding of employment and/or lower labour income in the importing country. The job losses and/or the fall in workers' income could negate the increase in household savings led by lower consumption of imported mobile phones. Domestic savings could remain unchanged; however, domestic investments may come down. Therefore, while tariffs helped achieve the primary objective of reducing CAD, it was achieved by lowering domestic investments, creating higher unemployment than before.

At the same time, a section of the domestic manufacturers may find an opportunity to capture market share. This may take care of the job losses and lower investments that happened at the importing domestic companies. Domestic investments, thus, could remain unchanged, and domestic savings could be higher, leading to lower CAD. Nevertheless, it would still lead to lower economic growth because the domestic manufacturing of mobile phones will be certainly less efficient than importing of those phones. This has to be the case, or else those mobile phones would never have been imported in the first place.

The complications do not end here. Let's consider a two-open-country world—ABC and XYZ. What ABC exports are imported by XYZ, and vice versa. If ABC exports more than it imports, then it runs a current account surplus (assuming balanced income and transfer accounts), which is exactly matched by the CAD of XYZ. ABC invests its surpluses in XYZ, helping to balance its BoP and also to finance XYZ's CAD. Now, if XYZ for some reason decides to impose to an extent tariff on a certain basket of imports, such that its total imports bill declines, it implies a corresponding fall in ABC's exports. Thus, ABC's exporters, along with XYZ's importers, lose business. As companies lose business in both nations, there may be a second round of impact which may extend to hurting other exports and imports in each nation, as consumers/investors adjust their consumption/investment behaviours. In an extreme situation, ABC could retaliate by imposing more tariffs on XYZ's exports, creating a vicious cycle that may continue unless trade is halted between the two nations. Obviously, this would hurt the national income of both countries badly.

Lastly, what would happen if the targeted imported item—on which tariff is hiked or imposed—turns out to be a 'Giffin good' or an investment avenue for households? Let's consider gold. While the government may be right in considering gold imports a burden on the country's finances, the household sector may behave very differently, especially if it considers gold purchases as investments rather than as consumption. As a result, even if the government hikes import duty on gold, the demand for gold may remain unchanged, pushing the import bill for gold higher, given the higher tariffs. This is exactly what happened during the 2011–13 period, when households viewed gold as an asset to battle very high inflation in India. As households chose to continue to demand and import gold at even higher prices, the imports bill continued to rise even though the household sector's real income was lower than before. Under such policies, CAD widens as household consumption rises with tariffs. With no change in domestic production and investments, domestic savings will fall to match the higher CAD.

There could thus be a number of possible outcomes of import tariff imposition or hikes; the outcomes are extremely difficult to predict at the time of implementation of these policies. Total spending on the imported items on which tariffs are hiked or imposed may go down, go up or remain unchanged, depending on the price elasticity of those items. In any case, if the policy is effective in containing CAD through import tariffs, real economic growth would be adversely affected.

Currency Devaluation versus Depreciation

There are three major currency regimes followed by every country in the world. At one extreme is the fixed exchange rate policy and at the other the free-floating exchange rate policy. Most developing and emerging market economics, however, fall in the middle of these two purist systems. They follow the managed exchange rate policy, also called the crawling exchange rate system, depending on the flexibility allowed in the currency market. When a country decides or chooses to weaken the value of its domestic currency in a fixed exchange rate system, it is called 'devaluation'. However, when the domestic currency weakens due to market forces under a floating exchange rate system—whether managed, crawling or free-floating—it is called 'depreciation'. In other words, currency devaluation is a planned policy while currency depreciation is unplanned. In both cases the domestic currency weakens, reducing its purchasing power.

How does currency devaluation affect CAD? Let us assume that the INR is fixed at 50 against the USD and the RBI follows a fixed exchange rate policy. One INR is thus equivalent to 2 American cents. Further, assume that rather than imposing customs duty, the RBI decides to devalue INR and reduces its value by 20 per cent against USD. How does it do that? One fine day, the RBI will announce that it will purchase or sell unlimited amounts of INR at 20 per cent lower than its existing rate. Accordingly, if anyone wants to sell USD, they will get INR 60 in exchange for 1 USD, and if anyone wants to purchase USDs against INRs, they will have to pay INR 60 for 1 USD. This is how the exchange rate is set under a fixed rate policy.

It means that all exporters who have earned USDs in exchange for their goods and services will get more INRs for the same amount of USDs, while all importers who pay in USDs will be discouraged because they will have to pay more INRs to buy the same amount of USDs to purchase foreign goods and services. Therefore, currency devaluation is beneficial for exporters and harmful for importers.

In terms of goods and services, let us assume that it costs INR 50 to manufacture a unit of clothing in India and that the same unit of clothing costs $1 in the US. The piece of clothing would have the same price in the international markets. If Indian exporters sell this unit of clothing in the international markets, they will earn $1, and if Indian importers purchase this piece of clothing, it will cost them $1 (or INR 50).

After the currency devaluation of 20 per cent, one INR will be equivalent to 1.67 American cents. The same unit of clothing manufactured in India would then cost INR 50 or $0.83 instead of the $1 before. Therefore, the cost of the same unit of clothing has dropped by 17 per cent in the international markets for Indian exporters. American clothing, on the other hand, which cost $1 in the international market, is now worth INR 60. So, the price of American clothing has increased by 20 per cent for Indian importers.

Like import tariffs, currency devaluation (or depreciation) thus not only makes imported items expensive for Indians but also makes Indian commodities cheaper in the international markets. Moreover, since currency weakness is valid for all exported and imported goods and services, devaluation is a much more powerful policy than higher custom duties.

The impact of a weaker currency on CAD works in the same way. With imports becoming more expensive, Indian household real income falls. Although the argument related to price elasticity of imported commodities on which tariffs are imposed is no more valid in this case, the import bill—in nominal terms—could fall or remain unchanged.

Nevertheless, with the fall in prices of Indian commodities in the international markets, higher demand for Indian goods and services is likely to lead to higher exports. Again, while the quantity of demand for Indian goods and services goes up, the nominal value of exports may go down, go up or remain unchanged.

Like tariffs, there is no certainty that India's CAD will narrow due to a weaker currency; however, there are three important things to note:

1. Devaluation of currency is more powerful than changing of tariffs because it works on both exports and imports;
2. Like tariffs, the lower value of currency will necessarily have an adverse impact on consumers' purchasing power; and
3. Currency devaluation is more likely to yield better results than currency depreciation.

The first of these points is explained above. With respect to the second point, the adverse impact on consumers' purchasing power in the case of higher tariffs was on account of the fact that even though nominal variables don't change, the higher prices of imported goods would most likely hurt real consumption growth. However, in the case of currency devaluation, not only do imports become more expensive but exports become cheaper also, benefiting the producers. Nevertheless, as the Theory of Everything suggests, if a weaker currency helps to narrow CAD, either total investments will be lower or domestic savings higher.

Currency devaluation is likely more effective than currency depreciation because of several factors:

1. A depreciation in the domestic currency could be a result of turmoil in the global economic environment, which may fail to boost exports;
2. If depreciation is the result of a global event or development, INR would not be the only currency to lose its value against the USD. Most currencies would lose their value against the USD, which will not lead to any relative weakness in INR; and
3. INR could weaken because of a domestic uncertainty. In that case, CAD could narrow because of lower imports; however, it will be a consequence of weak domestic growth rather than a result of currency depreciation.

In contrast, when a country chooses to devalue its currency, none of the above factors needs to hold. This explains why currency depreciation fails to lead to the results described in the textbooks. The reason is that currencies of other exporter economies may also weaken.

During the past two decades, globalization has increased considerably, and so has movement of the currencies of developing and emerging markets against the safe-haven currencies such as the USD, the Japanese yen (JPY) and the Swiss franc (CHF). Therefore, most of the episodes of INR depreciation in the twenty-first century have coincided with depreciation in many other currencies.

Since 2000, there have been three such episodes—in 2008–09, 2012–16 and 2020. The first episode was on account of the great financial crisis, the second on account of the Euro crisis and the third due to COVID-19.

INR depreciated at an average of 8.3 per cent in 2008 and 2009; however, there were at least seven more currencies, such as the Indonesian rupiah (IDR), the Mexican peso (MXN), the Great Britain pound (GBP), the New Zealand dollar (NZD), the South African rand (ZAR) and the South Korean won (KRW), which weakened more than 6.5 per cent during the two-year period.

Similarly, at the time of the Euro crisis, INR depreciated at an average of 7.7 per cent during the five years between 2012 and 2016. At the same time, there were at least thirteen more currencies which depreciated, including the Brazilian real (which recorded an average fall of 15 per cent) and the ZAR, which weakened more than 5 per cent per annum during the period against USD.

And of course, COVID-19 has hurt different nations to different degrees; however, most emerging market currencies weakened against the USD in the year 2020.

In short, all the episodes of INR depreciation in the past two decades were on account of global events, and they happened along with depreciation in several other developing market currencies. Also, these episodes were affected by weak global economic activity. Not surprisingly then, these features reduced the efficacy of INR depreciation meaningfully.

Overall, the Theory of Everything equation not only helps one understand the economic behaviour of domestic participants but also explains that external balances are a direct outcome of these domestic behaviours. Further, while the current account balance receives a lot of attention in debates on economic growth, the financial/capital account is as important, and foreign exchange reserves (FXR) are the final outcome of all activities of a nation vis-à-vis the rest of the world.

Key Lessons from the Chapter

- Foreign capital flows or financial account balances are more important than current account balances in the context of the impact of BoP on domestic currencies.
- For any central bank, there are two options for creating money in the domestic market—acquisition of foreign assets and acquisition of domestic assets. For any central bank which intervenes in the FX market, it is the foreign capital inflows that decide its ability to purchase/sell domestic assets.
- The idea of using FXR to fund domestic investments is a non-starter. Not only is the beneficial impact, in terms of real GDP growth, unlikely to be very large, but the related macro-adjustments—in terms of lower private sector surplus or higher CAD or both—may not be acceptable to the authorities.
- FDIs are the preferred form of foreign capital inflows; however, unlike generally perceived, they do not necessarily lead to higher GDP growth. Depending on the existing conditions—in terms of the savings–investments balance, capacity utilization and sensitivity of investment demand to interest rates—FDIs may or may not have a positive impact on the domestic economy.
- Since the 1950s, India has been consistently a foreign trade-deficit nation on merchandise. During the past seventy-one years, India has run a surplus on its merchandise trade only twice—in FY73 and FY77.
- It is not a coincidence that India's non-oil trade balance deteriorated substantially since FY04 when the country entered a high-growth phase. Higher growth, especially led by investments, usually results in higher CAD. Consumption-led growth during the past decade has affected India's CAD to the extent that the country witnessed a small deficit on consumption trade for the first time post-liberalization.

- Any policy to narrow the trade deficit, and thus CAD, will necessarily lead to a fall in investments, a rise in domestic savings or a combination of both. Be it higher tariffs or a weaker currency, there will be several unintended consequences which make the final outcome highly uncertain and complex. Nevertheless, currency devaluation is likely to yield better results than tariff hikes or currency depreciation. Consumers' purchasing power, however, will be adversely affected.

Chapter 6

THE INDIAN ECONOMY: PAST, PRESENT AND FUTURE

Non-economist: OK. So, you have told me about the household sector, then the corporate sector, the government and finally the external sector. This is too much. What is the bottom line? How do you process all this information and summarize it?

Me: Yes. That's what this chapter is all about. I combine what we have learnt so far and discuss the implications for the Indian economy—

Non-economist: Great. Let's get on with it. Am already sort of tired.

Me: Remember the two complications associated with economic analysis in the first chapter—interlinkages between the different economic participants and the role of the financial markets. The first complication is covered in this chapter.

Non-economist: OK. So, let me understand. You combine the learnings from the financial positions of all three domestic economic agents, discuss their interlinkages and summarize it all to explain the implications for the Indian economy. That's interesting.

Me: Yes. I am happy you find it interesting because this is not a very usual or well-known approach to understanding the Indian economy. Not only do I explain the past and the present of the Indian economy using the sectoral financial balance sheets, but I also discuss the possible scenarios that could occur over the next two decades.

Non-economist: So, are you going to tell me how India can grow faster and for a long time in this chapter? You should have put that at the start of this book.

Me: Yes, I will discuss that. But we need to remember that there are no short cuts and no free lunches. Let me explain.

Combining our learnings from the previous four chapters covering all four participants and their economic activities, the evolution of the Indian economy during the past two decades is described in this chapter. The strengths and weaknesses of each domestic participant—the household, corporate and government sectors—are listed, which helps to create alternative scenarios of how the Indian economy could evolve during the 2020s and the 2030s decades. Unless the structural issues are acknowledged, it is impossible to work on policies to address them. If a step backward allows us to run faster over a longer period of time, the idea must not be rejected. The 2020s decade, thus, should be seen as the 'Healing Decade'—to address the weak financial position of the household, unlisted companies and government sectors, which will pave the way for economically strong 2030s and future decades. The authorities have to create a long-term vision and embark on this difficult task. If a nation is to grow at 8 per cent for decades, all its economic participants will have to be in a strong financial position.

Instead of focusing on just one section of the society—how to increase the living standards of the poor or improve the finances of the public sector—the financial position of all three domestic economic participants, along with the role of the foreign sector (that is, the outside world), is discussed at length in this book. The implications of economic policies are often measured against just one aspect which is directly targeted. This may be either due to total ignorance or due to political considerations or simply a result of lazy analysis. Nevertheless, as explained in the previous chapters, economics is almost always about the trade-offs.

One reason the subject is found boring or probably irrelevant to discuss is that the debate ends, in most cases, without any definite conclusions. It is not that conclusions cannot be arrived at; however, to achieve that, wide-ranging related questions must be answered. Who has the time to hear these questions, let alone answer and debate them? For some, it is absolutely unnecessary to go into every detail. One of the biggest enemies of the analyst is over-researching, which may not only waste precious time but may also discourage the researcher from finishing the study that has been embarked on. Nevertheless, under-research or lack of research is equally harmful, and sometimes worse. Policies based on incomplete analysis or on one-sided interactions may not only fail to yield the desired results but may also lead to unwanted results. If the authorities are not careful, in their bid to achieve their desired objective, more of the same will be repeated, leading to serious adverse consequences.

Having explained each sector of the economy in detail, this chapter intends to link them together to understand the likely growth trajectory for the economy, with key conclusions. But before that, it must be noted that the behaviour of a nation's economic participants is an important determinant of economic growth. There is an established literature, almost wholeheartedly believed in by many well-known commentators, which concludes that the emotional state of the economic participants is the key driver of economic cycles. When the participants feel extremely excited or excessively depressed, they overdo whatever they are already doing, and peaks and troughs are created and stretched. This is almost inevitable. You cannot believe that an economy without emotions can exist—not in a human world. However, the inevitability of economic cycles implies booms and busts. There cannot be a bust without a corresponding boom, and a super-cycle cannot be achieved without a period of extremely subdued activity. This is a very important point, which I will return to in this chapter later.

As mentioned in Chapter 1, economic analysis gets complicated because of two factors: the interconnectedness between the different economic participants (which can be also called trade-offs) and the role of the financial markets (and their connection with the real economy). Without a clear understanding of these two complications, it is almost impossible to get a good hold on any economy, let alone make projections. The first complication is covered in this chapter, the latter is discussed in the next.

Who Bore the Brunt of COVID-19-led Income Losses?

Post-2019, no analysis would be complete without recognizing the changes brought about by the world-shaking event called the novel coronavirus (COVID-19) pandemic. As soon as the disease spread, parallels were drawn with the Spanish flu of the early twentieth century. Compared to many other Asian countries, while the Indian economy was hit with a delay (beginning March 2020), the authorities implemented one of the strictest lockdowns in the world, which continued for almost three months, followed by a few months of partial lockdowns. While COVID-19 affected human lives, this sudden stop to economic activities created massive dents in the livelihood of the domestic economic agents and large income losses for them. Learning from the first wave, and with better preparations, although the second COVID-19 (starting March 2021) wave was more severe in terms of its spread and loss of human lives, the economic losses were contained as there were no national lockdowns. To make an informed judgement on the future trajectory of India's growth, therefore, it is necessary to understand the true extent of income/output losses incurred by each domestic participant because of COVID-19 and its impact on the external sector.

As discussed earlier, if the private sector turns weak, the government sector must step in to stop the economic collapse. If the government can save the economy from falling into a serious crisis and provide the private sector the necessary time and support to come back on its feet, the latter can eventually take back its role in building the nation. The government then can take a back seat again and consolidate its finances. This is the broad philosophy along which modern economies are run these days. Of course, such policies come with their own sets of consequences, which too shape the future (discussed in the next chapter).

As more and more nations implemented lockdowns to contain the spread of the pandemic, governments across the world stepped in to save the livelihoods of the general population and to support companies. According to the IMF, the global fiscal deficit surged from 3.6 per cent of GDP in CY19 to 9.6 per cent of GDP in CY20, before retreating to 4.7 per cent of GDP in CY22.[1] There was, however, a massive difference between the advanced economies (AEs) and emerging market economies (EMEs). The former witnessed a tripling of their fiscal deficit—from 3 per cent of GDP in CY19 to 10.2 per cent of GDP in CY20—which eased quickly to 4.3 per cent of GDP in CY22. For EMEs, in contrast, while fiscal deficit almost doubled, from 4.5 per cent to 8.6 per cent of GDP, it fell to 5.2 per cent of GDP in CY22.

Although fiscal deficit widened almost everywhere, the true extent of economic support differed widely among nations, leading to serious consequences for their future growth. A comparison of fifteen large major economies reveals that income losses were as much as 11.3 per cent of gross domestic income (GDI) in FY21 in India, which was the highest after the deficit of 14.3 per cent of GDI in Spain. At the other end of the spectrum was South Korea, where the losses amounted to just 2.5 per cent of GDI (Exhibit 6.1).

These calculations suggest that governments incurred anywhere between 40 per cent and 260 per cent of GDI in economic losses in most nations, except in India and Russia, where the governments suffered only 33 per cent and 21 per cent in FY21, respectively (Mexico's government did not suffer any income losses in CY20).

Exhibit 6.1: Who bore the brunt of COVID-19-led income losses in FY21?

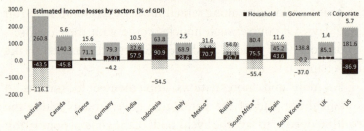

* FY basis estimates are prepared for all using quarterly data except Mexico, South Africa and South Korea, for which CY data is used (CY20 = FY21). Income losses are estimated comparing the actual income vis-à-vis a counterfactual No-COVID-19 scenario, which is prepared assuming the average growth in the three years (FY18–FY20) prior to the pandemic.
Source: CSO, various national sources, author's estimates.

At the other extreme were Australia, Canada, South Korea and the US, where the governments incurred more than 100 per cent in losses, overstimulating the economy. Not surprisingly then, while the share of private sector (household + corporate) losses ranged between 15 per cent and 55 per cent of FY21 income losses in five developed European nations, the private sector benefited in Australia, Canada, South Korea and the US. In other words, since the governments in Australia, Canada, South Korea and the US overstimulated their economies, their private sectors had more income growth than otherwise (actual > No-COVID-19 scenario) in FY21.

There was a marked contrast between AEs and EMEs in the matter of the household sector. Irrespective of whether the governments supported the sector or not, the household sector suffered disproportionately in four of the five EMEs covered in this exercise. The benefits of larger fiscal stimuli in Indonesia and South Africa were largely reaped by their corporate sectors and were hardly shared with households.

This means that the COVID-19-induced income losses were largely borne by the private sector in EMEs, including India, of which households incurred the largest chunk of the losses. This was in stark contrast to AEs. The income losses for the private sector were among the highest (at 68 per cent, or 7.7 per cent of GDP) in India, following 79 per cent in Russia and 99 per cent in Mexico).

The situation was not very different in FY22 during the second COVID-19 wave. Although the income losses were much lower than in FY21, the losses were again largely borne by the household sector in India.

Notwithstanding the limited fiscal stimulus in India, the surge in fiscal deficit and government debt was severe, like in other nations. It is almost certain that the GoI will remain in consolidation mode over many years to come back to the pre-COVID-19 debt ratios. This being so, the burden of pushing economic growth higher falls on the private sector. Does the Indian private sector have the strength to support higher growth on a sustainable basis in the coming years? This is what we discuss next.

Household versus Government versus Corporate

It is now time to compile all our learnings and make conclusions on *'how strong or weak our domestic participants are'*. This is important because it is almost impossible to achieve 8 per cent or higher growth on a sustainable basis for any economy unless all the three engines—consumption, investments and trade—are firing. And for these activities to be strong, the financial position of all the three domestic participants has to be strong.

Will Household Finances Improve or Continue Their Deterioration Path in the 2020s?

Household consumption was a primary driver of economic growth in India during the pre-COVID-19 period. The concern, however, was that the growth in household income lagged consumption growth, because of which household savings were coming down. Higher growth in consumption vis-à-vis income during the 2010s decade happened for the first time in the past seven decades (since Independence), and the consistent fall in household savings was also unprecedented. Still, almost unbelievably, these developments are rarely discussed in any economic debate.

Not only this, household leverage rose from 17 per cent of PDI in FY00 to 32 per cent of PDI in FY10 to 43 per cent in FY20. Although this expansion in household credit in the past few years is largely attributable to the expansion of the borrower base, which is comforting, an analysis of the debt-service ratio reveals that household leverage in India is not as low as the headline numbers suggest. Since the cost of servicing debt in India is very high—due to lower maturity periods and higher interest rates—compared with the cost in other major economies of the world, the threshold of peak household leverage in India is likely to be between 60 per cent and 80 per cent of PDI, based on DSR of 15 per cent and 20 per cent, respectively.

The financial position of Indian households, thus, was clearly unsatisfactory before COVID-19, and the pandemic has led to its further deterioration. Although household savings increased in FY21, it is estimated to have fallen sharply in FY22 and FY23. Further, household leverage has increased to 45 per cent of PDI in FY22.

An important indicator to gauge potential household demand over the next few years is 'excess savings'. Excess savings is the difference between actual savings and estimated household savings in the counterfactual (no-COVID-19) world. The latter is based on the assumption that had COVID-19 not happened, household income and savings would have tracked the same path (one of growth) as in the pre-pandemic years (FY18–FY20). The accumulation of these excess savings over a period of time is 'cumulative excess savings'.

According to the IMF,[2] 'As economies reopen, the release of excess savings accumulated during the pandemic could further fuel private spending.' This, along with accommodative monetary and fiscal policies, has led to concern about the possibility of persistently high inflation. Therefore, excess household savings has become an important indicator to understand the likely future trajectory of economic growth and inflation, and needs to be tracked closely.

Comparing actual household savings in FY21 vis-à-vis their pre-COVID-19 trends, it is clear that there were no excess household savings in India in FY21. In stark contrast to excess savings of 7–14 per cent of PDI in the advanced economies, India's excess household savings were just 0.1 per cent of PDI in FY21, implying that actual household savings in FY21 were almost similar (in absolute terms) to the no-COVID-19 scenario. Similarly, excess household savings in Indonesia were –5.5 per cent of PDI (Exhibit 6.2).

An interesting feature of India's savings was that while financial savings had seen excess build-up, lower physical savings dragged down household total excess savings in India. Many commentators look at the rising bank deposits, high currency holdings and increasing equity market to conclude that excess savings are high and rising in India as well. However,

Exhibit 6.2: Unlike rich nations, there were no excess household savings in India or Indonesia

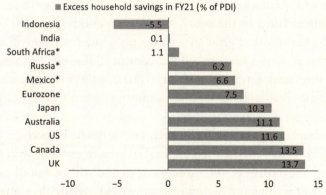

* FY basis estimates are prepared for all using quarterly data except Russia, South Africa and Mexico for which CY data is taken (CY20 = FY21)
Source: Various national sources, author's estimates

financial savings account for only 30–40 per cent of household total savings. On an aggregate basis, it is clear that there were negligible excess household savings in India.

The debate about the overheating of the economy and the resurgence of inflation in advanced economies hinges on the fact that there is a large build-up in cumulative excess savings in these nations. The situation seems to be at the other extreme in EMEs. There are no large excess savings in three out of five EMEs covered in our sample (India, Indonesia and South Africa), which alleviates fear of overheating of the economy and concerns about inflation in these nations.

In fact, I hope that COVID-19 may have acted as the necessary trigger to nudge India's household sector into realizing the extent of deterioration in their finances over the past decade. Such difficult times may remind individuals of the virtue of savings and the risks of leverage. If so, the financial position of the Indian household sector could improve over the years. However, the inevitable side effect of this improvement would be weak growth in household consumption, which will hurt real GDP growth.

On the contrary, it is possible that people will forget about all the economic lessons of COVID-19 and become financially irresponsible with a greater zeal to enjoy life, given its uncertainty, in the post-COVID-19 period. If so, not only will consumption grow at a faster pace but leverage will also continue to rise towards 60 per cent of PDI—my estimate of its threshold limit. But without faster growth in household income (that is, faster than consumption growth), these trends will be totally unsustainable.

Higher consumption growth and household leverage will lead to better-than-anticipated GDP growth over the next few years. Nevertheless, the subsequent period will be full of pain, as lower savings and higher leverage would prepare the stage for India's own slowdown. As we know, higher debt has been a key factor at the centre of all financial crises in the world during the past four decades, and the future is unlikely to be different in this regard.

Fiscal Consolidation Is Inevitable, Implying Weak Growth in Government Spending

Apart from personal consumption, government spending was the other key driver of GDP growth in the pre-COVID-19 period. As explained earlier, fiscal policies in India were highly geared towards encouraging consumption, which had the side-effect of lower household savings in the country. Notwithstanding a lower fiscal deficit, a faster decline in the household surplus (net financial savings) implied that India's government (Centre and the states) almost entirely absorbed the household surplus in the country. This was in contrast to its absorption of only 53 per cent of the household surplus in FY08 and an average of 80 per cent in the eight years between FY04 and FY11.

This interaction between fiscal policies and household finances strengthened further during the COVID-19 period. One of the most important contributors to excess household savings across the world was fiscal transfers, leading to huge government dis-savings. A cross-country analysis confirms a strong positive relationship between the cumulative fiscal support and excess savings during the period. The greater the fiscal support, the higher the extent of excess household savings in an economy (Exhibit 6.3). In short, excess household savings were the mirror image of large government dis-savings, which occurred due to huge fiscal stimuli. Gross domestic savings declined in most countries in FY21.

The absence of excess household savings in India was in line with the low fiscal stimulus in FY21, amounting to just 3.6 per cent of GDP. At the other end were Canada and the US, where the cumulative fiscal support amounted to 13–14 per cent of GDP, leading to the very high cumulative excess savings in these countries.

Exhibit 6.3: Excess household savings were directly a result of fiscal stimuli . . .

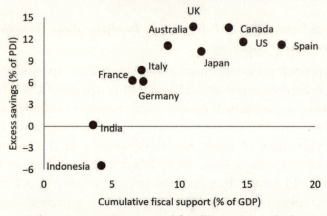

FY basis estimates are prepared for all using quarterly data
Source: Various national sources, author's estimates

If household finances were adversely hit by the pandemic, so were government finances. The combined adjusted fiscal deficit in India rose from 8.3 per cent of GDP in FY20 to 12.4 per cent of GDP in FY21, and the true government debt rose from 74.9 per cent of GDP to 87.4 per cent of GDP during the corresponding period. The government thus revised its fiscal deficit road map in 2021. From as high as 9.5 per cent of GDP in FY21RE, it was targeted to fall towards 4.5 per cent of GDP by FY26. Further, the Central government also announced that states can also run higher fiscal deficits of up to 3.5 per cent of GDP by FY26 (including an additional 0.5 per cent of GDP based on power sector reforms). This broadly means that (1) the Centre is in no hurry to reach its fiscal deficit anywhere close to the pre-COVID-19 level of 3.5 per cent of GDP or its original recommendation of 3 per cent of GDP under the FRBM Act; and (2) the combined fiscal deficit of the general government is targeted at 7.5–8 per cent of GDP by FY26, and likely 6–7 per cent of GDP by the end of the decade.

As far as GDP growth is concerned, an obvious question relates to the likely trajectory of government spending with the revised guidelines of the FRBM Act. Only faster growth in government spending will create a growth multiplier in the economy in the post-COVID-19 period. However, under the revised fiscal deficit targets, fiscal spending during the post-COVID-19 period (FY23–FY27) is likely to grow at around 10 per cent, against 12.5 per cent during the pre-COVID-19 period. Even the 10 per cent is based on an assumption of a sharp improvement in receipt buoyancy (measured as the ratio between the government's receipts growth and nominal GDP growth), which may also be a little optimistic.

Therefore, whether or not the government offered a massive stimulus on account of COVID-19, most governments will practise fiscal consolidation during the next many years and India will be no different. It may take at least a decade for the Indian government to narrow its debt to GDP ratio from the current levels to the pre-COVID-19 level (of around 70 per cent of GDP) and (at least) another decade to fall back to its long-determined target of 60 per cent of GDP. And all this assumes that the consolidation will be gradual, without risking any major reduction in growth in spending.

Will Corporate and Household Investments Rise Sharply?

Overall, both key drivers of economic growth during the pre-COVID-19 period—household consumption and government spending—are likely to grow slowly (= deterioration), compared to their pre-COVID-19 trajectories. The only way real GDP growth can then be maintained at about 7 per cent (same as in the pre-COVID-19 years) is if the corporate and household sectors increase their investments in the 2020s decade to offset the adverse impact of weak household consumption and government spending.

Let's talk about corporate investments first. India's listed corporate sector has come out stronger from COVID-19. The profits of listed companies rose from around 2.2 per cent of GDP between CY17 and CY20 to a nine-year high of 3.8 per cent of GDP each in CY21 and CY22. Further, listed non-financial companies have also deleveraged for the past many years, bringing down their debt from the peak of 25 per cent of GDP in FY14 to 20 per cent of GDP in FY21. Based on these facts, it is widely argued that the corporate sector could pick up the slack in household consumption and government spending.

Although listed companies have shown massive improvement in their balance sheets, it doesn't inspire confidence that India's corporate sector will grow its investments at a faster pace anytime in the near future. There are two reasons for this scepticism: (1) the much-larger unlisted corporate sector has suffered disproportionately due to COVID-19; and (2) if non-corporate demand (household and government) is expected to remain weak for the next few years, why would companies grow their investments at a faster rate, even if they are in a better financial position?

These arguments have already been discussed in Chapter 3. One reason record-high corporate profits in the US have failed to convert into a commensurate rise in corporate investments is the lack of demand. The average growth in private consumption in the US was just 4 per cent following the great financial crisis, against around 6 per cent in the period preceding the crisis. My fear is that this scenario might play out in India too.

The only other way that India can grow faster than or at a similar pace as it did in the pre-COVID-19 period is if residential (or household) investments make a very strong comeback. As explained in Chapter 2, household income, housing prices and borrowing interest rates are the primary drivers of residential real estate demand. While housing prices and interest rates have been favourable over the past few years, weak household income could act as a serious constraint to a sustained recovery in India's residential real estate sector. It is unclear if this situation will improve significantly in the coming years.

Can Exports Make Up for Weak Domestic Demand?

In 2020, Shoumitro Chatterjee, of Pennsylvania State University, and Arvind Subramanian, of Ashoka University and India's former chief economic adviser, co-authored a working paper on India's export performance since the early 1990s.[3] 'Between 1995 and 2018, India's overall export growth has averaged 13.4 percent annually, the third-best performance in the world among the top 50 exporters, nearly twice the average world growth and not far behind China's growth of just over 15 percent,' they wrote. It is also well established that many Asian nations have successfully transitioned to developed or high-income economies through exports-led growth. There is no doubt that the foreign market is much bigger than any single domestic economy. Be it the US or China, the rest of the world is much bigger than any economy individually. Not only are the domestic and international historical evidence in favour of exports-led growth, but the recent trends also provide some confidence. After stagnating at $300 bn for almost a decade, India's merchandise exports crossed $400 bn in FY22 for the first time ever and rose further in FY23.

One shortcoming of the paper by Chatterjee and Subramanian was the lack of discussion on imports. The authors looked at the share of investments, government consumption and exports in India's growth, but totally ignored imports. Imports are either consumed or invested (used further in the production process) in an economy, on account of which they are deducted from the sum of consumption, investments and exports to arrive at the GDP. Several studies have found that a significant portion of imports are used as raw materials in India, a part of which are re-exported. So exports and imports move in tandem in India. Not only have exports risen to all-time highs in FY22 and FY23 but imports have also posted all-time high levels. Consequently, India's merchandise trade deficit has also increased to all-time highs of about $25 bn/month in the last few months of FY22 and the first half of FY23. What matters for economic growth, therefore, is not exports but the trade balance (or current account balance).

There is no doubt that rising exports played a critical role in the transition of the four Asian tigers between the 1960s and 1990s into high-income countries and also in China since the 1980s in its growth miracle. However, as discussed in Chapter 5, exports growth (or the current account balance) is not independent of the behaviour of the domestic economic participants. At any point in time, no resource is lying idle in the economy. Every resource is either consumed or saved. The savings are either invested domestically or sent abroad. Therefore, if foreign demand for Indian goods and services increases for some reasons, there are only two possible options by which this demand can be met.

First, higher external demand can replace domestic demand. Historical evidence suggests a very strong and robust inverse relationship between the share of private consumption in GDP and the current account balance (this will be discussed in Chapter 8). Since labour is the largest input cost for producers, any policies to keep labour wages low would automatically give an edge to domestic producers, improving their competitiveness vis-à- vis the foreign producers. However, this will restrict domestic consumption spending. In light of India's current economic strategy, it is highly unclear as to how higher exports will become the main growth engine.

Second, with no reduction in domestic demand, higher export demand can be met through higher debt. This is probably one of the most acceptable forms of expansion in the present context, especially considering India's low leverage ratio (which, as shown in the previous chapters, is not really true). The borrowed money, however, needs to be converted into goods and services to be exported—the former (leverage) is financial in nature and the latter (exports) is physical (remember

Lesson#1 discussed in Chapter 1). Since we assumed that production efficiency and domestic demand are unchanged, the producer will have to import these goods and services using the borrowed money to meet his export orders. Thus, the trade balance deteriorates initially. This is exactly what happened in the previous episodes of higher investments in India.

Notably though, neither South Korea nor Taiwan (two of the four Asian tigers) transitioned successfully into high-income countries based on debt. Even after three decades of double-digit growth in these economies, their debt to GDP ratios were below 120 per cent of GDP in the early 1990s, much lower than India's current debt ratio. It is only China in the past three decades that has accumulated massive debt to grow quickly. However, any serious analysis will indicate that India must avoid following China's growth path.

Overall, external trade (led by exports) can drive economic growth, assuming that other economic policies (such as treatment of the household sector, preference to the corporate sector [producers] and the fiscal deficit) are also in line with this model. This is not the case in India, and doesn't appear to be happening anytime soon.

Moreover, protectionism has increased greatly in the past decade, which makes it difficult for any large economy to follow an export-led growth model currently. The import intensity of global growth—an indicator of trade openness—has declined sharply in the 2010s decade, leading to a fall in the global imports to GDP ratio. One reason that China and Germany were able to grow their economies through trade was the sharp surge in the trade/import intensity of global growth in the 1990s and 2000s decades. Measured as the percentage change in the volume of imports of goods and services over real GDP growth, the import intensity of global GDP growth has fallen from 2.4x each in the 1990s and the 2000s decades to 1.5x in the 2010s decade. It was higher, at 1.6x, in the first half of the 2010s decade but as low as 1.1x in the second half of the decade, similar to what it was in the 1970s and 1980s (Exhibit 6.4). Accordingly, the global imports to GDP ratio, which rose sharply in the 1970s decade, stagnated in the 1980s and surged continuously over the next two decades to its peak of 26 per cent in CY08, stood at 22 per cent in 2019.

Another way to look the falling import intensity is that while global real GDP growth (based on market exchange rates) averaged 2.8 per cent between 2012 and 2018, only slightly lower than the 3.1 per cent during the period 2002 to 2008, real imports growth almost halved during the former period (3.6 per cent average) from the latter period (7.1 per cent average).

This deterioration in the import intensity of global growth is an important recent characteristic of the global economy because it raises doubts as to the ability of any economy (other than those that have already walked that path) to be able to capitalize on the exports-led model now. A look at India's top seven export-trading partners reveals that they are also

Exhibit 6.4: Import intensity of global growth has weakened sharply in the post–2008 period

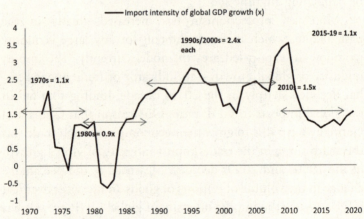

Growth in volume of goods and services imports/Real GDP growth (based on market exchange rates)
Source: World Bank, IMF, UNCTAD, author's estimates

witnessing similar trends. Protectionism, probably implicit, is a reality. If so, it may be very difficult for India to replicate the China or east Asian economic growth models in the 2020s or 2030s decades (discussed further in Chapter 8).

So, What Are the Possible Economic Scenarios?

Overall, the base-case scenario hoped for and projected in this book is that household consumption and government spending are likely to grow slowly over the next few years compared to the pre-COVID-19 period. Due to the better listed corporate sector and some favourable terms in the housing market, there is still a likelihood that investments may grow decently in the coming years. However, it is highly unlikely that investments will offset the adverse impact of weak consumption demand. Therefore, real GDP growth over the next few years is likely to be subdued, at 4–6 per cent, compared with the average of about 7 per cent in the pre-COVID-19 years.

Alternatively, if households continue to behave financially irresponsibly and ignore the virtues of saving and low debt, consumption growth may help drive real GDP growth to similar or even higher than pre-COVID-19 levels. However, the low income growth implies a continued decline in household savings, which will act as an automatic constraint on investment growth. Historical evidence from the past two centuries confirms that most nations in the world (with the clear exception of the US) have not successfully transitioned from low-income to middle- or high-income countries based on consumption growth. Investments/exports have been the key driver of growth in most successful nations. Therefore, from the long-term perspective, the base-case scenario is preferred over the alternative scenario, even though it implies weak growth over the next few years.

In the third possible scenario, consumption growth remains strong and investments also pick up. It may turn out that corporate and household investments rise quickly and, along with high consumption growth (led by the financially irresponsible behaviour of consumers), support India's GDP growth. That can definitely happen; however, there is again a trade-off, as suggested by history. Since Independence, India's investment rate has risen sharply during three periods—one in the late 1980s, and the other two in quick succession in the mid-2000s and early 2010s decades. Higher investments were not the only common thread in these three episodes.

India's investment rate increased from 18 per cent of GDP in FY84 to 26 per cent of GDP in FY91. During that period, India's real GDP growth (on three-year centred moving average basis) crossed 6 per cent for the first time since the 1950s. As investments created the virtuous cycle of higher corporate profits, higher employment, higher household income and higher economic growth, gross domestic savings also improved during the period. Nevertheless, the rise in savings lagged the rise in investments. In other words, CAD also widened—from 1.5 per cent of GDP in early 1980s to 2 per cent of GDP, and then to 3 per cent of GDP in FY91 (the highest since the 1960s)—with the higher rate of investments. This doubling of CAD cost the Indian economy dearly as the Soviet Union—India's largest trading partner at that time— came apart in the early 1990s. Similarly, during the second and third episodes, India's CAD widened with higher investments.

Thus, whenever India's investments have grown strongly, savings have also improved; however, the current account balance has worsened. More worryingly, the worsening of CAD has been faster over the decades. In the late 1980s, foreign savings (or wider CAD) supported almost 20 per cent of the higher investments rate (CAD widened by 1.5pp of GDP vs an increase of 8pp of GDP in investments); their contribution increased to a third in the mid-2000s (3.6pp of GDP vs 11pp of GDP) and accounted for more than 60 per cent of the expansion in the investments rate in the early 2010s (2.5pp of GDP vs 4pp of GDP). None of these episodes have ended well.

The trade-off between higher investments and higher CAD, is thus very real in India. The Theory of Everything identity helps understand this relationship between savings, investments and CAD.

Total investments = Domestic savings + CAD

Or, CAB = (Household savings – Household investments) + (Corporate savings – Corporate investments) + (Government savings – Government investments)

Or, CAB = Household net lending(+)/borrowings(–) + Corporate net lending(+)/borrowings(–) + Government net lending(+)/borrowings(–)

Generally, the household sector is a net lender in an economy and the government a net borrower. Therefore, the lower the fiscal deficit and the higher the household surplus, the more the domestic resources available for the corporate sector to invest. Since external balance is a reflection of net balances of each domestic participant, their changing financial positions reveal important information about their economic behaviours. There are four particular rules:

1. Continuous fall in household savings is a clear sign of their irresponsible financial behaviour, indicating impending difficulties.
2. The higher the ratio of fiscal deficit to household surplus (or its NFS), the more worrying it is.
3. The higher the net borrowings or deficit (investments – savings) of the corporate sector, the more confident it is and the higher the GDP growth is likely to be. If the corporate sector is a net lender/saver (that is, investments < savings), it suggests extreme caution at their end and likely weak GDP growth.
4. A continuous rise in CAD indicates an unsustainable growth model. Either the pace of surge in investments is too quick or the fall in savings is concerning. A continuous improvement in current account balance, on the other

hand, suggests cautious approach of economic agents, driving weak GDP growth.

Lastly, it is probable, as mentioned in Chapter 1, that higher labour productivity growth led by better TFP growth may boost GDP growth. While this is an ideal way to improve, this is not reliable because of its unpredictability, and it should not stand in the way of improving the sectoral financial balance sheets.

Overall, higher growth led by household consumption and government spending in the near future is likely to be highly unsustainable, and unlikely to continue for long. On the other hand, an improvement in the financial position of household and government sectors will likely lead to slower growth in the near future, with a promise to create an 8 per cent growth environment after a few years.

Near Future Must Include the 'Healing Decade' to Achieve 'Economically Strong Decade(s)' Later

Back in 2017, when the economy was grappling with the after-effects of demonetization and coming to terms with the newly introduced GST, Raamdeo Agrawal, Co-founder and Chairman of Motilal Oswal Financial Services, wrote a piece for the *Economic Times* titled 'Funding the Failures for Creating "Jobful" Growth'.[4] Although Agrawal focused on better and more efficient utilization of domestic savings in the country to fund equity/seed capital for businesses, my discussions with him centred on another important lesson—that failure is not bad, it is inevitable, it is necessary and it should be embraced. Failure precedes success. Not only is this true for individuals and companies but also for the government and the broad macroeconomy at large.

I read about economic cycles for the first time in Hyman Minsky's classic 1986 book, *Stabilizing an Unstable Economy*.[5] After reading him and others such as George Akerlof and Robert Shiller,[6] I totally bought the idea that a stable economy is just a fancy concept. One key reason for the instability Minsky talked about is the hunger to grow fast—faster than your neighbours, your colleagues, your competitors, your counterparts and the rest of the world. There is no way this hunger can and should disappear. This hunger is the mother of all innovation—not only in the financial markets but in other segments of the economy and of human life as well. Without this hunger, the world economy will stagnate and the standard of living will stagnate or worse, deteriorate.

However, with this hunger, economic cycles are inevitable. There is no need to be afraid of the downsides because they are the harbinger of good times. The key conclusion of the analysis contained in this book is that there are a few structural issues in the economy that must be addressed as soon as possible. Slower growth would be a direct consequence of these changes. However, once the adjustment process is complete, the economy is most likely to be reset to grow in the high single digits for a longer period of time. Thus, the 2020s decade should be seen as the 'Healing Decade', which will make it possible for India to witness 'Economically Strong Decade(s)' thereafter. In particular, the multi-decade vision, which I talked about in Chapter 1, to achieve 8 per cent growth on a sustainable basis must address four key structural issues over the next few years:

1. The household sector must become financially responsible

Whether we like it or not, greed among common citizens, especially in an economy where they are largely reliant on their bank accounts on a rainy day, is not good. Indian households have maintained their consumption amid weak income growth, which has led to lower savings and higher leverage. Although this combination leads to higher growth, it is extremely risky and unsustainable.

In this context, there are only two possible scenarios in the future—either household income grows faster or private spending weakens. It is almost impossible for households to continue with their financially irresponsible behaviour into the 2020s decade and beyond. There is a simple exercise that can help explain this.

Let's assume that from FY23 onward, households decide to go back to the pre-COVID-19 period in terms of their economic behaviour. It means that (nominal) PCE grows at an average of 12 per cent between FY24 and FY30, and (nominal) PDI grows at 10.6 per cent. If so, household savings (estimated using the unofficial direct methodology) will fall to 21 per cent of PDI by the end of the 2020s decade, as against 24 per cent of PDI in FY20. Although it is possible that corporate savings will rise, gross domestic savings are most likely to be lower. In that case, either investments will be lower or, if investments are maintained (or increased), CAD will widen. The former implies slower potential output growth and the latter means a repeat of the early 2010s, which will end badly.

Further, if consumption growth has to be maintained with slower income growth, household leverage will grow at 14 per cent during the 2020s decade, same as in the late 2010s decade. If so, household debt to PDI ratio will reach 60 per cent in early 2030s, which marks the alarming threshold as per my estimate (assuming a DSR of 15 per cent as the threshold).

Therefore, whether households realize it or not, unless their income grows substantially faster or the DSR improves significantly, it will be difficult for them to maintain their consumption growth at the late-2010s-decade level without commensurate rise in income. Further, neither can household savings continue to fall for long nor can household leverage afford to rise for more than a few years. Households will have to become more responsible in their financial behaviour— voluntarily or by being forced to.

More important, the fiscal and monetary policies have to align with this objective. As discussed in Chapter 4, the government must not adopt policies to incentivize private consumption or discourage personal savings. Although these policies might help support private spending, and thus GDP growth, they create serious imbalances over the medium-to-long term. Unfortunately, this realization does not seem to have sunk in at this stage.

2. Government finances must consolidate in the least disruptive manner

COVID-19 has hurt the financial position of governments everywhere in the world. As the Indian government works to lower its debt level, there are seven ways in which this objective can be achieved. Not all of them are feasible or valid for India—the final choice could be between the bad and the worse. India's economic growth in the 2020s decade will depend on which choice the government makes to consolidate its financial position.

The first of these options—**running high primary surpluses**—has the potential to kill economic growth and might push the economy into a must-avoid vicious cycle. This is one of the most destructive of all the options and should be avoided at all costs. Primary surplus is the difference between the total receipts and the non-interest spending of the government. During the past five decades, the Indian government (Union + states) has run a primary surplus only once—in FY08. More important, during the 2010s decade, the primary deficit averaged 3 per cent of GDP. As mentioned above, even without the targeting of a primary surplus, fiscal spending is likely to grow more slowly during the 2020s decade than during the pre-COVID-19 period. Moreover, attainment of primary surplus may be a self-defeating objective since lower fiscal spending could send the economy into a vicious cycle of slower growth, requiring more fiscal tightening to achieve primary surplus, which will push the economy further into slower growth.

The second option—**higher GDP growth**—is no more certain than a hope because, as discussed above, economic growth is most likely to be weaker in the 2020s decade than in the previous decades. The two key drivers of GDP growth—private consumption and government spending—are likely to see retrenchment in the post-COVID-19 era. And investments (corporate/household) are unlikely to offset their impact. Therefore, this option cannot be relied upon.

The third option—**financial repression**—is a potent and tested choice among policymakers to reduce the debt to GDP ratio. Financial repression is defined as policies that are against the savers and favour borrowers. Effectively, savers earn lower returns under such policies (often negative real returns) that allow lenders to provide cheap loans to the borrowers, reducing the burden of repayments. Carmen Reinhart and Belen Sbrancia[7] explained financial repression as a policy of regulating the financial markets, including directed lending to the government by captive domestic audiences (such as pension funds), explicit or implicit caps on interest rates, regulation of cross-border capital movements and (generally) a tighter connection between the government and banks. In their working paper a decade ago, the authors concluded that during 1945–80, the annual liquidation of government debts via negative real interest rates amounted to 3 to 4 per cent of GDP for the UK and the US, and as much as 5 per cent of GDP for Australia and Italy. With the quick and sudden surge in public debt due to COVID-19, this policy seems very likely to be adopted by many economies, including the US.

Financial repression is not new for India. The captive market for government bonds in India has always existed, with banks, pension funds and insurance accounting for as much as 75 per cent of all government bonds (Centre + states) in the country. Therefore, the more pertinent question for India is, *'How much more juice is left to be extracted via financial repression in India?'* If interest rates are kept artificially low for too long, it may encourage borrowings and support government finances, but the lack of sufficient financial savings in the nation could lead to another set of problems in the form of too much reliance on foreign capital. Therefore, while this option may be considered very practically in advanced economies, it may not yield large benefits for India.

The fourth option—**to ask the RBI to forgo its government securities**—is too controversial. Since the RBI holds 10.6 per cent of the outstanding government securities in India (totalling ₹14.1 tn as at end March 2023), the RBI and the GoI could get into a bilateral agreement and decide to extinguish a part of the G-secs held by the former. This thought, however, is impractical. Keeping aside the moral issues, even if the RBI agrees to simply extinguish a part of its assets held as G-secs, it will also have to adjust its liabilities to match its balance sheet. Leaving aside minor items, the RBI has only three key items on its liabilities side: notes in circulation, bank reserves (statutory + excess) and non-monetary liabilities (called 'other liabilities'). Notes in circulation are held by the public; bank reserves are actually assets of the banking sector; and non-monetary liabilities include revaluation changes and contingency reserves, which are a part of RBI's capital. It is not possible for the RBI to extinguish the first two items, and a large reduction in the third component will make India's central bank highly vulnerable. It seems highly improbable that this option will be put into practice.

The fifth option—**inflating away debt**—is potentially, to say the least, a very risky bet. How does inflation affect government debt? Well, higher inflation means higher prices of goods and services, which would attract a fixed rate of tax (called goods and services tax [GST] or value-added tax [VAT] in India). As prices go up, so do the tax receipts, assuming no change in demand. Similarly, as inflation goes up, workers demand more remuneration, leading to higher income tax collections (this transmission, however, seems to be doubtful in a large labour-surplus nation such as India). For India, this option is very risky as inflation has always been a key macro-challenge for the economy. Reinhart and Sbrancia stated in their paper that financial repression is most successful in liquidating debt when accompanied by inflation. This seems more problematic as inflation has surged dramatically in the post-COVID-19 period, and is seen as the biggest threat to the macroeconomic stability.

The next option—**higher tax rates**—is already in practice in India (and some other nations), but the manner in which it is done is likely to be more harmful than beneficial for the Indian economy. There are two ways in which tax collections can be raised—by hiking tax rates (personal/corporate/indirect) or by widening the tax base. Widening of the tax base is always more preferable to hiking of tax rates to avoid raising the burden on the same taxpayers. Although the GoI has taken numerous measures over the years to increase tax collections, total tax receipts have been stable, at between 15 per cent and 18 per cent of GDP since FY05 (with the highest ratio of 17.8 per cent in FY22, compared to its previous peak of 17.6 per cent of GDP in FY08). One of the clearly visible policies used by the GoI in the past few years has been the increase in effective tax rates[8] for individual income taxpayers, by levying surcharges ranging from 10 per cent to 37 per cent on individuals earning annual income of over ₹50 lakh. Consequently, the effective top tax rate for high-income individuals (earning more than ₹5 crore) has surged to as much as 42.7 per cent, from 33 per cent (39 per cent under the new tax regime).

Not only income tax rates, but indirect tax rates have also remained elevated. As the Centre facilitated market borrowings totalling ₹1.1 tn and ₹1.59 tn for states in lieu of GST compensation shortfalls in FY21 and FY22, respectively, the compensation cess, which was to have been dismantled after five years (that is, in June 2022), has now been extended till March 2026 to recover the states' borrowings. Like financial repression, higher individual tax rates are a reality in India and may continue in the future too.

Lastly, there is always an option for any government to **explicitly default or restructure its debt**. This option also seems impossible in the case of India because (1) the debt levels are not so alarmingly high; and (2) historical episodes establish the government's commitment to meet its obligations at all costs.

Overall, rather than relying too much on primary surpluses, financial repression or higher tax rates, a combination of these policies is likely to be deployed to achieve lower government debt to GDP ratios in the 2020s decade. With these choices, India's government debt to GDP ratio could fall to 80 per cent of GDP by the late 2020s and touch 60 per cent of GDP, but not before the late 2040s. Thus, while fiscal spending will not be a significant driver of GDP growth in the 2020s decade, the path taken to achieve this consolidation will be important.

3. Policymakers must not encourage household borrowings over the industrial/corporate borrowings

During the past few years, household leverage has increased rapidly in India while the corporate sector has deleveraged. Between FY15 and FY22, while household debt has risen from 27 per cent of GDP to 35.6 per cent of GDP, non-financial corporate debt has fallen from 65 per cent of GDP to 56 per cent. Notably, these trends are not entirely driven by the agents themselves—the regulators have also contributed to them. Not only have various fiscal policies incentivized household consumption and discouraged household savings during the past many years, the monetary policy also appears to have encouraged lenders to push consumer credit.

Recently, the RBI has been very active with its non-interest rate tools and several important policy actions have happened through numerous other measures listed under a separate policy document titled 'The Statement on Development and Regulatory Policies', beginning October 2016. Several monetary policy measures have been adopted to ease loan availability to the household sector (individuals and MSMEs) in the pre-COVID-19 period.

Between 2017 and early 2020, the risk weights on certain categories of housing loans were reduced, the risk weights on certain categories of consumer credit were reduced, the fixed limit on collateral-free mandated agricultural loans was increased and regulatory relaxations (with several extensions) were announced to handle the deteriorating situation of MSMEs in the country. Consequently, bank loans to MSMEs (manufacturing + services) picked up after 2017. The MSME loan growth was as high as 25 per cent in late 2013 and early 2014, which weakened continuously to 5 per cent in mid-2016, before demonetization was announced. At least partly supported by RBI measures, MSME loans grew at an average of 10 per cent during the next two years (2018 and 2019).

Observers may sympathize with the RBI, seeing the necessity on its part to ease the financial stress on MSMEs which were adversely hurt by demonetization and GST implementation. However, the support has continued even after two and three years of these events, and MSME lending was weakening much before any of these events.

This is not to conclude that all debt is bad and must be avoided at all times. Higher debt is nothing but borrowings from the future, and therefore must be utilized as efficiently as possible. Whether more debt is good or bad depends on the efficiency with which it is utilized (more on this in Chapter 8). If it is used for unproductive purposes, it is definitely going to add to the burden at a later stage.

Since more than half of household debt is on account of consumption demand, policies should incentivize industrial/corporate loans based on their viability, as they are likely to be more productive. During the past many years, almost all the large banks in the country have adopted models to increase their retail loan book while their industrial/corporate book has shrunk significantly (or grown slowly). While the regulation to raise funding through non-bank sources has contributed to this trend, the incentives to encourage household loans are surprising.

4. Corporate sector needs to align with the national objectives

As discussed earlier, higher corporate profits have failed to lead to higher corporate investments. This is a serious issue which must be tackled as soon as possible, because without higher corporate spending, economic growth could decline into a vicious cycle of slow growth. A look at the economic history of various successful Asian economies shows how the governments in South Korea, China and other economies coerced their companies into meeting the national objectives. By having a very large share of PSUs in the domestic corporate sector and tight control over the financial sector, the government can definitely decide on allocation of resources in the country. With the rising competition intensity and the globalized nature of today's economies, these policies are unlikely to be adopted. In fact, the trend has been to minimize government intervention wherever possible. Since this is highly efficient, there is no reason to go back to a socialist model. However, without strong confidence and aligning of objectives of all the economic participants, it has never been possible for any economy to successfully transition from low-income to high-income, and India would not be an outlier in this respect. Instead of spending its way out, the government needs to play a much more important and active role of being a facilitator to encourage higher corporate spending (that is, investments). Serious deliberations must be held to invite the best minds to bring into alignment our corporate and national objectives.

Overall, I present an argument that it is all right for an economy to grow at a slower pace for a limited period of time provided it clears the way for faster growth rates over the longer term. This might sound controversial and utterly insensitive; however, taking a breather is not necessarily troublesome if it helps you run faster. Remember, '*There cannot be a bust without a corresponding boom and a super cycle cannot be achieved without a period of extremely subdued activity.*' During the 2010s decade, especially the last six to seven years, a number of imbalances have been created in the economy, most of which are linked with the household and the government sectors. With COVID-19, the government has got its clear mandate to consolidate during the next decade; however, households also must change course and behave in a financially responsible manner by being more cautious about their borrowings and thoughtful about their savings rather than chase consumption. The authorities should help the people achieve these objectives by neither implementing policies that encourage consumption along with discouraging savings, nor by pushing the lenders towards Indian households. My recommendations will almost certainly lead to slower GDP growth in the 2020s decade. Nevertheless, once the financial balance sheets are strengthened, the following decades could witness super-economic cycles.

A new challenge, however, has emerged in the past few decades, which makes 'acceptance of pain' more difficult—the burgeoning financialization of the economies. As soon as the economic cycle appears to be turning southwards, the financial markets—being forward-looking—turn cautious and the confidence of the participating agents deteriorate very quickly. Such sharp movements not only create huge volatility and uncertainties but they also make it difficult to implement the needed adjustments. The financialization of the economy has restricted its ability to self-correct, as the policymakers (both fiscal and monetary) rush to intervene in the adjustment process.

What is the way out, then? How long and how many times can the central banks interject these necessary adjustment processes? Can these adjustments be deferred, and thus avoided permanently? This is what is discussed in the next, penultimate chapter.

Key Lessons from the Chapter

- Unlike in most advanced nations, the fiscal stimulus was very limited in India in FY21. It means that as much as 68 per cent of the income losses in India were borne by the private sector, of which the bulk was suffered by the households. With governments likely to remain in consolidation mode during the next many years, the onus of higher growth rests on the private sector.
- There were no excess household savings in India in FY21, in contrast to the situation in most advanced nations. So the challenges for the Indian economy in the near future will be slower growth, compared to overheating in the advanced economies.
- With weak household spending and fiscal consolidation, lower demand may constrain the willingness of listed companies to increase investments, notwithstanding their improved financial position.
- Alternatively, consumption growth may continue to support GDP growth, leading to weak investments due to lower savings. Or, investments may also pick up, funded by foreign savings, creating external imbalances. While GDP growth will be higher in these alternative scenarios, such growth will be highly unsustainable, making it last for only a few years.
- Increased protectionism has made it very difficult for any large economy such as India to follow an export-led growth model. Further, foreign trade can drive economic growth only if other economic policies, such as treatment of the household sector, preferences extended to the corporate

sector (producers) and the fiscal deficit are also in line with this model. This is not the case in India, and doesn't appear to be happening anytime soon.

- The 2020s decade should be seen as the 'Healing Decade', which will make it possible for India to witness 'Economically Strong Decade(s)' thereafter. In particular, a multi-decade vision that I recommend for India to achieve an 8 per cent growth on a sustainable basis needs to address four key structural issues: (1) the household sector must become financially responsible; (2) government finances must consolidate in the least disruptive manner; (3) policymakers must not encourage household borrowings over industrial/corporate borrowings; and (4) the corporate sector needs to align with the national objectives.

Chapter 7

ROLE OF FINANCIAL MARKETS IN THE REAL ECONOMY

Non-economist: I thought the book ended with Chapter 6. What more is left now?

Me: Remember I discussed two complications at the beginning of this book? The first is the interconnectedness among the different economic participants, which I have discussed, and the second is the growing role of the financial markets in the real economy. I will talk about the latter in this penultimate chapter.

Non-economist: Oh yes, you mentioned it. Financial markets . . . That's interesting. But you are an economist. What do you know about the financial markets?

Me: I think I can shed some light on the connection between the equity/bond markets and the real economy.

Non-economist: What is there to discuss? Financial markets mirror economic performance and they are its leading indicator as well. They are the greatest innovation. All nations need strong stock markets and well-developed bond markets. The US Federal Reserve was right in going all out in CY20. I don't know why the RBI did not do that.

Me: Considering the massive size of the financial markets, it is important not to lose sight of the real economy. The relationship between the financial markets and the real economy has weakened considerably since 2008. And central bank policies have a great role to play in that. Rising uncertainty and vulnerability on this front also make it pertinent to isolate (to the extent possible) the domestic economy from the unprecedented monetary policies of the Western world. It is not easy, but not impossible either. Let me explain.

The evolution of the financial markets—equity/stock and debt/ bonds—during the past four decades has been extraordinary. And with their rise, their connection with the real economy has also taken centre stage. Since it is easier to influence the financial markets than the real economy, their buoyancy must not be confused with a vibrant real economy. In this chapter, the role of the financial markets in India's real economy is discussed. It is safe to conclude that the debt market plays a much more important role in India than the equity markets, whose influence on the real economy remains limited. The two markets are directly linked through the financial sector's exposure to the capital markets. But we must be careful not to overemphasize these impacts, as the relationship between the financial markets and the real economy has weakened globally since 2008. The unprecedented monetary policies of the Western world due to the pandemic has increased volatility and uncertainty in the global financial markets, and more so for developing economies such as India. It is, therefore, extremely important for the domestic authorities to plan to mitigate India's potential vulnerability resulting from these global monetary policies. It will not be easy to make the necessary decisions and there will be no free lunches, but the outcome of better stability will be worth it.

How significant is the impact of financial markets on the real economy? This is not an easy question to answer, especially in the case of India.

Financial markets are not new to the world economy, but their expansion and increasing discussion of them in mainstream economics are. 'Planet Finance is beginning to dwarf Planet Earth. And Planet Finance seems to spin faster too,' said Niall Ferguson.[1] To update his data points, world economic output in CY21 was about $96 tn. Global equity market capitalization crossed $100 tn for the first time in CY20, reaching an all-time high of 128 per cent of GDP, and stayed at 127 per cent of GDP in CY21 as well. The total outstanding value of debt (loans +

domestic and international debt securities) amounted to more than $230 tn or 264 per cent of GDP in CY21. Interestingly, since CY06 (the last year for which data was used by Ferguson), global economic output has increased by almost 85 per cent, equity markets have risen by 2.5x and debt markets by a factor of 2.3x. In short, during this period of time, expansion of the financial markets has outpaced expansion of the real economy by a factor of anywhere between 2.7x and 2.9x.

During the past four decades, financial markets have increasingly become an integral part of economic analysis. Though financial markets include hundreds of different products, the analysis in this chapter is limited to two broad financial markets—the equity and bond markets. The connection between currency and economic activity has been discussed in Chapter 5.

The difference between equity/stock markets and the real economy has never been so stark as it has been in the past few years. What has changed? What is the real connection between stock markets and the real economy? How exactly are the two connected? Why is it that equity markets have recovered so strongly after COVID-19 while the real economy has lagged significantly? This chapter begins with a discussion on equity markets, after which the role of debt markets in India's economic growth is discussed.

Equity Markets and the Real Economy

The concept of the bourse (or the exchange) was 'invented' in the medieval Low Countries (most notably in predominantly Dutch-speaking cities like Bruges and Antwerp) before the birth of formal stock exchanges in the 17th century. Until the early 1600s, a bourse was not exactly a stock exchange in its modern sense. With the founding of the Dutch East India Company (VOC) in 1602 and the rise of Dutch capital markets in the early 17th century, the 'old' bourse (a place to trade commodities, government and municipal bonds) found a new purpose—a formal exchange

> that specializes in creating and sustaining secondary markets in the securities (such as bonds and shares of stock) issued by corporations—or a stock exchange as we know it today.
> – Wikipedia[2]

Although many companies were listed on the Amsterdam stock exchange, the Dutch East India Company (Vereenigde Oost-Indische Compagnie [VOC]) and the Dutch West India Company (WIC) were the two largest and most important companies, founded in 1602 and 1621, respectively. According to Dr Bryan Taylor,[3] chief economist, Global Financial Data, 'the VOC introduced limited liability for its shareholders which enabled the firm to fund large scale operations'. The primary objectives of establishing a stock exchange were to fund large-scale operations and to limit the liabilities for investors while providing them handsome returns as well for the risks undertaken. The average dividend paid by VOC to its shareholders over the course of its existence of about 200 years averaged 18 per cent of capital, implying a dividend yield of 5–7 per cent, according to Dr Taylor.

In one of the oldest books on the stock markets,[4] written in 1688, author Joseph de la Vega explained the working of the world's first important stock exchange:

> This enigmatic business [that is, the inner workings of the stock exchange in Amsterdam, primarily the practice of VOC and WIC stock trading] which is at once the fairest and most deceitful in Europe, the noblest and the most infamous in the world, the finest and the most vulgar on earth. It is a quintessence of academic learning and a paragon of fraudulence; it is a touchstone for the intelligent and a tombstone for the audacious, a treasury of usefulness and a source of disaster . . .

There is no doubt that financial markets have become an integral part of the real economy. However, the strength of this relationship in any country depends on a number of factors, and its volatility makes this analysis very difficult.

Using firm-level data, a 1990 Brookings Paper[5] concluded that the stock market may not be a complete sideshow, nor is it very central for investment decisions. A 1996 World Bank study[6] concluded that the cross-country regressions suggest a positive and robust association between the stock markets and long-term economic growth. In 1999, Federal Reserve Bank of New York[7] also addressed the role of stock markets on consumption and arrived at this conclusion: 'Spending growth in recent years has surely been augmented by market gains, but the effect is found to be rather unstable and hard to pin down. The contemporaneous response of consumption growth to an unexpected change in wealth is uncertain and the response appears very short-lived.' In 2001, in a research note titled 'Financial Development and Economic Growth: An Egg-and-Chicken Problem?',[8] the authors, using data for nine OECD countries and China, made the following conclusion: 'There is little support for the hypothesis that finance "leads" growth, and caution must be exercised in making general conclusions about this relationship.'

In contrast, the National Bureau of Economic Research, in its 2019/2020 working paper,[9] found that for every dollar of increased stock market wealth, consumer spending increases by 3.2 per cent and payroll by 1.7 per cent, unless countered by monetary policy. Research papers investigating the same relationship for India also came up with such contradictory results.[10]

In the past fifteen years or so, the entry of central banks with their newly found tools of flushing the system with almost unlimited and uninterrupted liquidity has changed the workings of stock (and debt) markets in an unsustainable manner. Once upon a time, a good part of the equity market fed on innovation, product differentiation, superior knowledge and risk-taking abilities of companies. As Joseph de la Vega said in the seventeenth century, volatility and greed, risk and reward were always a part of the stock markets. Greed led to innovation, and that was rewarded by investors. At the same time, being the most risky asset class, stocks were always associated with volatility. However, serious problems arise when rewards become available without innovation and risks are minimized by attempts to artificially support markets.

It is argued that the stock market is a reflection of investors' confidence in the real economy. If stock markets are moving up, it reflects the growing optimism and high confidence among the investors, who are becoming wealthier. However, there is an important nuance that is ignored in these discussions. Stock market movements are a reflection of the performance of listed companies, not of the entire corporate sector, let alone the economy. There could be, and there have been, periods of disconnect between the listed corporate sector and the rest of the economy. This means the more the listed companies are representative of the entire corporate sector, the more closely they will be associated with the real economy. Similarly, optimism and high confidence among investors may simply imply more wealth creation for the rich section of the society rather than a reflection of the general mood. The wider the retail participation in the equity markets, the larger the wealth effect, and thus the more important the role of the financial markets in an economy. How strong then is the relationship between movements in the Indian stock market and the country's real economy?

When demonetization was announced on 8 November 2016 and GST implemented from 1 July 2017, the theme of 'value migration' was very popular in India. In his book *Value Migration: How to Think Several Moves ahead of the Competition*, Adrian Slywotzky[11] defined 'value migration' as a flow of economic and shareholder value away from obsolete business models to new, more effective designs that are better able to satisfy the most important priorities of customers. This is a part of 'creative destruction', a term coined by the Austrian economist Joseph Schumpeter in 1942. Schumpeter told us to embrace failure, without which it would be difficult to succeed. And when 'creative destruction' is complemented by 'effective construction' of new businesses, it leads to 'value migration'.

In 2017, it was largely believed in India that the dual policies of demonetization and GST would have the likely effect of formalizing a large part of the informal economy. Within the formal sector, the listed corporate sector stands to benefit in terms of market share, turning large into larger. I explained in Chapter 3 that the listed NFCs account for 25–35 per cent of the entire NFC sector's GVA, implying 12–15 per cent of India's national GVA. Therefore, it is very likely that while the listed companies may perform better, helping the stock markets to move higher, the rest of the economy may remain a laggard, pulling down the real economy.

Although the effectiveness of demonetization and GST in bringing about a wave of formalization is debatable (at least regarding the pace at which it happened), COVID-19 was almost certainly able to achieve this objective. Based on about 2,800 listed NFCs, we find that their nominal GVA grew 7.7 per cent between CY14 and CY16, against their average growth of 8.6 per cent between CY17 and CY19. At the same time, the share of aggregate sales of listed NFCs fell continuously from 42 per cent of GDP in CY12 to 27 per cent in CY16, before picking up slightly to about 30 per cent in CY19. Post-COVID-19, however, listed companies have posted a remarkable comeback, while the rest of India continued to lag behind. Between Q3CY20 and Q4CY22, the GVA of listed companies grew at an average of about 19 per cent, compared to an average growth of 14 per cent in the rest of the economy. Further, sales of listed NFCs have also increased to an eight-year high of 33 per cent of GDP in CY22.

The larger and more diversified a company is, the more options it has for manoeuvre. Even if one assumes that COVID-19 affected the top line (sales) of all companies (listed and unlisted) in a similar fashion (which, in itself, is a questionable assumption), the ability of the larger and diversified companies to adjust their expenditure items and thus maintain the bottom line (profits) is exponentially greater than that of small firms. Further, since listed companies are answerable to their shareholders and face higher public scrutiny, delivering a stable bottom line is important for them. The better recovery/performance of the listed NFCs allowed a strong recovery in the equity market, while the gradual revival in GDP growth was the result of weak growth in the rest of India. Therefore, there was a large disconnect between the stock markets and the real economy. It was based on the fact that the performance of the listed companies and that of the rest of the economy were very different.

Thus stock markets are not really a reflection of confidence in the real economy. If the real economy is doing better/worse, it is highly likely that the equity markets will also perform well/bad. However, the positive/adverse impact of the equity markets may not necessarily have a substantial impact on the real economy. The massive fiscal and monetary stimulus have also played a big role in driving this divergence between the equity markets and the real economy. The real economy is more affected by the fiscal policy and the financial markets more easily influenced by the monetary policy (domestic as well as international). Monetary policies primarily work through the financial markets, which, in turn, are supposed to affect the real economy. However, this bridge connecting monetary easing with improvement in the real economy seems to have developed a barricade that severely limits the pass-through. Consequently, the monetary policy is increasingly ineffective in reviving the real economy, while the financial markets are growing disproportionately.

This chapter not only seeks to explore the interlinkages and relationships between the financial markets—equity/stock and debt/bonds—and the real economy, but also discusses the likely impact of the global monetary easing. The latter has played a critical role in weakening the relationship between these two sectors, and at the same time led to increased vulnerabilities and uncertainties over a longer period of time.

There are direct and indirect connections between the financial markets and the real economy. My analysis suggests that while the direct connections—the impact of equity market on consumption and investments—are not very strong in India, the indirect relationship could be more critical and important.

The impact of stock markets on consumption spending is directly proportional to the potential size of the wealth effect and the role of dividends in household income. To understand if the wealth effect is really large or not, we analyse the exposure of the household sector to the equity markets. Using data from the household financial balance sheets released by the RBI, one can estimate the share of equity holdings in total household financial assets. The larger the equity exposure of households, the more significant could be the wealth effect and thus the more important the impact of movements in the stock markets on consumption.

According to the RBI, Indian households held only 7–9 per cent of their gross financial assets in equity during the decade between FY12 and FY21. This ratio was at its peak of 8.6 per cent each in FY18 and FY19, which eased slightly to 8.2 per cent in FY21 (the latest available data). A comparison of the share of equity holdings in the total financial assets held by households in select major economies of the world suggests that Indian households are the most risk-averse, while Chinese and US households are the least risk-averse (Exhibit 7.1). Equity holdings accounted for 52 per cent and 46 per cent of all financial assets for Chinese and US households, respectively, while the share was as low as 7 per cent in India. With such low equity holdings, the wealth effect is much smaller in India than in the US.

Exhibit 7.1: Comparison of the share of equity holdings in total financial assets of household sector (%)

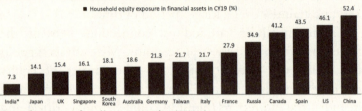

Data for CY19 for all except India (FY20)
Source: RBI, various national sources, author's calculations

A look at the investors in equity markets in select economies suggests that households hold 10–20 per cent of total market capitalization in India, Japan and some European nations, while the ratio is more than double, at about 40 per cent, in the US. Foreigners hold almost a quarter of India's equity, higher than 15–20 per cent in the US, Japan and Germany, but lower than a third in the UK.

Further, the share of dividends (or distributed income by corporations) in household income is less than 2 per cent in India, vis-à-vis above 7 per cent in the US and the UK, and more than 10 per cent in some European nations.

Since the wealth effect is rather small in India, the stock markets may not have a meaningful direct impact on consumption. Further, equities are generally held by high-net-worth individuals in a country. According to the Distributional Financial Accounts published by the US Federal Reserve,[12] more than half of corporate equities held by households in the US is held by the top 1 per cent (99th to 100th wealth percentiles) of households by wealth, and the top 10 per cent (90th to 100th wealth percentiles) of household accounts for about 90 per cent of equity holdings. The bottom 50 per cent households by wealth hold less than 1 per cent of equity markets.

There are two more things to keep in mind while assessing the likely impact of stock market movements on consumption. One, there is a large difference between notional vs realized capital gains and losses. Whenever the stock market moves sharply (upwards or downwards), it creates very large notional (paper) changes in equity holders' wealth. However, it is very likely that only a small portion of these notional changes are actually realized. If so, the real impact of the large and quick movements in the stock markets would have only small wealth effects, unless the gains are permanent (this could be a subject of further research). Two, according to an economic theory called 'life-cycle hypothesis', consumers tend to smoothen out their consumption patterns throughout their lifetime. Therefore, temporary events (such as a rapid surge or a quick collapse in the stock markets) are unlikely to have any major impact on consumption patterns. In fact, even without these temporary events, consumers behave in a very cautious manner. During every boom period, as the income starts growing faster, savings rise before consumption does in the initial period. It is only when higher income growth sustains for a long-enough period of time that consumption growth picks up, stabilizing the savings ratio. In contrast, if income grows slowly, consumers may try to smooth consumption through higher debt or a drawdown in savings initially. However, the longer these trends sustain, the more likely will be their impact on consumption.

To get an idea of the likely impact of stock market movements on investments, the amount of capital raised through equity issuances and its share in total resources mobilized by the corporate sector in a country is examined. If a larger share of resources is mobilized through the equity markets, stock market movements are likely to have a more influential role in investments.

It is widely acknowledged that there is a serious lack of equity capital in India. Most of the financing happens through the debt channels, which is not ideal. India needs equity capital to replace debt. There are several advantages of equity vis-à-vis debt capital. More equity capital displays a higher risk appetite, which encourages innovation. Debt capital is more burdensome, involving fixed repayments. Equity financing encourages an entrepreneurial culture and is more progressive in nature. The fact that it primarily provides financing at the initial phase of a venture makes it necessary and desirable for any economy. Further, if a firm or a person is able to secure equity capital, it becomes easier to raise debt. Therefore, although traditional debt investors (such as banks) may resist new-age entrepreneurs initially, they can feel more comfortable extending credit to those companies which have attracted equity investors.

There are several ways in which a registered company can raise funds through the stock markets. An unlisted company (or a private company) can choose to go public by offering shares in a new stock issuance called initial public offering (IPO); an existing listed company could offer a new issuance to investors under a follow-on public offer (FPO); a company can raise funds through a rights issue (offered at a discounted price) made to existing investors or shareholders; a company can choose to issue shares to a large private equity fund or to a set of pre-identified qualified institutional investors under private allotments (PAs) or qualified institutional placements (QIPs).

An analysis of the total resources raised by the corporate sector from the financial markets in India reveals that the average share of equity financing (comprising public issues, rights issues, QIPs and private placements) was around 27 per cent during the recent few years, better than the 15 per cent in the first half of the 2010s decade but lower than the share of around 40 per cent in the late 2000s decade. This means that debt continues to remain the dominant form of capital issuance in India (Exhibit 7.2). In other words, notwithstanding the buoyancy in the equity markets and more IPOs in FY22 than earlier, total resources raised through equity issues (including private placements) were at a five-year low of 1 per cent of GDP (Exhibit 7.3).

Role of Financial Markets in the Real Economy

Exhibit 7.2: Share of equity and debt in total resources raised from the primary market (%)

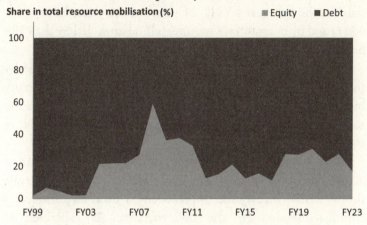

Exhibit 7.3: Total resources raised through equity issuances (% of GDP)

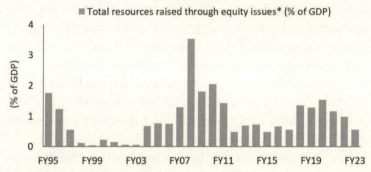

* Including private placements
Source: RBI, SEBI, MOFSL

What, however, has changed is the financing available for new ideas. Although there was no significant increase in the share of equity issuances in the total resources mobilized by the corporate sector, the amount raised through IPOs amounted to 1.1 tn in FY22, more than 3x of the FY21 figure (₹ 310 bn) and almost 4x of the amount raised in the previous years (average of ₹215 bn in FY19 and FY20). But a large number of the IPOs were made by the fintech industry. For instance, IPOs totalling ₹363 bn were made in November 2021 (more than in the full year FY21), of which more than 80 per cent was raised by e-commerce or fintech industries, led by the ₹183 bn issuance of One97 Communications Ltd.

If the share of risk capital in the total resources raised by the corporate sector increases further and remains consistently high, it can provide a tailwind to the economy. But this is too early to conclude so and it would be premature to include it in the base-case scenario at this stage.

This is more so because the buoyancy in equity markets across the world at this point is not entirely driven by strong fundamentals but by the unprecedented fiscal and monetary stimuli provided by the policymakers. As explained in Chapter 3, corporate profits tend to improve due to higher fiscal deficit. The jump in the fiscal deficit in CY20 and CY21 has proved beneficial to corporate profits, which, along with cheap and abundant liquidity, is reflected in the global equity markets. Unless the reversal of economic stimuli are offset by corresponding improvements in consumption, investments and thus corporate earnings, equity markets may find it extremely difficult to sustain their rally. This was amply clear in 2022, as global central banks started hiking rates and governments began their fiscal consolidation.

So does this mean that the stock market does not play an important role in India? Of course not. It is important and it has the potential to become a tailwind for India. However, there are a few facts to remember. One, unlike in the US and some other highly capitalistic economies, exposure of the retail/household sector to equity markets is very limited in India. It confirms a weak wealth effect, and thus a limited impact of the movements in stock markets on consumption. Two, India needs risk capital, and the trends of the past few quarters have been encouraging. The rising share of equity in the total resources raised by the corporate sector and increasing retail participation are welcome signs. Nevertheless, these trends need to sustain for at least a few more years to have significant economic impact. Three, the recent trends are highly uncertain because they are led by the unprecedented—and hopefully, temporary—economic stimuli. Overall, the rally in the equity markets is encouraging and the markets are important. However, the direct linkages between the equity market and the real economy are much weaker in India than in many other capitalist societies such as the North American nations.

This conclusion is linked with Lesson#1 mentioned in Chapter 1, which differentiated between financial and physical investments. Availability of capital—domestic or foreign—doesn't guarantee higher investments, and thus GDP growth. Buoyant stock markets may help companies raise capital and also help bring in the volatile foreign capital flows. However, whether they convert into higher physical investments is dependent on a number of other factors, as discussed above.

The indirect linkages, however, are more important. But before we delve into that, let us examine the role of debt markets in India. Is the direct economic impact of debt markets as muted as the direct impact of equity markets in India, or is it different? What are the key indicators to analyse in order to understand the likely influence of the debt markets on India's real economy?

Bond Markets and the Real Economy

Consumption was the primary driver of India's economic growth during the 2010s decade, while investments lagged significantly. Since consumption growth outpaced income growth, household savings declined during the period, dragging down domestic savings. A policy advocated by many government officials and most market participants to tackle this lack of investments is for the RBI to cut interest rates or ease monetary policy. Since investments are debt-oriented, lower borrowing costs would be an incentive for investors to borrow and invest. After all, corporate debt in India has also fallen dramatically during the past many years.

All this is true. However, just like lower interest rates incentivize borrowings and investments, they also reduce returns on savings, discouraging savers. Household savings in India fell gradually over the past many years to their lowest level in two decades and only barely stabilized before COVID-19. While corporate debt has fallen in India, total debt to GDP ratio has been stable since the household sector has added leverage. How then will the recommendation of an easy monetary policy (or lower interest rates) for India help?

Household savings consist of two components in India—financial and physical (primarily, residential real estate). During the 2010s decade, both financial and physical savings fell. Gross financial savings were down from their peak of 21 per cent in the mid-2000s decade to 14–15 per cent of PDI, and physical savings were down from their peak of around 20 per cent in FY12 to 14–15 per cent of PDI. Higher interest rates boost returns on financial savings, while lower interest rates push physical savings higher. Since physical savings are higher than net financial savings, it is argued that lower interest rates could boost total household savings in India.

We have already shown in Chapter 2 that interest rates are one of the determinants of physical savings. Income and housing prices also influence real estate demand. In this section, we analyse the potential influence of interest rates on household financial savings.

A look at the share of interest-earning assets in household GFS in India and its comparison with its share in other countries is a good starting point (Exhibit 7.4). The long-term (safe) assets held by households are largely in the form of deposits, insurance and pensions funds, all of which earn higher returns when interest rates rise. While equity holdings accounted for only about 8 per cent of GFS for Indian households, long-term assets accounted for as much as 74 per cent. In contrast, but unsurprisingly, Chinese and US households have the lowest share of long-term assets compared to households in other countries. The share of long-term assets in the total financial assets for US households is about 46 per cent, the same as the share of equity holdings, while it is the lowest, at less than 40 per cent, for Chinese households.

Exhibit 7.4: A comparison of the share of long-term assets in household gross financial savings (%)

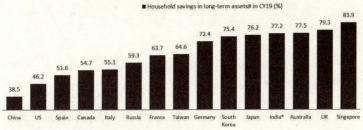

Deposits, insurance and pension funds
Data for CY19 for all except India (FY20)
Source: RBI, various national sources, author's calculations

A comparison of growth in household term deposits vis-à-vis the weighted nominal deposit rate (WNDR[13]) during the past three decades suggests a strong positive correlation. Important, while household deposits share a good positive correlation with the nominal deposit rate, they do not tend to share a similarly strong relationship with weighted real deposit rates (WRDR). From the late 1990s to the mid-2000s decade, as WNDR starting coming off, so did household deposit growth. The two—WNDR and household deposit growth—moved together right up to FY19, after which they moved in opposite directions, as deposits surged and nominal interest rates came down (Exhibit 7.5).

The comparison with WRDR, however, was not so straight forward. Household deposits grew slowly between the late 1990s and mid-2000s decade when real deposit rates surged. Similarly, between FY15 and FY19, while real rates increased

Exhibit 7.5: Households' bank deposits share a strong correlation with nominal, not real, interest rates

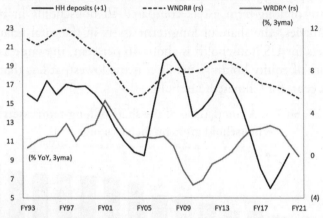

Household (HH) deposits growth is leading by 1 year
3-yr moving average (3yma)
Weighted nominal deposit rate (WNDR) is derived from RBI data on household deposits by maturity
^ WNDR deflated by CPI
Source: RBI, author's estimates

sharply, household deposits grew slowly. The only period when household deposits and WRDR moved together was between FY09 and FY14, when India's inflation averaged 10 per cent per annum. Thus, we believe that this is a perfect case of 'money illusion'; Indian citizens seem to have the tendency to think of their returns and money in nominal terms rather than in real terms.

In short, interest rates affect household financial savings in India because a large part of GFS is debt-oriented. This is a key reason why an easy monetary policy for India during a time when savings are falling is not recommended. Ideally, both financial and physical savings need to rise. However, the potential multiplier of financial savings could be much higher than that of physical savings. Therefore, lower interest rates do not provide a credible solution to India's economic issues. Although it *may* boost physical savings, which account for about two-thirds of total household savings, its adverse impact on financial savings could more than negate the gains, dragging down total savings in the country.

Additionally, although India's headline household debt seems low, its debt service ratio is quite high. Consequently, the authorities need to be mindful of encouraging further household leverage.

During the past decade or so, the Indian banking system has undergone massive transformation. The RBI introduced the base lending rate (BLR) in 2010 and then shifted to the marginal cost of lending rate (MCLR) in 2016. In October 2019, the repo-linked lending rate (RLLR) was introduced, under which most banks have linked their retail loans to the repo rate. RLLR increases transparency and makes changes in the lending rates more predictable for retail borrowers. Further, the resetting of lending rates usually happens within three to six months of changes in the repo rate, while there was a longer and uncertain lag under MCLR.

This means that banks do not have much flexibility in the matter of lending rates on retail loans, although they have full discretion on deposit rates. Since household financial savings have fallen in the past decade, it would not be desirable to keep monetary policy easy significantly (unless demanded by exceptional situations like the pandemic). At the same time, with weak investments, lending rates also should not be very high (which, however, is constrained by lower savings). This combination of higher deposit rates and lower lending rates, as suggested by the broad macroeconomic trends, implies a reduction in the interest margin or bank spread.

Surprisingly, though, bank margins for private sector banks have seen a significant jump during the past few years, but the margins for public sector banks have been stable. Since PvSBs are gaining market share (as discussed in Chapter 3), margins for the banking system as a whole have increased (Exhibit 7.6). The only way margins can expand is if deposit rates

Exhibit 7.6: Interest rate spread has risen continuously for Indian PvSBs, in the past many years ...

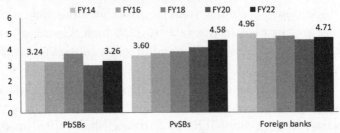

* Based on weighted lending rate on outstanding loans and weighted deposit rate on outstanding rupee term deposits
Source: RBI, author's estimates

reduce slower than the cuts in lending rates, or if lending rates increase faster than deposit rates. None of these combinations is appropriate in the current context of India's macroeconomic fundamentals. The margins have started falling in FY23, but it has to continue for many years to have any meaningful impact.

World Bank data confirms that the bank spread in India is not very high compared to the bank spreads in other emerging markets. At 3.4 per cent during the pre-COVID-19 years, the interest margin for Indian banks was in the middle in the emerging markets' pack. Interestingly, though, India was among the very few major nations where the spread had widened in the 2010s decade.

Consequently, not only do Indian policymakers need to keep a leash on lower interest rates due to falling savings, but also consider inflationary trends while deliberating economic policies. To my mind, while CY20 and CY21 were different and justified quick fiscal and monetary stimulus, there is no need for India to continue with an easy monetary policy outside these exceptional circumstances, irrespective of what the other economies are practising.

It is commonplace to argue that if the US can ease its monetary policy substantially, then why not India? Such comparisons reflect extremely poor understanding of the two economies. An easy monetary (and fiscal) policy is not suited for India vis-à-vis the US because of the massive differences between the household financial position in the two countries. Not only is the composition of their financial savings very different but the overall financial positions of households in the two economies are quite the opposite of each other.

During the past decade or so, Indian households have grown their consumption faster than their income, leading to lower savings, and have also taken on more debt. In contrast, US households have increased their savings and reduced their leverage. Therefore, while the Indian authorities need to encourage savings and discourage consumption, the job of the US policymakers is exactly the opposite—to incentivize consumption. With these differences, it is difficult to recommend an easy monetary policy or lower interest rates for India.

The trade-off between incentivizing borrowers and discouraging savers by means of easy monetary policy is extremely important in India, since savings have fallen dramatically during the past many years. Efforts to push savings higher without a commensurate rise in investments will lead to slower GDP growth and lower CAD (probably, a current account surplus if it sustains for some years). In contrast, a revival in investments without a corresponding increase in savings will push GDP growth higher and widen CAD. The former will be similar to the FY00–FY03 episode, while the latter will rhyme with the FY10–FY13 period in India. None of these episodes will be long-lasting. Surplus funds will pull down interest rates in the former scenario, and after a period of weak activity, GDP growth will pick up. In contrast, rising imbalances will drive growth slower in the latter scenario. This book argues that the former episode is a more favourable option to drive higher growth over a longer period of time, thus leading to the 'healing' I recommend in the 2020s decade.

Overall, it is clear that unlike in the US, equity markets in India are unlikely to influence the real economy directly in a significant manner. On the contrary, debt markets look more important. Of course, what connects them is the leverage. If a large number of positions in the stock market are backed by leverage, which was the case in the mid-2000s decade in the US, a sharp fall in the equity markets could spill over to the credit markets and thus threaten financial sector stability. According to RBI, the total exposure of banks to the capital markets[14] was only about 1 per cent of their total loan book in FY21 and FY22, the lowest in seventeen years, and down from a peak of 2–2.5 per cent a decade ago. A sharp correction in equities is thus unlikely to rattle the credit markets, and thus the real economy. A major disturbance in the debt markets, however, could have more widespread consequences.

What about the Indirect Role of Financial Markets?

Since Indian households park most of their financial savings into debt markets, the role of long-term financial institutions such as insurance, pension and provident funds is also important. From a long-term perspective, low interest rates also hurt the ability of these institutions to earn handsome returns on their investments, forcing them to increase their risk appetite, and thus, vulnerability, to meet their obligations. Such institutions primarily manage the retirement funds of citizens, and any adverse impact on their financial position must be dealt with carefully.

The exposure of insurance funds in India to the stock market has remained broadly stable at around 20 per cent of their total assets in the past decade, while the exposure has increased from negligible in FY12 to about 5 per cent in FY21 for P&PFs. A large part of such savings are thus primarily invested into safe and liquid assets (primarily government bonds) with a fixed rate of return. In India, investors earned 8.15 per cent on employees' provident fund schemes in FY23, down from 8.5 per cent in FY21 but higher than the multi-decade low of 8.1 per cent in FY22. Since the return on these risk-free assets is directly linked with the policy interest rates managed by the RBI, a loose monetary policy tends to reduce the return on investments for insurance/pension funds. However, these institutions are bound to meet their obligations to their investors, which are fixed in nature. Therefore, when interest rates are low in these safe and liquid assets, retirement funds start moving into risky assets, including equity markets, and also into other geographies, seeking higher interest rates on their investments. It is then inevitable that the vulnerability of these institutions also rises. This indirect impact due to the rising exposure of long-term institutions to equity markets (and risky assets, in general) represents an indirect impact, which has increased, and may be more important than the direct impact on the economy.

In its 2021 Global Financial Stability Report[15] (GSFR), the International Monetary Fund noted:

> [P]ension funds have increased their share of investments in alternative assets such as private equity, infrastructure, and real estate—strategies with greater leverage and liquidity risks—in an attempt to meet their return targets . . . Insurers have also increased their investments in less liquid and riskier lower-rated corporate bonds, foreign bonds, and other illiquid exposures . . .

Importantly, these concerns did not originate after the COVID-19-related monetary easing but were raised earlier too. The IMF discussed these issues in its October 2019 GSFR,[16] which was highlighted in RBI's July 2020 Financial Stability Report (FSR)[17] too. The IMF succinctly captured the entire issue in the summary of Chapter 3 of the report, aptly titled 'Falling Rates, Rising Risks'. It said:

> Lower-for-longer yields may prompt institutional investors to seek riskier and more illiquid investments to earn their targeted return. This increased risk-taking may lead to a

further build-up of vulnerabilities among investment funds, pension funds, and life insurers, with grim implications for financial stability. Furthermore, institutional investors' strategies to search for yield may introduce additional risks. Low yields promote an increase in portfolio similarities among investment funds, which may amplify market sell-offs in the event of adverse shocks. . .

In June 2019, a US Federal Reserve staff's research paper[18] also highlighted this issue: 'The shift of funds into riskier investments raises concerns regarding the potential impact of sharp declines in asset values or low returns on state and local finances.'

Of course, these issues were relegated to the back burner during the COVID-19 period. Nevertheless, they are among the very serious indirect adverse impacts of an easy monetary policy pursued for a long period of time, which will play out with a considerable lag (of decades, possibly) across the world. And this will not only impact other nations, but will also be more adverse for the domestic financial sector in the advanced economies experiencing exceptionally low interest rates for a long period of time. The concern is that if and when such adversity happens, it would dwarf the 2008 episode.

Spillover Effect of US Federal Reserve Policies on Other Economies

It would not be an exaggeration to state that financial markets are considered as important as—and sometimes more important than—the real economy. This is certainly true for most of us employed in this industry and is probably true for extremely capitalistic countries such as the US. It is, therefore, not surprising that American policymakers go all out to save their financial markets during economic slowdowns. This is not true of the Indian economy, and the lack of serious focus on the part of policymakers on saving the financial markets during the turmoil is also not surprising. However, given the size of the US economy, the spillover effects of its policies on the rest of the world are serious.

The world economy in the first two decades of the twenty-first century has been very different from what it was in the previous decades/centuries in terms of handling of macroeconomic balances. In almost total disregard of the writings of Hyman Minsky and John Schumpeter, global policymakers have resisted the painful economic adjustments linked with the process of addressing the removal of excesses. This is very unlike in the earlier times, when removal of economic excesses and the related pain were an acceptable and practical solution to the economic malaise. Most of us seem to be living in a fancy world, where economic growth is believed to be permanent and entrenched but slowdowns are supposed to be temporary and short. Economic booms and busts are as real and unavoidable as day and night, happiness and sadness, life and death. If there is anything natural in the subject of economics, it is the inevitability of growth and decline episodes. You may wish to have the former and not the latter, and may also delay the latter from occurring. However, you cannot prevent it. And the more you delay it, the worse it is likely to be, whenever it happens, like a rolling snowball.

Since the great financial crisis in 2008, interest rates have come down dramatically in the US and other advanced nations. Along with other policy tools, central banks across the globe have eased monetary policy to a never-before extent. What was started by Japan in the early 2000s decade, and which was seen as exceptional then, has engulfed the entire Western world since 2008, which again saw another extreme during COVID-19. So what are its implications?

Central bank policies have become the key drivers of financial markets across the world, in the hope that it would help achieve the desirable effects on the real economy. Although these policies have failed to yield the desired results (which, I believe, is higher GDP growth with inflation close to the targeted levels), they have certainly helped stabilize the world economy, although in an increasingly unbalanced and delicate manner. Consequently, rather than rethinking the whole strategy during the COVID-19 pandemic, central banks doubled down on their policies. While the strategy is being championed by the US Federal Reserve, it is being followed by many other central banks in the world, to different degrees.

But central banks don't invest in equity markets. So, how can they be the key driver of stock markets? The short answer is indirectly: by supporting the financial sector with cheap and almost unlimited liquidity. During difficult economic situations, a central bank supports the financial sector in the hope that as the lender community stabilizes, it will start pushing more credit into the real economy, leading to higher growth. Thus, monetary policy broadly addresses the supply side of financing, while it is almost ineffective as far as the demand side of the economy is concerned (this is true as of now, though I would not be surprised but more worried if it changes in the future). In particular, the central bank policy is very simple: reduce interest rates and make sufficient liquidity available for the financial sector. This objective is achieved by creating excess reserves (primarily) on the liabilities side, and by buying domestic/foreign securities on asset side. Since central banks in the advanced Western economies do not intervene in their currency markets, they do not accumulate foreign exchange reserves; and thus, buying domestic securities is the only option available to them (this was covered in Chapter 5).

Since 2008, most of these central banks have added to lenders' liquidity by purchasing a portion of their financial assets (government and/or non-government securities), reducing interest rates to encourage borrowings and also announcing additional liquidity windows for the financial sector to draw money from at (very) low interest rates. The lenders are then expected to utilize the additional liquidity to fund investment opportunities in the real economy. The lenders may do so;

however, there are many other ways to deploy this additional liquidity. One of the obvious places to park a good portion of this new liquidity is the financial markets—leading to higher equity markets, lower bond yields, inflated commodity (fuel and non-fuel) cycles and, of course, the rise of totally unconventional instruments such as crypto currencies. These are some unintended but serious consequences of the glut in liquidity created by the Western world, with the US leading from the front.

Besides rapid asset inflation, this set of central bank policies creates multiple other problems, some of which are specific to a set of countries, while others are more global in nature. An easy monetary policy carried on for a long time by central banks in the advanced economies leaves the currency-market-intervening central banks with the undesirable options of either supporting domestic interest rates or currencies to ease domestic financial conditions. As a result, the extent of monetary easing in economies with currency-market-intervening central banks is much lower than in the advanced nations.

Although the RBI does not manage the level of the rupee against the US dollar, its stated policy has been to intervene in the FX market to mitigate volatility in the rupee. Therefore, RBI also faces the challenges faced by other currency-managing central banks—to a lesser extent though, which restrict its ability to stimulate the domestic economy at a rapid pace during difficult times.

When central banks in advanced economies supply excess liquidity to their domestic markets, a part of the additional liquidity is parked in EM assets.[19] Unlike many advanced economies in the Western world, central banks in the currency-market-intervening economies (mostly, but not limited to, emerging markets) accumulate foreign exchange reserves. When easy monetary policy in one part of the world leads to higher foreign capital flows in other nations, the countries with currency-market-intervening policies are left with the undesirable choice of either supporting their currency or supporting their domestic bond market. This choice is not only unwarranted in difficult times but also unfair on these countries because it was forced upon them by central banks in the non-currency-market-intervening nations. But, unfair as it is, this is the hard reality of the globalized world economy.

Due to very high foreign capital inflows, if currency-market-intervening central banks don't intervene in FX markets and stay out of them, their domestic currency will appreciate (as the demand for domestic assets has increased). By choosing not to intervene in FX markets, the size of these central banks' balance sheet does not change and their ability to support the domestic bond markets by intervening more in government securities (primarily) increases sharply, as in the non-FX-intervening nations. As a result, while domestic interest rates will come down, the domestic currency will tend to strengthen, offsetting the impact of lower interest rates.

In contrast, if a nation's central bank intervenes in FX markets and accumulates FXR to support the nation's domestic currency, its ability to purchase domestic securities will be limited because its balance sheet has already expanded to the extent of the increase in FX reserves. Thus, while the domestic currency may be stable, support to domestic interest rates will be limited.

These are the real-world trade-offs that all currency-market-intervening central banks have to face. And whether they like it or not, this is a choice forced upon them by the actions of central banks in the large non-currency-market-intervening advanced economies. Therefore, while the Western World gets the option to ease its domestic financial conditions significantly—weakening their currency as well as reducing their domestic interest rates substantially—the other set of central banks have to choose between these options, leading to only limited easing of their financial condition.

This is exactly what happened in India in FY21 and FY22. Record-high foreign capital inflows forced the RBI to accumulate about $100 bn worth of FXR during the year to mitigate the strengthening bias in the rupee. Due to the accumulation of FXR, RBI's balance sheet expanded. Consequently, it reduced the ability of RBI to purchase more sovereign securities, due to which the 10-year benchmark bond yield stayed stubbornly at around 6 per cent. Almost 90 per cent of the expansion in the RBI's balance sheet in FY21 was on account of strong foreign capital inflows (up by ₹6.3 tn), with 10 per cent accounted for by RBI's support to domestic sectors (through purchases of securities and loans and advances). In FY22, however, almost a third of the expansion in RBI's balance sheet was accounted for by the accumulation of FXR, while support to the domestic sectors accounted for almost half of the expansion (gold coins and bullion accounted for the rest).

Should the US Federal Reserve be more sympathetic in this matter towards the FX-intervening central bank nations? The answer to this question from most practical market participants would be no. After all, the responsibility of a central bank is towards the domestic economy rather than to the rest of the world. Why should any central bank consider the spillover impact of its policy on any other nation in the world? This may be a correct argument, but it would be highly unfair, uncooperative and irresponsible on the part of the US Federal Reserve not to consider it. This point can be explained by asking a simple question: 'How is quantitative easing (QE) different from subsidies/tariffs?'

On 30 October 1947, the General Agreement on Tariffs and Trade (GATT) was signed by twenty-three countries with the objective of minimizing barriers to international trade by eliminating or reducing quotas, tariffs and subsidies, while preserving significant regulations. In 1995, GATT was absorbed into the World Trade Organization (WTO), which extended it. By this time, 125 nations were signatories to its agreements, which covered about 90 per cent of global trade. In simple words, WTO claims to ensure free trade among all its members by ensuring that no nation is subsidizing its exporters or restricting imports using tariffs. In October 2019,[20] WTO recommended that India withdraw certain 'prohibited subsidies' under the Merchandise Exports from India Scheme (MEIS) within 120 days. Accordingly, India replaced MEIS with RoDTEP (Remission of Duties and Taxes on Export Products).

This global cooperation is not limited to international trade but is extended to various other areas through several international institutions such as the World Bank, the IMF, the World Health Organization (WHO), and the Bank for International Settlements, which prepare globally acceptable norms and rules for eradication of poverty, for the health sector, for the banking sector and other economic areas, which are to be implemented by member nations.

Unfortunately, massive overuse of monetary/fiscal easing has never been considered a contentious issue in global economics. Notwithstanding the large negative externalities of over-stimulus by the US for many other nations in the world, there is no platform for a discussion on bringing it under the umbrella of global cooperation. It is possible that the powerful nations will remain uncooperative in these areas, but then it is the responsibility of the affected nations to make the appropriate noises in protest.

'Isn't QE a direct way of favouring domestic participants at the cost of foreigners?' When the US Federal Reserve pumps in an immense amount of liquidity to support its domestic financial system, it creates significant negative externalities for many other nations of the world. The FX-intervening central banks are left with the unfair choice of either supporting their currency or supporting their domestic bond market. The easy monetary policy followed by the US Federal Reserve leads to a weaker US dollar and stronger other currencies (including those of emerging markets).

At the other end, when the US Federal Reserve decides to scale back its monetary stimulus, many emerging markets brace themselves for capital outflows and related volatility, similar to what was seen during the 2013 Taper Tantrum. As foreign capital flows out of emerging markets, their currencies would weaken substantially and the domestic financial markets would turn highly volatile. While the US Fed would still know what to do, the FX-intervening central banks would be crushed between (1) the pressure to keep raising interest rates to mitigate large foreign capital outflows and keep their currencies stable against the USD, and (2) the need to reduce interest rates to support the weakening domestic economy/financial markets due to rising uncertainties. No matter what the emerging markets do, their authorities tend to lose control of their economies and their financial markets because of the US's monetary policies.

Worse, as the world's rich nations launch unprecedented stimuli to support their consumer and producer communities, pressure mounts significantly on other governments to replicate the US policies. *If they can support private businesses and distribute free money to their citizens, why can't my government do the same?* This ideology may seem highly imprudent to the intellectual community; however, it would be an extremely difficult task to explain the nuances of it to the general voting class. In an extreme case, dissatisfaction among the general public may lead to political instability or social chaos.

Don't these indirect consequences of unprecedented economic stimuli by the US authorities amount to negative externalities? By crediting free money into citizens' bank accounts and creating a large positive wealth effect for domestic producers, won't these policies count as discriminatory and biased? How are these policies different from other governments subsidizing their exporters or restricting imports using tariffs?

If the latter is unfair, the former set of policies should also be objected to and prohibited.

The primary objective of all international institutions is to ensure a level playing field for all nations, for which uniform and strict ground rules are set. Being the world's largest economy and the sole issuer of the leading global currency (that is, the US dollar), US economic policies have widespread implications and have the potential to impact the rest of the world. It is only sensible then for the US to be more responsible in setting its policies. In case it fails to behave in a fair manner, it becomes the responsibility of the rest of the world and the various international institutions to get the US to toe the line.

Of course, this is not the first time someone has mentioned these issues. Dr Raghuram Rajan, former governor of the RBI, former IMF chief economist and director of research, had raised this issue at several forums. Dr Prachi Mishra, along with Dr Rajan, had authored a working paper[21] discussing a framework to internalize these spillovers to improve the collective outcomes. Dr Martin Wolf, the chief economics commentator at the *Financial Times*, London, and the winner of the Commander of the British Empire in 2000 'for services to financial journalism', has followed this story for half a century and has written extensively on it over the past quarter of a century. In short, neither are these spillovers new nor have they gone unnoticed. But the powerful continue to dominate the rules, as one would generally expect. Of course, in this process, life becomes more difficult for policymakers in many other nations.

What Can Indian Policymakers Do to Mitigate These Spillover Impacts?

Isn't there any option for India and other emerging markets to fight these unfair practices of the US Federal Reserve? Of course, there is, and it is a very simple one too.

'When we float, we regain monetary policy autonomy, and then RBI can actually focus on Indian CPI inflation.' This idea from Dr Ajay Shah is so simple and so effective that I fail to understand any resistance to it.

Dr Shah is a well-known financial markets expert and economist based out of Mumbai (shifted from New Delhi recently). He has worked at the ministry of finance and I am fortunate to be in touch with him. I met him for the first time in his office on 20 September 2019; he happened to have read some of my notes and had agreed to meet me. I remember the date because the finance minister had announced a reduction in corporate income taxes on the very same day (you may want to go back to the beginning of this book). As we continued to interact through email and over the phone, I was amazed by the clarity of his thoughts and some of his exceptional policy recommendations.

When I wrote an article about the spillover effect of the US monetary policy on emerging markets in a newspaper, Dr Shah was quick to point out how poor the general understanding of the subject is. His theory is very simple: 'When RBI manages USD/INR, we "import" US monetary policy.' As explained earlier, when the US Federal Reserve lowers interest rates or implements large quantitative easing measures, it will divert a portion of the new liquidity into other nations, including India. As more foreign capital flows in, it tends to strengthen the Indian rupee. Dr Shah is of the opinion that this is a natural phenomenon and should not be interfered with. Instead of fighting with the consequences, RBI must accept these spillovers. The best way to handle these situations for India (or any other EM) is for the RBI to stop intervening in the FX market and become a non-FX-intervening central bank. This policy will allow the RBI to support the domestic bond market more effectively, practise an independent monetary policy and also help the currency to be market-determined.

Let's consider two examples—one in mid-2013 when the Taper Tantrum led to massive capital outflows and thus large rupee depreciation, and the other in late 2020, when high foreign capital inflows led to sharp rupee appreciation.

In mid-2013, when the Indian rupee was depreciating very quickly, the RBI undertook several measures to defend the currency. As Dr Shah stated in his blog,[22] 'Many components of a currency defence are effectively an interest rate defence. At a difficult time in the economy, defending the rupee by raising rates hurts the domestic economy further.' As massive capital outflows happened, a number of restrictions and capital controls were implemented, along with interest rate hikes. This policy of hiking interest rates was a consequence of the RBI defending the rupee, which, as Dr Shah argued, was highly ineffective. His broad argument is that since capital controls, restrictions and interest rate hikes were ineffective in containing the rupee depreciation, the collateral damage—in the form of an adverse impact on equities, a sharp surge in short-term rates (the 91-day treasury bill rate surged from 7.5 per cent to around 12 per cent during the period) and the related economic impact—was more significant. Had the RBI not intervened in the FX market to fight the depreciation, the rupee would have weakened in a similar manner, but the adverse impact on the domestic economy (due to the sharp surge in domestic interest rates) would have been lower.

Similarly, as COVID-19 hit the world economy, the capital outflows in early-2020 led to rupee depreciation (from 71 against the US dollar in January 2020 to a peak of 76.81 in April 2020). However, as the US monetary policy unleashed its QE, a huge amount of foreign capital flows made its way into the rest of the world, including India, beginning mid-2020, which took the INR back to 72.7 by early 2021. Of course, the RBI first utilized and then accumulated record FXR during the episode, to mitigate the rupee movements. Had the RBI not intervened, the rupee may have behaved similarly or moved more but it could have supported the domestic bond market more effectively by buying G-secs, which was the need of the hour. Over time, as a stronger currency would have led to deterioration in India's external balance and made foreign investors more wary of rupee depreciation, market forces would have led to the rupee weakening, which is exactly what happened in 2022.

Therefore, as RBI intervenes in the FX market in many different situations, its ability to conduct an independent monetary policy becomes highly restricted. During periods of large capital inflows, its policy to mitigate the strengthening bias in the rupee by accumulating FXR limits its ability to support the domestic bond market as much. On the contrary, during episodes of massive capital outflows, the monetary tightening to stop foreign investors hurt the domestic economy even further.

Dr Shah provides a simple solution: let the rupee be market-determined, accept the spillover from foreign monetary policies and focus entirely on the domestic monetary policy. In short, instead of blaming the US Federal Reserve, the RBI should become a non-FX-intervening central bank. Of course, some parties would lose with such a change, but as explained, matters would be more predictable and likely to be beneficial on a net basis from a longer-period perspective.

Notwithstanding its simplicity, this policy is likely to be highly unpopular. Since most of the successful Asian economies during the past century have managed (or controlled) their currencies, the idea of a free-floating currency in India may be unthinkable. But what such preconceived notions and ideology fail to see are the changing reality and rising complications of globalization. With QE now the mainstream policy rather than an exception, and given the rising role of financial markets (through which the monetary policy works), it is time to rethink, relearn and adapt. Given the changing realities, it is worth discussing whether the key lessons from the past successes of nations are still valid. How relevant and practical are those lessons for India today? That's what is discussed in the next and final chapter of this book.

Key Lessons from the Chapter

- The primary purpose of the financial markets is to generate a source of financing for the companies to raise funds to undertake long-term projects and to limit liability for their shareholders along with bringing them maximum returns. Additionally, these markets provide a venue to savers to diversify their financial investments (savings) and also create a wealth effect.
- There is no disconnect between better performance of the equity markets and weak real economy. The former is a reflection of the performance of listed companies, which have witnessed a very strong revival in their financial position and account for around 11 per cent of national GVA. Since the rest of the sectors saw weaker recovery, real economic growth remains weak.
- Our analysis suggests that while the equity market may not be very influential in impacting real economic growth, the debt market is more important in India.
- Our analysis suggests that Indian savers are under a 'money illusion', tending to look at nominal returns more than real returns. Given the need to encourage both investments and savings in the country, there is no obvious argument for monetary easing in India. The situation suggests that a narrowing of bank margins could help; however, they have widened in the past few years in the country.
- The adoption of unconventional monetary easing by the US Federal Reserve has serious consequences for most emerging markets with currency-market-intervening central banks. While the former gets to ease its monetary policy significantly, the latter have to make a difficult

and unfair choice between supporting their currency or supporting their domestic bond markets.
- While serious efforts have to be made to bring more cooperation and responsibility among the global monetary policy authorities and the spillover effect of their policies, emerging markets such as India should move towards accepting these spillovers by choosing to allow their currency to be market-determined, while also practising an independent monetary policy. This will bring its own share of problems for some participants; however, the net economic impact over the longer term may be beneficial.

Chapter 8

LESSONS FOR THE FUTURE FROM THE PAST

Non-economist: If only India could grow at 8 per cent or more, all our economic problems would be solved. That should be our only focus and we must spend all our energies to achieve that at any cost.

Me: This is a classic 'chicken or egg' problem. How can the economy grow at 8 per cent if household and government finances are stretched?

Non-economist: Debt can be a solution. The regulators must reduce interest rates sharply and encourage borrowings.

Me: Really? And I thought one lesson from the worst financial crisis in seven decades was to keep a lid on debt. Has higher debt really led to higher and more stable growth globally?

Non-economist: Of course, look at China. Look at the US. Why can't the Indian government spend more? That can help sustain both consumption and investment.

Me: Do you really think the success of the East Asian nations between the 1960s and 1980s was predicated on debt growth? Moreover, are the twenty-first-century American policies relevant for India? Or should we look back at the key policies of nineteenth-century US? Are those policies relevant today? We need to be very careful when we make comparisons.

Non-economist: You sound right. But, then, how did Korea or Taiwan grow so fast for decades? And what were the common economic policies followed by successful nations across the world?

Me: That's exactly what I end this book with. The key lessons from the economic history of a large set of successful nations are surprisingly very similar. Is India following any of these lessons? Can India follow any of these policies? Let's discuss.

There are two established growth models in the world—the East Asian growth model (EAGM) and American growth model (AGM). This chapter seeks to explain the key characteristics of these two models. During India's high-growth phase, there were many similarities it shared with EAGM; however, they appear more coincidental than planned. The persistently high fiscal deficits, the increasingly independent financial sector, the lack of alignment between the corporate sector's objectives and the national objectives, and the willingness to keep both consumption and investments high, reflect the inability of the Indian economy to follow EAGM. Further, the high level of socialism, abundant labour supply, inability to run high external deficits and a large unorganized workforce make it difficult for India to follow AGM too. In short, India does not seem to be following any of the two established growth models. More worryingly, there seems to be a lack of coherence on long-term economic growth vision. Is it creating and following a new growth model? More questions than answers bring in scepticism.

The conclusions of this book will not be acceptable to many and I foresee many counter-arguments, two of which will be more prominent than others. First, the massive wave of digitalization in the country is expected to bring in growth benefits and the production-linked incentive (PLI) scheme for a few sectors could revive the long-dead investment cycle. While both these developments are beneficial, their economic impact will be limited.

From the labour-market perspective, real GDP growth can also be defined simply as a function of growth in labour employment and growth in productivity. As highlighted in Chapter 1, the massive wave of digitalization could help push the productivity growth higher, boosting the real GDP growth. One of the biggest achievements of the Indian government has been financial inclusion—to open accounts in financial institutions (FIs) for a large section of the population.

According to the World Bank's 2021[1] (2017) Global Findex database, as much as 77 per cent (80 per cent) of respondents in India said they had an account with an FI, higher than the world average of 74 per cent (67 per cent), significantly higher than the median ratio of 58 per cent (56 per cent) for lower-middle-income countries (LMICs) and fifth highest among thirty-six LMICs (Mongolia reported 98 per cent respondents with FI accounts, Iran 90 per cent, Sri Lanka 89 per cent and Ukraine 84 per cent). Therefore, India has scored very high in terms of financial inclusion. Nevertheless, one of the criticisms of this policy is that a lot of these accounts either have zero balance or are dormant.

The 2021 Global Findex database shows that although India, among the LMICs, has a very high share of respondents with FI accounts, the percentage of these respondents who have made one or more withdrawals from these accounts in the past twelve months was only 39 per cent (42 per cent), the seventh lowest among thirty-six LMICs (it was as high as 93.8 per cent in Mongolia), and to be compared to the median ratio of 46 per cent for LMICs and 67 per cent for the world. This is strange. If an account has been opened and money is deposited, some sort of withdrawal (cash, electronic or any-time money) is sure to happen.

Further, while the ratio of respondents with FI accounts has increased by around 45 per cent in India since 2014 (when the second Global Findex publication was released), the ratio of account holders who have withdrawn money from their accounts has remained broadly unchanged in India (at around 40 per cent).

Moreover, while the number of digital payment transactions in the country has grown exponentially in the past few years, currency with the public also increased, to its post-Independence highest level of 14.4 per cent of GDP in FY21, and stayed elevated at 13.4 per cent of GDP and 12.4 per cent of GDP in FY22 and FY23 respectively (the third-fourth highest since FY56 when it was 14.2 per cent of GDP); it has been at an average of 11 per cent during the past 2010s decade.

By providing infrastructure for smooth digital payments, the authorities have certainly helped improve the efficiency of companies by connecting them with suppliers, consumers, employees, lenders and other markets. This may not only improve the efficiency of the corporate sector and provide massive convenience to all the involved parties, but also make it much more affordable to carry out transactions. Eventually, this may lead to better total factor productivity (TFP) and better profitability for the corporate sector.

As discussed in Chapter 3, corporate profits have risen continuously during the past two decades almost everywhere in the world. However, corporate spending/investments have failed to match this rise in profitability. Similarly, even if digital payments systems help improve corporate profits further, why would that lead to higher investments, unless either domestic demand picks up and/or export orders increase? Digitalization does little to affect domestic/external consumer demand.

That is exactly where the second counter-argument comes in. The GoI announced PLI schemes for a few sectors in 2020, entailing total costs of up to ₹2 tn spread over five years. Incidentally, this was not a new scheme, and the outlays under PLIs do not count as new spending by the government. India, after an order from WTO in October 2019,[2] decided to replace its earlier Merchandise Exports from India Scheme (MEIS) with its Remission of Duties and Taxes on Export Products (RoDTEP) scheme. However, the allocation under RoDTEP was only about ₹100 bn, 25 per cent of the allocation under MEIS and 20 per cent of the proposed allocation when the scheme was initially announced in 2019. According to some news reports,[3] NITI Aayog allegedly proposed on 6 August 2020 that once the RoDTEP scheme replaces the MEIS, the annual 'savings' of ₹400 bn be utilized to roll out PLI schemes in 'sectors of strength to create global champions'.

On 21 March 2020,[4] the Union cabinet approved a PLI scheme for large-scale electronics manufacturing (mobile phones and electronic components). As the name suggests, the scheme proposed PLIs of 4 per cent to 6 per cent on incremental sales (over 2019–20 as the base year) of goods under the target segments to boost domestic manufacturing, reduce imports, promote exports and attract large-scale investments. If all this was achieved, it would lead to higher employment and help create a virtuous economic growth cycle. In a press conference on 1 August 2020,[5] it was stated that the scheme (applicable only on mobile phone and electronic components manufacturing) was expected to lead to total production of ₹11.5 tn, more than 60 per cent of which would be contributed by export orders of ₹7 tn. It was also expected to bring in additional investments to the tune of ₹110 bn and generate as many as 1.2 mn direct and indirect employment opportunities.

The scheme was hailed by industry associations, economists and financial markets alike. On 11 November 2020,[6] the PLI scheme was extended to thirteen sectors with a total outlay of ₹1.97 tn over five years (including the earlier scheme announced on electronics manufacturing). Almost half of these outlays were allocated to two sectors—automobiles and auto components (₹570 bn) and mobile manufacturing and specified electronic components (₹409 bn).

The idea of the PLI scheme is a noble one and fed on the 'China Plus One' strategy, which gained momentum after COVID-19 in 2020. Economists also did not want to miss an opportunity to be positive on India's growth story. The Economic Survey 2020–21 expected the PLI scheme to make India an integral part of the global supply chain, and market economists like me too echoed the same views.

Once again, while the financial markets and manufacturers rightly welcomed the move, the economic implications are unlikely to be as dramatic. Let me take you back to the Theory of Everything equation one more time. To make it simple, we replace current account as the difference between exports and imports only. The identity then can be reclassified as:

Total investments + Exports of goods & services = Domestic savings + Imports of goods & services

PLI is expected to boost domestic manufacturing—the majority of the output to be exported—and reduce import intensity in the targeted sectors. As the equation shows, PLI is expected to increase the left-hand side of the equation and aims to reduce imports on the right-hand side. So if this identity has to hold, domestic savings have to rise disproportionately (equal to the sum of the rise in investments and exports, and make up for the fall in imports). Does PLI support this? Of course; as profitability picks up and employment is generated, corporate and household savings will rise. However, unless the authorities implement targeted policies, it is almost impossible for domestic savings to match or exceed (which is required in this case) the rise in investments. As discussed in Chapter 6, during three episodes in the past four decades, higher investments in India have coincided with (1) higher domestic savings but which were lower than the rise in investments; and thus, (2) higher imports and CAD.

So is there no way out? Of course, there is. However, it calls for a long-term vision spanning the next few decades. The country's economic policies will have to be based on this vision and they will not be iron-clad. The authorities need to be flexible, they should be willing to learn, unlearn, relearn and adapt using existing and new knowledge. The PLI scheme is kind of a replica of the incentives provided under the East Asian growth model. But these successful nations did this on a much larger scale and such incentives were just one part of their massive plan.

As repeatedly mentioned, trade-offs are inevitable in economics. As a policy is implemented to benefit one segment of the society, it may have an adverse impact on the behaviour of some other participants. The key is to ensure that the economy continues to gain on a net basis without even attempting to support all segments of the society. However, this is exactly where political compulsions come in. It is not going to be an easy task. Had it been easy, all or more nations would have done it. Only a handful of economies have achieved this feat, and it was certainly very difficult for them too. While it is almost impossible to attain a 'please-all' objective in the short term, it can be achieved over a longer time horizon as the entire economy is pulled up. And that's why, unless a long-term economic growth vision is in place and the authorities are willing (and capable) to take some very difficult decisions, it will be only a pipe dream that India joins the league of economically successful nations.

East Asian versus American Growth Model

In one way or the other, the growth models adopted by most of the successful economies in the world were similar. What we know as the East Asian growth model is applicable to almost all Asian nations, and similar practices had been followed by some European nations (Russia, Germany, etc.) too. In his highly influential work *High Wages Versus High Savings in a Globalized World*, Professor Michael Pettis[7] argues that there are broadly two kinds of economic growth models followed in the world—the one which has been adopted by almost all nations after World War II, the EAGM, and the other model practised by the US in the nineteenth century. He calls them 'high-savings' versus 'high-wages' economic growth models.

Under EAGM, a set of policies is implemented to push domestic savings and total investments higher; nevertheless, savings growth outpaces investments, and thus these countries run a current account surplus. Further, the state has large control over allocation of resources through direct control of financial institutions and/or a deep presence of public sector units, PSUs (also called state-owned enterprises). The fiscal deficit is kept in strict check and the education standards (called 'human capital', in economics parlance) are pretty high. At the same time, household wage growth in these economies is much lower, which makes production of goods and services more competitive in the international market. Countries following this growth model are also engaged in subsidizing their exporters and/or restricting imports.

In contrast, the US was largely a trade-deficit nation during most of the nineteenth century.[8] Between 1800 and 1870, average US trade deficit amounted to 2.2 per cent of GDP, which turned into an average trade surplus of about 1.1 per cent of GDP during the subsequent century (1870–1970), till the 'Gold Standard' was abandoned. Although it ran trade surpluses in the latter part of the nineteenth century, the US continued to run a current account deficit[9] till World War I because of the rising deficit on account of the services and income accounts. A CAD implies that US investments were higher than domestic savings in the nineteenth and early twentieth century, in contrast to what happened in countries that followed EAGM. Further, although the US government also invested heavily in the initial phases, the financial and non-financial companies were largely run by the private sector. Household wage growth, thus, in stark contrast under EAGM, was much higher and not suppressed, as it was under EAGM.

Treatment of the Household Sector

As Professor Pettis puts it, one of the biggest differences between the two economic growth models lies in their treatment of the household sector. Under EAGM, a number of policies are adopted to make domestic goods and services more competitive in the international market. One of the most commonly used methods to achieve this is to lower labour costs, that is, household wages. As the cost of the most important and biggest raw material in the production of goods and services falls, the latter become cheaper, making them attractive for the rest of the world to buy. The side-effect of lowering wages and salaries, however, is the direct adverse impact on the domestic demand for goods and services. Therefore, under EAGM, the economic policies replace domestic demand with larger external demand for domestically produced goods and services. The household sector is suppressed to improve the current account balance.

In contrast, household wages were kept at high levels under AGM, which drove productivity and efficiency gains. The objective of the US was never to boost savings, hurt domestic demand and to replace it with external demand, or a current account surplus. Instead, domestic demand for goods and services became the primary driver of high growth in the US.

There are many policies that helped to boost domestic savings under the EAGM. Since the household sector is the largest saver in any country, one might think that the authorities have to push the household sector to increase gross domestic savings. In stark contrast, the trick to boost GDS is to reduce the share of consumption, and thus, the share of the household sector, in the nation's GDP. Since GDS is the difference between income and total final consumption in a country, any step to reduce the share of consumption will automatically boost savings. Of course, total income (or GDP) has to grow, or the model would be unsustainable.

Since the household sector is by far the largest consumer in an economy and their consumption is directly linked with income, the best way to lower the share of the household sector in the national income is to reduce the consumption ratio in the country. Historical evidence suggests that one of the most effective policies to increase GDS, and thus the current account balance, is to shift income/resources from households to the corporate sector. Since households consume a large part of their income, and companies, by definition, do not consume their income, lower household income will reduce the consumption ratio in an economy and GDS will be boosted by higher corporate income/savings. It might sound outrageous, but if you give it a thought and also look at the data, you will have no option but to believe it. Exhibit 8.1 below plots the share of private final consumption expenditure (PFCE) vis-à-vis the current account balance in 147 nations across the world. The inverse correlation is very strong. The lower the household share in GDP, the higher the current account balance, led by higher savings.

The Theory of Everything equation also suggests the same. If a policy is implemented to boost the savings ratio, then either investments will go up or the current account balance will improve, or both will happen. There is no other way to match this identity. A lower consumption ratio is equivalent to a lower share of the household sector, which means higher savings, and thus a higher current accounts balance.

There may be a case, however, wherein although savings increase, investments rise at a faster pace, and thus the current account balance deteriorates. This was the case in the Indian economy during all high-investment-rate episodes since the 1980s. It is, in fact, very natural at the beginning of the

Exhibit 8.1: Strong inverse correlation between private consumption and current account balance

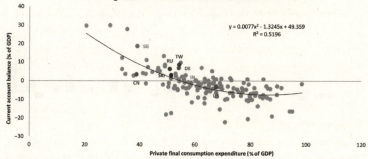

Each data point represents an average of the past two decades (2000–2019)

Source: World Bank, Taiwan National Statistics, author's calculations

transformation of an economy. As the economy develops its investment capacity, it is very likely to import excessively initially. Because the technical know-how or the required machinery may be unavailable domestically, a willingness to boost domestic capacity leads to higher imports in the initial stages of development. Not surprisingly, thus, as the East Asian tigers (such as Hong Kong, Singapore, South Korea and Taiwan) moved to a higher growth path in the late 1950s and early 1960s, all of them witnessed higher CAD or external deficit.

All the East Asian tigers posted average CADs of 2 per cent to 10 per cent of GDP in the 1960s, with Singapore and South Korea running CADs up to the mid-1980s (Exhibit 8.2). Considering the large current account surplus and the highly export-oriented nature of these nations in the twenty-first century, this fact may come as a surprise to many readers. Even China posted small deficits or marginal surpluses on the current account till the 1980s, after which it turned into a large surplus nation. India, on the other hand, never experienced very high CAD, as it doesn't appear to have followed the EAGM to replace domestic demand with exports.

In short, few nations have successfully achieved developed-economy status by approaching a consistent and long-term

Exhibit 8.2: Current account balances of East Asian tigers, India and China since 1960s

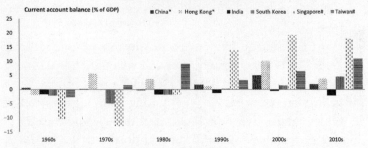

* Net exports of goods and services for 1960s and 1970s, # Net exports of goods and services in 1960s
Source: IMF, various national sources, World Bank

plan to suppress the household sector to achieve a lower consumption rate. To keep domestic growth high and boost savings in the economy, highly efficient investments were undertaken and domestic demand was replaced by exports. This model led to high CAD initially, but eventually the economies turned into large surplus nations. An obvious question, then, is how to suppress consumption and how to boost domestic savings.

There are many policies, as explained by Professor Pettis, that various economies have successfully adopted to achieve this objective. However, most of these policies have been implemented under authoritarian political structures. Since these policies tend to benefit or support the corporate sector (and the public sector, due to the large share of PSUs/SoEs) at the cost of households, it may be politically difficult to implement them and extract the desired results under a democratic regime. It is not that no democratic nation has been able to implement these growth models; however, there were some special circumstances or situations that made these policies implementable and successful for them. Often, commentators compare various economic policies without considering them in the right context. It would be up to the authorities in any country to judge whether these policies make sense for them in today's environment.

There have been four major policies adopted to suppress the household sector:

First, based on the marginal propensity to save and consume, any policy to increase income inequality would reduce private consumption and boost domestic savings in a country. Since the savings propensity is very low among poor households and very high among rich households and the corporate sector, a transfer of resources to the latter will do the trick. Although this is a socially controversial and undesirable policy, it can be achieved when the rich households and corporate sector benefit more than poor households. Regressive tax policies or high tax exemptions are examples of such a policy.

Second, as already mentioned, lowering of wages is the most direct way to reduce the share of the household sector in an economy. In a labour-surplus nation such as China and India, this is not difficult to achieve. However, this is also true for most underdeveloped economies, including Bangladesh, Pakistan and Vietnam. Therefore, some extra efforts and focus are required to beat the competition. One interesting example to learn from is that of Germany, which, through the Hartz reforms in 2003–05, achieved massive improvement in its competitiveness. The primary purpose of these reforms was to tackle the very high levels of unemployment in the economy in the 1990s and early 2000s. However, improved competitiveness also created the perfect scenario to turn Germany from a current account deficit (up to the early 2000s) nation to a very large surplus nation during the past two decades. Germany's unemployment rate was more than 10 per cent in the late 1990s and around 12 per cent even in 2005. However, after complete implementation of the Hartz reforms, employment picked up significantly, helping to reduce the unemployment rate closer to 6 per cent.

It is very likely that while the authorities attempt to reduce consumption for the nation to become more export-oriented, the latter does not happen at the same pace as reduction of consumption and the policy backfires initially. This is where a multi-pronged focus, patience and a long-term vision come into the picture.

Third, an undervalued (or weaker) currency also helps a long way in improving the competitiveness of domestic goods and services in the international market and in transferring resources from the household (consumer) to the corporate sector (producer).

We have already discussed how various trade policies work. Although they are broadly believed to work directly through exports and imports, all trade policies, such as tariffs and/or currency intervention, affect the behaviour and economic decisions of domestic participants. As the currency is maintained at weaker-than-otherwise levels, it adversely impacts the real income of the household sector and reduces import demand. At the same time, producers are encouraged to sell their products in the external market; these products are not only more competitive in the international market because of the undervalued currency, but will also earn exporters higher-than-otherwise income when they convert foreign currency into domestic units. As a result of this policy, the central bank is likely to accumulate a large quantity of foreign exchange reserves. The effectiveness of this policy measure can be gauged from the fact that three of the four East Asian tigers (Hong Kong, Singapore and Taiwan) and China continue to maintain a pegged (undervalued) currency against the US dollar.

Lastly, Professor Pettis also talks about 'financial repression' as a successful policy in achieving the objective of higher domestic savings. To refresh our memory, financial repression consists of all policies that result in savers earning lower returns and borrowers being able to borrow at lower rates. Since households are the net savers in an economy and the corporate/government sectors the major borrowers, the policy of financial repression hurts the former and benefits the latter sectors. The effects of financial repression are thus similar to the other policies mentioned above. Financial repression effectively transfers resources from the household to the corporate and/or government sectors.

Successful economies have chosen to implement all these policies together to achieve their desired objective rather than being selective in their policy decisions. Together, these policies not only led to weaker household consumption in those countries, which reduced the need to import, but they also made domestic products more competitive in the rest of the world. The ultimate objective of these policies was to transfer resources to the corporate sector, which boosted corporate savings and thus GDS. Consequently, not only does the share of household consumption fall but the share of household in GDS also declines rapidly. In South Korea, the share of households in GDS has fallen from 50 per cent in the 1970s to less than 20 per cent currently; in Taiwan, from more than 60 per cent in the 1980s to less than 40 per cent; and in China, from 55 per cent in the early 1990s to 45 per cent in 2007–08 and then stabilized at 45–50 per cent since then. The share of the household sector in GDS has come down in India too—from 80 per cent in the early 1990s to 60 per cent currently; however, in comparison with these other countries it continues to remain very high.

Overall, reduction in the share of consumption in an economy helps boost the savings rate, which eventually leads to higher external surpluses. There was a strong pattern among numerous successful economies of several policies being adopted to suppress the household sector (the major consumer in an economy) and transfer the resources to the corporate/government sector. Instead of choosing one over the other, several complementary economic policies, reinforcing each other, were adopted to achieve this objective.

State Control to Align Corporate Sector with Rational Objectives

Corporate profits have risen almost continuously over the past two decades across economies; however, the pick-up in corporate investments has failed to match this rise in profitability. In fact, it has actually weakened in some nations. How then did the successful Asian or other economies ensure that when resources were transferred to the corporate sector under EAGM, the sector also invested? It was ensured by aligning the objectives of the companies with the national priorities, many a times forcibly.

It is not a coincidence that most successful economies have had a large presence of PSUs/SOEs. To ensure that domestic companies are aligned with the national objectives, the governments not only had good influence over the domestic corporate sector but also controlled the financial sector to allocate resources accordingly. These policies may be considered outdated these days and India seems to be moving away from this path. We often hear, 'The government has no business to be in business.' However, history is full of examples where national governments have been proactive in controlling and forcing their large and strategically important industries to be in line with the national objectives.

South Korea provides an interesting example. After the May 1961 coup, Park Chung Hee ruled South Korea as head of a military dictatorship and then served as the president of the country from 1963 until his assassination in 1979. Joe Studwell, in his extremely insightful book *How Asia Works?*, explains how South Korea became a global force in manufacturing and a major exporter under Park Chung Hee. Here is an excerpt[10] from the book:

> Most developing state dictators just lock up political dissidents. Park also locked up businessmen whose attention he wanted to grasp . . . Park had no more success than any other dictator in cowing those fighting for transparency and institutional development—including democracy. But he discovered that entrepreneurs, so long as they were still allowed to make money, could be bent to his will quite easily.

The objective of higher growth in South Korea was achieved primarily by forcing companies to work for the nation. It created many unexpected benefits as well, which were initiated by Chung's vision but accomplished by the industrialists' hard work.

Not only was coercion (the stick) used to align businesses and their owners with the national objectives but enough incentives (the carrot) were also provided to ensure that the industrialists remained highly motivated and competitive to carry on with the national objectives. Once an industry or sector was chosen as a priority by the authorities, their businessmen were incentivized in various ways, most of them financial, to encourage them to participate.

Since the financial sector is also largely controlled by the government under EAGM, availability of bank finance on easy terms becomes the most important criterion for businesses to thrive. But this is not sufficient. As Chung realized, businessmen had to find the opportunity profitable enough. And therefore, other incentives such as tax exemption, lower utility rates and various rebates on related imports, along with subsidies/incentives for exports, were provided. As a World Bank[11] study noted, governments in many East Asian economies linked financial incentives with the foreign exchange earnings of industries. In other words, the more you exported, the more 'carrots' you are eligible to get.

Since the goods and services produced for exports have to compete with products from the rest of the world, the industries have to be careful about the quality of their products, along with ensuring their affordability. Although the government can help in making a product more affordable by using the policies discussed earlier, it is almost entirely the responsibility of the producers to deliver products of the best quality, which are not only able to compete with similar products in the international market but are also attractive enough to attract customers by diverting them away from the competing products.

This is important, because had the authorities linked their incentives to either production of goods and services, or employment, or investments, or any other domestically determined factor, the producers would not have cared as much about the quality of their products. Higher tariffs or import restrictions may have allowed the producers to continue making inferior-quality products, creating a glut in the domestic market without improving their efficiency or competitiveness but at the same time allowing them to benefit from the government incentives. This was never the intention under EAGM. By suppressing the household sector, it was clear that these economies chose to replace domestic demand with exports, and that's why linking of all the incentives with exports (or foreign exchange earnings) was the best way to achieve their objectives.

This is where India's PLI is lacking. Unlike East Asian economies, the GoI has linked financial incentives with domestic production, which is expected to replace imports and eventually be exported. However, the linking factor is 'domestic production', not foreign exchange earnings or exports. What if the Indian industrialists replace imports with domestic production but fail to win export orders? What if lower-quality substitutes are dumped in the domestic market, making consumers worse off than before? One may argue that linking production to exports may lead to higher imports, as had been the case in most East Asian nations as well. However, it would certainly ensure best quality goods and services.

What about Government Finances?

Besides these policies, one more similarity among almost all successful nations, irrespective of their growth model, was the government's tight control of its own financial position, also called fiscal balance. Ranging from the US in the late eighteenth/early nineteenth centuries to Japan in the late nineteenth century to South Korea in the second half of the twentieth century and China in the late twentieth century, the fiscal deficit, and thus government debt, in almost all these countries was extremely contained. In fact, except for the European nations, which were almost always at war with one another, fiscal recklessness was never a common phenomenon during the initial stages of development in nations that achieved economic success.

Exhibit 8.3 compares the long-term trends in fiscal balance as a percentage of GDP in six major Asian economies, including India. Except for South Korea and India, the other four nations—China, Hong Kong, Singapore and Taiwan—experienced fiscal surplus (or marginal deficits) in the 1960s and 1970s. Further, while South Korea ran high fiscal deficits—amounting to around 10 per cent of GDP in the 1950s—it was quickly consolidated to less than 3–4 per cent in the 1970s and was almost balanced in the 1980s.

India, on the contrary, has run a persistent and high fiscal deficit during the past seven decades. The Central government's fiscal deficit averaged 4 per cent of GDP between the 1950s and 1970. Since we have general government data for 1980 onward, we know that it has been stubbornly consistent at around 7–9 per cent during the past four decades.

While every economics student and market participant is aware of the concept of fiscal balance and its implications, it is interesting to note that the concept of 'fiscal deficit' is not very old in India. Until 1991–92, the Union Budget documents did not mention or report the fiscal balance. Instead, the 'budgeted or uncovered deficit' was reported. Fiscal deficit made its first appearance in the Economic Survey 1990–91,

Exhibit 8.3: India has run an extremely persistent and high fiscal deficit since the 1960s

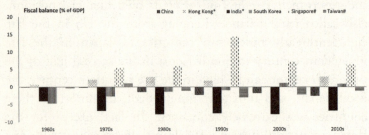

* Financial year (April–March) data; Calendar year for others
India/China data is only central government up to 1970/1981 and general government since then
Source: IMF, World Bank, various national sources, author's research

under the shadow of the impending IMF structural adjustment programme in 1991, by the then finance minister, Dr Manmohan Singh, and later made its way into Union Budget documents in 1991–92.[12] Therefore, while it may be difficult to find old research documents commenting on fiscal deficit, discussions on government debt were ubiquitous.

It is a common practice to compare the twenty-first-century policies of the US or Japan with India's. Considering their very different economic structures and level of development, the fiscal balances in these economies ought to be very different as well. Therefore, one may question the relevance of comparing the twenty-first-century fiscal balances of the US (or of Japan) with India's.

A better way to compare the economies is to compare their build-up in government debt when they were at a similar development stage, say, immediately post-Independence or liberalization. The US became independent in 1776; in Japan, a political revolution (called Meiji Restoration) in 1868 led to the demise of the military government in the country; in South Korea, Park Chung Hee changed the country's economic fate in the 1960s. These stages in economic structure and development were more similar to those of India in the 1950s, immediately after Independence. Therefore, it may be more useful to compare India's government debt since the 1950s with US government debt in the early nineteenth century, with Japanese government debt during the late nineteenth century and with trends in the East Asian economies since the second half of the twentieth century.

Thanks to the excellent work done by IMF researchers to assemble a wide array of historical sources and publish a working paper,[13] historical data on public debt since 1800 across many countries is available. Consequently, one can compare government debt during the first seventy years of Independence in the US, government debt after the end of military rule in Japan, and government debt in other Asian economies (including India) since the 1950s (Exhibit 8.4).

As expected, India's government debt since Independence has been very high compared with all other countries and has been remarkably stable at around 70 per cent of GDP for the past three decades up to FY19. The Japanese government debt was around 40 per cent in the 1870s (after the Meiji Restoration); however, it reduced to 20 per cent by the end of the nineteenth century. Though it rose sharply to 70 per cent of GDP during World War I, it came down quickly towards 30 per cent by the early 1920s.

Similarly, US government debt was 40 per cent, as per the first record available for 1791, which was reduced to 20 per cent by the end of the eighteenth century. It was reduced further, to below 10 per cent of GDP, by the mid-1820s and stayed in the low single digits before the Civil War broke out in the 1860s. The situation was no different in the East Asian countries, where government debt was extremely stable at very low levels (less than 20 per cent of GDP) till the end of the twentieth century.

Exhibit 8.4: Comparison of government debt in India with selected countries

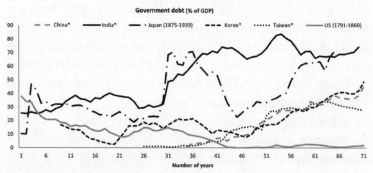

India's data is for the Central government up to 1980 (Year = 30) and for the general government since
* 1950–2020 period (FY51–FY21 for India)
Data begins from 1984 (China), 1958 (South Korea) and 1975 (Taiwan)
Source: IMF, World Bank, various national sources, author's research

Controlled fiscal deficits, and therefore lower government debt, allowed these countries to allocate resources towards building their soft infrastructure (human capital) and physical infrastructure (investments) and to facilitate an enabling economic environment for the private sector to boom. Since Asian economies suppressed the household sector, which led to higher corporate savings (and thus GDS), lower borrowings by the government implies that surplus funds were available for the private businesses to avail of. As discussed in Chapter 4, the fiscal deficit in India has been almost equivalent to the entire household surplus during the past three decades. In contrast, the government absorbed only about 30 per cent (on an average) of the household surplus in South Korea between 1975 and the early 1990s, after which the government of South Korea has run fiscal surpluses.

What about International Trade Policies?

As discussed above, the successful East Asian economies did not always have current account surpluses. There were high external deficits during the initial phases of development because of higher imports. However, this doesn't mean that these economies practised free trade. Instead, large export subsidies, in the form of various financial and non-financial incentives, and high import barriers were very common. From the European economies in the seventeenth and eighteenth centuries to the US in the nineteenth century to many Asian economies in the twentieth, the 'protectionism' provided to various infant industries at their initial stages of development was a common characteristic across high-growth nations.

The 'infant industry' argument is simple and important, especially in the context of developing economies in their initial stages of development. In order to encourage strategic industries domestically, various kinds of protection are provided by national governments to protect them from more efficient and advanced foreign competition. Not only are these domestic producers saved from imported competition but they are also encouraged and made competitive using several financial and non-financial incentives. Also, while one might think that China is the front leader when it comes to these policies, any student of economic history would agree that protectionism is one of the oldest and the most common economic policies adopted by most Western nations too.

Mehdi Shafaeddin, a Swiss-Iranian development economist, who served as senior economist, executive direction and management, United Nations Conference on Trade and Development (UNCTAD), has worked extensively on trade liberalization and industrialization. He says:[14]

> The United States was the motherland of infant industry protection not only at the intellectual level but also in actual fact. Despite the fact that the Industrial Revolution contributed to the rapid industrialization of Great Britain, its industrial sector benefited from trade protection and other forms of government intervention in the trade flow . . .
>
> With the exception of Hong Kong, no country has developed its industrial base without prior infant industry protection.

The British protected their manufacturing segment from its superior Dutch counterparts in the eighteenth century in the same way that the US protected its manufacturers from the more efficient English manufacturers in the nineteenth century. The British also saved their garments industry from superior Indian textiles by imposing heavy tariffs on imports of the latter into England and by dumping their inferior-quality goods in India. The early history of the US again provides evidence of how protectionism helped and lack of tariffs was harmful.

George Friedrich List, a German-American economist, advocated imposition of tariffs on imported goods while supporting free trade of domestic goods, and stated that the cost of a tariff should be seen as an investment in a nation's future productivity.[15] List noted that after the Peace of Paris treaty in the late eighteenth century, which ended the American Revolutionary War, English-manufactured goods obtained free admission in the United States of North America, which was almost impossible for the American manufacturers to bear.[16] An orator in the Congress said after the crisis:[17]

> We did buy, according to the advice of modern theorists, where we could buy the cheapest, and our markets were flooded with foreign goods. Our merchants, even those who thought to enrich themselves by importation, became bankrupt; and all these causes together were so detrimental to agriculture, that landed property became very generally worthless, and consequently bankruptcy became general even among our landowners . . .

Not surprisingly, then, the US Congress was inundated with petitions from all the states in favour of protective measures for the internal industry, and Washington did just that by levying light duties on imports of the most important manufactured articles under the first American tariff in 1789.

For a couple of decades, tariffs were kept at lower levels and reduced for many articles, under coercion by powerful private interests. The irony of these events, however, unfolded in the imposition of tariffs and other trade restrictions by Great Britain on foods and grain (famously called the Corn Laws) between 1815 and 1846. This incident allowed approval of higher tariffs by the US Congress, which were supplemented by the tariffs of 1828.

List was careful in the matter of protectionism and the infant industry argument. He never advocated across-the-board protectionism, nor was he against international trade. He maintained that protectionism should be temporary, targeted and not excessive, and that after a point trade should be liberalized selectively and gradually, aiming at the ultimate goal of free trade when all nations have reached the same level of development.[18]

In contrast, David Ricardo, in his famous comparative trade theory, underlined the free trade philosophy, proving that countries should engage in production of those goods in which they possess comparative advantage. If each country specializes in its comparative advantage, global production of goods would be maximized and all countries would tend to benefit.

The idea that countries get richer by practising free trade has very little empirical evidence, and it is far more likely that countries benefit from free trade only after they get rich. It is not surprising then that liberal trade policies are all advocated by the rich Western world, and that almost all nations in the world have practised protectionism in their initial stages of development.

Notably, in contrast to Britain and the US, the Ottoman empire, which controlled much of south-eastern Europe, western Asia and northern Africa between the fourteenth and early twentieth centuries, practised free trade, which, according to economic historian Paul Bairoch, led to its de-industrialization.[19] In contrast to the protectionism of China, Japan and Spain, the Ottoman empire had a liberal trade policy and was open to foreign imports. This has origins in capitulations by the Ottoman empire, dating back to the first commercial treaties signed with France in 1536, taken further ahead with capitulations in 1673 and 1740, which lowered duties to 3 per cent for imports and exports. The liberal Ottoman policies were praised by British economists such as J.R. McCulloch in his *Dictionary of Commerce* (1834), but later highlighted by British politicians such as Prime Minister Benjamin Disraeli, who cited the Ottoman empire as 'an instance of the injury done by unrestrained competition' in the 1846 Corn Laws debate. He said:

> There has been free trade in Turkey, and what has it produced? It has destroyed some of the finest manufactures of the world. As late as 1812 these manufactures existed; but they have been destroyed. That was the consequences of

competition in Turkey, and its effects have been as pernicious as the effects of the contrary principle in Spain . . .

Free trade is almost universally considered the advocated norm in economics these days. Nevertheless, going back into history, this was never the case. Michael Hudson summarizes the point succinctly in the preface to the second edition of his classic book *Trade, Development and Foreign Debt*:[20]

> Historically, first England and later the United State endowed themselves with capital, by means of protectionist policies and their own credit creation. England put forth the argument for free trade to persuade other countries not to adopt the strategy that had enabled it to overtake Holland and France.

Not only economic thinking, but the means to achieve economic objectives have also undergone a massive change. While import tariffs were the dominant form of protectionism before the 1970s, undervaluation of the currency replaced it once exchange rates became flexible. Maintaining an undervalued currency against the US dollar, which is still managed by many economies such as China, Hong Kong, Singapore and Taiwan, is one of the most potent policies to support exporters (producers). When a country manages its currency by keeping it undervalued, it is similar to infant industry tariffs and has the same effect. But is it now possible?

Was Private Debt High in These Successful Nations?

Not only government debt, but private debt too was not significantly high in South Korea and Taiwan during their high-growth phases. With government debt contained at below 20 per cent of GDP in both nations in the early 1990s, household debt was under 40 per cent and under 50 per cent of GDP, respectively, in South Korea and Taiwan, while corporate debt was under 80 per cent and around 75 per cent, respectively, towards the end of their three-decade episodes of high growth. In contrast, while government debt in China was also contained, corporate debt (including SOEs') rose to 100 per cent of GDP in the early 2000s and had risen sharply to 160 per cent of GDP by the mid-2010s decade.

During the past few years, debt growth in India has remained extremely subdued. Prior to the pandemic, the entire focus of several policymakers' meetings was to lift debt growth in the country. These debates were partly misleading because household debt in India was broadly assumed to be at low levels of 10–11 per cent of GDP (RBI had not started publishing its estimates of the household financial balance sheet at that time) and there were no clear estimates of corporate debt in the country. The basic assumption in such meetings was that India's leverage was too low, especially compared with other economies. If only debt growth could be pushed higher in India, it would take care of GDP growth—that was the belief.

Unlike China and many other nations today, the economic performance of South Korea and Taiwan between the 1950s and early 1990s clearly shows that higher leverage is not the only possible way to grow fast. Even after almost three successive decades of high single-digit growth, the total non-financial sector's (government + household + corporate) debt in these two countries was less than 150 per cent of GDP. In contrast, although household debt in India is around 35 per cent of GDP, the non-financial sector's total debt amounted to more than 150 per cent of GDP in 2019, and was around 160 per cent of GDP as of December 2022. Should our policymakers then be so comfortable in pushing household debt higher? As explained earlier in this book, although household debt seems to be low in India compared with other nations, it is a combination of higher interest rates and low maturity that keeps the threshold at a lower level in India.

What Can Be Done Then?

The question then is, 'Is there any other way India can grow faster?' Yes, India can grow faster without pushing debt higher by ensuring better and efficient allocation of domestic resources in the country. In economics parlance, this is estimated as the incremental capital-output ratio (ICOR). While this is easier said than done, it is not impossible, and the current government, with its very strong mandate, is the best hope for achieving this objective.

ICOR measures capital productivity in an economy by linking investments to the changes in GDP. In particular, ICOR measures the units of investment required to produce an additional unit of GDP growth. An ICOR of, say, 3x implies that three units of investment are required to produce an additional unit of GDP growth, while an ICOR of 5x means that the country needs five units of investments to produce the same effect. The lower the ICOR, the more efficient the capital, and vice versa.

Almost all high-growth episodes across the world since the seventeenth century have entailed improvement in capital productivity by more efficient reallocation of domestic resources. As countries divert resources from the less productive agriculture sector to industrial activity, it is almost obvious that higher growth will be achieved. Be it Russia from the 1930s to the 1970s, Brazil in the 1950s and 1960s, the East Asian economies from the late 1950s to the early 1990s, or China since the 1980s, every country has witnessed higher growth as a result of rapid industrialization. As better technology or equipment becomes available, existing resources are more efficiently utilized, which leads to more resources, leading to higher growth.

A comparison of most of the Asian economies indicates that the pattern has been very similar. Not only were these economies able to push the investment rate higher but they also improved on capital productivity, reflected in their lower ICOR. The ICOR averaged 2–3x between the 1960s and the 1980s in Hong Kong, Singapore and South Korea, with an average of 4.5x in Taiwan. Even in China, ICOR was about

3x in the 1990s and the 2000s decade. This combination of higher investments and lower ICOR for a prolonged period helped these nations successfully transition from low-income to high-income economies. In contrast, India's ICOR was 5.1x in the 2000s decade and stabilized at those levels up to FY19. According to the government's second advance estimates,[21] the ICOR was 5.1x in FY23, after a turmoil in the FY20–FY22 period.

What Are the Lessons for India?

If we look at India's high-growth episode in the mid-2000s decade, it is easy to find various traits of EAGM. India's domestic savings increased rapidly from 25 per cent of GDP in early 2000s decade to its peak of 37 per cent of GDP in FY08. At the same time, India's investments also increased rapidly from 24 per cent to 38.1 per cent of GDP. As had happened in most East Asian economies, India's CAD widened, from a surplus in the first three years of the twenty-first century to a deficit of 1.3 per cent of GDP in FY08. This was not because of low exports growth. In fact, exports growth was markedly high during the period; however, imports grew even faster, pushing the trade deficit higher.

At the same time, the share of PFCE fell rapidly, from 65 per cent in the early 2000s decade to an all-time low of 56 per cent of GDP in FY11. Further, as the fiscal deficit also narrowed significantly, government dis-savings also reduced. In other words, as the share of households fell, the corporate sector surged during the first decade of the century. Corporate profits almost doubled, from 4.4 per cent of GDP in the 1990s to 8.1 per cent of GDP in the 2000s decade, and peaked at 12.3 per cent of GDP in FY08. Corporate investments also grew rapidly during the high-growth phase—at an average of 32 per cent during FY04–09 against the 22 per cent growth in total investments. Moreover, like in most successful nations, the share of households in India's GDS fell, from 85–90 per cent in the early 2000s decade to 55–60 per cent in FY07–08, while it increased from 30 per cent to over 40 per cent for the corporate sector during the period. This is exactly the script that played out in South Korea and Taiwan in the 1960s and 1970s.

There were, however, some notable differences. It is highly arguable that India saw exceptionally high growth in the mid-2000s decade because of its domestic policies or its long-term vision. More likely, India was part of the global high-growth phase—almost all countries in the world posted higher growth during this period.

There were several differences in India's high-growth phase and the multi-decadal high-growth witnessed in several Asian countries during the second half of the twentieth century.

First, although the share of the household sector declined in the Indian economy, it was more a result of global growth than of India's policies. There were no direct policies to lower labour wages in the country and make domestic goods and services more competitive than in the rest of the world.

Second, it is also difficult to link the high growth seen in India's exports during the period with domestic initiatives or direct support. Rather, the fact that the rupee strengthened during the high-growth phase was a strong signal that India's high growth was more a result of the global tide than of any attempted efforts.

Third, although the high investments rate (around 40 per cent of GDP) is cheered in India and argued to be a key factor for the high growth, such high investment rates are unusual. The efficiency of India's investments (measured by ICOR) was also closer to averaged 5.1x in the 2000s decade, compared to 4x in Taiwan, and 3x in South Korea and China during their high growth phases.

Fourth, while the financial position of the government improved during the period, aggregate government debt was down from around 80 per cent of GDP to under 70 per cent of

GDP in FY08—it was still too high and further improvement was desired.

In short, while the high-growth phase of FY04–08 in India reflected several traits of EAGM, one cannot say that India followed EAGM. The similarities seem to be more coincidental than planned. As global growth collapsed in 2008, this conclusion was entirely supported by the response of Indian policymakers. The massive expansion in fiscal deficit in 2009–13 created growth at the cost of overheating of the economy and boosting of consumption growth. Consequently, inflation clocked an average of 10 per cent during the FY09–14 period and the current account widened to a record-high of 4–5 per cent of GDP. The expansion in CAD was partly because of a surge in investments and partly because of a shortfall in savings, as implementation of the sixth pay commission (with huge arrears) and higher allocation to the demand-driven rural employment guarantee programme continued to raise consumption. The share of PFCE also rose gradually, from 56 per cent in FY11 to 61 per cent of GDP in FY20. A comparison of the 2000s decade vis-à-vis the 2010s decades confirms two conclusions: either India's growth model shifted abruptly from EAGM in the 2000s decade to a consumption-led one in the 2010s decade, or there was no growth model in the 2000s decade and the policymakers were taking one step at a time with the sole objective of maintaining short-term growth. Both conclusions reveal the nation's serious lack of patience, long-term vision and ability to handle difficult periods.

Overall, there are no examples of successful nations in recent economic history (say twentieth century) which have grown out of their low-income status by boosting consumption rather than investments/exports. And if higher consumption is based on debt and past savings, then any gains will only prove to be transitory. The word 'transitory' does not necessarily mean a few months or quarters but means the situation may continue for many years before hurting growth potential significantly for a much longer period. The historical lessons are very clear: (1) Keep the government financial position in check and improve the quality of spending by investing in soft (health, education, etc.) and physical infrastructure. (2) The government should be a facilitator and enabler of private investments in the country rather than itself being the primary investor. If needed, it must align the corporate sector objectives with the national objectives. (3) The private sector requires support, especially at the initial stages of development. Therefore, protectionism is neither bad nor orthodox; excessive, prolonged and unconditional support, however, is a serious burden on any nation. (4) High debt is not a solution to achieve high growth for decades. In fact, prolonged periods of high growth can never be achieved with excess debt. (5) Better allocation of resources leading to higher efficiency of investments holds the key.

These are some of the common policies that have been implemented by almost all successful nations in the world. The key difference between the two models of economic development, as classified by Professor Pettis, however, lies in their treatment of the household sector.

So Does India Follow Any Growth Model at All?

Many commentators have talked about India creating and adopting a new economic growth model, based entirely on the services sector rather than on the manufacturing sector, as was followed under EAGM and AGM. While the optimism is appreciated, there are many unanswered questions. With its low education standards, how can India continue to grow its services sector as strongly as it has in the past fifteen years or so? Software services and telecommunications have been among the most favourable services industries in the country. What about the lagging health infrastructure or education quality? Since the services sector is more productivity-oriented, can India afford to choose a productivity-led model with such large employment requirements? Since the services sector requires a highly skilled workforce, what future does it hold for India's abundant low-skilled workforce? It is not surprising that there are no precedents to follow if India is to take this path. Because there are more questions than answers, these arguments attract serious scepticism. I am not saying that India cannot follow a new model; however, it is absolutely necessary to find answers to these questions by an open debate, keeping a comprehensive vision and road map. I am not sure if we have these things in place.

Instead, the economic policy framework remains as confused and muddled as ever in India. With the acceleration of the Mahatma Gandhi National Rural Employment Guarantee Act (MGNREGA) after the great financial crisis, the focus has decidedly shifted to the agricultural sector, in particular, and the rural sector, in general. With unconditional income support having been made available under PM-KISAN, the change in ideology is firmly established. The nation has firmly moved towards the redistribution economic model.

The confusion, however, comes from recent actions of the GoI, in the form of a large cut in corporate income taxes (remember the example with which this book began). Such pro-corporate policies could lead to substantial efficiency and competitive gains; however, they have to be complemented with several other policies, all with the same objective—to push corporate income/savings higher with an assurance of higher spending on their part—with exceptional attention on improving the efficiency of investments. As explained already, the 'please all' model has never worked and actually reflects absence of a long-term economic vision.

Can India follow EAGM or AGM at this stage? It can, but it would be difficult. There are several tough policies to be implemented under any of these models, which may be highly unpopular for any government. The only way to ensure continuity of these hard choices is to implement them effectively and wait for them to yield high growth over the long term. It is not a coincidence that most of the nations that adopted EAGM successfully did not have democratic government structures in place. Democracy has many benefits, but it has its own disadvantages when it comes to implementing and sustaining unpopular policies. In contrast, decision-making—whether right or wrong—is much easier in an undemocratic setting.

Further, the global environment has been set in a manner that may see Indian policymakers failing to adopt the required policies, even though several other nations openly implemented them a few decades ago and some continue to do so. Do you think that if India wants to encourage a domestic industry to compete in the foreign markets, it can directly support the industry with financial and non-financial incentives? Is it really possible today to build a high-protection wall to support domestic manufacturers and then to collapse it if it leads to more inefficiencies in the system? Not only will these decisions be seriously challenged in the so-called equitable economic environment of today, but reversal of these domestic policies may also be very difficult because of internal political compulsions.

The fact is, the rules of the game are still set by the advanced nations and emerging economies such as India are still on the receiving end in several matters. What otherwise explains the absence of application of equality and cooperation in the monetary policies area?

One of the most important characteristics of the Indian economy is its demography. With one of the youngest populations in the world and its large pool of working people, India's demography is in stark contrast to those of most advanced nations at this stage, which are witnessing ageing populations and declining working-age populations. It is then not surprising to see many smart and talented Indians moving to advanced nations in search of a better and more prosperous future. While this is a sensible thing to do on the part of these individuals, it is extremely debilitating for the nation. Imposition of higher taxes on the rich to continue its redistribution of wealth and its muddled economic policies are unlikely to yield any fruits for the economy.

The 2020s decade will be full of challenges and opportunities. How India leverages these opportunities will depend on how its policymakers address those challenges. Together, their decisions will decide the fate of not only the 2020s decade but also the 2030s decade. This book firmly argues that the current decade should be a 'Healing Decade', wherein the authorities get their act together, create a multi-decade vision for obtaining a seat for India at the high-income nations table, choose a crystal-clear growth model, address the fundamental issues and bet on the country's long-term prospects. Without accepting and addressing their weaknesses, no one has ever been to learn and explore their strengths. That's exactly what we also need to do for the nation too.

Key Lessons from the Chapter

- Neither the current wave of digitalization nor the various incentive schemes are a substitute for the weak financial balance sheets of the domestic economic agents.
- In one way or the other, the growth models adopted by most successful economies in the world were similar to each other. There are two established growth models in the World—the East Asian growth model and the American growth model. One of the biggest differences between these two economic growth models lies in their treatment of the household sector. While households are suppressed in favour of the corporate sector under EAGM, they are the key drivers of growth in the latter.
- The four key policies used to achieve growth under EAGM were higher inequality, lower household wages, undervalued (or weaker) currency and financial repression. Lower consumption leading to lower share of households, and increase in GDS by increasing the share of companies.

Weak domestic demand is replaced with higher external demand, leading to current account surpluses. At the initial stages of development, however, many successful nations witnessed high CAD, only to turn it into a surplus at a later stage.
- By keeping good control on the financial sector and a high share of PSUs, several nations align their corporate sector with the national objectives. Many countries used the carrot-and-stick approach to make private businesses play an important role in national growth.
- Notwithstanding the choice of growth model, government finances were kept under strict check in the initial decades of these countries' Independence and development. India, in contrast, has seen persistent and high fiscal deficits during the past seven decades. Not only government debt but private debt too was kept in check by most economies (with the exception of China) in the initial stages of their development.
- The idea that countries get richer by practising free trade has little empirical evidence to back it, and it is far more likely that countries benefit from free trade only after they get rich.
- Although the high-growth phase of FY04–08 in India reflected several traits of EAGM, it is extremely difficult to conclude that India followed EAGM. The similarity seems to be more coincidental than planned.
- The 'please all' model has never worked anywhere and actually reflects absence of a long-term economic vision. Not only does the government want to keep consumption growth high by supporting the farm sector but it also wants to incentivize companies through income tax cuts. Considering the current global environment and India's development stage, it is highly difficult for it to follow EAGM.

APPENDICES

Appendix 1: Household financial position in nominal/current terms since 1950–51 (₹ tn)

	GDP	PDI	PFCE	Total savings	GFS	Financial liabilities	NFS	Investment*	Outstanding Debt
1950–51	0.10	0.09	0.09		0.00		0.00	0.01	
1951–52	0.11	0.10	0.10	0.01	0.00	0.00	0.00	0.01	0.01
1952–53	0.11	0.10	0.10	0.01	0.00	0.00	0.00	0.01	0.01
1953–54	0.12	0.11	0.11	0.01	0.00	0.00	0.00	0.01	0.01
1954–55	0.11	0.10	0.10	0.01	0.01	0.00	0.00	0.00	0.01
1955–56	0.11	0.10	0.10	0.01	0.00	0.00	0.00	0.01	0.01
1956–57	0.14	0.12	0.12	0.01	0.00	0.00	0.00	0.01	0.01
1957–58	0.14	0.12	0.12	0.01	0.00	0.00	0.00	0.01	0.01
1958–59	0.16	0.14	0.14	0.01	0.00	0.00	0.00	0.01	0.01
1959–60	0.16	0.14	0.15	0.01	0.01	0.00	0.00	0.01	0.02
1960–61	0.18	0.16	0.16	0.01	0.01	0.00	0.00	0.01	0.02
1961–62	0.19	0.16	0.17	0.01	0.01	0.00	0.01	0.01	0.02
1962–63	0.20	0.17	0.18	0.02	0.01	0.00	0.01	0.01	0.02
1963–64	0.23	0.20	0.19	0.02	0.01	0.00	0.01	0.01	0.02
1964–65	0.27	0.23	0.23	0.02	0.01	0.00	0.01	0.01	0.03
1965–66	0.29	0.24	0.24	0.02	0.01	0.00	0.01	0.02	0.03

Appendix 1 (continued)

	GDP	PDI	PFCE	Total savings	GFS	Financial liabilities	NFS	Investment*	Outstanding Debt
1966–67	0.33	0.28	0.28	0.03	0.01	0.00	0.01	0.02	0.03
1967–68	0.38	0.33	0.34	0.03	0.01	0.00	0.01	0.02	0.04
1968–69	0.41	0.35	0.34	0.03	0.01	0.01	0.01	0.02	0.04
1969–70	0.45	0.38	0.36	0.04	0.02	0.01	0.01	0.03	0.05
1970–71	0.48	0.40	0.38	0.05	0.02	0.01	0.02	0.03	0.05
1971–72	0.51	0.42	0.41	0.05	0.02	0.01	0.02	0.04	0.06
1972–73	0.56	0.47	0.46	0.06	0.03	0.01	0.02	0.03	0.07
1973–74	0.68	0.58	0.55	0.07	0.04	0.01	0.03	0.04	0.08
1974–75	0.81	0.67	0.67	0.09	0.03	0.01	0.03	0.06	0.08
1975–76	0.87	0.72	0.68	0.10	0.05	0.01	0.04	0.06	0.09
1976–77	0.93	0.76	0.71	0.12	0.07	0.01	0.05	0.06	0.11
1977–78	1.06	0.88	0.82	0.13	0.07	0.02	0.05	0.08	0.13
1978–79	1.15	0.95	0.89	0.17	0.09	0.03	0.07	0.10	0.15
1979–80	1.26	1.03	0.97	0.17	0.10	0.04	0.07	0.10	0.19
1980–81	1.50	1.28	1.18	0.18	0.12	0.04	0.09	0.10	0.22
1981–82	1.76	1.47	1.36	0.19	0.14	0.04	0.10	0.09	0.26
1982–83	1.97	1.63	1.50	0.22	0.16	0.04	0.13	0.09	0.30
1983–84	2.29	1.93	1.75	0.27	0.19	0.05	0.14	0.14	0.35
1984–85	2.57	2.15	1.94	0.33	0.24	0.06	0.18	0.15	0.41
1985–86	2.90	2.38	2.14	0.37	0.26	0.07	0.19	0.18	0.48

	GDP	PDI	PFCE	Total savings	GFS	Financial liabilities	NFS	Investment*	Outstanding Debt
1986–87	3.24	2.66	2.40	0.42	0.32	0.09	0.23	0.19	0.56
1987–88	3.68	3.01	2.67	0.57	0.36	0.09	0.27	0.30	0.66
1988–89	4.37	3.57	3.10	0.67	0.40	0.13	0.27	0.40	0.78
1989–90	5.02	4.09	3.47	0.83	0.48	0.10	0.38	0.45	0.89
1990–91	5.86	4.80	3.99	1.09	0.59	0.09	0.50	0.59	0.98
1991–92	6.74	5.48	4.58	1.06	0.68	0.06	0.62	0.44	1.04
1992–93	7.75	6.39	5.16	1.28	0.80	0.15	0.65	0.63	1.19
1993–94	8.91	7.39	5.91	1.51	1.10	0.15	0.95	0.57	1.34
1994–95	10.46	8.68	6.87	1.87	1.46	0.25	1.21	0.66	1.59
1995–96	12.27	9.92	7.92	1.99	1.24	0.19	1.06	0.93	1.77
1996–97	14.19	11.84	9.29	2.25	1.59	0.17	1.42	0.83	1.94
1997–98	15.72	13.05	10.19	2.84	1.72	0.25	1.47	1.37	2.19
1998–99	18.03	15.23	11.66	3.52	2.07	0.27	1.80	1.72	2.46
1999–00	20.23	16.71	13.13	4.32	2.36	0.36	2.00	2.32	2.82
2000–01	21.77	18.31	14.07	4.64	2.47	0.32	2.16	2.49	3.14
2001–02	23.56	20.17	15.32	5.32	2.86	0.52	2.34	2.98	3.65
2002–03	25.36	21.36	16.20	5.74	3.23	0.60	2.63	3.11	4.26
2003–04	28.42	23.56	17.71	6.64	3.89	0.70	3.19	3.44	4.96
2004–05	32.42	25.82	19.18	7.54	4.47	1.22	3.26	4.29	6.17
2005–06	36.93	29.11	21.53	8.31	5.84	1.85	3.99	4.32	8.02

Appendix 1 (continued)

	GDP	PDI	PFCE	Total savings	GFS	Financial liabilities	NFS	Investment*	Outstanding Debt
2006-07	42.95	33.29	24.77	9.73	7.65	2.84	4.80	4.93	10.87
2007-08	49.87	37.35	28.41	11.42	7.72	1.90	5.83	5.60	12.77
2008-09	56.30	45.31	32.49	13.49	7.27	1.65	5.61	7.88	14.42
2009-10	64.78	51.98	37.08	16.75	9.90	2.05	7.84	8.90	16.47
2010-11	77.84	60.04	43.60	18.32	10.80	2.83	7.97	10.35	19.30
2011-12	87.36	70.35	49.10	20.66	9.33	2.90	6.43	13.89	23.36
2012-13	99.44	79.81	56.14	22.35	10.64	3.30	7.34	14.65	28.28
2013-14	112.34	90.10	64.76	22.85	11.91	3.59	8.32	14.16	31.11
2014-15	124.68	98.43	72.47	24.39	12.57	3.77	8.80	15.13	33.82
2015-16	137.72	107.82	81.26	24.75	14.96	3.85	11.11	13.18	38.54
2016-17	153.92	119.70	91.27	27.87	16.15	4.69	11.46	15.95	44.83
2017-18	170.90	132.87	100.36	32.97	20.56	7.51	13.06	19.44	52.38
2018-19	189.00	149.90	112.05	38.45	22.64	7.71	14.92	23.09	63.30
2019-20	201.04	161.43	122.45	38.45	23.25	7.75	15.50	22.52	69.85
2020-21	198.30	165.30	121.50	44.35	30.54	7.78	22.77	21.19	77.72
2021-22	234.71	185.24	143.44	46.20	25.98	8.07	17.91	27.69	83.65

Second revised estimates for 2020-21 and First revised estimates for 2021-22

Total savings = NFS + investments

* Household investments = Physical savings

n/a = not available

Source: CSO, RBI, author's estimates

Appendix 2: Household financial position since 1950–51

	Real/constant prices			Nominal/current prices						
	Real GDP	Real PDI	Real PFCE	PDI	PFCE	Total savings	NFS	Investment*	Debt
	% YoY			% of GDP			% of PDI		
1951–52	2.9	2.0	6.4	87.1	107.0	6.4	0.0	6.4	10.1
1952–53	2.6	3.9	4.0	88.5	107.1	7.4	0.9	6.5	10.1
1953–54	6.2	7.1	6.0	89.4	106.0	5.8	0.8	5.0	9.8
1954–55	4.8	3.9	3.3	88.5	105.4	7.7	2.8	5.0	11.0
1955–56	3.2	2.7	1.0	88.4	103.6	10.5	4.4	6.1	12.1
1956–57	5.6	6.0	4.4	88.8	102.1	10.3	2.9	7.4	10.8
1957–58	-0.4	-1.3	-2.0	88.1	101.4	8.7	2.7	6.0	11.0
1958–59	7.4	7.8	9.2	88.6	102.7	7.2	2.7	4.5	10.4
1959–60	2.6	2.0	1.1	88.2	101.8	8.7	3.0	5.8	10.7
1960–61	5.5	5.3	5.7	86.7	102.2	7.3	2.4	5.0	11.9
1961–62	3.7	2.1	1.7	85.9	101.8	7.8	3.2	4.6	12.1
1962–63	2.9	2.4	1.3	85.1	100.7	8.8	2.9	5.9	12.7
1963–64	6.0	6.1	3.7	84.1	98.5	8.1	3.8	4.3	12.6
1964–65	7.5	6.3	6.0	85.1	98.2	8.0	2.9	5.1	11.7
1965–66	-2.6	-0.5	0.1	84.7	98.8	9.7	3.5	6.2	12.1
1966–67	-0.1	-0.5	1.3	85.6	100.6	11.0	2.8	8.2	11.9

Appendix 2 (continued)

	Real/constant prices			Nominal/current prices					
	Real GDP	Real PDI	Real PFCE	PDI	PFCE	Total savings	NFS	Investment*	Debt
		% YoY		% of GDP			% of PDI		
1967–68	7.8	5.0	5.7	86.5	101.2	9.8	2.5	7.3	11.0
1968–69	3.4	7.9	2.6	86.0	96.3	9.4	2.3	7.1	11.9
1969–70	6.5	4.7	3.7	85.2	95.4	11.3	2.2	9.1	12.8
1970–71	5.2	2.6	3.4	84.1	96.1	11.7	3.8	7.9	13.6
1971–72	1.6	0.2	1.9	83.2	97.8	12.5	3.8	8.7	14.5
1972–73	−0.6	1.2	0.7	83.7	97.3	11.8	5.0	6.8	14.4
1973–74	3.3	4.6	2.5	84.6	95.3	12.5	4.8	7.6	13.0
1974–75	1.2	−4.0	−0.1	83.4	99.2	13.2	3.9	9.4	12.3
1975–76	9.1	9.9	5.7	82.6	95.4	13.8	5.6	8.2	13.1
1976–77	1.7	4.5	2.0	81.6	93.1	15.1	6.8	8.3	14.2
1977–78	7.3	8.7	8.2	83.4	92.7	15.0	6.2	8.9	14.2
1978–79	5.7	4.9	6.1	82.7	93.8	17.5	7.1	10.4	16.1
1979–80	−5.2	−1.9	−2.2	82.2	93.5	16.4	6.5	9.9	18.2
1980–81	6.7	10.2	9.0	85.3	92.5	14.2	6.7	7.4	17.5
1981–82	6.0	4.8	4.3	83.8	92.1	12.9	6.5	6.4	17.9
1982–83	3.5	1.3	1.0	82.9	91.9	13.4	7.7	5.7	18.3
1983–84	7.3	8.8	7.8	84.2	91.0	14.1	7.0	7.1	18.2
1984–85	3.8	3.8	2.9	83.8	90.2	15.2	8.3	6.9	19.0

	Real/constant prices			Nominal/current prices						
	Real GDP	Real PDI	Real PFCE	PDI	PFCE	Total savings	NFS	Investment*	Debt
	% YoY			% of GDP			% of PDI		
1985–86	5.3	4.3	4.2	82.1	90.1	15.4	7.8	7.6	20.1
1986–87	4.8	2.8	3.2	82.0	90.4	15.9	8.8	7.1	21.2
1987–88	4.0	5.6	3.4	81.8	88.5	19.0	8.9	10.1	21.8
1988–89	9.6	8.0	6.2	81.6	87.1	18.8	7.6	11.2	22.0
1989–90	5.9	7.8	5.0	81.5	84.8	20.3	9.3	11.0	21.7
1990–91	5.5	6.6	4.5	81.8	83.1	22.6	10.3	12.3	20.4
1991–92	1.1	1.6	2.2	81.3	83.5	19.3	11.3	7.9	19.0
1992–93	5.5	6.0	2.6	82.4	80.8	20.0	10.2	9.8	18.6
1993–94	4.8	5.5	4.3	83.0	80.0	20.5	12.8	7.7	18.1
1994–95	6.7	5.9	4.9	83.0	79.2	21.6	13.9	7.7	18.3
1995–96	7.6	5.2	6.1	80.8	79.9	20.0	10.7	9.4	17.9
1996–97	7.5	9.7	7.8	83.4	78.4	19.0	12.0	7.0	16.4
1997–98	4.0	3.5	3.0	83.0	78.1	21.8	11.3	10.5	16.8
1998–99	6.2	8.6	6.5	84.5	76.6	23.1	11.8	11.3	16.1
1999–00	8.8	3.4	6.1	82.6	78.5	25.9	12.0	13.9	16.9
2000–01	3.8	5.8	3.4	84.1	76.8	25.4	11.8	13.6	17.1
2001–02	4.8	7.2	6.0	85.6	75.9	26.4	11.6	14.8	18.1
2002–03	3.8	3.0	2.9	84.2	75.9	26.9	12.3	14.6	19.9

Appendix 2 (continued)

	Real/constant prices			Nominal/current prices					
	Real GDP	Real PDI	Real PFCE	PDI	PFCE	Total savings	NFS	Investment*	Debt
	% YoY			% of GDP			% of PDI		
2003–04	7.9	6.9	5.9	82.9	75.2	28.2	13.6	14.6	21.0
2004–05	7.9	6.5	5.2	79.6	74.3	29.2	12.6	16.6	23.9
2005–06	9.3	9.1	8.6	78.8	74.0	28.5	13.7	14.8	27.6
2006–07	9.3	7.8	8.5	77.5	74.4	29.2	14.4	14.8	32.6
2007–08	9.8	7.0	9.4	74.9	76.1	30.6	15.6	15.0	34.2
2008–09	3.9	13.7	7.2	80.5	71.7	29.8	12.4	17.4	31.8
2009–10	8.5	8.0	7.4	80.2	71.3	32.2	15.1	17.1	31.7
2010–11	10.3	6.7	8.7	77.1	72.6	30.5	13.3	17.2	32.1
2011–12	6.6	8.6	9.3	80.5	69.8	29.4	9.1	19.7	33.2
2012–13	5.5	4.7	5.5	80.3	70.3	28.0	9.2	18.4	35.4
2013–14	6.4	5.0	7.3	80.2	71.9	25.4	9.2	15.7	34.5
2014–15	7.4	3.9	6.4	78.9	73.6	24.8	8.9	15.4	34.4
2015–16	8.0	5.4	7.9	78.3	75.4	23.0	10.3	12.2	35.7
2016–17	8.3	6.9	8.1	77.8	76.2	23.3	9.6	13.3	37.4
2017–18	6.8	7.2	6.2	77.7	75.5	24.8	9.8	14.6	39.4
2018–19	6.5	8.2	7.1	79.3	74.8	25.6	10.0	15.4	42.2
2019–20	3.9	3.6	5.2	80.3	75.9	23.8	9.6	14.0	43.3

Appendix 3: Essay on of Debt Service Ratio (DSR) for Indian Households

	Real/constant prices			Nominal/current prices				
	Real GDP	Real PDI	Real PFCE	PDI	PFCE	Total savings	NFS	Investment*	Debt
	% YoY			% of GDP			% of PDI		
2020–21	-5.8	-2.2	-5.2	83.4	73.5	26.8	13.8	12.8	47.0
2021–22	9.1	5.6	11.2	78.9	77.4	24.9	9.7	14.9	45.2
	Decadal average								
1950s	3.9	3.8	3.7	88.4	104.0	8.1	2.2	5.9	10.7
1960s	4.1	3.9	3.2	85.5	99.4	9.1	2.8	6.3	12.1
1970s	2.9	3.1	2.8	83.1	95.4	14.0	5.4	8.6	14.4
1980s	5.7	5.7	4.7	82.9	89.8	15.9	7.9	8.1	19.8
1990s	5.8	5.6	4.8	82.6	79.8	21.4	11.6	9.7	17.8
2000s	6.9	7.5	6.4	80.8	74.5	28.6	13.3	15.3	25.8
2010s	6.9	6.0	7.2	79.0	73.6	25.8	9.9	15.6	36.8

Second revised estimates for 2020-21 and First revised estimates for 2021-22
Total savings = NFS + investments
* Household investments = Physical savings
n/a = not available
Source: CSO, RBI, author's estimates

Appendix 3: Estimation of Debt Service Ratio (DSR) for Indian Households

In order to address the lack of data on average maturity of loans, I use an RBI publication called *Statistical Tables related to Banks in India*. It contains the maturity profile of banks' total loan book (not household loans) under eight different baskets: 1–14 days, 15–28 days, 29 days to 3 months, 3–6 months, 6–12 months, 1–3 years, 3–5 years and over 5 years. Taking the mid-point of each period (and eight years for loans with maturity of over five years), I find that the average maturity of bank loans ranged from 2.5 years to 3.2 years during the past two decades. Considering that household loans comprise housing loans, which are generally of longer maturity, I assume that the average maturity of bank loans to the household sector was one and a half years more than the average maturity of loans. It means that the average maturity of bank loans to the household sector ranged from 4.0 years to 4.7 years during the past two decades.

Further, since 97 per cent of outstanding housing loans to individuals with HFCs were of over seven years' maturity as at end-FY21 (and the ratio has been similar in the previous years), I have assumed their average maturity at ten years for HFCs. Lastly, since no such information is available for NBFC loans to the household sector, I have assumed it to be same as that of bank loans.

When I combine this information on the maturity profile of banks/NBFCs (4.0 years to 4.7 years) and HFCs (ten years), an estimate of the average maturity of household debt in the country can be prepared. This methodology suggests that the average maturity of household debt in India ranged between 4.5 years and 5.3 years during FY02 and FY22. To put it in perspective, the average maturity of household debt in seventeen advanced nations, for which DSR is calculated by BIS, is estimated at close to thirteen years.

Further, I use RBI data on banks' exposure to the household sector to estimate the interest rate on household loans every year. This data is also available for the past two decades. Since there are no details on the effective interest rates charged by HFCs and NBFCs, I assume the banks' interest rate as the final interest rate on Indian household debt (effective interest rate for non-bank lenders, however, is likely to be higher than the rate for banks). Since the average maturity of household debt has been about five years during the past two decades, I use the debt-weighted average interest rate for the last five years on a rotating basis as a proxy of the effective interest rate.

Now, with the information available on household debt, household income, effective interest rate and maturity, I can prepare estimates of the debt service ratio (DSR) for Indian households using equation (1) above and compare it with its counterparts in other nations.

Appendix 4: Deriving India's Corporate Profits from the Theory of Everything (% of GDP)

	Equation (4)			Equation (6)			Common items		Corporate profits
	Total net investments#	HH total savings	Govt savings	Corporate net investments#	HH fin savings	Core FD*	CAD	Dividends paid	
1989–90	20.9	16.5	-1.2	8.1	7.7	5.3	2.0	0.1	3.8
1990–91	23.3	18.5	-1.4	9.8	8.6	5.2	3.0	0.3	3.6
1991–92	18.4	15.7	-0.9	8.9	9.4	4.1	0.3	0.3	3.7
1992–93	19.6	16.5	-0.8	8.5	8.6	4.0	1.6	0.3	2.6
1993–94	18.8	17.0	-1.9	9.7	10.8	4.8	0.4	0.4	3.8
1994–95	21.4	17.9	-1.5	12.2	11.7	4.6	1.0	0.6	4.7
1995–96	21.9	16.2	-1.1	11.9	8.8	3.8	1.6	0.6	6.0
1996–97	20.1	15.8	-1.4	12.2	10.2	3.7	1.1	0.6	5.2
1997–98	22.0	18.1	-1.8	10.9	9.5	4.4	1.3	0.6	5.1
1998–99	20.7	19.5	-3.6	9.0	10.2	6.0	0.9	0.7	4.6
1999–00	23.3	21.7	-4.0	9.5	10.4	6.5	1.0	0.7	5.3
2000–01	20.6	21.3	-4.3	6.7	10.1	7.0	0.5	0.8	3.9
2001–02	20.4	23.1	-4.7	5.2	10.7	7.5	-0.7	1.0	3.7
2002–03	21.0	22.2	-4.1	5.7	10.2	7.4	-1.2	1.1	5.3
2003–04	23.4	23.1	-2.8	6.7	11.2	7.6	-2.3	1.1	6.5
2004–05	29.8	23.5	-2.0	11.8	10.0	6.7	0.4	1.2	9.3
2005–06	31.0	22.3	-1.8	15.4	10.4	5.5	1.2	1.5	10.9
2006–07	30.5	21.2	-0.9	15.2	9.6	4.6	1.0	1.6	10.8

	Equation (4)			Equation (6)				Common items		Corporate profits
	Total net investments#	HH total savings	Govt savings	Corporate net investments#	HH fin savings	Core FD*	CAD	Dividends paid		
2007–08	33.5	20.6	0.5	17.4	9.2	4.2	1.3	1.2		12.3
2008–09	32.5	25.2	-2.5	14.3	10.9	6.4	2.3	1.1		8.7
2009–10	33.0	24.8	-2.7	15.2	10.9	6.6	2.8	1.1		9.2
2010–11	34.2	24.0	-0.5	16.9	10.4	4.2	2.9	1.2		8.9
2011–12	33.3	23.6	-1.8	13.9	7.7	5.3	4.3	1.2		8.4
2012–13	33.0	22.5	-1.6	14.8	7.7	5.0	4.8	1.1		8.4
2013–14	28.0	20.3	-1.5	11.9	7.7	5.1	1.7	1.3		8.8
2014–15	27.6	19.6	-1.4	11.9	7.4	4.9	1.3	1.5		9.6
2015–16	26.1	18.0	-1.2	12.9	8.4	4.8	1.0	1.6		9.9
2016–17	26.0	18.1	-0.8	11.9	7.7	4.5	0.6	1.5		9.6
2017–18	28.1	19.3	-1.2	13.0	7.9	4.9	1.8	1.3		9.5
2018–19	28.0	20.3	-1.4	12.2	8.1	4.9	2.1	1.4		8.2
2019–20	24.4	19.1	-2.8	9.6	7.9	6.4	0.9	1.4		8.6
2020–21	21.3	22.4	-6.7	6.8	11.7	10.5	-0.9	1.4		8.0
2021–22	25.1	19.7	-2.7	9.1	7.9	6.9	1.2	1.5		8.4

Second revised estimates for 2020-21 and First revised estimates for 2021-22
Adjusted by corporate depreciation and include valuables and E&O
* Core fiscal deficit (FD) = Government investments − Savings
Source: CSO, MOFSL, RBI, author's estimates

Appendix 5: Financial Position of India's Corporate Sector (% of GDP)

	Profits (% of GDP)					Debt (% of GDP)			
	Total	BSE500 companies	ow: NIFTY50	Non-BSE500 listed	Unlisted companies	Total*	BSE500 companies	ow: NIFTY50	Other companies
1989–90	3.8	0.3		0.1	3.5	18.6	5.4		13.2
1990–91	3.6	0.9		0.2	2.5	19.6	6.4		13.2
1991–92	3.7	1.0		0.3	2.3	23.7	6.8		16.9
1992–93	2.6	0.9		0.3	1.5	25.2	6.8		18.5
1993–94	3.8	1.2		0.5	2.1	26.4	6.6		19.8
1994–95	4.7	1.9		0.7	2.1	31.7	7.7		24.0
1995–96	6.0	1.9		0.6	3.4	35.9	7.9		28.1
1996–97	5.2	1.8		0.3	3.1	36.7	8.1		28.6
1997–98	5.1	1.9		0.2	2.9	38.2	8.7		29.6
1998–99	4.6	1.6	0.8	0.0	2.9	39.8	8.4	3.3	31.5
1999–00	5.3	1.7	1.0	0.0	3.5	38.9	7.9	3.1	31.0
2000–01	3.9	1.9	1.0	0.0	1.9	43.3	8.0	2.9	35.4
2001–02	3.7	2.0	1.2	−0.2	1.9	49.7	8.9	3.7	40.8
2002–03	5.3	2.7	1.5	−0.2	2.7	50.7	8.4	3.7	42.3
2003–04	6.5	3.2	1.7	0.2	3.0	47.6	7.8	3.7	39.8
2004–05	9.3	3.7	2.0	0.5	5.1	45.2	7.5	3.5	37.7
2005–06	10.9	3.8	2.2	0.6	6.5	46.8	8.3	3.7	38.5
2006–07	10.8	4.5	2.4	0.9	5.4	52.5	9.8	4.7	42.7

	Profits (% of GDP)					Debt (% of GDP)		
	Total	BSE500 companies	ow: NIFTY50	Non-BSE500 listed	Unlisted companies	Total*	BSE500 companies	ow: NIFTY50	Other companies
2007–08	12.3	5.0	2.7	1.0	6.3	63.8	12.3	6.2	51.5
2008–09	8.7	3.9	2.1	0.7	4.1	64.0	14.7	7.5	49.3
2009–10	9.2	4.6	2.5	0.7	3.9	67.6	13.7	6.5	53.9
2010–11	8.9	4.4	2.4	0.8	3.8	68.8	13.7	6.8	55.0
2011–12	8.4	4.1	2.5	0.4	3.9	70.1	15.9	7.9	54.1
2012–13	8.4	3.8	2.3	0.2	4.4	69.7	16.0	7.9	53.7
2013–14	8.8	3.7	2.3	0.2	4.9	61.6	16.8	8.4	44.8
2014–15	9.6	3.2	2.1	0.2	6.2	65.0	16.4	8.7	48.6
2015–16	9.9	2.9	2.0	0.0	7.0	61.6	14.8	7.8	46.8
2016–17	9.6	3.1	1.9	0.0	6.5	53.1	14.5	7.8	38.6
2017–18	9.5	2.7	1.8	−0.1	6.9	64.3	14.1	8.0	50.2
2018–19	8.2	2.8	1.7	−0.3	5.7	57.4	15.0	8.6	42.3
2019–20	8.6	2.0	1.6	−0.4	7.0	58.3	15.7	9.4	42.6
2020–21	8.0	3.3	2.0	0.0	4.7	61.0	15.4	9.1	45.5
2021–22	8.4	4.3	2.5	0.3	3.9	55.6	13.3	7.9	42.3

* RBI data available up to 2020–21; BIS data is used to estimate FY22 Corporate debt data prior to 2011-12 is from the RBI data on private corporate statistics.

Listed/BSE500/NIFTY50 companies for all years are as per January 2023

Source: CSO, MOFSL, RBI, BIS, author's estimates

Appendix 6: Major Receipts Components of the Combined Government

	Total spending	Total receipts	Fiscal deficit*	Direct taxes	Indirect taxes	Non-tax revenue receipts	Non-debt capital receipts	Debt receipts*
		% of GDP				% of total receipts#		
1970–71	19.9	15.1	4.8	8.4	41.4	14.4	11.5	24.3
1971–72	22.2	16.7	5.4	6.8	42.5	13.2	13.0	24.6
1972–73	23.8	17.5	6.3	8.0	40.1	15.5	10.0	26.4
1973–74	21.2	16.6	4.7	9.5	41.2	15.6	11.7	22.0
1974–75	20.9	16.5	4.4	9.8	44.6	15.7	8.8	21.1
1975–76	23.8	19.0	4.8	10.7	43.2	16.7	9.3	20.1
1976–77	24.7	19.0	5.7	10.1	43.1	16.5	7.2	23.1
1977–78	24.5	19.1	5.4	9.4	41.5	17.1	9.9	22.1
1978–79	27.0	19.7	7.3	8.3	41.7	15.1	7.9	27.0
1979–80	26.9	19.5	7.4	8.4	43.7	14.9	5.5	27.5
1980–81	26.6	18.5	8.0	7.5	41.2	15.5	6.3	29.6
1981–82	25.5	18.3	7.2	8.3	45.3	13.0	5.0	28.4
1982–83	27.0	19.1	7.9	7.6	43.4	13.2	6.4	29.4
1983–84	26.8	18.3	8.5	7.4	43.7	11.7	5.8	31.5
1984–85	28.8	18.8	10.0	6.6	41.7	11.9	5.1	34.7

	Total spending	Total receipts	Fiscal deficit*	Direct taxes	Indirect taxes	Non-tax revenue receipts	Non-debt capital receipts	Debt receipts*
		% of GDP				% of total receipts#		
1985–86	29.8	19.6	10.1	6.8	43.2	12.0	4.1	34.0
1986–87	31.4	20.4	11.0	6.4	42.2	12.0	4.4	35.0
1987–88	30.7	20.3	10.4	6.3	44.1	11.2	4.6	33.8
1988–89	29.6	19.8	9.7	7.1	44.7	10.6	4.6	33.0
1989–90	30.5	20.3	10.2	6.7	43.9	12.1	3.9	33.3
1990–91	29.7	18.9	10.8	8.1	42.2	9.2	4.1	36.3
1991–92	28.5	20.4	8.1	9.8	43.7	11.5	6.5	28.6
1992–93	27.2	19.4	7.9	10.4	43.9	11.9	4.9	28.9
1993–94	26.8	17.8	9.0	10.5	40.4	11.7	3.6	33.8
1994–95	27.0	18.8	8.2	12.0	39.9	12.1	5.9	30.2
1995–96	25.5	18.0	7.5	13.3	42.1	12.2	3.3	29.2
1996–97	25.0	17.8	7.3	13.3	42.3	11.5	3.9	29.1
1997–98	25.9	17.5	8.4	14.0	39.0	11.1	3.6	32.3
1998–99	26.9	16.6	10.3	11.6	35.8	10.0	4.2	38.5
1999–00	26.7	17.0	9.6	12.8	37.4	10.8	2.8	36.1
2000–01	27.1	17.6	9.5	13.8	37.3	10.4	3.6	35.0

Appendix 6 (continued)

	Total spending	Total receipts	Fiscal deficit*	Direct taxes	Indirect taxes	Non-tax revenue receipts	Non-debt capital receipts	Debt receipts*
	% of GDP					% of total receipts#		
2001–02	27.3	17.4	10.0	13.2	34.8	11.2	4.3	36.4
2002–03	27.8	18.7	9.1	14.0	34.9	11.4	5.7	34.0
2003–04	27.9	21.0	6.9	15.0	33.6	10.4	12.0	29.1
2004–05	26.8	20.6	6.2	17.4	36.5	11.9	8.3	25.9
2005–06	25.6	19.2	6.4	19.9	41.0	11.9	2.2	25.0
2006–07	25.5	20.3	5.1	23.6	42.6	12.2	1.5	20.1
2007–08	26.2	22.1	4.1	26.1	41.2	12.8	4.5	15.5
2008–09	28.1	19.7	8.4	23.0	35.5	10.5	1.1	29.8
2009–10	28.2	18.8	9.3	22.9	31.2	10.7	2.0	33.2
2010–11	27.3	20.4	6.9	23.7	35.3	14.2	1.6	25.3
2011–12	27.4	19.6	7.8	23.7	36.8	8.8	1.8	28.7
2012–13	26.8	19.9	6.9	24.2	39.3	9.2	1.5	25.8
2013–14	26.4	19.7	6.7	24.5	37.9	10.9	1.3	25.4
2014–15	26.2	19.5	6.7	24.2	37.9	10.2	1.9	25.8
2015–16	27.0	20.1	6.9	23.0	39.0	10.7	1.6	25.7
2016–17	27.3	20.4	7.0	22.8	39.7	10.4	1.6	25.5

	Total spending	Total receipts	Fiscal deficit*	Direct taxes	Indirect taxes	Non-tax revenue receipts	Non-debt capital receipts	Debt receipts*
	% of GDP					% of total receipts#		
2017–18	26.3	20.5	5.9	25.2	41.2	8.1	3.2	22.3
2018–19	26.4	20.5	5.9	25.7	40.1	9.0	2.8	22.3
2019–20	26.9	19.6	7.3	22.3	37.8	10.8	2.0	27.1
2020–21	31.7	18.4	13.2	17.4	33.6	6.0	1.0	41.9
2021–22	29.9	20.7	9.4	22.2	37.4	8.3	0.7	31.4
	Decadal average							
1970s	23.5	17.9	5.6	8.9	42.3	15.5	9.5	23.8
1980s	28.7	19.4	9.3	7.1	43.3	12.3	5.0	32.3
1990s	26.9	18.2	8.7	11.6	40.7	11.2	4.3	32.3
2000s	27.1	19.6	7.5	18.9	36.9	11.3	4.5	28.4
2010s	26.8	20.0	6.8	23.9	38.5	10.2	1.9	25.4

* Reported Fiscal deficit = Debt receipts
# Including debt receipts
Source: CSO, RBI, author's estimates

Appendix 7: Understanding the Economic Classification of Central Government Spending

Since 1957–58, the economic division of the ministry of finance has been preparing an economic classification of Central government budgetary transactions to make the Budget a more useful tool of economic analysis. This classification involves arranging of the expenditures and receipts of the Central government, including those of the railways and posts and telecommunications, by significant economic categories, distinguishing current from capital outlays, spending on goods and services from transfers to individuals and institutions, tax receipts from other receipts, and borrowings from intergovernmental loans and grants, etc. In this manner, the flows into and out of the Central government can be related to important categories of transactions influencing the behaviour of other sectors of the economy.

Separately, the CSO also publishes economically classified data on the total expenditure of the general government under National Account Statistics, which has been available on a regular basis for every year since FY81. Since the national-income type of government account is the most prevalent form of economic classification, the methodology and concepts used in this analysis are those used in the national income accounting system.

- **Item 1: Government final consumption expenditure (GFCE)** – It comprises wages and salaries paid to employees and current expenditure incurred on purchases of commodities and services. This indicates the value of the available supplies of goods and factors drawn for the government's current use, for developmental as well as non-developmental purposes.
- **Item 2: Transfer payments** – These expenditures do not involve direct demand on goods and services; they are mere transfers intended to add to the incomes of others.

While current transfers supplement the income accounts of recipients, capital transfers are intended to assist capital expenditure. Current transfers comprise interest payments, current grants to states, Union Territories, local authorities and non-profit institutions, subsidies, pensions and transfer payments to others.

- **Item 3: Gross capital formation (GCF)** – Total capital outlays representing physical asset formation by administration and departmental commercial undertakings and capital transfers. A distinction between administration and departmental commercial undertakings in respect of capital expenditure is not very meaningful, for the reason that the entire expenditure on capital formation is a final expenditure which is a charge on the national product and for which the government has to find resources either from its own savings or by drawing on private savings.
- **Item 4: Financial investments and loans to the rest of the economy** – Loans have been allocated between those meant for capital formation and those for other purposes. Investments in shares and loans for capital formation indicate the extent to which the government promotes capital formation in the rest of the economy through financial assistance, in addition to the capital formation directly undertaken by it.

Appendix 8: Economic Classification of General Government Spending (% of total spending)

% of total spending	GFCE	GCF	Final outlays	Current Transfers	Capital Transfers	Total transfers	Fin invt & loans
1980–81	37.8	8.5	46.3	25.8	3.8	29.6	24.1
1984–85	37.4	8.3	45.7	29.3	3.7	33.0	21.3
1989–90	40.8	6.1	46.8	33.8	4.9	38.7	14.4
1990–91	41.7	6.9	48.5	32.2	4.7	36.9	14.6
1991–92	43.0	7.1	50.1	34.6	4.2	38.8	11.0
1992–93	45.0	7.5	52.5	33.2	4.5	37.7	9.8
1993–94	42.5	6.5	49.0	29.9	4.4	34.3	16.7
1994–95	42.7	7.0	49.7	32.9	5.7	38.6	11.7
1995–96	44.8	6.7	51.4	32.7	6.1	38.8	9.7
1996–97	45.0	6.9	51.9	34.7	5.8	40.5	7.7
1997–98	46.6	5.8	52.4	33.6	5.0	38.5	9.1
1998–99	49.0	6.4	55.4	31.4	6.2	37.6	7.0
1999–00	48.4	7.9	56.2	30.7	5.0	35.7	8.1
2000–01	45.3	8.0	53.2	33.0	5.0	38.0	8.8
2001–02	44.9	8.0	52.8	34.9	4.9	39.8	7.3
2002–03	44.3	7.4	51.7	35.7	6.5	42.3	6.0
2003–04	40.9	7.5	48.4	33.6	6.3	39.9	11.7
2004–05	40.0	11.6	51.6	32.9	5.1	38.0	10.4
2005–06	39.7	12.5	52.2	34.8	6.8	41.6	6.2
2006–07	38.2	13.0	51.2	36.5	7.7	44.2	4.6

% of total spending	GFCE	GCF	Final outlays	Current Transfers	Capital Transfers	Total transfers	Fin invt & loans
2007–08	37.8	13.2	51.0	35.5	6.6	42.1	7.0
2008–09	34.0	11.0	45.0	37.3	9.4	46.6	8.4
2009–10	35.5	9.3	44.9	39.4	10.9	50.3	4.8
2010–11	35.6	9.1	44.7	38.8	10.2	49.0	6.3
2011–12	33.6	10.8	44.4	39.6	9.9	49.5	6.1
2012–13	34.3	11.2	45.5	42.0	8.3	50.3	4.2
2013–14	33.5	11.5	45.0	41.7	7.9	49.6	5.4
2014–15	33.1	11.4	44.5	43.4	7.5	50.9	4.5
2015–16	31.7	11.5	43.2	41.0	6.6	47.6	9.2
2016–17	32.3	12.0	44.3	39.9	8.0	48.0	7.8
2017–18	33.8	11.3	45.0	39.5	8.2	47.7	7.3
2018–19	34.4	11.0	45.4	39.7	7.4	47.1	7.5
2019–20	34.5	10.4	44.9	43.1	6.1	49.2	5.9
2020–21	30.0	9.3	39.3	44.0	10.4	54.4	6.2
2021–22	30.7	11.4	42.1	42.7	7.1	49.7	8.2
Decadal average							
1980s	39.5	8.2	47.7	28.6	3.6	32.3	20.0
1990s	44.9	6.9	51.7	32.6	5.1	37.8	10.5
2000s	40.1	10.1	50.2	35.4	6.9	42.3	7.5
2010s	33.7	11.0	44.7	40.9	8.0	48.9	6.4

Second revised estimates for 2020-21 and First revised estimates for 2021-22

Source: CSO, author's estimates

Appendix 9: Major Spending Areas/Components of the Combined Government (% of total spending)

	National security^	Interest payments	Subsidy	Rural development*	Pension	Education & health#	Transport	Others
1990–91	12.2	14.3	7.0	13.4	3.0	15.2	4.2	28.0
1991–92	12.0	16.1	6.4	13.2	3.2	15.2	3.5	29.1
1992–93	12.2	17.3	5.1	14.5	3.5	15.4	4.0	27.5
1993–94	12.9	18.0	4.9	14.6	3.6	15.7	3.4	27.1
1994–95	11.7	18.5	4.2	13.5	3.6	15.2	3.3	29.0
1995–96	12.1	18.8	4.0	13.0	3.9	15.2	3.2	29.3
1996–97	12.0	19.6	4.4	12.0	4.2	15.6	3.3	28.6
1997–98	12.5	19.2	4.6	11.7	4.5	15.5	3.4	27.2
1998–99	12.0	19.2	4.9	12.0	5.4	16.0	3.2	25.3
1999–00	12.7	20.5	4.5	11.9	6.9	16.9	3.5	25.3
2000–01	12.4	21.2	4.5	11.0	6.7	17.0	4.7	25.5
2001–02	12.3	22.1	4.8	10.4	6.2	16.1	4.8	25.7
2002–03	11.6	22.5	6.2	10.6	6.1	15.6	4.7	28.3

	National security^	Interest payments	Subsidy	Rural development*	Pension	Education & health#	Transport	Others
2003–04	11.0	22.4	5.6	10.1	5.9	14.9	4.4	33.2
2004–05	12.2	22.2	5.3	10.6	6.4	15.3	4.8	30.6
2005–06	12.1	21.5	5.0	11.8	6.4	16.0	5.7	22.8
2006–07	11.2	21.1	5.2	12.0	6.3	16.1	6.0	24.0
2007–08	10.1	19.8	5.4	12.4	6.2	15.8	5.7	25.6
2008–09	10.5	17.9	8.2	13.7	6.2	16.2	5.2	22.9
2009–10	11.4	17.2	7.7	12.6	7.6	16.5	5.8	21.8
2010–11	10.8	16.4	8.2	12.7	7.8	17.0	5.9	21.6
2011–12	10.9	16.7	9.1	11.6	7.9	17.0	5.6	21.6
2012–13	10.6	17.0	9.6	11.1	8.0	17.1	5.2	21.7
2013–14	10.7	18.0	8.6	10.7	8.0	17.2	5.6	21.6
2014–15	10.7	17.9	7.9	12.7	8.5	17.1	5.7	19.9
2015–16	10.2	17.4	7.1	12.5	8.1	16.5	5.8	22.3
2016–17	10.1	17.2	8.5	13.4	8.5	16.4	5.8	19.9
2017–18	10.4	18.1	7.1	14.3	9.4	16.6	5.7	18.5

Appendix 9 (continued)

	National security^	Interest payments	Subsidy	Rural development*	Pension	Education & health#	Transport	Others
2018–19	10.2	17.9	7.2	14.0	9.5	17.0	6.2	18.0
2019–20	10.4	17.7	6.5	13.8	9.8	16.8	5.9	19.1
2020–21	9.1	16.9	8.4	13.7	9.2	14.6	6.3	21.4
2021–22	8.9	17.4	7.4	11.9	8.9	15.1	7.7	22.3
Decadal average								
1990s	12.2	18.2	5.0	13.0	4.2	15.6	3.5	27.6
2000s	11.5	20.8	5.8	11.5	6.4	15.9	5.2	26.1
2010s	10.5	17.4	8.0	12.7	8.5	16.9	5.7	20.4

^ Defense and Police
* Including Agriculture & allied activities, Rural development and Irrigation
# Including water sanitation & supply
Source: MOSPI, Budget documents, author's calculations

Appendix 10: Understanding the Formal Accounting System of India's Government

According to the office of the Chief Controller of Accounts (CCA), the accounts of the government are kept in three parts:
1. Consolidated Fund of India
2. Contingency Fund of India and
3. Public Account

Consolidated Fund of India

All revenues received by the government by way of taxes, like income tax, central excise, customs and other receipts flowing to the government in connection with the conduct of government business, that is, non-tax revenues are credited into the Consolidated Fund constituted under Article 266 (1) of the Constitution of India. Similarly, all loans raised by the government by issue of public notifications, treasury bills (internal debt) and loans obtained from foreign governments and international institutions (external debt) are credited into this fund. All expenditure of the government is incurred from this fund, and no amount can be withdrawn from the Fund without authorization from Parliament.

Contingency Fund of India

Article 267(I) of the Constitution provides that:

> Parliament may by law establish a Contingency Fund in the nature of an imprest to be entitled the Contingency Fund of India into which shall be paid from time to time such sums as may be determined by such law, and the said Fund shall be placed at the disposal of the President to enable advances to be made by him out of such Fund for the purposes of meeting unforeseen expenditure pending authorisation of such expenditure by Parliament by law under Article 115 or Article 116.

Appendix 10

Public Account

In the Public Account constituted under Article 266 (2) of the Constitution, the transactions relate to debt other than those included in the Consolidated Fund of India. The transactions under debt, deposits and advances in this part are those in respect of which government incurs a liability to repay the money received or has a claim to recover the amounts paid. The transactions relating to 'remittance' and 'suspense' shall embrace all adjusting heads. The initial debits or credits to these heads will be cleared eventually by corresponding receipts or payments. The receipts under Public Account do not constitute the normal receipts of the government. Parliamentary authorization for payments from the Public Account is therefore not required.

Appendix 11: Estimating Adjusted Fiscal Deficit (AFD) from Reported Fiscal Deficit (RFD) of the Central Government

	Reported fiscal deficit		Recap bonds	Subsidy arrears*	NSSF loans to FCI	FSBs/EBRs	Other securities#	Adjusted fiscal deficit	
	INR bn	% of GDP			INR bn			INR bn	% of GDP
1980–81	83	5.5	0	0	0	0	2	84	5.6
1985–86	219	7.5	0	0	0	0	5	224	7.7
1990–91	446	7.6	7	0	0	0	6	459	7.8
1995–96	602	4.9	9	0	0	0	26	637	5.2
1996–97	667	4.7	15	0	0	0	0	682	4.8
1997–98	889	5.7	27	130	0	0	0	1,046	6.7
1998–99	1,133	6.3	4	64	0	0	60	1,261	7.0
1999–00	1,047	5.2	2	62	0	0	50	1,162	5.7
2000–01	1,188	5.5	8	0	0	0	26	1,222	5.6
2001–02	1,410	6.0	23	90	0	0	4	1,526	6.5
2002–03	1,451	5.7	8	0	0	0	25	1,484	5.8
2003–04	1,233	4.3	–1	24	0	0	36	1,292	4.5
2004–05	1,258	3.9	–1	34	0	0	8	1,299	4.0
2005–06	1,464	4.0	5	232	0	0	106	1,807	4.9

Appendix 11 (continued)

	Reported fiscal deficit		Recap bonds	Subsidy arrears*	NSSF loans to FCI	FSBs/EBRs	Other securities#	Adjusted fiscal deficit	
	INR bn	% of GDP			INR bn			INR bn	% of GDP
2006–07	1,426	3.3	162	329	0	0	6	1,923	4.5
2007–08	1,269	2.5	0	281	0	0	100	1,650	3.3
2008–09	3,370	6.0	0	1,064	0	0	12	4,446	7.9
2009–10	4,185	6.5	0	326	0	0	40	4,550	7.0
2010–11	3,736	4.8	0	274	0	0	94	4,103	5.3
2011–12	5,160	5.9	0	608	0	0	19	5,787	6.6
2012–13	4,902	4.9	0	716	0	0	46	5,664	5.7
2013–14	5,029	4.5	0	800	0	0	6	5,835	5.2
2014–15	5,107	4.1	0	513	0	0	62	5,682	4.6
2015–16	5,328	3.9	0	608	0	0	513	6,449	4.7
2016–17	5,356	3.5	0	516	700	92	23	6,687	4.3
2017–18	5,911	3.5	800	432	510	151	417	8,220	4.8
2018–19	6,494	3.4	1,105	674	700	656	495	10,125	5.4
2019–20	9,337	4.6	758	253	636	220	326	11,530	5.7
2020–21	18,183	9.2	200	250	-2,546	267	227	16,581	8.4
2021–22	15,871	6.8	0	200	0	8	-62	16,017	6.8

	Reported fiscal deficit		Recap bonds	Subsidy arrears*	NSSF loans to FCI	FSBs/EBRs	Other securities#	Adjusted fiscal deficit	
	INR bn	% of GDP			INR bn			INR bn	% of GDP
					Decadal average				
1980s		6.6	0.0	0.0	0.0	0.0	0.2		6.8
1990s		5.7	0.1	0.2	0.0	0.0	0.2		6.3
2000s		4.8	0.1	0.6	0.0	0.0	0.1		5.4
2010s		4.3	0.2	0.4	0.2	0.1	0.2		5.2

* Fuel & Fertilizer subsidies
# Including NSSF loans to PSUs other than FCIs
~ GoI paid-off all FCI arrears in 4QFY21
Source: Budget documents, author's estimates

Appendix 12: Reconciliation of the Different Estimates of Union Government Liabilities and Estimation of the Adjusted Debt

	GoI debt*		Add: External debt~	Add: FSBs	GoI debt#	Less: NSSF loans –States / PSUs$	GoI debt@	Add: NSSF-FCI / Annuity	Adjusted GoI debt	
	INR bn	% of GDP	INR bn						INR bn	% of GDP
1980–81	0.6	39.9	0.0	0.0	0.6	0.0	0.6	0.0	0.6	41.4
1985–86	1.4	47.5	0.1	0.0	1.5	0.0	1.5	0.0	1.5	52.4
1990–91	3.1	53.7	0.3	0.0	3.5	0.0	3.5	0.0	3.5	59.6
1991–92	3.5	52.6	0.7	0.0	4.3	0.0	4.3	0.0	4.3	63.4
1992–93	4.0	51.9	0.8	0.0	4.8	0.0	4.8	0.0	4.8	62.1
1993–94	4.8	53.6	0.8	0.0	5.6	0.0	5.6	0.0	5.6	62.6
1994–95	5.4	51.5	0.9	0.0	6.3	0.0	6.3	0.0	6.3	60.3
1995–96	6.1	49.4	1.0	0.0	7.0	0.0	7.0	0.0	7.0	57.3
1996–97	6.8	47.6	1.0	0.0	7.7	0.0	7.7	0.0	7.7	54.3
1997–98	7.8	49.5	1.1	0.0	8.8	0.0	8.8	0.0	8.8	56.2
1998–99	8.9	49.5	1.2	0.0	10.1	0.0	10.1	0.0	10.1	56.1
1999–00	10.2	50.5	1.3	0.0	11.5	0.3	11.2	0.0	11.2	55.5
2000–01	11.7	53.7	1.2	0.0	12.9	0.6	12.3	0.0	12.3	56.6

	GoI debt*		Add: External debt~	Add: FSBs	GoI debt#	Less: NSSF loans –States / PSUs$	GoI debt@	Add: NSSF-FCI / Annuity	Adjusted GoI debt	
	INR bn	% of GDP							INR bn	% of GDP
					INR bn					
2001–02	13.7	58.0	1.3	0.0	14.9	1.0	14.0	0.0	14.0	59.4
2002–03	15.6	61.5	1.4	0.0	17.0	1.5	15.5	0.0	15.5	61.0
2003–04	17.4	61.1	1.4	0.0	18.7	2.2	16.6	0.0	16.6	58.4
2004–05	19.9	61.5	1.3	0.0	21.2	3.7	17.6	0.0	17.6	54.2
2005–06	22.6	61.2	1.0	0.0	23.6	4.2	19.4	0.0	19.4	52.5
2006–07	25.4	59.1	1.0	0.0	26.4	5.2	21.2	0.0	21.2	49.4
2007–08	28.4	56.9	1.0	0.0	29.4	6.3	23.1	0.0	23.1	46.3
2008–09	31.6	56.1	1.4	0.0	33.0	5.5	27.5	0.0	27.5	48.9
2009–10	35.3	54.5	1.2	0.0	36.5	4.9	31.6	0.1	31.6	48.8
2010–11	39.4	50.6	1.2	0.0	40.6	5.3	35.3	0.1	35.4	45.5
2011–12	45.2	51.7	1.5	0.0	46.7	5.2	41.5	0.1	41.6	47.6
2012–13	50.7	51.0	1.5	0.0	52.3	5.2	47.1	0.1	47.1	47.4
2013–14	56.7	50.5	1.9	0.0	58.6	5.2	53.4	0.1	53.5	47.6
2014–15	62.4	50.1	1.7	0.0	64.1	5.4	58.7	0.1	58.7	47.1
2015–16	69.0	50.1	2.0	0.0	71.0	5.7	65.3	0.1	65.3	47.4

Appendix 12 (continued)

	GoI debt*		Add: External debt~	Add: FSBs	GoI debt#	Less: NSSF loans –States / PSUs$	GoI debt@	Add: NSSF-FCI / Annuity	Adjusted GoI debt	
	INR bn	% of GDP				INR bn			INR bn	% of GDP
2016–17	74.5	48.4	1.8	0.1	76.3	6.1	70.3	0.8	71.0	46.1
2017–18	82.4	48.2	2.0	0.2	84.5	6.7	77.9	1.7	79.5	46.5
2018–19	90.8	48.1	2.0	0.9	93.8	7.4	86.4	2.3	88.7	46.9
2019–20	102.2	50.8	2.9	1.1	106.2	8.6	97.5	3.0	100.5	48.5
2020–21	120.8	60.9	2.7	1.4	124.9	7.8	117.1	0.4	117.5	59.0
2021–22	135.7	57.8	3.9	1.4	141.0	4.8	136.2	0.4	136.6	58.2

* As per Union Budget documents
~ Difference between External debt at current market exchange rate and at historical prices
\# According to RBI estimates
$ Including balances under market stabilization scheme (MSS) and cash balances
@ As per Ministry of Finance
Source: Budget documents, RBI, MOF, author's estimates

Appendix 13: Key Concepts in BoP and International Investment Position (IIP)

According to the sixth edition of the *Balance of Payments and International Investment Position Manual* (BPM6), 'The balance of payments is a statistical statement that summarizes transactions between residents and nonresidents during a period. It consists of the goods and services account, the primary income account, the Secondary income account, the capital account, and the financial account.'

Current Account

The current account shows flows of goods, services, primary income and secondary income between residents and non-residents. The current account balance shows the difference between the sum of exports and income receivable and the sum of imports and income payable (exports and imports refer to both goods and services, while income refers to both primary and secondary income).

Goods and Services Account

The goods and services account shows transactions on items that are outcomes of production activities, in which an enterprise uses inputs (intermediate inputs, labour, produced and non-produced assets) in order to transform them into outputs that can be supplied to other units. Goods and services represent outcomes of the production process. In contrast, when other resources, such as labour, land, natural resources or financial resources, are supplied, they are shown in other accounts. *Goods* are physically produced items over which ownership rights can be established and whose economic ownership can be passed from one institutional unit to another by their engaging in transactions. *Services* are the result of a production activity that changes the conditions of the consuming units or facilitates the exchange of products or financial assets. Services are not generally separate items over which ownership rights can be established and cannot generally be separated from their production.

Primary Income Account

Primary income (also called 'income' account) represents the return that accrues to institutional units for their contribution to the production process or for provision of financial assets and renting of natural resources to other institutional units. Two types of primary income are distinguished: (a) income associated with the production process; and (b) income associated with ownership of financial and other non-produced assets.

Secondary Income (Transfers) Account

Secondary income (also called 'transfers') account must be distinguished from primary income account. Transfers account captures the further redistribution of income through current transfers, such as by governments or charitable organizations, while the income account captures the returns for provision of labour, financial assets and renting of natural resources. Whereas the primary income account affects national income, transfers, together with (primary) income, affects gross national disposable income. Capital transfers do not affect disposable income and, hence, are recorded in the capital account.

Capital Account

The capital account shows the credit and debit entries for non-produced non-financial assets and capital transfers between residents and non-residents. It records acquisitions and disposals of non-produced non-financial assets, such as land sold to embassies and sale of leases and licenses, as well as capital transfers—that is, the provision of resources for capital purposes by one party without anything of economic value being supplied as a direct return to that party.

Financial Account

The financial account shows the net acquisition and disposal of financial assets and liabilities. These transactions appear in the balance of payments and, because of their effect on the stock of assets and liabilities, are also in the integrated IIP statement.

Foreign Direct Investments (FDI)

Direct investment is a category of cross-border investment associated with a resident in one economy having control or a significant degree of influence on the management of an enterprise that is resident in another economy. As well as funds, direct investors may supply additional contributions such as know-how, technology, management and marketing. Furthermore, enterprises in a direct investment relationship are more likely to trade with and finance each other.

Foreign Portfolio Investments (FPI)

In contrast to direct investors, portfolio investors typically have less of a role in the decision-making of the enterprise with potentially important implications for future flows and for the volatility of the price and volume of positions. Portfolio investment differs from other kinds of investment in that it provides a direct way to access the financial markets, and thus can provide liquidity and flexibility. It is associated with the financial markets and with their specialized service providers, such as exchanges, dealers and regulators.

Reserve Assets

Reserve assets are those external assets that are readily available to and controlled by the monetary authorities for meeting the balance of payments financing needs, for intervention in exchange markets to influence the currency exchange rate, and for other related purposes (such as for maintaining confidence in the currency and the economy, and for serving as a basis for foreign borrowings).

International Investments Position

IIP is a statistical statement that shows at a point in time the value and composition of: (a) financial assets of residents in an economy that are claims on non-residents and gold bullion held as reserve assets, and (b) liabilities of residents of an economy to non-residents. The difference between an economy's external financial assets and liabilities is the economy's net IIP, which may be positive or negative. The IIP is a subset of the national balance sheet. The net IIP plus the value of non-financial assets equals the net worth of the economy, which is the balancing item in the national balance sheet.

Appendix 14: India's Merchandise Trade Deficit by Broad Baskets (% of GDP)

	Merchandise trade balance	Oil	Non-oil trade balance					
			Total non-oil	Consumption	Ow: Agri, etc.	Investments	Ow: Engineering goods	Valuables
1970–71	−0.2	−0.3	0.1					
1971–72	−0.4	−0.4	−0.1					
1972–73	0.2	−0.3	0.5					
1973–74	−0.6	−0.8	0.2					
1974–75	−1.5	−1.4	−0.1					
1975–76	−1.4	−1.4	0.0					
1976–77	0.1	−1.5	1.6					
1977–78	−0.6	−1.5	0.9					
1978–79	−1.0	−1.5	0.5					
1979–80	−2.2	−2.6	0.4					
1980–81	−4.0	−3.6	−0.4					
1981–82	−3.4	−2.9	−0.5					
1982–83	−2.8	−2.3	−0.6					
1983–84	−2.7	−1.4	−1.3					
1984–85	−2.1	−1.4	−0.7					
1985–86	−3.1	−1.5	−1.6					

Appendix 14 (continued)

	Merchandise trade balance	Oil	Non-oil trade balance					
			Total non-oil	Consumption	Ow: Agri, etc.	Investments	Ow: Engineering goods	Valuables
1986–87	-2.4	-0.8	-1.6					
1987–88	-1.8	-0.9	-0.9					
1988–89	-1.9	-0.9	-1.0					
1989–90	-1.6	-1.1	-0.4					
1990–91	-1.8	-1.7	-0.1					
1991–92	-0.6	-1.8	1.3	3.3	1.0	-2.3	-1.5	0.3
1992–93	-1.3	-2.1	0.8	3.0	0.8	-2.5	-1.4	0.2
1993–94	-0.4	-1.9	1.5	3.3	1.1	-2.3	-1.6	0.5
1994–95	-0.7	-1.7	1.0	3.0	0.7	-2.7	-1.8	0.7
1995–96	-1.4	-2.0	0.6	3.5	1.2	-3.5	-2.3	0.6
1996–97	-1.4	-2.4	1.0	3.6	1.3	-2.8	-1.9	0.2
1997–98	-1.6	-1.9	0.3	3.2	1.1	-2.6	-1.5	-0.3
1998–99	-2.2	-1.5	-0.7	2.6	0.6	-2.6	-1.6	-0.7
1999–00	-2.8	-2.7	-0.1	2.3	0.5	-1.9	-0.9	-0.6
2000–01	-1.3	-2.9	1.7	2.9	0.8	-0.8	-0.4	-0.4
2001–02	-1.6	-2.4	0.9	2.3	0.6	-1.0	-0.6	-0.4
2002–03	-1.7	-2.9	1.2	2.2	0.6	-0.7	-0.6	-0.3

	Merchandise trade balance	Oil	Non-oil trade balance					
			Total non-oil	Consumption	Ow: Agri, etc.	Investments	Ow: Engineering goods	Valuables
2003–04	−2.4	−2.8	0.4	1.7	0.5	−0.7	−0.7	−0.6
2004–05	−3.9	−3.2	−0.7	1.3	0.5	−1.1	−0.8	−1.0
2005–06	−5.6	−3.9	−1.7	1.3	0.7	−2.4	−1.7	−0.6
2006–07	−6.3	−4.1	−2.2	1.1	0.7	−2.7	−1.8	−0.7
2007–08	−7.3	−4.2	−3.1	1.1	1.0	−3.6	−2.7	−0.5
2008–09	−9.7	−5.4	−4.3	1.1	0.8	−4.3	−2.4	−0.9
2009–10	−8.1	−4.4	−3.8	0.7	0.4	−3.2	−2.1	−1.2
2010–11	−7.1	−3.8	−3.2	1.0	0.7	−2.1	−1.3	−2.2
2011–12	−10.1	−5.4	−4.6	1.3	1.2	−3.5	−1.8	−2.4
2012–13	−10.4	−5.6	−4.8	1.3	1.2	−4.2	−1.6	−1.9
2013–14	−7.2	−5.5	−1.7	1.7	1.5	−2.6	−0.7	−0.8
2014–15	−6.7	−4.0	−2.8	0.9	0.9	−2.6	−0.4	−1.1
2015–16	−5.6	−2.5	−3.1	0.2	0.5	−2.6	−0.9	−0.8
2016–17	−4.7	−2.4	−2.3	0.1	0.3	−1.9	−0.5	−0.4
2017–18	−6.1	−2.7	−3.4	−0.2	0.5	−2.0	−0.5	−1.3
2018–19	−6.8	−3.5	−3.3	−0.1	0.7	−2.4	−0.8	−0.9
2019–20	−5.7	−3.1	−2.5	−0.1	0.5	−1.8	−0.8	−0.7

Appendix 14 (continued)

	Merchandise trade balance	Oil	Non-oil trade balance					
			Total non-oil	Consumption	Ow: Agri, etc.	Investments	Ow: Engineering goods	Valuables
2020–21	–3.8	–2.1	–1.7	0.1	0.7	–0.7	–0.2	–1.1
2021–22	–6.1	–3.0	–3.1	–0.2	0.5	–1.5	0.2	–1.3
Decadal average							
1970s	–0.8	–1.2	0.4					
1980s	–2.6	–1.7	–0.9					
1990s	–1.4	–2.0	0.6	3.1	0.9	–2.6	–1.6	0.1
2000s	–4.8	–3.6	–1.2	1.6	0.7	–2.1	–1.4	–0.6
2010s	–7.0	–3.9	–3.2	0.6	0.8	–2.6	–0.9	–1.2

Consumption basket is broadly classified into four sub-components: agriculture & allied products, electronic goods, textiles, including readymade garments, and others (leather & leather manufacturers, cosmetics/toiletries, essential oils, handicrafts, sports goods, footwear of rubber/canvas, paper/wood products, stationary items, newsprint and handloom products).

Investment basket consists of ores & minerals, chemical & related products (excluding cosmetics/toiletries and essential oils), engineering goods and others (rubber manufactured goods, glass/ceramics, plastic & linoleum products, computer software in physical form; graphite, explosives & accessories, granite, natural resources & products, moulded & extruded goods, optical items and other commodities).

Break-up of non-oil trade deficit is not available before FY92

Source: Reserve Bank of India (RBI), Ministry of Commerce, Author's estimates

ACKNOWLEDGEMENTS

My thanks are due to countless people who have helped me achieve my dream of writing this book. I am thankful to God Almighty and my parents, who have made me what I am. It would not have been possible to write and get this book published without the perseverance I learned from my parents. And I can never sufficiently emphasize the role of good fortune in my life.

My wife and life, Archita Nanda, patiently bore with me while I was working on the book and had little time for family. I cannot thank enough my seven-year-old daughter, who sacrificed her playtime with me and whose innocent smile and hugs wiped away my tiredness many a time.

I want to thank all my employers and colleagues past and present who welcomed me into their fold and gave me many opportunities to learn. My current employer, Motilal Oswal Financial Services Ltd, where I have spent more than seven years now, deserves special mention for providing me a platform to do my work independently, spread my wings and fly high. Thank you Mr Raamdeo Agrawal for showing interest in my work, and thank you Mr Rajat Rajgarhia for giving me the independence and placing confidence in me.

I want to acknowledge the help rendered by Dr Pronab Sen, who heard me for hours and answered my questions patiently whenever I reached out to him. It was under his guidance that I was able to connect the dots, think clearly and write this book.

I am obliged to Dr Rathin Roy, who not only helped me connect with my publisher but also shared his views with me in long discussions. We have known each other just a couple of years and I am surprised at the connect we have made in such a short time.

I owe thanks to various other people who knowingly or not helped me in this endeavour. Mr Shankar Sharma and Ms Devina Mehra for giving the best possible start to my career, Dr Michael Pettis for inspiring me with his outstanding work, which he shared freely with hundreds of thousands like me through his blog, Dr Rajiv Kumar, Dr Ajay Shah, Dr Martin Wolf, Dr Viral Acharya, Professor Chetan Ghate and many others.

I was also fortunate to find great support from my industry, be it from Navneet Munot, Suyash Choudhary, Anirudha Dutta and Shreyash Devalkar, who shared their wisdom and helped me improve, or from Sankaren Naren, Prashant Jain and Vetri Subramaniam, whose words of encouragement motivated me to keep striving.

Of course, I cannot thank enough my publisher, Krishan Chopra, Jaishree Ram Mohan and several other people at Bloomsbury who worked in the background to make this book a reality.

Lastly, I want to thank several other people who have helped me throughout my career and inspired me to do this work. I learned every time you answered my questions and I felt confident or became aware of my shortcomings when you questioned me.

NOTES

Chapter 1

1. United Nations, 'Inequality – Bridging the Divide, UN75 2020 and Beyond'. Source: https://www.un.org/en/un75/inequality-bridging-divide
2. World GDP per capita (constant 2015 US$), World Bank Development indicators.
3. 'Corporate tax rates slashed to 22% for domestic companies and 15% for new domestic manufacturing companies and other fiscal reliefs', Ministry of Finance, 20 September 2019, PIB, New Delhi.
4. Strictly speaking, the efficiency of spending by one sector is very different from that by another agent. For instance, corporate spending (that is, investments) can be very different from household or government consumption spending. Therefore, the actual impact of such a policy on economic growth is unlikely to be nil.
5. Without any other tax changes, if the government is supposed to earn ₹100 on corporate income, the GoI will collect lower, say, only ₹95, after the reduction in corporate tax rate cut. Effectively, the GoI has transferred ₹5 from its own treasury to the companies, which is called 'transfer of resources from the Government to the corporate sector'.
6. Net impact will include the likely impact of any policy on not only the targeted sector (companies, in this example), but also the indirect consequences on other economic participants. This is one of the key themes of this book, which is explored in detail in the subsequent chapters.
7. If the GoI accepts a higher fiscal deficit or creates higher uncertainty about the supply of government bonds, the fixed income market participants may not cheer the policy.
8. The GoI follows a financial year of twelve months ending March of the following year. Thus, FY19 (or 2018–19) runs from April 2018 to Mar 2019.

9. 'Report on Municipal Finances', Reserve Bank of India, 10 November 2022.
10. United Nations, World Population Prospects 2022.
11. Following the EU-KLEMS (Capital, Labour, Energy, Material and Services) methodology, the RBI had funded a project on productivity measurement in 2009. Its first report, 'Estimates of Productivity Growth for the Indian Economy', which contained time series data of productivity growth for the period 1980–81 to 2008–09, was published in 2014. The report has been updated almost annually since then, with the recent update released in October 2022, containing data up to 2019–20.
12. M. McLeay, A. Radia and R. Thomas, 'Money Creation in the Modern Economy', Bank of England, *Quarterly Bulletin*, Vol. 49, No. 2, 2014: 14–27. Source: https://www.bankofengland.co.uk/-/media/boe/files/quarterly-bulletin/2014/money-creation-in-the-modern-economy.pdf
13. The definition of core fiscal deficit could be different at different places. In this book, core fiscal deficit is defined as (government investments – savings [= total income – government final consumption expenditure]), which is lower than fiscal deficit (government spending – total receipts) because it excludes government transfers, which, as discussed in Chapter 4, are a large portion of government spending.
14. This section of the book is heavily influenced by the writings of Professor Michael Pettis (at Peking University, Beijing, China) and the likes of Dr Richard Koo, Chief Economist at Nomura Research Institute and the late Dr Hyman Minsky, among others.
15. Niall Fergusson, *The Ascent of Money: A Financial History of the World*, November 2008.
16. 'Monthly Information Bulletin on Corporate Sector, January 2023', Government of India, Ministry of Corporate Affairs, 1 March 2023.

Chapter 2

1. 'Periodic Labour Force Survey (PLFS), July 2021 – June 2022', Government of India, Annual Report, February 2023.

2. 'Employment by sex and status in employment – ILO modelled estimates, Nov. 2022 (thousands), Annual', International Labour Organization (ILO), last updated in February 2023.
3. 'Share of employment outside the formal sector by sex and economic activity', ILO, last updated May 2023.
4. Nominal PDI is deflated by private final consumption expenditure (PFCE) deflator to arrive at real PDI, and GDP deflator is used to arrive at real GDP from nominal GDP.
5. 'First revised estimates of national income, consumption expenditure, saving and capital formation for 2021–22', National Statistics Office, Government of India, 28 February 2023.
6. 'Report of the High Level Committee on Estimation of Savings and Investment', Government of India, March 2009.
7. 'Report on the Pilot Survey of Income, Consumption and Savings – Part II: Methodological Study (September 1983–December 1984), Department of Statistics, report No. 398, NSSO, September 1995.
8. The quasi corporate sector was shifted from the household to the corporate sector in SNA under the new 2011–12 base.
9. 'Report on Trend & Progress of Housing in India 2022', National Housing Bank, March 2023.
10. 'Residential Asset Price Monitoring Survey (RAPMS)' is a quarterly survey conducted by RBI since July 2010. Source: https://www.rbi.org.in/Scripts/BS_PressReleaseDisplay.aspx?prid=47578
11. RBI's House Price Index (HPI) is based on property transaction registration data obtained from the departments of registration and stamps of state governments from ten selected cities. The coverage of property registration data is more robust as compared to property loan data collected from banks/HFCs for preparation of the residential property price index (RPPI) as all house transactions are not financed by banks/HFCs. However, RAPMS also has the advantage of capturing additional information such as loan amount, EMI, income of the borrower, etc. A comparison of All-India RPPI with All-India HPI indicated that both indices tend to move in a similar direction. The annual growth in RPPI and HPI also moved together in most quarters.

12. This may not necessarily be the case if new borrowers are less creditworthy than existing borrowers, same borrowers are getting new loans by opening new accounts and if the existing borrowers' debt is much lower than the potential. However, the absence of details restricts our analysis, which comes with this limitation.
13. Mathias Drehmann and Mikael Juselius, 'Do debt service costs affect macroeconomic and financial stability?', *BIS Quarterly Review*, September 2012. Source: https://www.bis.org/publ/qtrpdf/r_qt1209e.html
14. 'China 2018 Financial Stability Report', People's Bank of China.
15. 'Press note on Second advance estimates of National income 2022-23', National Statistics Office, Ministry of Statistics & Programme implementation, Government of India, 28 February 2023.

Chapter 3

1. Corporate savings are not equal to corporate profits. The former is the sum of retained profits (profit after taxes *minus* dividends) and depreciation.
2. Some of the recent popular books on India's financial sector are: *Overdraft: Saving the Indian Saver* by Dr Urjit Patel, former governor, RBI; *Quest for Restoring Financial Stability in India* by Dr Viral Acharya, former deputy governor, RBI; *Pandemonium: The Great Indian Banking Tragedy* by Tamal Bandyopadhyay; *Hits and Misses: The Indian Banking Story* by Madan Sabnavis, chief economist, CARE Ratings; and *I Do What I Do* by Dr Raghuram Rajan, former governor, RBI.
3. The first report covered data for the period 1951–52 to 1993–94. Prior to the release of 'Financial Stocks and Flows of the Indian Economy 2011–12 to 2017–18', the RBI published only financial flows, titled 'Flow of Funds Account of India'.
4. See, for instance, V. Viral Acharya and G. Raghuram Rajan, 'Indian Banking: A Time to Reform?', The University of Chicago Booth School of Business, 21 September 2020.
5. Urjit Patel, 'The cul-de-sac in Indian Banking: A dominant government sector, limited fiscal space and independent regulation (Is there an "impossible trilemma"?)', Session VI

Keynote: Financial Sector, 19th Annual Conference on Indian Economic Policy, Stanford, 3–4 June 2019.
6. 'Report of the Internal Working Group to Review Extant Ownership Guidelines and Corporate Structure for Indian Private Sector Banks', Reserve Bank of India, 20 November, 2020.
7. V. Viral Acharya and G. Raghuram Rajan, 'Do We Really Need Indian Corporations in Banking?', NYU Stern School of Business, 23 November 2020.
8. Amol Agrawal, 'Banks: Governance, Not Ownership, Is Key', *Hindustan Times*, 26 November 2020.
9. C.P. Chandrashekhar, 'Extending Private Banking', *Economics & Political Weekly*, Vol. 46, Issue no. 11, 12 March 2011.
10. Stephanie Findlay and Hudson Lockett, '"Modi's Rockefeller": Gautam Adani and the Concentration of Power in India', *Financial Times*, 13 November 2020.
11. 'Monthly Information Bulletin on Corporate Sector, January 2023', Government of India, Ministry of Corporate Affairs, 1 March 2023.
12. A. David Levy, Martin P. Farnham and Samira Rajan, 'Where Profits Come from? Answering the critical question that few ever ask', The Jerome Levy Forecasting Center, LLC, 1997.
13. The treatment of DDT was changed in 2020. DDT now is paid by the recipient (that is, shareholder) and not the payer (that is, company).
14. Whenever I talk of corporate debt, I refer to the debt of non-financial companies (NFCs) only. Since the financial sector is in the business of lending, estimating or analysing its aggregate debt does not make much sense for the purpose of this book.
15. Chen Sally, Kim Minsuk, Otte Marijn, Wiseman Kevin, and Zdzienicka Aleksandra, 'Private Sector Deleveraging and Growth Following Busts', IMF Working Paper, WP/15/35, February 2015.
16. Milton Friedman, *Capitalism and Freedom*, University of Chicago Press, 1962.

Chapter 4

1. Excluding grants from the Centre to the states, which are actually spent by the states. In this chapter, general government is the same as combined government of the Centre and states. GoI is the same as the Union or Central government. Also, a mention of government is the same as general government.
2. 'Centre Clears Entire GST Compensation Due Till Date (31 MAY, 2022)', Press Information Bureau, 31 May 2022. Source: https://pib.gov.in/PressReleasePage.aspx?PRID=1829777
3. 'Centre Releases Rs. 17,000 Crore of GST Compensation to States/UTs', Press Information Bureau, 25 November 2022. Source: https://pib.gov.in/PressReleasePage.aspx?PRID=1878840
4. Central/state excise duty and VAT would be continued on five petroleum products (petroleum crude, high speed diesel, motor spirit [commonly known as petrol], natural gas and aviation turbine fuel), which would be subject to levy of GST whenever notified on the recommendation of the GST Council. Tobacco products could be subjected to both central excise duty and GST. Alcoholic liquor for human consumption had been kept outside the ambit of GST.
5. One of the largest off-budget transactions since FY17 has been on account of food subsidy. A major part of the food subsidy was reflected on the balance sheet of Food Corporation of India (FCI), the wholly owned arm of GoI, to carry out the national food subsidy programme, which ideally should have been a part of the fiscal maths. The government cleared all FCI dues in one stroke in FY21, which not only improved its fiscal accounting but also raised its fiscal deficit in FY21.
6. Standing Committee on Chemicals & Fertilizers (2020–21), 17th Lok Sabha, March 2021. Source: http://164.100.47.193/lsscommittee/Chemicals%20&%20Fertilizers/17_Chemicals_And_Fertilizers_20.pdf.
7. Source: https://www.business-standard.com/article/economy-policy/india-may-start-fy22-with-almost-nil-fertiliser-subsidy-arrears-120111201707_1.html
8. Source: https://indianexpress.com/article/india/significant-increase-in-fertiliser-subsidy-as-budget-sidesteps-reform-7170744/

9. While GoI cleared all FCI dues in FY21, year-wise adjusted fiscal deficits are presented to understand the true picture of public finances over the years.
10. Statement 1(i) of the Union Budget on 'Statement of liabilities of the central government' (published with the Budget documents every year), Status Paper on Government Debt 2018–19, Ministry of Finance. Source: https://dea.gov.in/public-debt-management (available for 2020–21 on 13 April 2022); and 'Combined liabilities of the central and state governments', RBI Database on Indian Economy (DBIE).
11. I am thankful to Subhash Chandra Garg, former economic affairs secretary and finance secretary of India, for sharing his knowledge in his blog.
12. '*Suit boot ki Sarkar*' is a phrase accusing the government of favoritism towards the corporate sector. '*Garibo ka masiha*' and/or '*Robin Hood Sarkar*' refers to a pro-poor government which prioritizes the poor or farmers in the country over other sections of the society.
13. 'State Finances: A Study of Budgets 2019–20', RBI Annual Publications, 30 September 2019; the 2020–21 version was released on 27 October 2020.
14. Ali Wyne, Graham T. Allison, and Robert Blackwill, *Lee Kuan Yew: The Grand Master's Insights on China, the United States, and the World*, MIT Press, 2012.

Chapter 5

1. According as recent data available up to March 2023. For almost a year between June 2021 and June 2022, India became the fourth largest holder of FX reserves, beating Russia. The latter, however, regained its fourth spot in July 2022.
2. M. McLeay, A. Radia and R. Thomas (2014), 'Money creation in the modern Economy', Bank of England, *Quarterly Bulletin*, Vol. 49, No. 2, Pages 14–27. Source: https://www.bankofengland.co.uk/-/media/boe/files/quarterly-bulletin/2014/money-creation-in-the-modern-economy.pdf
3. 'India Must Use Forex for Better Infrastructure', 13 March 2009. Source: https://www.livemint.com/Politics/HMzP3rlvj55yTABq7JMgyO/India-must-use-forex-for-better-infrastructure.html

4. Shankar Acharya, 'Forex for infrastructure, anyone?', *Business Standard*, 26 October 2004. Source: https://www.business-standard.com/article/opinion/shankar-acharya-forex-for-infrastructure-anyone-104102601029_1.html
5. Arvind Panagariya, 'Muddled on Forex for Infrastructure', *Economic Times*, 12 January 2005. Source: https://economictimes.indiatimes.com/muddled-on-forex-for-infrastructure/articleshow/987668.cms?utm_source=contentofinterest&utm_medium=text&utm_campaign=cppst
6. Arvind Panagariya, *India: The Emerging Giant*, Oxford University Press, 2008.
7. Deepak Lal, Suman Berry and Devendra Kumar Pant, '*The Real Exchange Rate, Fiscal Deficits and Capital Flows India 1981–2000*', *Economics and Political Weekly*, 22 November 2003.
8. Vijay Joshi and Sanjeev Sanyal, *Foreign Inflows and Macroeconomic Policy in India*, 2004.
9. Ibid.
10. Dr Pronab Sen, 'Foreign Direct Investment: A Solution to BOP Problems?', *Economics and Political Weekly*, Special Articles, 29 July 1995.
11. RBI Annual Report 2021–22, 27 May 2022. P. 163, para. VII.29.
12. Michael Pettis, *The Great Rebalancing: Trade, Conflict, and the Perilous Road Ahead for the World Economy*, Princeton University Press, 2013.

Chapter 6

1. 'On the Path to Policy Normalization', IMF, *Fiscal Monitor*, April 2023.
2. *World Economic Outlook*, Chapter 2, titled 'Inflation scares', International Monetary Fund, October 2021.
3. S. Chatterjee and A. Subramanian, '*India's Export-Led Growth: Exemplar and Exception*', Ashoka Centre for Economic Policy, Ashoka University, Working Paper 1, October 2020.
4. R. Agrawal, 'Funding the failures for creating "jobful" growth', *Economic Times*, 19 September 2017. Source: https://economictimes.indiatimes.com/markets/stocks/news/

how-to-use–12t-savings-for-big-growth-with-loads-of-jobs/articleshow/60509288.cms?from=mdr
5. Hyman Minsky, *Stabilizing an Unstable Economy*, 1986.
6. George Akerlof, Robert J. Shiller, *Animal Spirits*, 2009.
7. Carmen M. Reinhart and M. Belen Sbrancia, 'The Liquidation of Government Debt', IMF Working Paper, WP/15/7, January 2015.
8. Income Tax department, Government of India. Source: https://incometaxindia.gov.in/Pages/charts-and-tables.aspx

Chapter 7

1. Niall Fergusson, *The Ascent of Money: A Financial History of the World*, November 2008.
2. Wikipedia, entry on 'stock market'.
3. B. Taylor, '*The* First *and the Greatest: The Rise and Fall of the Vereenigde Oost-Indische Compagnie (United East India Company)*', Global Financial Data, November 2013.
4. Wikipedia, entry on 'stock broker'.
5. R. Morck, A. Sheifer and R.W. Vishny, 'The Stock Market and Investment: Is the market a Sideshow?', Brookings Paper on Economic Activity, 2, 1990.
6. R. Levine and S. Zervos, 'Stock Market Development and Long-run growth', World Bank Policy Research Working Paper, 1582, March 1996.
7. S. Ludvigson and C. Steindal, 'How Important Is the Stock Market Effect on Consumption?', *Federal Reserve Bank of New York Economic Policy Review*, July 1999.
8. Jordan Z. Shan, Alan G. Morris, and Fiona Sun, 'Financial Development and Economic Growth: An Egg-and-Chicken Problem?', *International Advances in Economic Research* 9(3): 443–54, August 2001.
9. G. Chodorwo-Reich, P.T. Nenov and A. Simsek, 'Stock Market wealth and the Real Economy: A Local Labor Market Approach', Working Paper 25959, National Bureau of Economic Research, June 2019, revised February 2020.
10. S.R. Paramati and R. Gupta, 'An Empirical Analysis of Stock Market Performance and Economic Growth: Evidence from India', *International Research Journal of Finance and Economics*

ISSN 1450–2887, Issue 73, 2011 and, S. Palamalai, 'Stock Market Development and Economic Growth in India: An Empirical Analysis', *International Journal of Finance & Banking Studies* (2147–4486), January 2016.

11. Adrian Slywotzky, *Value Migration: How to Think Several Moves Ahead of the Competition*, Harvard Business Review Press, 1995.
12. US Federal Reserve, DFA: Distributional Financial Accounts.
13. Calculated using annual data available in RBI database on maturity-wise household deposits and the corresponding deposit interest rates.
14. The prudential capital market exposure norms—in terms of base and coverage—prescribed for banks, were modified and came into effect on 1 April 2007. Source: https://rbi.org.in/Scripts/BS_ViewMasCirculardetails.aspx?id=9875
15. 'Preempting a Legacy of Vulnerabilities', International Monetary Fund (IMF), Global Financial Stability Report, April 2021.
16. 'Lower for longer', International Monetary Fund (IMF), Global Financial Stability Report, October 2019.
17. RBI Financial Stability Report, Issue no. 21, July 2020.
18. L. Lina, M. Pritsker, A. Zlate, K. Anadu and J. Bohn, 'Reach for Yield by U.S. Public Pension Funds', Finance and Economics Discussion Series 2019–048. Washington, board of governors of the Federal Reserve System.
19. Please note that by advanced economies I mean countries with non-FX intervening central banks. Similarly, by EMs, I mean countries with FX-intervening central banks, which may include some advanced nations. This is true only for this section.
20. 'India – Export related measures, Report of the Panel', World Trade Organization, WT/DS541/R, 31 October 2019. Source: https://www.wto.org/english/tratop_e/dispu_e/541r_e.pdf
21. P. Mishra and R. Rajan, 'Rule of the Monetary Game', RBI Working Paper Series, WPS (DEPR): 04/2016, March 2016.
22. A. Shah, 'Lessons from the Indian currency defence of 2013', The Leap Blog, 27 June 2015.

Chapter 8

1. Global Findex Report 2021, launched by the World Bank on 29 June 2022. This was the fourth round of the survey. It began in 2011, which was followed by the second round in 2014 and the third one in 2017.
2. 'India – Export related measures, Report of the Panel', World Trade Organization, WT/DS541/R, 31 October 2019. Source: https://www.wto.org/english/tratop_e/dispu_e/541r_e.pdf
3. Source: https://www.financialexpress.com/economy/cut-in-benefits-new-export-scheme-to-cost-govt-just-rs–10000-crore/2052223/
4. 'Cabinet approves Production Linked Incentive Scheme for Large Scale Electronics Manufacturing', Government of India, 21 March 2020. Source: https://pib.gov.in/PressReleasePage.aspx?PRID=1607487
5. 'PLI Scheme to herald a new era in mobile phone and electronic components manufacturing', Government of India, 1 August 2020. Source: https://www.pib.gov.in/PressReleasePage.aspx?PRID=1642823
6. 'Cabinet approves PLI Scheme to 10 key Sectors for Enhancing India's Manufacturing Capabilities and Enhancing Exports – Atmanirbhar Bharat', Government of India, 11 November 2020. Source: https://www.pib.gov.in/PressReleasePage.aspx?PRID=1671912
7. Michael Pettis, 'High Wages Versus High Savings in a Globalized World', Blog on Carnegie Endowment for International Peace. Source: https://carnegieendowment.org/chinafinancialmarkets/75972
8. Brian Reinbold and Yi Wen, 'Historical U.S. Trade Deficits', Economic Research, Federal Reserve Bank of St Louis, no. 13, 2019. Source: https://research.stlouisfed.org/publications/economic-synopses/2019/05/17/historical-u-s-trade-deficits
9. Matthew Simon, 'The United States Balance of Payments, 1861–1900', Pace College, Volume: *Trends in the American Economy in the Nineteenth Century*, 1960. Source: https://www.nber.org/system/files/chapters/c2492/c2492.pdf
10. Joe Studwell, *How Asia Works, Success and failure in the world's most dynamic region*, Grove Press, 2013, pp. 110–114.

11. *A World Bank Policy Research Report: The East Asian miracle, Economic Growth and Public Policy*, Oxford University Press, 1993.
12. S. Gupta and K. Singh, 'Fiscal deficits and its Trends in India', *International Journal of Business and Management Invention*, Volume 5, Issue 11, November 2016. Source: https://www.ijbmi.org/papers/Vol(5)11/H0511063075.pdf
13. P. Mauro, R. Romeu, A. Binder and A. Zaman, 'A Modern History of Fiscal Prudence and Profligacy', IMF Working Paper No. 13/5, International Monetary Fund, Washington DC, 2013.
14. Mehdi Shafaeddin, 'How did developed countries industrialize?: The History of Trade and Industrial Policy: The Cases of Great Britain and the USA', UNCTAD Discussion Paper no. 139, December 1998. Source: https://unctad.org/system/files/official-document/dp_139.en.pdf
15. Wikipedia Page, Friedrich List.
16. Friedrich List, *The National System of Political Economy*, JB Lippincott and Co., Philadelphia, 1856.
17. Ibid.
18. Mehdi Shafaeddin, 'What did Frederick List actually say?: Some clarifications on the infant industry argument', UNCTAD Discussion Papers no. 149, July 2000. Source: https://unctad.org/system/files/official-document/dp_149.en.pdf
19. Wikipedia, 'Economic History of the Ottoman Empire'. Source: https://en.wikipedia.org/wiki/Economic_history_of_the_Ottoman_Empire
20. Michael Hudson, *Trade, Development and Foreign Debt: How trade and development concentrate economic power in the hands of dominant nations*, ISLET, preface to the Second edition published in 2009, first published in 1992.
21. Press note on Second advance estimates of National income 2022-23', National Statistics Office, Ministry of Statistics & Programme implementation, Government of India, 28 February 2023.

INDEX

Adjusted fiscal deficit (AFD), 155, 163, 172, 173
Agrawal, Amol, 111
Agrawal, Raamdeo, 254
Ahmedabad University, 111
Akerlof, George, 255
Amazon, 127
American growth model (AGM), 305, 335, 336
Amsterdam stock exchange, 270
Asian Development Bank (ADB), 166

Balance of Payments and International Investment Position Manual, 193
Bank for International Settlements (BIS), 87, 92
Bharatiya Janata Party (BJP), 2, 175
Bharat Petroleum Corporation Ltd (BPCL), 164
Bond markets, 281–290
British empire, 298
BSE500, 132, 135

Capital consumption allowances, 118
Capitalism and Freedom, 147
Central Bank of the Republic of China, 196
Central bank policies, 292
Central public sector enterprises (CPSEs), 22, 51, 157, 165, 189, 191
Central Statistics Office (CSO), 67, 68, 70
Chandrashekhar, C.P., 111
Chartered accountants (CAs), 66
Chatterjee, Shoumitro, 247
Chidambaram, P., 206
'China Plus One' strategy, 308
Classification of the Functions of Government (COFOG), 159
Consolidated Fund of India (CFI), 154, 164
Consumption-related trade, 218
Core fiscal deficit, 35, 117, 118, 120, 121, 149, 209
Corporate
  Act, 113
  bonds, 107
  debt, 130, 134
  exports, 131
  investments, 131
  profits, 131, 145, 318
  tax collection, 126–127
  taxes, 133
COVID-19, 69, 71, 97, 98, 104, 112, 123, 133, 134, 139, 141, 154, 167, 172, 187, 190, 211, 215, 217, 230, 236, 240, 257, 258, 264, 269, 273, 289, 291, 292, 308
  induced income loss, 236, 238
current account deficit (CAD), 18, 19, 29–38, 42, 55, 105, 116–118, 120–124, 128, 149, 174, 194, 195, 197–199,

202, 205–209, 211, 215, 219–226, 228, 229, 231, 232, 252, 253, 256, 287, 309, 311, 314, 315, 332, 334, 339

Debt capital, 277
Debt service ratio (DSR), 92–96, 240
Dictionary of Commerce, 331
Disraeli, Benjamin, 331
Dividends
    distribution tax, 119
    paid, 118
Domestic money supply, 198

East Asian growth model (EAGM), 305, 310, 311, 318, 320, 334–336
European Central Bank (ECB), 196
Export-Import (EXIM) Bank, 166
External commercial borrowings (ECBs), 107
Extra budgetary resources (EBRs), 166

Farm loan waivers, 178
Financial markets, 288–289
Financial repression, 258
Financial Stability Report (FSR), 289
Financial Times, 111, 298
Fiscal deficit, 120
fiscal flexibility, 182
Flipkart, 127
follow-on public offer (FPO), 278
Food Corporation of India (FCI), 165, 166, 167, 171, 173
Foreign direct investments (FDI), 28, 192, 198, 211–214, 231

Foreign exchange reserves (FXR), 198, 199, 209, 211, 215, 230
    policies, 196, 197, 205
Foreign portfolio investments (FPIs), 211
FRBM Act, 168
Friedman, Milton, 147
Fully serviced bonds (FSBs), 166

Gandhi, Indira, 111
Global corporate profits, 144
Global Financial Data, 270
Goods and services tax (GST), 154, 272
Goyal, Piyush, 177
Gross capital formation (GCF), 79, 159, 224, 361
Gross domestic savings (GDS), 19, 75, 116, 184, 243, 252, 256, 312
Gross financial savings (GFS), 59, 62, 74–78, 107, 282, 284
Gross fixed capital formation (GFCF), 79, 117

High Level Committee on Estimation of Savings and Investment, 72, 79
High tax exemptions, 316
Hindustan Petroleum Corporation Ltd (HPCL), 164
Household consumption, 238
    components, 69
    debt, 98, 100
    trends, 69
Household debt
    estimation, 87–90
    trends, 87–90
Households
    finances, 97
    financial savings, 75

income, 66, 99
   components, 65–69
   trends, 65–69
   investment, 60
   non-financial savings, 78
   physical savings, 79, 80
   savers, 76
House price index (HPI), 84
House price to income (HPTI) ratio, 85, 86
Housing loans account, 89
How Asia Works, 319

Incremental capital-output ratio (ICOR), 326
Indian Oil Corporation (IOC), 164
Industrial Development Bank of India (IDBI), 166
Insurance funds and pension and provident funds, 77–78
Intellectual property rights, 79
Interest payments, 60, 64
Interim budget, 176, 180
International Labour Organization (ILO), 67
International trade policies, 328

Lakshmi Vilas Bank (LVB), 109
Loans, 64
   to income ratio, 85
   to value ratio, 85
Lower middle income countries (LMICs), 306

Mahatma Gandhi National Rural Employment Guarantee Act (MGNREGA), 336
Medical health insurance schemes, 58
Merchandise Exports from India Scheme (MEIS), 295, 307

Micro, small and medium enterprises (MSMEs), 113
Mishra, Prachi, 298
Modern Monetary Theory (MMT), 163
Modi, Nirav, 178
Motilal Oswal Financial Services, 80, 254

NABARD All India Rural Financial Inclusion Survey, 182
National Bureau of Economic Research, 271
National Highways Authority of India (NHAI), 165
National Housing Bank (NHB), 83, 89, 109
National Income Accounts (NIA), 59, 61
National Sample Survey Office (NSSO), 73
National Small Savings Fund (NSSF), 165, 170
Netflix, 178
New-age cash-burning companies, 127
New market stabilization scheme, 204
NIFTY50, 112, 129, 130, 132, 133, 134, 135
NITI Aayog, 307
Non-banking financial companies (NBFCs), 25, 88–90, 107, 165, 217, 350, 351
Non-government non-financial (NGNF) sector, 107, 108

Ola, 127
One97 Communications Ltd, 280
Ottoman empire: liberal policies, 330, 331

Panagariya, Arvind, 207
Patel, Urjit, 110
Personal disposable income (PDI), 67, 84, 98
Pettis, Michael, 222, 310, 311, 315, 317, 335
PLI scheme, 308
Power Finance Corporation (PFC), 165
Pradhan Mantri Garib Kalyan Yojana (PMGKY), 187
Pradhan Mantri Kisan Samman Nidhi (PM-KISAN), 7, 180
Pradhan Mantri Shram-Yogi Maandhan, 180
Private final consumption expenditure (PFCE), 313
Private sector banks (PvSBs), 107, 109–110, 285–286
Public Provident Fund (PPF), 58, 77
Public sector banks (PbSBs), 107, 109–110, 164
Punjab Mercantile Cooperative (PMC) Bank, 109

Rajan, Raghuram, 107, 110, 111
real estate sector, 82
Regressive tax policies, 316
Reliance Jio, 215
Remission of Duties and Taxes on Export Products (RoDTEP) scheme, 296, 307
Reported fiscal deficit (RFD), 155, 163, 166
Reserve Bank of India (RBI), 9, 75, 93, 98, 209, 275
    data, 138
    governors, 107
Residential asset price monitoring survey (RAPMS), 84, 85
Residential property, 83

Residential property price index (RPPI), 85

Scheduled commercial banks (SCBs), 83
Sen, Pronab, 31, 211
Shares and debentures, 77
Shiller, Robert, 255
Short-term borrowings, 108
Sitharaman, Nirmala, 2
Small finance banks (SFBs), 110
Software services and telecommunications, 335
Special purpose vehicles (SPVs), 166
Stabilizing an Unstable Economy, 254
Swiggy, 127
Swiss National Bank (SNB), 196

Taylor, Bryan, 270
Total factor productivity (TFP), 307
Trade, Development and Foreign Debt, 331

Uber, 127
Union Budgets, 172, 175
    documents, 168, 322
United Nations Conference on Trade and Development (UNCTAD), 328

Wolf, Martin, 298
World Health Organization (WHO), 296
World Trade Organization (WTO), 295

YES Bank, 109
Yew, Lee Kuan, 186

ABOUT THE AUTHOR

Nikhil Gupta is Chief Economist and Senior Group Vice-President at Motilal Oswal Financial Services. He is a frequent contributor to business newspapers and a participant in consultations with RBI, NITI Aayog and other institutions on economic outlook. He was born in 1985 in New Delhi and holds an MA in economics from the prestigious Gokhale Institute of Politics and Economics, Pune. As a part of India's financial sector, Nikhil started his career tracking the US macroeconomic developments at First Global Securities Ltd, Mumbai, before he moved on to cover the Indian economy. For the past seven years, he has handled the Economics desk at Motilal Oswal, where he covers data releases, writes thematic research reports and keeps his clientele updated of such developments.